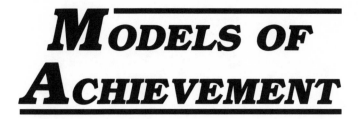

MODELS OF ACHIEVEMENT

Reflections of Eminent Women in Psychology

VOLUME 2

MODELS OF ACHIEVEMENT

Reflections of Eminent Women in Psychology

VOLUME 2

Edited by

Agnes N. O'Connell
Nancy Felipe Russo

 LAWRENCE ERLBAUM ASSOCIATES, PUBLISHERS
1988 Hillsdale, New Jersey   Hove and London

Copyright © 1988 by Lawrence Erlbaum Associates, Inc.
All rights reserved. No part of this book may be reproduced in
any form, by photostat, microform, retrieval system, or any other
means, without the prior written permission of the publisher.

Lawrence Erlbaum Associates, Inc., Publishers
365 Broadway
Hillsdale, New Jersey 07642

Library of Congress Cataloging-in-Publication Data
(Revised for vol. 2)

Models of achievement.

  Vol. 2 has imprint: Hillsdale, N.J.: L. Erlbaum
Associates.
  Includes bibliographies and indexes.
  1. Women psychologists—United States—Biography.
2. Psychology—United States—History—20th century.
3. Sex discrimination in psychology—United States.
I. O'Connell, Agnes N. II. Russo, Nancy Felipe,
1943–
BF109.A1M6 1983   150'.88042   82-23583
ISBN 0-231-05312-6 (v. 1: alk. paper)
ISBN 0-231-05313-4 (pbk.: v. 1)
ISBN 0-8058-0083-2 (L. Erlbaum Associates: v. 2)
ISBN 0-8058-0322-X (pbk)

Printed in the United States of America
10 9 8 7 6 5 4 3 2 1

Contents

PART III
Personal Perspectives: Autobiographical Sketches

PART IV
Perspectives on Patterns of Achievement

Foreword

As a student and also as a teacher of the history of psychology, I have always enjoyed reading about the lives and accomplishments of eminent psychologists. Early in my career, however, I was chagrined to discover the paucity of published material about the lives and works of women psychologists. Although women have been active participants in psychology since the inception of the field, their contributions have not been appropriately recognized.

Agnes N. O'Connell and Nancy Felipe Russo, themselves models of achievement in psychology, have played leadership roles in helping to correct the historical record. Volume 1 of *Models of Achievement: Reflections of Eminent Women in Psychology*, published in 1983, was an important step toward recognizing and recording the contributions of women in the history of psychology. Volume 2, another important scholarly contribution, is greeted with great enthusiasm.

This book presents in their own style the life stories of 17 eminent women who have made noteworthy advances in both theory and research in mid-20th century psychology. These stories provide fascinating and informative reading for both students and professionals and also for historians of psychology as the centennial year (1992) of the American Psychological Association approaches. O'Connell and Russo's second volume is unique in presenting the autobiographies of the five living women to have attained the office of president of that organization: Anne Anastasi, Florence L. Denmark, Janet Taylor Spence, Bonnie R. Strickland,

and Leona E. Tyler. The volume is also especially significant in preserving the contributions of two minority women who have achieved distinction in psychology: Martha E. Bernal and Carolyn Robertson Payton.

Each autobiography is idiosyncratic, and each is rich in detail. The personalities of the women, their family relationships, and the encouragement and support they enjoyed in their scholarly pursuits are strikingly diverse. All, however, share a common trait: a tremendous persistence in overcoming obstacles to achieve their goals. Their stories document the many gains women have made in this century. In addition, they reveal strategies for coping with various challenges in pursuing one's familial and career goals. Many valuable lessons may be gleaned from the perceptions, objectives, and attainments of these remarkable people.

The autobiographies are enhanced by the insights of O'Connell's penetrating analyses and synthesis of personal and professional commonalities and differences in these women's lives and experiences. The women's eminence is made more evident by Russo's informative discussion of the societal context and its relationship to development of the field and women's contributions to it.

In recording the continuing achievements of these eminent women in the development of psychology, Volume 2 of *Models of Achievement: Reflections of Eminent Women in Psychology* is indeed an eloquent testimonial to the 17 autobiographers themselves. It will surely serve as an energizing source of pride and inspiration to all readers.

Virginia Staudt Sexton, PhD
St. John's University

Preface

The first volume of *Models of Achievement: Reflections of Eminent Women in Psychology* (O'Connell & Russo, 1983) was the outcome of an idea long in incubation. The idea began to germinate more than a decade ago with an article on foremothers (Bernstein & Russo, 1974) and with a series of workshops at the regional and national psychological conventions on gender-specific barriers to research (O'Connell et al., 1978). The idea for preserving information about eminent women in psychology was first realized in a special issue of the *Psychology of Women Quarterly* that contained biographies of seven distinguished women (O'Connell & Russo, 1980).

An additional realization of our idea to preserve and publicize the lives and achievements of women psychologists came when we organized symposia on eminent women in which three or four women presented brief sketches of their lives and careers. These symposia were held at the annual meetings of the American Psychological Association (APA) 1979 through 1981, at the annual meeting of the Southeastern Psychological Association in 1980, and at the annual meeting of the Eastern Psychological Association in 1980.

The positive response to the symposia confirmed our belief that there was a great demand for knowledge about women's contributions in psychology—contributions viewed from the perspective of the women themselves. The models-of-achievement project thus produced a book with expanded, more comprehensive versions of these presentations. The expanded autobiographies, a chapter on the social and historical context, and a chapter analyzing the similarities and differences in the lives and careers of 17 eminent women appear in the first volume.

Publication of the first volume increased rather than satisfied demand for knowledge about the lives of women in psychology. Our students asked us, "What about contemporary women? What are the similarities and differences among women past and present?" The convention symposia were so well received that we were barraged with letters and phone calls with suggestions for others who merit recognition. Because we are committed to the goal of bringing the lives and achievements of eminent women to as many of our colleagues and students as possible and because many people demand information on role models, we continued to organize symposia and to prepare this second book. This volume contains expanded autobiographies of a selection of 17 eminent women who presented brief autobiographical sketches at the annual meetings of the APA between 1981 and 1987 and at the annual meeting of the Eastern Psychological Association in 1983.

Overall, the goals of the first and second volumes are similar: to provide a sense of history and purpose; to increase the visibility of distinguished women; and to serve as a source of inspiration to students and colleagues. This second volume, however, takes a step toward responding to requests for autobiographies of more contemporary role models.

Thus, this volume contains an even greater number of autobiographies of younger eminent women. Twelve of the women were born between 1915 and 1936 and earned their doctorates between 1942 and 1967; 13 of the women in the first volume were born between 1897 and 1913 and earned their doctorates between 1927 and 1939. In addition to responding to reader demand for information about more contemporary women, the autobiographies in this volume shed light on how historical events such as the Great Depression, World War II, and the women's movement have affected lives, opportunities, and achievements. Analyses of the autobiographies provide transhistorical and time-specific profiles of eminent women in psychology.

This volume is appropriate as supplementary reading in a variety of psychology courses, including psychology of women, sex roles, history of psychology, and personality. The book is also particularly useful in introductory psychology, social psychology, and counseling and career development courses and is appropriate for women's studies courses in departments of women's studies, sociology, education, and history. For individual use, we hope that it will be a thoughtful gift for aspiring young psychologists and for women who may be feeling alone or isolated in their professions. Whether this book is used as supplementary text or as "extracurricular" bedside reading, the descriptions of the creative, productive, and professionally rewarding interactions among colleagues of both sexes found in these autobiographies should serve to inspire both male and female readers (O'Connell & Russo, 1983).

Our work to preserve a history of psychology that includes the vision of women as psychologists and that serves as a source of inspiration continues. This work has generated an enthusiastic response from numerous sources. Psi Chi, the National Honor Society in Psychology, continues to generously sponsor the symposia on eminent women that we organize, as it has since their inception in 1979. Psi Chi has been instrumental in making these symposia an exciting, ongoing tradition at the annual meetings of APA. In addition to three APA groups—the Committee on Women in Psychology, the Board of Social and Ethical Responsibility, and the Board of Ethnic Minority Affairs—various APA divisions have provided support and encouragement over the years, including the Division of General Psychology, the Division of the Teaching of Psychology, the Division of Developmental Psychology, the Society for the Psychological Study of Social Issues, the Division of Adult Development and Aging, the Division of the History of Psychology, and the Division of the Psychology of Women.

We are particularly grateful to the distinguished Virginia Staudt Sexton for her Foreword, which is the most recent expression of the longstanding encouragement and support she has given us. We thank our colleagues, students, and numerous reviewers of the first volume for encouraging us to continue in this work. Thanks also are extended to Larry Erlbaum and his staff.

A special acknowledgment goes to the illustrious contributors who expanded and revised their autobiographies with patience and cooperation and to Alberta Siegel for handling the Lois Meek Stolz manuscript during the production process. We also appreciate the efforts of Barbara Priestner-Werte for her valuable assistance in the content analyses of the autobiographies and that of Adrienne Thompson for her secretarial assistance. Thomas D. O'Connell and Allen Meyer provided valuable comments on the chapters, and Karen Applegate, Ria Hermann, and Barbara Priestner-Werte provided invaluable research assistance. We also thank Rick Sample and the APA library for access to materials. Background research was made possible by a minigrant from the College of Liberal Arts and

Sciences at Arizona State University. Content analyses were made possible by a separately budgeted research grant from Montclair State College.

Agnes N. O'Connell
Montclair State College

Nancy Felipe Russo
Arizona State University

REFERENCES

Bernstein, M. D., & Russo, N. F. (1974). The history of psychology revisited: Or, Up with our foremothers. *American Psychologist, 29,* 130–134.

O'Connell, A. N., Alpert, J., Richardson, M. S., Rotter, N., Ruble, D. N., & Unger, R. K. (1978). Gender-specific barriers to research in psychology: Report of the Task Force on Women Doing Research—APA Division 35. *JSAS: Catalog of Selected Documents in Psychology* (Ms. No. 1753) 8.

O'Connell, A. N., & Russo, N. F. (Eds.). (1980). *Eminent women in psychology: Models of achievement* [Special issue]. *Psychology of Women Quarterly, 5*(1).

O'Connell, A. N., & Russo, N. F. (Eds.). (1983). *Models of achievement: Reflections of eminent women in psychology.* New York: Columbia University Press.

PART I

GENERAL INTRODUCTION

CHAPTER 1

A New Vision
of Women in Psychology

Agnes N. O'Connell
Nancy Felipe Russo

The purpose of these volumes is to present a new way of looking at women in psychology and in society. One way this new vision can be brought into sharp focus is by preserving and making visible the often unrecognized and undervalued accomplishments of women in the field. Women have made significant contributions to the cornerstones of thinking in psychology since its inception, but appropriate acknowledgment has not yet been made. These autobiographies respond to the historical neglect of women's roles and contributions and give these remarkable women the opportunity to define and interpret their experiences in their own words. From these autobiographies and accomplishments, a new vision of women in psychology begins to emerge.

An outcome of this new vision is the illumination of women as role models. Role models are needed to aid in the acculturation of women into psychology. The professional advantages of same-sex role models in the lives of prominent women have been well documented (e.g., Almquist & Angrist, 1975; Goldstein, 1979), and these advantages also apply to reading about distinguished women (Walum, cited in Douvan, 1974). Although the number of women psychologists is increasing, there are still too few to fill the need for role models. In 1984, women earned 50.1% of the doctorates awarded in psychology (APA [American Psychological Association] Committee on Women in Psychology, 1986). The majority of psychology students in graduate schools are women (all subfields combined). Yet ironically, only one in four full-time faculty members is a woman, and the role models available in graduate departments

continue to be predominantly men. For women to see the realization of their own aspirations in the lives of other women is a crucial
source of support and inspiration during difficult times (Douvan,
1974). Much wisdom and inspiration are to be gained from the
varied combinations of perseverance, determination, dedication,
humility, humor, and achievement contained in the lives of these
eminent women.

In this volume, the new vision is shaped by the lives of women
who are more contemporary than those whose autobiographies are
contained in our earlier work. The inclusion of younger eminent
women reflects the response to requests from colleagues and
students as well as our own interest in examining the historical
evolution of the lives and achievements of women in psychology.
Thirteen of the 17 women in the first volume were born between
1897 and 1913 and earned their doctorates between 1927 and 1939.
In contrast, 12 of the 17 women in this volume were born between
1915 and 1936 and earned their doctorates between 1942 and 1967.

The criteria for choosing the women in this volume include a sus-
tained record of achievement over a significant period of time;
achievement that has withstood the clarifying filter of time; being
a pioneer; being a leader or expert. These women represent a wide
range of subdisciplines, remarkable accomplishments, and varying life styles. They are women of great creative achievements
whose lives do not follow the beaten path. They are women whose
indomitable spirit make the pursuit of challenge and achievement
possible in the face of discrimination, humiliation, trivialization, and
other barriers.

Some come from professional families; some from poor and disadvantaged backgrounds. They have experienced sexism, racism,
anti-Semitism, and issues of acculturation in their educational and
professional pursuits and in their daily lives. They have overcome
these barriers with courage and grace. Despite obstacles, they have
made extraordinary contributions to psychology in academe, industry, and government. Their work reaches the highest standards
of excellence—whether it is in theoretical or applied or in traditional
or emerging areas. Their personal lives represent a cross-section
of the life styles available to women in the 20th century. They are
single, married and childless, married with children, single parents,
and grandmothers.

Our invitation to participate in the celebration of eminent wom-
en and their work by contributing an autobiography to these volumes generated a variety of responses—from gracious acceptance
to strong resistance. Despite their undeniable accomplishments,

several of the women perceived their leadership and contributions to psychology as "serendipitous," the result of "chance encounters," "luck," or the "interaction of time, place, people, and circumstances" and expressed feelings of embarrassment or surprise at our invitation. These disclaimers of ability reflect humility and an attributional style that did not exclude these women from high achievement. "Luck" requires being prepared to respond to opportunity's knock, is difficult to separate from strategy, and may very well be the residue of skill.

Close examination of their autobiographies reveals that these women are in charge of their lives. Each is unique in her definition of fulfillment and the specific configuration of her choices, but they all possess the remarkable strength, talent, resiliency, and flexibility to influence as well as be influenced by their surroundings.

Historical events shaped the nature and number of opportunities open to these women. The affluence and optimism following World War I gave way to hard times during the depression of the 1930s. World War II brought educational and employment opportunities for women, but its aftermath brought retrenchment. It was not until the women's movement of the 1960s and 1970s that new gains were made, and women in psychology played a role in forging those gains.

Since the 1970s, five women have achieved the distinction of serving as president of APA: Anne Anastasi (1972), Leona E. Tyler (1973), Florence L. Denmark (1980), Janet Taylor Spence (1984), and Bonnie R. Strickland (1987). Their autobiographies are contained in this volume. Only two other women, Mary Whiton Calkins (1905) and Margaret Floy Washburn (1921), have achieved that distinction since APA was founded in 1892. Their biographies are contained in a special issue of *Psychology of Women Quarterly* (O'Connell & Russo, 1980).

The impact of the gains of the 1960s and the 1970s is evident in many of the autobiographies presented here. Yet, decades after the resurgence of the women's movement, equality is yet to be fully realized. What is required is a revolution of vision, a new way of perceiving women. What is required is the perception of women as exemplars, as fully functioning, competent, capable contributors to psychology and to society—without the covert reservations of societal or cultural stereotypes. It will take wisdom, dedication, and energy to ensure a future marked by excellence, progress, and opportunity.

The lessons contained in these autobiographies provide a foundation for achieving this new vision and these goals. To clarify the lessons to be learned, this book considers the contributions of women in psychology from three levels of analysis. Nancy Felipe Russo presents the universal level in a chapter on the social and historical context. Agnes N. O'Connell presents the group level in a chapter on the similarities and differences in the lives of these eminent women. The distinguished women themselves present the individual level in their autobiographies.

We hope that the lessons contained in the lives of these distinguished women will be learned wisely and well by both women and men. We also hope that these volumes will be the catalyst for a rippling revolution of vision, a new way of looking at women in psychology and in society, a new vision of women as exemplars and major contributors across time.

REFERENCES

Almquist, E. M., & Angrist, S. S. (1985). *Careers and contingencies.* Amherst: University of Massachusetts Press.

APA Committee on Women in Psychology. (1986). *Report on women in psychology.* Washington, DC: American Psychological Association.

Douvan, E. (1974). The role of models in women's professional development. *Psychology of Women Quarterly, 1,* 5–20.

Goldstein, E. (1979). Effect of same-sex and cross-sex role models on the subsequent academic productivity of scholars. *American Psychologist, 34* (5), 407–410.

O'Connell, A. N., Russo, N. F. (Eds.). (1980). *Eminent women in psychology: Models of achievement* [Special issue]. *Psychology of Women Quarterly, 5*(1).

PART II

HISTORICAL PERSPECTIVES

CHAPTER 2

Women's Participation in Psychology: Reflecting and Shaping the Social Context

Nancy Felipe Russo

Women's entry into and participation in psychology are integrally linked with a myriad of overlapping and interweaving social and economic factors that have shaped America culture in the 20th century. These factors include women's struggle for suffrage, reform movements (including the progressive education and child welfare movements), the expansion of higher education, the trend toward professionalism, World War I, the Great Depression, World War II and its social and economic aftermath, the civil rights movement, and the resurgence of the women's movement in the *1960s* and 1970s.

Psychology in the United States began its growth at the end of the 19th century, at a time of great economic and social change, when belief in women's innate altruism and moral superiority was used to justify women's participation in public life and societal reform (Hymowitz & Weissman, 1978). The early feminists who organized the 1848 Seneca Falls Convention wanted suffrage as a means to ensure equality for women. But political realities led them to exploit (and thus reinforce) the rhetoric of the reform movements. It was argued that the vote was needed so that "women could 'stand maternal watch for the nation's children' at the ballot box" (Ryan, 1983, p. 214). Women's access to higher education, better conditions of employment, and equal political rights were all justified as means to expand the maternal domain and enable women to "clean up" society (Klein, 1984; Ryan, 1983).

The increased emphasis on child welfare was accompanied by

a societal trend toward professionalism in the 20th century. A belief in a "professional approach to child care" emerged, and science was used to argue for women's greater access to higher education. The role of "mother" became viewed as "a scientific vocation that required intelligence and training" in order to produce vigorous, healthy male citizens to serve in the nation's armed forces in World War I (Filene, 1975). The goal of melding science and motherhood in the service of child welfare provided a rationale for women's higher education and legitimized women's participation in the world of work.

THE EMERGENCE OF APPLIED PSYCHOLOGY

What women were doing in applied settings was considered to be secondary to the "real" psychology that was developing in academic settings in which women were more likely to be excluded from regular faculty appointments. Yet, as described by Russo (1983), during the first three decades of the 20th century, society's interest in progressive education and in child welfare stimulated psychological research on child development, mental retardation, and mental testing. Women found opportunities for education and employment in these areas of applied psychology, which were considered congruent with women's special talents, interests, and abilities.

The psychological clinics and child guidance and child welfare institutes that emerged from these movements provided supportive work environments for women. The first psychological clinic, established by Lightner Witmer at the University of Pennsylvania in 1896, was founded "for the study and treatment of children who were mentally or morally retarded and of those who had physical defects that slowed development or progress" (French, 1984, p. 976). In 1900, Anna McKeag became the first person to receive a PhD from the clinic. Eight of Witmer's first 25 doctoral students were women (French, 1984). Women became pioneers in the development and application of psychological tests and have continued to make major contributions to tests and measurements in psychology (Denmark, 1980; Russo & Denmark, 1987; Russo & O'Connell, 1980; Sexton, 1969, 1973–1974). In this volume are Anne Anastasi, Marie Skodak Crissey, Erika Fromm, Olga E. deCillis Engelhardt, Jane Loevinger, Patricia Cain Smith, Frances K. Graham, Martha T. Mednick, Janet Taylor Spence, Bonnie R.

Strickland, and Leona E. Tyler—all have made contributions to tests and measurements in psychology. Crissey's autobiography, in particular, discusses the evolution of research with intelligence tests in the 1930s.

In 1909, the Juvenile Psychopathic Institute, considered to be the first mental health clinic, was established in Chicago by psychiatrist William Healy and psychologists Augusta F. Bronner and Grace Fernald. Child guidance clinics spread in the 1920s; in 1924, child guidance clinicians founded the American Orthopsychiatric Association. In 1931, Bronner became its president (Reisman, 1976).

The institutes for child study that spread during the 1920s enabled women to pursue scientific research in child development. Such institutes created a source of employment for women who were typically denied access to regular faculty positions in academe (outside the women's colleges), giving them access to stimulating colleagues and research facilities. The list of women associated with these institutes reads like a *Who's Who* of women psychologists and includes Lois Hayden Meek Stolz, Tyler, Crissey, and Dorothy Hansen Eichorn, who are included in this volume.

Thus, the progressive education and child welfare movements provided educational and employment opportunities for women while shaping their aspirations and interests as well. Further, these movements led to the establishment of institutional structures encouraging sex segregation in psychology that was not to be challenged effectively until the women's movement reemerged in the 1960s and 1970s. Their impact can be seen in the higher proportions of doctorates awarded to women from 1920 to 1974 in subfields specializing in knowledge related to these movements: developmental (48%), school (32%), education (25%), clinical (24%), and counseling and guidance (24%). In contrast, 6% of the PhDs in industrial-organizational psychology went to women (Russo, 1984).

WOMEN AND SCIENTIFIC PSYCHOLOGY

As higher education expanded in the 1920s and 1930s, so too did opportunities for women's education. Women began to trickle into all fields of science but particularly into those congruent with society's conceptions of women's abilities—psychology, sociology, economics, and applied chemistry in home economics (Rossiter, 1974; Solomon, 1985). As we have seen, the demand for applied psychological knowledge related to topics considered to be in women's traditional domain created applied subfields that provided a place for women psychologists to pursue research in areas congruent with society's gender stereotypes, and female scientists have continued to choose psychology in greater proportions than male scientists. In the years between 1920 and 1974, before the major impact of the women's movement on science, 5.7% of the PhDs awarded to men were in psychology compared to 15.2% of PhDs awarded to women. In 1983, 1 in 4 female doctoral scientists were in psychology compared to 1 in 10 male doctoral scientists (National Science Foundation [NSF], 1986).

The disadvantaged status of women in academe has affected women's ability to fulfill their scientific potential in psychology. In 1984, 50.1% of PhD recipients in psychology were women, but only 22% of the full-time positions in psychology departments were occupied by women—a proportion unchanged from the 1940s. Women in academe are more likely to hold part-time positions (41%) compared to full-time positions (22%; Pion, Bramblett, Wicherski, & Stapp, 1985). Of the 5,300 women employed in doctoral psychology departments, 43.4% were tenured compared to 71.1% of men. Women continue to be concentrated in lower ranks. Of the 7,500 doctoral psychologists holding the rank of full professor in 1983, only 12% were women. The salary gap between women and men persists, even when years of experience are controlled (Russo, Olmedo, Stapp, & Fulcher, 1981).

The beginning of the 20th century, particularly during the 1920s, was a time when science enjoyed immense prestige, when the prefacing of a statement with the phrase "Science teaches us" was sufficient to silence argument (Kargon, 1974, p. 33) The scientific community was mindful of the use of science as a tool for social change. As J. Playfair McMurrich proclaims in his 1923 presidential address to the American Association for the Advancement of Science, "The world accepts with tranquility the shattering of many old beliefs, providing that the necessity for their destruction is vouched for by competent scientific opinion" (Kargon, 1974, p. 33). Science was seen as a tool for implementing democratic ideals. As psychologist James Cattell proclaimed, "The applications of science have abolished slavery and serfdom, the need of child labor, the subjection of women; they have made possible universal education, democracy and equality of opportunity, and have given us so much of these as we have" (Cattell, 1925/1974, pp. 63–64). It was in the 1920s that the science of psychology began to capture the imagination of the public and the psychologist became the "expert" in matters ranging from the home to the workplace.

In this context, the use of scientific psychology to buttress or break stereotypes about women takes on new import. Scientific traditions have extensive historical roots in a mythology that defines scientific values—objectivity, reason, and mind—as "male." If women's gains are to be maintained, understanding how scientific psychology has been used to rationalize sex discrimination is essential. Equally important, however, is understanding how that same scientific ideology—founded on reason and objectivity—has also been a powerful tool for exposing myths perpetuated under the guise of scientific "fact." When women overcame educational barriers and obtained scientific credentials and knowledge, they also acquired the skills and power to challenge the use of pseudoscientific "facts" to rationalize gender stereotyping and discrimination.

The end of the 19th century was a time when the fledgling science of psychology was used to perpetuate gender and sex-role stereotypes that supported the status quo, including the belief that developing women's intellectual capabilities was incompatible with the qualities needed to meet obligations of their roles as mothers and wives (Lewin, 1984; Rosenberg, 1982; Welter, 1966). For example, the founder of the American Psychological Association (APA), G. Stanley Hall, warned that women competing with men "in the world" would cause "race suicide" as maternal urges became neglected (Shields, 1975a, 1975b).

Early women psychologists thus faced barriers that were justified in the name of "scientific" psychology—and some used their scientific knowledge and skills to put such myths to scientific test. Pioneer Helen Thompson Woolley, who in 1903 was the first person to receive a psychology doctorate from the University of Chicago, was also the first to use her scientific skills to rebut the myths of "scientific psychology" about sex differences (Rosenberg, 1982).

Influenced by the work of Woolley, Leta Stetter Hollingworth (EdD, Columbia, 1916) also used her scientific expertise to rebut myths about women. Known for her distinguished contributions to child psychology and education, Hollingworth was the first to use the term *gifted*, and her book on adolescence became a classic (Benjamin, 1975). She demanded that psychology apply scientific rigor in research on women. Her rigorous empirical research on mental and physical performance during the menstrual cycle, on the variability hypothesis (which erroneously explained men's higher status due to greater male variability), and on women's sex roles directly confronted the myths of the time (Shields, 1975b).

The first two decades of the 20th century were an active period for research that challenged myths and shibboleths about women. Feminist critiques of psychology played a critical but unacknowledged role in eroding the armchair psychology of the 19th century and in promoting the transition to empiricism in the social sciences of the 1920s (Rossiter, 1982, p. 115).

In the 1970s, research on the psychology of women again emerged to challenge traditional assumptions. A landmark event marking the resurgence of the field was a 1974 research conference on future directions in research in the psychology of women. The conference, organized by Julia Sherman and Florence L. Denmark, reflected an interest in the field at the federal level and was funded by the National Institute of Mental Health. The resulting book (Sherman & Denmark, 1978) was dedicated to Hollingworth.

Women's greater participation in behavioral and social sciences has been associated with a devaluation of those fields, which in turn has affected access to public funding sources, such as the NSF, for scientific research by women. This devaluation can be seen in the 1947 debates on the bill to establish NSF: Representative Clarence J. Brown (Rep.–OH) argued that if social sciences were included, the result would be "a lot of short-haired women and long-haired men messing into everybody's personal affairs" (Heckler, 1980, p. 145). Similar arguments against the inclusion of social sciences in NSF programs were repeated in the 1960s, when the director of NSF sought to broaden the mandate of the organization, and in the 1970s, when Senator Edward Kennedy (Dem.–MA) proposed legislation to establish special programs to increase women's participation in science (Russo & Cassidy, 1983).

MINORITY WOMEN

The NSF estimates that of the 13,800 women holding psychology doctorates in 1984, 7.2% were members of minority groups—3.6% Black, 2.2% Asian, and 1.2% Hispanic. The proportion of Native American women holding doctorates in the field is a fraction of a percent (NSF, 1986). Our first volume included the autobiographies of Ruth W. Howard (Beckham), the first black woman to receive a PhD in psychology (Howard, 1983), and Mamie Phipps Clark, whose co-authored research (with her husband Kenneth Clark)—cited in *Brown v. the Board of Education*—was instrumental in the United States Supreme Court ruling to desegregate U.S. schools (Clark, 1983). This volume chronicles the lives and careers of Carolyn Robertson Payton, recipient of the APA Distinguished Professional

Contributions Award and Director of the Peace Corps under President Jimmy Carter. Martha E. Bernal was the first woman of Mexican-American descent to obtain a PhD in psychology. Bernal later became a highly cited contributor to behavior therapy and parenting literatures as well as a leader in advocating advancement in the status of Hispanic psychologists. Such stories are sources of information as well as inspiration to future generations of men and women in psychology.

THE 1920s—
THE DECADE THAT ROARED

World War I opened opportunities for women to contribute at every level of society and was a countervailing force to the pattern of segregation of the sexes. Women's participation in the war effort, the passage of the Nineteenth Amendment, and the high societal value placed on what was considered "women's work" in the progressive education and child guidance movements began a legacy of optimism and opportunity for the generations of women that followed.

The assumption that marriage should take precedence over a career was accepted by the majority of both sexes at the turn of the century. Professional women were viewed by themselves and by others as atypical for their sex (Solomon, 1985). In the 1920s, however, as higher education expanded, the proportion of married women obtaining doctorates began to increase. For the first time, the question of whether to choose marriage *or* work became how to manage marriage *and* work—a question that gained import as increasing numbers of married women entered the labor force and that persists to this day. The question was particularly relevant for women psychologists: During this period, although their actual numbers were small, approximately one in four were married (Rossiter, 1982).

The optimism of the 1920s was accompanied by a diffusion of focus for the women's movement. Ironically, women's political participation in reform movements led to passage of reform legislation and political appointments to "women's jobs" that were created to implement that legislation. Legislators, fearing that women's suffrage would lead to severe political consequences, became responsive to women's issues—the Equal Rights Amendment to the Constitution of the United States was introduced in 1923. However, women did not maintain their organizations and vigilance in the context of this optimism. Research on women's voting patterns at the time revealed that they voted the same as their husbands, and women's issues were not on their husbands' political agenda. Political attention to women's issues began a decline that became a plummet in the 1930s.

THE GREAT DEPRESSION

The economic crash of 1929 and the consequent Great Depression of the 1930s brought a sudden reversal to the optimism of the 1920s and to opportunity for women. The reversal is a stark reminder of the vulnerability of the status of women living under a constitution that does not protect women's rights. As male unemployment levels increased during the Great Depression, women entered the workforce to support their families. White-collar fields expanded at the same time that industrial employment declined. The tenacity of sex segregation in the workforce explains the paradox of opportunity for women increasing at the same time that men could not find jobs. The trend of marriage and career aspirations in the 1920s continued into the 1930s—by 1938, 36% of women professionals were married (Rossiter, 1982).

Government, business, and public leaders combined to insist that female employment was only acceptable before marriage. Employed married women were described as "thieving parasites who held jobs "that rightfully belonged to the God-intended providers of the household' " (Klein, 1984, p. 42). The New Deal institutionalized sex discrimination in multiple ways. Although not specifically directed to limit the employment of female psychologists, such pervasive, socially approved sex discrimination had an impact on all women in society, no matter how educated or skilled.

In 1932, Section 213 of the Economy Act specified that spouses of government employees were to be those first dismissed in any necessary workforce reductions (Rossiter, 1982). Almost every state had legislation introduced to restrict the employment of married women, and the concept of the "family wage" became entrenched in the marketplace. Other reforms that established basic institutional structures in U.S. society—including unemployment compensation and social security—were designed to enable men to serve as sole support of their families. It was not until the late 1970s, when the rise of single-headed households and the feminization of poverty could be ignored only with great societal peril, did the basic assumptions of such institutions begin to be questioned.

It was during the 1930s that universities began to pass anti-nepotism rules that limited the employment of women in professional married couples, and it was assumed that the husband's career would have priority. Anti-nepotism rules were particularly hard on the large number of married couples in psychology. Such rules kept Mednick and Spence from obtaining faculty appointments. In 1976, a study by the American Association of University Women found that one of every four institutions still had anti-nepotism policies. Such policies were more likely to be found in large, co-educational, public institutions in which larger numbers of psychologists were likely to be employed (Howard, 1978).

Little has been written about women psychologists in the decade of the 1930s, which included the beginning of the immigration of Jewish contributors to psychology. These contributors, who came to the United States to escape Nazism, included Hedda Bolgar, Else Frenkel-Brunswik, Margaret Mahler, Eugenia Hanfmann, and Erika Fromm. The autobiographies of Hanfmann and Fromm are included in our first and second volumes, respectively. In her autobiography in our first volume, Mary Henle talked about the anti-Semitism in the United States that has affected the careers of Jewish psychologists.

It was also during the 1930s that psychoanalysis increased its influence on American culture. As early as 1918, however, it had been used to specifically label the activities of American feminists as "very largely a compensation for a strong but imperfectly repressed masochistic tendency" (Ryan, 1983). Although interpretations of Sigmund Freud's work reinforced stereotypical conceptions of women and came to be a powerful tool against women's advancement, numerous women were involved in his early psychoanalytic circle. Some of them, including Frieda Fromm-Reichmann, Karen Horney, Melanie Klein, and Clara Thompson, challenged the givens of the Freudian psychoanalytic scheme that had added new dimensions to the myths held about women at the time (Russo & O'Connell, 1980). As Mednick points out in her autobiography, the visibility of these women established a place for women in psychoanalysis: "Because of them, it never occurred [to me] that women did not belong in psychology" (chapter 16).

When the backlashes developed against women's employment in the 1930s and against higher education in the 1940s, Freudian psychology was used to justify denial of women's equal access to education and to promote women's confinement to domesticity in order to avoid guilt and psychic conflicts engendered by participation in the workforce (Deutsch, 1944).

During the Depression, psychologists' employment opportunities were limited, salaries meager. Nonetheless, women continued to enter psychology: Of the 558 psychology doctorates granted between 1933 and 1937, one of every four went to a woman. Although graduate education stressed the ties betweeen psychology and science, societal demand for applied workers necessitated the development of applied training institutions such as Columbia Teachers College. By the end of the 1930s, although women comprised 30% of psychologists, they held 51% of psychology positions in applied settings (e.g., schools, educational systems, clinics, guidance centers, hospitals, and custodial institutions; Bryan, & Boring, 1946).

At the end of the 1930s, few women held positions of leadership in psychology. No woman had been elected to the presidency of APA since Margaret Washburn had held that office in 1921, when APA was a relatively small society with fewer than 400 members. Male-dominated nominating committees limited women's opportunities to hold office (Capshew & Laszlo, 1986).

Despite institutional, social, and psychological barriers, married women continued to participate in the labor force. At the end of the 1930s, 15.2% of all married women were employed. That figure changed drastically, however, as the 1930s negative view of employed, married women was overturned when wartime mobilization required the employment of women in the 1940s. Government and industry collaborated in the most intensive propaganda campaign in history to persuade married women not only to join the labor force but also to take on traditionally male jobs (Honey, 1984).

WORLD WAR II: A PARADOX
OF OPPORTUNITY AND SETBACKS

Although creating opportunities for women in the workforce—Loevinger points out in chapter 11 that in some situations, civilian employers even preferred to hire women in psychology (rather than men, who might be drafted)—World War II also contributed to sex segregation in psychology and undermined the position of women psychologists in the field. The war widened the gap between the status of male and female psychologists by employing the men in the war effort and by stimulating the growth of male-oriented subfields, particularly in industrial and personnel psychology.

Of 1,006 psychologists entering the armed forces, only 33 were women (Marquis, 1944). The autobiography of one of those women,

Mildred Mitchell, is included in our first volume. Civilian psychologists as well as military personnel received intensive training and research experiences. Psychologists became involved in devising personnel selection and training methods, in human factors research, and in civilian morale studies. This wartime experience stimulated male-dominated subfields of industrial and personnel psychology and created predominantly male social networks among researchers that shaped the postwar development of the field.

The APA played an active role in organizing psychologists during the war, but its initial efforts reflected the interests and expertise of male psychologists. During the 1939 APA convention, the APA contributed to the organization of an all-male Emergency Committee in Psychology that operated under the aegis of the National Research Council. Capshew and Laszlo (1986) and Walsh (1986) described how women psychologists had insisted they be included in wartime mobilization of psychology, but they were consistently rebuffed in their efforts by male colleagues who informed them that women's role was to "keep the home fires burning" (Schwesinger, 1943, p. 298) and who admonished them to "be good girls . . . and wait until plans could be shaped up to include [them]" (Schwesinger, 1943, p. 299). Women psychologists were told to seek volunteer work in their communities, whereas their male colleagues obtained paid employment in the military and in federal bureaucracies (Capshew & Laszlo, 1986).

In response, a New York group of women psychologists organized what became the National Council of Women Psychologists (NCWP; Portenier, n.d., p. 15). Hoping to bring scientific legitimization to the group, Florence Goodenough, a distinguished researcher in child development, was elected to serve as president. Helen Peak served as vice-president, Gladys C. Schwesinger served as Secretary, and Theodora M. Abel served as Treasurer. The NCWP quickly gained prominence and became acknowledged by invitations to send delegates to the Emergency Committee in Psychology (Capshew & Laszlo, 1986).

Capshew and Laszlo (1986) gave an account of how NCWP efforts were undercut, how its focus was diffused, and how its energies were channeled away from War Department work into local community activities. Several authors (e.g., Finison & Furumoto, 1978; Murphy, 1943; Portenier, n.d.) have summarized the research and service of women psychologists during the war years. These activities reflected the sex segregation of the subfields of psychology and focused on problems of civilian morale, relocation, refugees, children, and families in wartime. Tyler organized a counseling service for veterans. In a remarkable achievement, Stolz established the child care centers that were maintained at Kaiser shipyards during the war.

This is not to say that some women were not involved in every facet of the wartime effort of psychology (Russo & O'Connell, 1980). In her autobiography, Hanfmann (1983) communicated the excitement as well as the frustration of working as a psychologist for the OSS (Office of Strategic Services) when it was necessary to burn all records and notes at the end of the war.

During the war, women's scientific expertise was again called upon to defend women against myths and stereotypes. Georgene Seward, a student of Hollingworth, responded to the expressed concern about women's fitness to perform "men's" wartime work during the menstrual cycle. Seward (1944) conducted an exhaustive survey of the scientific literature and concluded that observed menstrual cycle effects were based on cultural stereotypes, not on physiological or psychological data. Ironically, despite repeated scientific rebuttal since the 1920s, myths about the impact of the menstrual cycle on women's performance continue to be revived to this day.

With the end of World War II, women's educational and career opportunities diminished. The message of the intense propaganda campaign that had formerly encouraged women to serve their country by working in the war effort now told women to serve their country and their men by returning to the home and having babies. There was a general acceptance of a male priority for education and jobs that became institutionalized in law in the form of veterans' preference. The outcome of the GI bill was to further widen the education gap by reducing women's access to higher education. By 1947, 69% of college males were veterans—49% of the total college enrollment (Solomon, 1985). This influx of older men, half of whom were married to wives engaged in "putting hubby through" (cf. Mednick, chap. 16), changed the character of higher education.

Although the Depression led to a skepticism regarding the merit of science, World War II restored confidence in it. After World War II, science and military applications were inextricably linked, and science was defined even more as a male activity. The war had created new and highly desirable positions in business and industry for male psychologists, most of which were not open to women. In 1944, female psychologists had a higher unemployment rate than at the beginning of the war (Walsh, 1986).

Given the military's stimulation of training and personnel psychology and the expectation that opportunities in business and industry were open to "men" (Marquis, 1944, p. 661), it is not surprising that industrial/organizational psychology remained the subfield of psychology with the highest proportion of men through the decade of the 1970s (Russo, 1984). Engelhardt and Smith are eminent exceptions.

The needs of male-oriented employment settings shaped the knowledge base of psychology, even in the applied areas in which women psychologists have traditionally participated. There were 16 million veterans of World War II and 4 million veterans of previous wars. The Veterans Administration cooperated with the U.S. Public Health Service to create funds for clinical training to serve the predominently male population of patients in need of mental health services. Experience in working with outpatients, women, and children was neglected (Reisman, 1976).

After World War II, the cult of femininity led to contradictions between idealized sex roles and the reality of women's interests, abilities, and aspirations. Despite the public ideology that extolled marriage and motherhood, the rate of female employment between 1940 and 1950 increased almost without interrruption. In 1950, one in three married women was employed, up from one in six in 1940 (Ryan, 1983). Mednick describes the conflicts and experiences during her clinical training and the negative attitudes expressed toward professional women during this period (chap. 16).

The NCWP continued after the war, developing several projects to promote the careers of women psychologists, organizing career-oriented sessions at APA annual meetings, and publishing a 1950 handbook on career issues (Walsh, 1986). However, these women were operating at a time when there was little societal support for such activities, and they were sensitive to the accusation that they were violating professional norms by pointing to discriminatory treatment. Thus, at the same time they endured blatant, sex-based inequities, they were told that *they* were being "divisive" and unprofessional by even noticing such treatment, let alone objecting to it and organizing for change.

The ideology of science joined with the norms of professionalism to pressure women in psychology to docilely accept limited opportunity and second-class status. The world of science was presented as value-free; merit was the measure of advancement. Without a feminist consciousness and group identity to enable women to examine their collective experiences and identify common inequities, any particular woman's lower status could be attributed to her personal characteristics, such as her ability, motivation, interest, and achievement. Mednick describes experiences during her clinical training that "only seemed strange at the time" (chap. 16); she reinterpreted these experiences when she attained a feminist consciousness. Lack of understanding of the dynamics of sex discrimination led to a lower salary for Denmark. It was not until the 1970s, with the wider societal and cultural support of the women's movement, that the number of women who had developed a feminist consciousness had become sufficient to organize effectively in psychology and to enact institutional changes in the discipline (Russo & Denmark, 1987).

THE REEMERGENCE
OF THE WOMEN'S MOVEMENT

The repressive climate for American women in the 1950s gave way to social reform and the civil rights movement. The frustrations and dissatisfactions of women in the 1950s were exposed in *The Feminine Mystique*, written by Betty Friedan (1963), Jane Loevinger's friend and teaching assistant at Berkeley. As Lillian E. Troll points out (chap. 8), that work became a catalyst for the resurgence of the women's movement. Friedan suggested that the generation of women who lived the feminine mystique provided negative role models for their daughters, who developed feminist aspirations from the ashes of their mothers' disappointments.

In 1961, President John F. Kennedy established the first President's Commission on the Status of Women, which called attention to sex bias in education, including vocational and guidance counseling, and identified the need to rebut myths and stereotypes about women (Peterson, 1983). Concern about women's rights received a boost from the civil rights movement when legal prohibition against sex discrimination in employment was included in the 1964 Civil Rights Act in an attempt to kill that legislation. During this period, careers of women in psychology once again began to receive attention and were the subject of workshops organized at the APA annual meetings (Sexton, 1973–1974).

The 1970s brought new opportunities for women in all fields. A feminist ideology arose to advocate equality for women and men, to promote women's solidarity, and to point to discrimination and inadequate social institutions to explain why women have been denied support in the home and access to the world of work. This ideology energized a protest movement that evolved into an organized and sophisticated political lobby on behalf of women's rights for their own sake (Klein, 1984; Tinker, 1983).

In 1970, psychologist Bernice Sandler, who had experienced sex discrimination in her search for an academic position, began to file class-action suits under the aegis of the Women's Equity Action League. Complaints were filed at over 250 colleges and universities and helped lead to the passage of Title IX of the Education Amendments of 1972, which prohibited sex discrimination in educational institutions receiving federal financial assistance (later restricted by the Supreme Court decision in *Grove City College v. Bell* and yet to be restored as of this writing). Sandler continued her leadership in promoting sex equity in education, in helping to draft the Women's Educational Equity Act of 1972, and in heading the Project on the Status and Education of Women of the Association of American Colleges (Milsap, 1983).

Beginning in the late 1960s, women again organized in psychology, this time in a more supportive climate and with an explicitly feminist stance. In 1969, the Association for Women in Psychology dramatically communicated their concern with inequities in the field at the annual convention of the APA. In response, in October 1970, APA established a task force charged with reporting on the status of women in psychology, with Helen Astin as Chair (Task Force on the Status of Women in Psychology, 1973). When the Task Force was discharged in 1972, and ad hoc Committee on the Status of Women was formed, chaired by Mednick, which became a continuing Committee on Women in Psychology (CWP) under Mednick's leadership in 1973. The mission of the committee was to "function as a catalyst, by means of interacting with and making recommendations to the various parts of the Association's governing structure" (Russo, 1984). Payton (in 1981) and Denmark (in 1983) also chaired CWP.

CWP recommended the establishment of the Division of the Psychology of Women (Division 35), which was formed in 1973 "to promote the research and study of women . . . to encourage the integration of this information about women with current psychological knowledge and beliefs in order to apply the gained knowledge to the society and its institutions" (Russo, 1984). Mednick, Denmark, and Carolyn Sherif (whose autobiography was included in our first volume) served as presidents of the division. Other eminent women in these volumes participating in the division include Thelma Alper, Engelhardt, Graham, Payton, Spence, Strickland, and Troll. For a description of the history of the division and of the evolution of the field, see Mednick (1978) and Denmark (1977).

These institutional structures—CWP and Division 35—provided a powerful lever for feminists to promote institutional change in that prestigious organization and to revitalize the science and practice of psychology for both sexes. In addition to having an impact on increasing women's participation in nearly all areas of the complex governance structure of APA (Russo, 1984), both Division 35 and CWP have played major roles in encouraging attention to the history of women in psychology (Russo & Denmark, 1987; O'Connell et al. 1978; O'Connell & Russo, 1980, 1983). Major institutional reforms include changes in APA accreditation standards for clinical, counseling, and school psychology doctoral programs so that numbers and distribution of women faculty and students as well as strategies for incorporating new research on women into the curriculum are examined (APA, 1983; Denmark, 1983). In 1977, the APA *Ethical Standards* were revised so that sexual contact between client and therapist would be designated as explicitly unethical in all circumstances. In 1981, sexual harassment of students was identified as explicitly unethical as well (Russo, 1984).

CURRENT STATUS AND PROSPECTS

Women's history in psychology calls attention to how the societal context affects the evolution of psychology and shapes women's contributions to it. Today the achievements of women psychologists are not seen as exceptions but rather as the result of the interaction of talent with opportunity. There is recognition that public intervention with regard to blatant inequities and discrimination is needed, and women have discovered the importance of working together. The consciousness of the women's movement continues and has become institutionalized in the interdisciplinary study of women's lives and experiences in the curricula of colleges and universities. In psychology, a new ideology that values both women and men is manifested in the vigor and expansion of the field of a feminist psychology of women that is challenging traditional paradigms in psychology. That challenge is critical to maintaining progress toward equality of women and men in psychology and society. It is clear from the historical pattern of setbacks and successes that women's progress cannot be taken for granted. Vigilance is indeed the price of maintaining progress. It is hoped that the historical knowledge of the contributions of women in psychology and the critical role that the use of feminist scholarship can play in supporting women's advancement in society will strengthen steps toward equality for future generations.

ACKNOWLEDGMENTS

I thank D. Allen Meyer and Agnes N. O'Connell for their reviews of this chapter. Thanks also go to Karen Applegate and Ria Hermann for helping to gather materials and to Michele Nymann for typing the manuscript. Background preparation for this work was supported by the Minigrant Program, College of Liberal Arts and Sciences, Arizona State University.

REFERENCES

American Psychological Association. (1983). *Accreditation handbook* (rev. ed.). Washington, DC: Author.

Benjamin, L. T., Jr. (1975). The pioneering work of Leta Hollingsworth in the psychology of women. *Nebraska History, 56,* 140–144.

Bryan, A. I., & Boring, E. G. (1946). Women in American psychology: Statistics from the OPP questionnaire. *Psychological Bulletin, 41,* 447–454.

Capshew, J. H. & Laszlo, A. C. (1986). "We would not take no for an answer": Women psychologists and gender politics during World War II. *Journal of Social Issues, 42,* 157–180.

Cattell, J. M. (1974). Some psychological experiments. Presidential address, American Association for the Advancement of Science. In R. H. Kargon, (Ed,), *The maturing of American science* (pp. 62–65). Washington, DC. (Original work published 1925)

Clark, M. P. (1983). Mamie Phipps Clark. In A. N. O'Connell & N. F. Russo (Eds.), *Models of achievement: Reflections of eminent women in psychology* (pp. 267–278). New York: Columbia University Press.

Denmark, F. L. (1977). The psychology of women: An overview of an emerging field. *Personality and Social Psychology Bulletin, 3,* 356–367.

Denmark, F. (1980). Psyche: From rocking the cradle to rocking the boat. *American Psychologist, 35,* 1057–1065.

Denmark, F. L. (1983). Integrating the psychology of women into introductory psychology. In C. J. Scheier & A. Rogers (Eds.), *The G. Stanley Hall Lecture Series.* (Vol. 3, pp. 33–75). Washington, DC: American Psychological Association.

Deutsch, H. (1944). *The psychology of women.* New York: Grune & Stratton.

Filene, P. G. (1975). *Him/her/self: Sex roles in modern America.* New York: Harcourt Brace Jovanovich.

Finison, L., Furomoto, L. (1978, August). *An historical perspective on psychology, social action, and women's rights.* Paper presented at the annual meeting of the American Psychological Association, Toronto, Canada.

French, J. L. (1984). On the conception, birth, and early development of school psychology. *American Psychologist, 39,* 976–987.

Friedan, B. (1963). *The feminine mystique.* New York: Norton.

Hanfmann, E. (1983). Eugenia Hanfmann. In A. N. O'Connell & N. F. Russo (Eds.), *Models of achievement: Reflections of eminent women in psychology* (pp. 141–154). New York: Columbia University Press.

Hechler, K. (1980). *Toward the endless frontier: History of the committee on science and technology, 1959–795.* Washington, DC: U.S. Government Printing Office.

Henle, M. (1983). Mary Henle. In A. N. O'Connell & N. F. Russo (Eds.), *Models of achievement: Reflections of eminent women in psychology* (pp. 220–232).

Honey, M. (1984). *Creating Rosie the Riveter: Class, gender and propaganda during World War II*. Amherst: University of Massachusetts Press.

Howard, S. (1978). *But we will persist. A comparative research report on the status of women in academe*. Washington, DC: American Association of University Women.

Howard, R. W. (1983). Ruth W. Howard. In A. N. O'Connell & N. F. Russo (Eds.), *Models of achievement: Reflections of eminent women in psychology* (pp. 55–68). New York: Columbia University Press.

Hymowitz, C., & Weissman, M. (1978). *A history of women in America*. New York: Bantam.

Kargon, R. H. (Ed.). (1974). *The maturing of American science*. Washington, DC: American Association for the Advancement of Science.

Klein, E. (1984). *Gender politics: From consciousness to mass politics*. Cambridge, MA: Harvard University Press.

Lewin, M. (Ed.). (1984). *In the shadow of the past: Psychology portrays the sexes*. New York: Columbia University Press.

Marquis, D. G. (1944). Post-war reemployment prospects in psychology. *Psychological Bulletin, 41*, 653–663.

Mednick, M. T. S. (1978). Now we are four: What should we be when we grow up? *Psychology of Women Quarterly, 3*, 123–138.

Milsap, M. (1983). Sex equity in education. In I. Tinker (Ed.), *Women in Washington: Advocates for public policy* (pp. 91–119). Beverly Hills, CA: Sage.

Murphy, G. (1943). Service of women psychologists to the war: Foreward. *Journal of Consulting Psychology, 7*, 249–251.

National Science Foundation. (1986). *Women and minorities in science and engineering*. Washington, DC: Author.

O'Connell, A. N., Alpert, J., Richardson, M. S., Rotter, N., Ruble, D. N. & Unger, R. K. (1978). Gender-specific barriers to research in psychology: Report of the Task Force on Women Doing Research—APA Division 35. *JSAS: Catalog of Selected Documents in Psychology* (Ms. No. 1753) *8*, 80.

O'Connell, A. N., & Russo, N. F. (Eds.). (1980). *Eminent women in psychology: Models of achievement*. New York: Human Sciences Press.

O'Connell, A. N., & Russo, N. F. (Eds.). (1983). *Models of achievement: Reflections of eminent women in psychology*. New York: Columbia University Press.

Peterson, E. (1983). The Kennedy Commission. Tinker In I. (Ed.), *Women in Washington: Advocates for public policy* (pp. 21–34). Beverly Hills, CA: Sage.

Pion, G., Bramblett, P., Wicherski, M., & Stapp, J. (1985). *Summary report of the 1984–85 Survey of Graduate Departments of Psychology*. Washington, DC: American Psychological Association.

Portenier, L. G. (Ed.). n.d. *International Council of Psychologists, Inc.: The first quarter-century, 1942–1967*. International Council of Psychologists, Inc.

Reisman, J. (1976). *A history of clinical psychology*. New York: Irvington.

Rosenberg, R. (1982). *Beyond separate spheres: Intellectual roots of modern feminism*. New Haven, CT: Yale University Press.

Rossiter, M. W. (1974). Women scientists in America before 1920. *American Scientist, 62*, 312–323.

Rossiter, M. W. (1982). *Women scientists in America: Struggles and strategies to 1940*. Baltimore: Johns Hopkins University Press.

Russo, N. F. (1983). Psychology's foremothers: Their achievements in context. In A. N. O'Connell & N. F. Russo (Eds.), *Models of achievement: Reflections of eminent women in psychology* (pp. 9–24). New York: Columbia University Press.

Russo, N. F. (1984). *Women in the American Psychological Association*. Washington DC: Women's Programs Office, American Psychological Association.

Russo, N. F., & Cassidy, M. M. (1983). Women in science and technology. In I. Tinker (Ed.), *Women in Washington: Advocates for public policy* (pp. 250–261). Beverly Hills, CA: Sage.

Russo, N. F., & Denmark, F. L. (1987). Contributions of women to psychology. *Annual Review of Psychology, 38*, 279–298.

Russo, N. F., & O'Connell, A. N. (1980). Models from our past: Psychology's foremothers. *Psychology of Women Quarterly, 5*, 11–54.

Russo, N. F., Olmedo, E., Stapp, J., & Fulcher, R. (1981). Women and minorities in psychology. *American Psychologist, 36*, 1315–1363.

Ryan, M. P. (1983). *Womanhood in America from colonial times to the present*. New York: Franklin Watts.

Schwesinger, G. (1943). Wartime organizational activities of women psychologists: II. The National Council of Women Psychologists. *Journal of Consulting Psychology, 7*, 298–299.

Seward, G. H. (1944). Psychological effects of the menstrual cycle on women workers. *Psychological Bulletin, 41*, 90–102.

Sexton, V. S. (1969). Women's accomplishments in American psychology: A brief survey. *Pakistan Journal of Psychology, 2*, 29–35.

Sexton, V. S. (1973–1974). Women in American psychology: An overview. *International Understanding, 10*, 66–77.

Sherman, J. A., & Denmark, F. L. (1978). *The psychology of women: Future directions in research*. New York: Psychological Dimensions, Inc.

Shields, S. A. (1975a). Functionalism, Darwinism and the psychology of women: A study of social myth. *American Psychologist, 30*, 739–754.

Shields, S. A. (1975b). Ms. Pilgrim's progress: The contributions of Leta Stetter Hollingworth to the psychology of women. *American Psychologist, 30*, 852–857.

Soloman, B. (1985). *In the company of educated women*. New Haven, CT: Yale University Press.

Task Force on the Status of Women in Psychology. (1973). Report of the Task Force on the Status of Women in Psychology. *American Psychologist, 28*, 611–616.

Tinker, I. (Ed.). (1983). *Women in Washington: Advocates for public policy*. Beverly Hills, CA: Sage.

Walsh, M. R. (1986). Academic professional women organizing for change: The struggle in psychology. *Journal of Social Issues, 41*, 17–27.

Welter, B. (1966). The cult of true womanhood: 1820–1860. *American Quarterly, 18*, 151–174.

PART III

PERSONAL PERSPECTIVES: AUTOBIOGRAPHICAL SKETCHES

CHAPTER 3

Lois Hayden Meek Stolz

Lois Hayden Meek Stolz

I have been asked to discuss whether being a woman fostered opportunities or problems or otherwise had an effect on my education, on my career, or on personal-professional adjustments. I frankly do not know. So I have decided to tell you something about my experiences, and let you make the decision. I say "something about my experiences" because I feel sure you would not want to know all that has happened in my 70 years of professional life.

> (I remember a story told me by Sidonie Gruenberg of the Child Study Association. Her youngest son asked her a question about sex. She said, "Why don't you ask your father, he is a biologist, that's his field." The son replied, "Oh, I don't want to know that much.")

When I finished high school, my one desire in life was to go to a "finishing school" to become beautiful and attractive. However, my father had other ideas. He said, in true late-Victorian style, "Every women should be able to earn her own living, if she has to." *If she has to*, that meant if her father or husband did not do the job. So, I was sent to the Washington, DC, Normal School, over my strong protests. To circumvent my father, I decided I would flunk out.

I probably would have succeeded if it had not been for a friend who decided she would never graduate if she sat in the back row with me. I followed her to the front row.

This was my undoing. As I listened, I began to learn about the world I lived in, rather than the academic world of the high school classical curriculum. All the teachers at the Normal School were women with excellent backgrounds and a verve for teaching. There I first met William James in a course given by the head of the school, Ann Goding. It was when I was practice-teaching under Rose Hardy that I first learned the importance of understanding causes of behavior.

I spent 9 years in the Washington, DC, public schools: For 4 years, I was a teacher; then, on the recommendation of Mr. Ely, the district superintendent, I became a demonstration teacher and supervisor for 5 years. During that time, I began teaching in the summer quarter at the University of Virginia on the recommendation of Ethel Summy of the DC public schools. I also went to George Washington University in late afternoons and completed work for the AB degree, *cum laude.*

At George Washington University, I first learned of John B. Watson and behaviorism. But I was influenced most by a professor of sociology, Robert Kern, who not only won me over as a major, but directed me toward a political liberalism that became an integral part of my philosophy for life.

Finally, my educational preparation led me to a PhD from Columbia University. Several factors brought this about. I had become interested in progressive education and had visited the Horace Mann School at Teachers College, Columbia University. In my demonstration classroom, I had begun experimenting, Then, in the summer of 1921, while I was at the University of Virginia, a family tragedy occurred. My only sibling, an older brother, died suddenly. Due to my grief, my father suggested that this might be a good time to take off for graduate study. At that time, Teachers College at Columbia University was the most outstanding college in the United States for graduate work in education. So I went.

I was almost 30 when I enrolled at Columbia, but this was not unusual, for most of the graduate students had had previous work experience. I planned to major in educational sociology, due to Robert Kern. That was lucky, for the chairman of that department was David Snedden. His idea was that women should not bother with higher degrees; their role was homemaking. So, he approved anything I wanted to take—what did it matter anyhow? This left me free to study with professors I had heard about: Edward Thorndike, R. S. Woodworth, Arthur Gates, Rudolph Pintner, Harry Hollingsworth, John Dewey, William Kilpatrick, Patty Hill. Such a feast!

It was during that year that my major interest turned from sociology to psychology. This was partly due of course to the outstanding psychology professors, but also due to one professor who was not so good: a woman who taught the course in child psychology. She was the co-author of the excellent text we used. But her lectures were boring—statistics—one could not find a child. I had acquired some ability to observe children, to understand a little of the causes of their behavior, and to help them with problems in behavior and learning. My negative response to this professor made me yearn to be able to teach such a course in a dynamic, interesting way.

At the end of that year I received the MA degree and was awarded a small scholarship for another year of study. In the summer at the University of Virginia, I decided not to return to Columbia the next fall, but to wait until I had accumulated more money. Professor Mabel Carney of Teachers College heard about my decision when she gave some lectures at the University of Virginia that summer. When she returned to New York, she talked with Professor Patty Hill. The result was that I received a letter from Professor Bagley offering me an assistantship, telling me I could keep the scholarship and continue my major in psychology.

So, due to two women professors, I returned to Teachers College; in 2 more years, I completed the doctoral examinations, finished my dissertation on learning of young children, and received the PhD degree. Now in my early 30s, I was ready for a career in psychology.

There was one more hurdle—a job. It finally narrowed to a choice between two: an assistant professorship at Teachers College and a job with the American Association of University Women (AAUW). It seemed that the Laura Spelman Rockefeller foundation had given a grant to the AAUW for a program to disseminate information about children to the college graduates in the branches of the Association. I had been interviewed by the Education Policy Committee of the Association. That was a meeting to remember, made up of outstanding leaders in women's education—among whom were M. Carey Thomas of Bryn Mawr, Ada Comstock of Radcliffe, Mary Woolley of Mt. Holyoke, Frances Fenton Bernard of Smith, and perhaps most important, Chairman Helen Thompson Woolley, an outstanding psychologist. It was Helen Thompson Woolley who had persuaded the association to adopt the program.

When I was offered the job, I went to Dr. Thorndike to ask his advice about which position to accept, the one at the AAUW or the one at Columbia. He did not hesitate: Take the AAUW position. I must admit I was surprised and chagrined. I asked him about his advice. He said (and I have remembered it through the years), "If you stay here, you will always be thought of as a bright young student. If you go out and do something worthwhile, and they really want you, they will bring you back and you will have status." Dr. Kilpatrick agreed.

So I went to AAUW in Washington, DC in 1924, not realizing how this would affect my career for the rest of my life. First, there was the influence of Helen Thompson Woolley, who became my advisor. Then, there was the child development movement promoted by the Laura Spelman Rockefeller Memorial, of which the AAUW program was a part. Through the leadership of Beardsley Ruml and Lawrence Frank, this program became the dominant influence on child research in the 1920s and 1930s through the establishment of institutes at several universities and through the activation of the dissemination of knowledge of child development to practitioners: parents, educators, pediatricians, nurses, dietitians, and others. It was at this time that attention was focused on the preschool years—before then, a relatively neglected period. Later in the 1930s, development in adolescence became a focus through grants to the Progressive Education Association and to the Institute of Child Welfare Research, University of California.

I became a part of this movement, was swept along by it, and at times did a little sweeping myself. The position at the AAUW had several advantages. I traveled extensively in the United States to visit branches; I had the opportunity not only to attend and participate in meetings, but to visit institutions and programs; and I met and came to know many leaders in the field: Bird Baldwin, Harold Jones, Herbert Stolz, George Stoddard, Arnold Gesell, Douglas Thom. There were women psychologists too: Mary Jones, Beth Wellman, Jean MacFarlane, Nancy Bayley, Elizabeth Woods, Rachel Stutsman, Ruth Updegraff, Florence Goodenough, and some 20 others I could list.

Shortly after I began work at the AAUW, I was invited, on the recommendation of Harold Rugg, to be chairman of a committee of the National Society for the Study of Education (NSSE) to prepare a yearbook on preschool and parent education. I was the first woman to be named chairman of a yearbook committee of the NSSE. The yearbook was presented in February 1929 by the committee that included Helen Thompson Woolley, Gesell, Baldwin, Hill, Edna White, and Thom. There were in addition 29 associate contributors, 20 of them women, 8 psychologists.

After 5 years with the AAUW, when I was in my 30s, I returned to Teachers College as a professor of education and as associate director of the Child Development Institute. This came about because Dr. Helen Thompson Woolley, who was then director, needed an associate director and recommended me. A few months later, Dr. Woolley became ill, and I was appointed director, I stayed at Columbia 10 years, 10 difficult years. The Great Depression of the 1930s—when all employees got a cut in salary; when the Laura Spelman Rockefeller Memorial went out of business; when the General Education Board financed us for 2 years on a limited budget to integrate the program of the institute into the college and then to close shop.

But there were rewarding experiences too for me, both in teaching and administration. We supervised some excellent PhD dissertations, including those of Lois Murphy, Gertrude Driscoll, Meta Rust, Ruth Arrington, and Mary Fisher Langmuir. Arthur Jersild and his associates published some important studies, as did Dr. Mary Swartz Rose and Elda Robb. We developed a syllabus for a major graduate course in child development; the Family Consultation Center was opened; a guidance nursery was developed. And when we closed, many of the programs of the institute had been integrated into the offerings of Teachers College.

During that decade there were many opportunities to contribute to the child development movement. One of the most exciting was helping to inaugurate the establishment of nursery schools for children of families on relief through the Federal Emergency Relief Administration and to serve on the advisory committee. It was also during the 1930s that I became interested in the development of children during adolescence through participating in the research program of the Progressive Education Association financed by the General Education Board.

However, when I had a delayed sabbatical leave from 1938 to 1939, I decided not to return to Columbia. Why? Well, as Dr. Agnes N. O'Connell lists it in the outline she sent us—Integration of Professional and Personal Life. I married Herbert R. Stolz, who had been the director of the Institute of Child Welfare Research, University of California at Berkeley. But as far as I can see, there was no conflict in roles between woman and psychologist, perhaps due to my middle age and previous experiences in psychology. I found plenty to do in California—including some activities that administrative work had kept me from: writing two books, working in institutes for teachers, beginning research on adolescent development, becoming active in the mental hygiene movement.

Then the war. The upsurge in employment of women created a demand for the care of children. Several organizations pressed the governor of California to do something about this. On their recommendation, he appointed me assistant to the governor in the area of Care of Children in Wartime. It was a difficult task with many frustrations, some due to competition between state departments for control of the program.

Then a telephone call from Edgar Kaiser took me to Portland, Oregon, to undertake the most exciting professional experience I have ever had. The project was to develop the Child Service Centers in two shipyards (under the management of Kaiser) that employed some 25,000 women. James Hymes joined me; together we did the job. By the end of the war, we had served over 3,800 different children, with almost 250,000 child care days, freeing just under 2 million woman-work-hours (see Hymes, 1978). And we had provided the best services I have ever seen—educational, psychological, nutritional, and medical.

Near the end of the war, there was another "lucky accident." Our friends, Roger and Louise Barker, drove from Stanford to our home in Oakland to ask a favor. Roger was scheduled to teach that summer at Stanford, but another offer intrigued him. However, Stanford would not release him unless he could find an acceptable substitute. Would I be that substitute? Finally I was persuaded, in spite of the 40-mile drive. Later Jack Hilgard made me a permanent fixture. Teaching and research—no administrative responsibilities. What heaven! Shortly after, I received a grant from the National Institute of Mental Health for the study of fathers and children separated by war. Then, with Alberta Siegel, I undertook a study of the effects on children of mothers' employment outside the home, in cooperation with the AAUW. Following this, I participated with Robert Sears and Wilbur Schramm in the study of influences on parent behavior. In all these investigations, graduate students participated.

In retrospect, I find three areas of influences that have determined where I was going in my professional life. The first is people: my father, two women friends, the women teachers at Normal School, the men professors at Columbia University, all had strong positive effects. Then two professors who had negative influences—a man who steered me out of sociology and a woman who made me want to teach a more dynamic course in child psychology. And the women in the AAUW, especially Helen Woolley and Ada Comstock.

The second influencing factor was related to the social conditions of the times, primarily the economic depression of the 1930s, the world war of the 1940s, and the adjustments following the war.

Another factor was the changes occurring in the professional fields. For me, probably the most decisive was the child development movement. But also there was progressive education and later the mental hygiene movement spearheaded by Clifford Beers.

And finally I suppose I should mention me. Qualities in my personality certainly were factors: a mid-Victorian drive to work, values for social justice, a strong liking for people—all may have helped or hindered on the way. Did the fact that I am a *woman* have anything to do with this? Yes. My father's attitude, the AAUW offer, the influence of Dr. Helen Thompson Woolley. But not, as I see it, in my being director of an institute, a chairman of an NSSE committee, a professor at Stanford University, or in my continuing relationships with students and in my commitment to the welfare of humankind.

REPRESENTATIVE PUBLICATIONS

Dillon, M. (1983, March 30). Stolz, 91, sees children as our prime resource. *Campus Report* (Stanford University), pp. 4–5.

Dillon, M. (1983, April 13). Stolz profoundly influenced child development research. *Campus Report* (Stanford University), pp. 4–5.

Hymes, J. L. (1978). Early childhood education: Living history interviews. Book 2. Care of the children of working mothers. Carmel, CA: Hacienda Press.

Meek, L. H. (1926). New ventures in education for university women. *Journal of American Association of University Women, 20,* 1, 17–19.

Meek, L. H. (1928). (Ed.) *Preschool and parental education* (The Twenty-Eighth Yearbook, National Society for the Study of Education: L. H. Meek, Chairman). Bloomington, IL: National Society for the Study of Education.

Meek, L. H. (1931). *How children build habits. Guidance materials for study groups* (No. 1). Washington, DC: American Association of University Women.

Meek, L. H. (1932). Psychology and the preschool child. In P. S. Achilles (Ed.), *Psychology at work* (pp. 3–32). New York: McGraw-Hill.

Meek, L. H., & Jersild, A. T. (1936). Mental development from two to twelve years. *Review of Educational Research, 6,* 1.

Meek, L. H. (1941). Patterns of growth during adolescence with implications for school procedures. *Journal of Progressive Education, 18*(1), 41–45.

Meek, L. H. (1950). *Your child's development and guidance.* Philadelphia: Lippincott. (Original work published 1940).

Owen, F. W., Adams, P. A., Forrest, T., Stolz, L. M., & Fisher, S. (1971). Learning disorders in children: Sibling studies. *Monographs of the Society for Research in Child Development, 36,* 4 (144).

Siegei, A. E., Stolz, L. M., Hitchcock, E. A., & Adamson, J. (1959). Dependence and independence in the children of working mothers. *Child Development, 30,* 533–546.

Stolz, H. R., & Stolz, L. M. (1944). Adolescent problems related to somatic variations. In H. E. Jones, et al. *43rd Yearbook of the National Society for the Study of Education: Part I* (pp. 80–99). Chicago: University of Chicago Press.

Stolz, H. R., & Stolz, L. M. (1951). *Somatic development of adolescent boys.* New York: MacMillan.

Stolz, H. R., & Stolz, L. M. (1971). Somatic development of adolescent boys. In M. C. Jones, N. Bayley, J. W. MacFarlane, & M. P. Honzik (Eds.), *The course of human development* (pp. 27–42). Waltham, MA: Xerox Publishing.

Stolz, L. M. (1943, November 7). The nursery comes to the shipyard. *New York Times Magazine,* pp. 20, 39.

Stolz, L. M. (1951). *The effect of mobilization and war on children* [Condensation of address made to the Midcentury White House Conference on Children and Youth, Washington, DC, December 1950]. *Journal of American Association of University Women, 44*, 134–140.

Stolz, L. M. (1954). *Father relations of war-born children: The effect of postwar adjustment of fathers on the behavior and personality of first children born while the fathers were at war.* Stanford, CA: Stanford University Press.

Stolz, L. M. (1955). Priorities for learning in a democracy. *Journal of American Association of University Women, 49*(1), 15–21.

Stolz, L. M. (1958). Youth: The Gesell Institute and its latest study. [A review of *Youth: The Years from Ten to Sixteen*] by Gesell, A., Ilg, F., and Ames, L. B. *Contemporary Psychology, 3*(1), 10–15.

Stolz, L. M. (1960). Effects of maternal employment on children: Evidence from research. *Child Development, 31*, 749–782.

Stolz, L. M. (1961). For better parents. [A review of *Education for Child Rearing* by Brim, O. G.] *Contemporary Psychology, 6*, 169–170.

Stolz, L. M. (1964). *Our changing understanding of children's fears.* New York: National Association for the Education of Young Children.

Stolz, L. M. (1966). Old and new directions in child development. *Merrill-Palmer Quarterly, 12*(3), 221–232.

Stolz, L. M. (1967). *Influences on parent behavior.* Stanford, CA: Stanford University Press.

Stolz, L. M. (1968). History of participation in the child development movement. In *Oral History Interviews* conducted by Milton J. E. Senn. Bethesda, MD: National Library of Medicine, National Institute of Health, U.S. Department of Health, Education and Welfare.

Stolz, L.M., & Zapoleon, M.W. (1971). Helen Thompson Woolley. In E.I. James, J. W. James, & P. S. Boyor (Eds.), *Notable American Women 1607–1950; a biographical dictionary* (Vol. 3, pp. 657–660). Cambridge, MA: Belknap.

Stolz, L. M. (1977–1978). An American child development pioneer: Lois Meek Stolz. In *Oral History Interviews* conducted by Ruby Takaniski (Ed.). Bethesda, MD: National Library of Medicine, National Institute of Health, U.S. Department of Health, Education and Welfare.

Stolz, L. M. (1978). The Kaiser Child Service Centers. In J. L. Hymes, Jr. (Ed.), *Living history interviews: Book 2. Care of children of working mothers* (pp. 27–56). Carmel, CA: Hacienda Press.

CHAPTER 4

Leona E. Tyler

Leona E. Tyler

My life has been divided into several distinct stages, differentiated not only by activities and surroundings but also by the way I saw myself and my place in the world. During most of these periods, the fact that I had been born female rather than male was not a very important part of the picture.

The first stage was the period in which I was mainly influenced by my parents and family. Born in 1906, I was a happy child in a closely knit family consisting of father, mother, and three younger brothers. I realize now that we were on the verge of poverty most of the time, but we never went hungry and we never were on welfare or any other form of public assistance. We prided ourselves on our ancestry, which we could trace back to the Revolution or earlier on both sides. We took for granted our superiority to our neighbors and classmates of the many European nationalities that made up the population of the Minnesota mining town in which we lived. No one from my parents' generation had gone to college, but my mother made up her mind that we should—and we did.

It might not seem obvious to those who do not know the area, the Mesabi Iron Range, that this remote region provided a very rich environment for the sort of child I was. The recent immigrants from many European countries had brought their cultures with them. Predominant nationalities were Italian, Finnish, Swedish, Norwegian, Serbian, and Croatian. There were many Cornish people from England, "Cousin Jacks" we called them. The tax revenues from the very productive mines were so large that there were palatial school buildings staffed by the best teachers available. Libraries were excellent. Music, which all my life was to be essential to me, flourished. Often when a concert was scheduled in the city, arrangements would be made for the artist to give a special program for schoolchildren. One of my precious memories is Schumann-Heink's concert for us on her last tour.

My mother was committed to the strictest kind of Fundamentalist Christianity, and as I reached adolescence, this became more and more of a sore point with me, as the prohibition against dancing placed severe limits on my social activity. I did not rebel; at least part of me assumed that she might be right. The general religious attitude and high moral principles instilled in me at that time have persisted long after their dogmatic foundation disintegrated.

Although I was always a good student and passed rapidly through the grades to graduate from high school at 15 and from college at 19, I was neither popular nor conspicuous as an adolescent. I did not take part in extracurricular activities. I was not elected to any offices. Most of my free time was spent reading or playing the piano. Aesthetic values, especially those involved in music, increasingly came to replace the family's religious and moral values. I became an "intellectual" who felt that she was cast in a different mold from the people around her and could not expect to be understood.

Gender was not the problem during this period. It was never emphasized in our family, my mother assuming that the passage of the Nineteenth Amendment had disposed of the myth of female inferiority for good. My father helped with the housework; my mother disciplined the children more firmly than he did. She did, of course, follow the Biblical injunctions about how women should behave. She never worked outside the home; she never learned to drive; "bobbed" hair was anathema to her. But she held my brothers and me to the same standards, academically and behaviorally.

My college years, 1921 to 1925, were a transition period, but the pattern set earlier was not broken during either the 2 years at Virginia Junior College in my home town or the 2 years at the University of Minnesota. The most significant experience was my encounter with chemistry, the first real science I had studied. It was an overpowering aesthetic experience to contemplate the universal order embodied in the periodic table of the elements, the similarity of atomic and astronomical structures, the generation of enormously complex organic substances from combinations of simple molecules. I decided that, of course, I would major in chemistry.

But when I started upper-division work at the university, I found that I lacked all the prerequisites for the advanced courses. I had never studied physics or mathematics beyond geometry. It would take several additional years to remedy these deficiencies. And I knew that my family's resources had been stretched to the limit to keep me at the university for 2 years. I must get my bachelor's degree and start earning my living. Teaching was an obvious choice, as the women in my family for two generations had been country school teachers during part of their lives. If I became a high school teacher, I would be a step up from them. I would major in English because I liked to read and had a vague idea of becoming a writer some day. I also took an advanced math course each term so that if sometime I found it possible to go back to chemistry, I would be prepared. Psychology never entered my mind as a major. The one course I had taken in junior college was of no interest whatsoever to me.

Teachers, mentors, or role models have never been very influential in my decisions. The only two college teachers I remember from my undergraduate years were Fred Cope, my chemistry instructor in junior college, and Dora V. Smith, who taught the English Methods course at the university; through Smith's efforts, I became vitally interested in and, I think, quite competent in the teaching of ninth graders to write. Throughout my life, my education has come from books rather than from teachers. What mattered to me in the courses I took was the reading list, not the instructor.

As I look back on my undergraduate years, the dominant impression is one of omnivorous reading. I had no trouble maintaining a respectable honors-level average in my courses, but I finished my assignments as quickly as possible so that I could settle down in the Arthur Upson Room at the university library, a beautifully furnished, richly supplied place for pleasure reading. There I could follow my own paths and discover books and authors with special meaning for me.

It was the next period of my life—after I started out at 19 as an independent person, a small-town junior high school teacher—that turned out to be a time of liberation and transformation. There were people who mattered to me during those years, although I should not call them mentors or role models. I discovered that I was not alone, that there were people who thought as I did. One was Madam Lombardi, my charismatic piano teacher, who with her husband had come over from Milan to start a new conservatory of music on the Mesabi Iron Range. I worked tremendously hard at the piano during those years but gradually recognized that my talent was not sufficient for a musical career. More important still was a colleague at the school where I taught. The son of highly educated parents and the product of a scientific education at a major university, somehow he had never exactly fit into the slots he was expected to fill and ended up a small-town shop teacher. He was as devoted to music as I was and used his electronic skills to build a superb record player. I spent long hours listening to records with him and talking about music, books, public affairs, and many other things. It was always a completely platonic affair. He was married with two children, and at that stage of my life I would have been horrified at the thought of being the occasion of a divorce and the breakup of a family. But slowly I found myself abandoning the dogmatic religion, the self-righteous intolerance, and the conservative ideology I had grown up with and becoming an avowed liberal, an internationalist, a supporter of unpopular causes.

The process was carried even further in my next teaching situation, where I became a member of a small, close social group consisting of a talented young organist, an enlightened journalist, and the journalist's naturalist wife. We read and discussed books, listened to music, took long walks and sometimes trips together. Here also the relationships were close friendships, not love affairs. The organist had no intention of getting married and in fact was in no position to do so. The journalist and his wife were a devoted couple. But it was intensely satisfying to me to have found a place where I really belonged. It was during these prepsychology years that I also became involved in the peace movement and found myself joining organizations, serving on committees, and playing a part in community affairs quite foreign to the style of life that had characterized my high school and college years.

There were complications. Because my meager 10-month salary was not sufficient to maintain me in independence during the summer, I returned to the family home during those months. Conflicts of values sometimes erupted into bitter arguments. The compromise I adopted was to conform behaviorally to my mother's demanding standards, not smoking or drinking or even cutting my hair. But I reserved the right to think as I pleased. It was not really a good solution. It seems strange from today's point of view that I did not find myself a summer job and leave home completely. But at the time I thought that the family would be hurt if I abandoned them—and I really loved them all. I enjoyed the leisure the summer months gave me to read and think and practice on the piano.

I never intended to be an English teacher all my life. I enjoyed some aspects of it, but the constant vigilance required to keep order in a junior high classroom was a continuing strain. Like most young teachers, I expected that I would eventually meet up with someone to marry and thus would be free to give up the effort. Somehow this did not happen for me, and by 1937, when I registered for a summer session Individual Differences course, I had tentatively decided to head for a master's degree in psychology and a career in the developing field of counseling.

It was the teacher of that first Individual Differences course, Donald G. Paterson, known to his friends as Pat, who changed the whole pattern of my life. He asked me to come in for an interview to discuss my plans, convinced me that I should be in full-time graduate work, arranged for me to get a teaching assistantship at the University of Minnesota to make this financially possible, and worked out with me a research plan that I could initiate during my last year of public school teaching. At the end of this one interview, I was no longer a struggling junior high teacher but a prospective psychologist. I was pleased but incredulous. I could not possibly be as able as he seemed to think I was, but I would do everything in my power not to disappoint him.

I can see now that the direction of my intellectual efforts for the rest of my life was set then. I saw dimly that what I most wanted to understand was the rich diversity of human individuality, which had first become apparent to me in the themes my ninth graders had written. My graduate program emphasized individual differences and gave me special training in counseling. My research, initiated with my master's thesis, entitled "An Interest Test for Girls," and carried on for many years afterward, was on the development and measurement of interests. As the years passed, these three threads—individual differences, counseling, and interest research—were woven together into complex patterns.

My two full-time graduate years, 1938 to 1940, were sheer delight for me. To be able to spend the best hours of the day reading and studying, free from the constraints of classrooms where I always felt uncertain as to whether I could control the situation, was almost too good to be true. I enjoyed my classes, my research activities, and the associations with other graduate students and faculty. The only problem was my home situation. To save money, I stayed at the family home in St. Paul, where the relationship with my mother was strained. From her point of view, psychology was a wicked subject. Darwin, Freud, and the later psychologists were enemies of everything she valued, and my choice of a psychology major meant that she had failed in her duty. I dealt with this conflict as well as I could, not very wisely I am afraid, and it constituted a spur to me to maximize the speed with which I finished the program and became independent again.

Two persons qualify as "mentors" during the graduate years, "Pat" Paterson, who had brought me into the profession and whose ideas and encouragement continued to support my decision, and "Mike" Elliott, whose philosophical and theoretical interests were like my own. I was not aware of any "role models." The only woman faculty member with whom I was associated was Florence Goodenough, and although I liked and admired her, I never thought of her as a model. Edna Heidbreder had left Minnesota before my time. If there was any sex discrimination, I did not see it. Among the 15 graduate assistants, 4 were women, and we were never treated any differently from the others, so far as I could see. My assumption that intelligent people no longer considered women inferior persisted. I never had occasion to question it.

At the end of the summer of 1940, I had completed my course work and PhD dissertation, and although I could not schedule my final oral examination or receive the degree until the next academic year, I was ready and eager to go to work on some college faculty. Here, as at the beginning of my graduate education, the way was cleared for me. The chairman of the psychology department at the University of Oregon wrote to the Minnesota chairman seeking a promising candidate for an instructorship. I was asked if I would like to go to Oregon, was recommended, and was accepted for the position before I had even filled out an application blank. It seems that the "old boy" network occasionally let an "old girl" through.

In my career as a psychologist from 1940 on, I can distinguish three qualitatively different periods. The first 10 years at Oregon were among the happiest of my life. For a confirmed aesthete and nature lover, the sheer physical beauty of the surroundings was a constant inspiration. I was surrounded by people I liked and who liked me—faculty members, graduate students, students in my classes. I was free to do the things I most wanted to do—initiate a research program, organize a part-time counseling service, write a new textbook on individual differences (Tyler, 1947). It may seem strange to today's academicians to hear that in those years, when I was an instructor and assistant professor, I considered myself a great success. My experience as a small-town public school teacher had given me no understanding of the structure of college faculties. The difference between assistant, associate, and full professors was lost on me. For me to be an accepted member of the university faculty seemed an enormous step up from my previous positions.

I realize now that my progress up the academic ladder was slower than it should have been and that sexist attitudes were undoubtedly involved, but at the time I did not notice them. I would have considered it bad manners to ask about my colleagues' salaries; we simply did not ask such questions in those days. I think I would have been content to maintain the status I had for the rest of my life.

As a pacifist, I was greatly troubled by the war. I was thankful that as a woman I was not called on to serve the military in any way. I did for a couple years teach mathematics courses to a contingent of recruits stationed at the university, and I organized the counseling service for veterans, but neither of these activities troubled my conscience because they were services to individuals, not to the war machine. I also volunteered time to provide counseling for men at a nearby camp for conscientious objectors.

During the next period, 1950 to 1965, the kinds of recognition I received undermined my concept of myself as a simple teacher, lucky to have landed in such pleasant surroundings. The first shock was to have my book, *The Psychology of Human Differences* (Tyler, 1947), accepted for publication in the prestigious Century Psychology Series. But the real turning point was the sabbatical year in London, 1951 to 1952. I did not have a grant of any sort but found that at the exchange rates then in force, I could live very comfortably on my half-salary. I had research data to analyze, and Hans Eysenck and his colleagues at Maudsley Hospital made me welcome to their statistical facilities and graduate seminars. The year was rewarding personally as well as professionally. I reveled in London's aesthetic delights—concerts, operas, plays, museums. There was a short but very intense love affair. I visited places on the continent I had always wished to see. I began writing another book, *The Work of the Counselor* (Tyler, 1953).

When I returned to the university in 1952, my position was subtly different from what it had been before. Although I was no more ambitious than I had ever been, I began to receive kinds of recognition I had never expected or sought, such as appointment to the Publications Board of the American Psychological Association (APA), requests to consult and teach summer school, election to office in state and regional associations. *The Work of the Counselor* was an immediate success, and I became known as an authority on counseling, in which I was heavily engaged at the time. Just when I was transformed in my own eyes from an ordinary to an influential psychologist I cannot remember precisely, but the transformation did take place. It did not change the core of my personality. I have never really felt like an important person, a leader in my field.

It was during this period that I reconciled myself to the fact that

I was probably going to be single all my life. Since childhood, I had always assumed that I would eventually meet a man whom I would marry; consciously or unconsciously, I had been looking for him. I had expected and wished to have children. The reasons why these plans had not worked out are too complex to be analyzed here. My adolescent maladjustment and the fact that during my most marriageable years I lived in small, remote towns far from intellectual centers played some part. Throughout the years, I have been involved in several close friendships with men who meant a great deal to me, but for various reasons they were not available as husbands—already married, homosexual, too young or too old, too poor. Adjustment to a permanently single life has many aspects, such as creating for oneself the sort of home one wishes to live in, making one's own travel arrangements, being one's own chauffeur, as well as sublimating sexual and maternal motivation. Being on my own has contributed to my success, although it is not the life I would have chosen. "*She* travels the fastest who travels alone," to adapt a famous quotation.

Sometime during the 1950s, the ideas generated by my research and writing, as well as my teaching and counseling, gradually coalesced into a search for a coherent theoretical system. I became convinced that research on individual differences, based as it is on normative measurement of hypothetical traits, was never going to give us understanding of individuality. In my presidential address to the Western Psychological Association in 1958, I proposed that individuality is a matter of *choice* and *organization* (Tyler, 1959). I came to see the vocational interests I had been studying as the directions one's choices had taken during development. The concept of multiple possibilities became the cornerstone of my thinking about individuality. Once more, a sabbatical year, this time at the University of Amsterdam from 1962 to 1963, gave me an opportunity to think about basic questions.

From 1965 to my retirement and on up to the present, the shape of my life was different because I was no longer primarily a teacher. From 1965 to 1971, when I retired, I was dean of the Graduate School at the University of Oregon. Like my previous promotions, this was a complete surprise to me. It was some time before I could bring myself to accept the offer and an even longer time before I could get used to the position, and I realized that I, like a lot of other people, had been assuming that such an administrative role was not suitable for a woman. Had the opportunity come 10 years later, after the resurgence of militant feminism, perhaps my struggle with myself would have been easier. What I had to get used to was having an influence on the policies, development, and structure of the university as a whole. At this time, under Arthur Fleming's dynamic leadership, the University of Oregon was undergoing a transformation from a minor to a major institution. The Graduate School, as the seeker and the custodian of research funds and the upholder of academic standards, played a large part in this transformation.

Furthermore, it was during this period that my participation in APA affairs became an important part of my life, so that my role in the profession was similar to my role at the university. I served on the Board of Directors, the Policy and Planning Board, for 3 years as president-elect, president, and past president, and later as a member of the Board of Social and Ethical Responsibility. I was an advisory editor for *Contemporary Psychology* and was often asked to evaluate submissions to other journals.

Throughout all these successive stages of my career as a psychologist, I have been a writer. That is why retirement did not constitute a new situation for me as it does for many academicians. I went right on writing. The focus of my efforts, however, has gradually changed from textbooks and revisions of textbooks to think pieces about psychology as a whole. Like so many people before, I have become more and more philosophical in my old age. The two books published since I retired (Tyler, 1978, 1983) are the most tangible results of this shift. Fortunately, the weakening of the deterministic, positivistic assumptions most psychologists had thought they must accept if a science of behavior was to be built made it more legitimate than it had been to theorize about human possibilities from which each individual selects a unique fraction. This is the heart of my system of ideas.

As I consider my relationship to the women's rights movement, it seems to me that I have occupied an ambiguous position. I was born too early or too late to participate fully. Coming to maturity soon after the women's suffrage movement had attained its aim, I assumed that women now no longer needed to struggle for rights. Reaching retirement at about the time when the new feminist movement had reached its peak, I had personally nothing to gain from it. But there is no doubt in my mind about the importance of the movement. For me, its most significant aspect is not the clamor over whether women should take on men's roles, but the emphasis on *solidarity*, women helping one another. This is a feeling that was foreign to most women of my generation. Although I served as adviser to the few women who entered our graduate program over the years, I took no responsibility for trying to increase their number or for getting more women appointed to the faculty.

Fighting for my own "rights" still does not appeal to me as a worthy cause; working for policies and practices to improve the position of all women does. I believe the emphasis our society is placing on all sorts of individual *rights* to be excessive, and I would like to see a shift toward concern for the common good. But that is a matter for another chapter, another occasion.

REFERENCES

Tyler, L. E. (1947). *The psychology of human differences.* New York: Appleton–Century–Crofts.

Tyler, L. E. (1953). *The work of the counselor.* New York: Appleton–Century–Crofts.

Tyler, L. E. (1959). Toward a workable psychology of individuality. *American Psychologist, 14*, 75–81.

Tyler, L. E. (1978). *Individuality: Human possibilities and personal choice in the psychological development of men and women.* San Francisco: Jossey-Bass.

Tyler, L. E. (1983). *Thinking creatively: a new approach to psychology and individual lives.* San Francisco: Jossey-Bass.

REPRESENTATIVE PUBLICATIONS

Tyler, L. E. (1945). Relationships between strong vocational interest scores and other attitude and personality measures. *Journal of Applied Psychology, 29*, 58–67.

Tyler, L. E. (1951). Individual differences. *Annual Review of Psychology, 2*, 95–112.

Tyler, L. E. (1951). The relationship of interests to abilities and reputation among first-grade children. *Educational and Psychological Measurement, 11*, 255–264.

Tyler, L. E. (1955). The development of "vocational interests": I. The organization of likes and dislikes in ten-year-old children. *Journal of Genetic Psychology, 86*, 33–44.

Tyler, L. E. (1958). Counseling. *Annual Review of Psychology, 9*, 375–390.

Tyler, L. E. (1959). Distinctive patterns of likes and dislikes over a twenty-two year period. *Journal of Counseling Psychology, 6*, 234–237.

Tyler, L. E. (1961). Research explorations in the realm of choice. *Journal of Counseling Psychology, 8*, 195–201.

Tyler, L. E. (1964). The antecedents of two varieties of interest pattern. *Genetic Psychology Monographs, 70*, 177–277.

Tyler, L. E. (Ed.). (1969). *Intelligence: Some recurring issues.* New York: Van Nostrand.

Tyler, L. E. (1972). Human abilities. *Annual Review of Psychology, 23*, 177–206.

Tyler, L. E. (1973). Design for a hopeful psychology. *American Psychologist, 28*, 1021–1029.

Tyler, L. E. (1974). *Individual differences: Abilities and motivational directions.* Englewood Cliffs, NJ: Prentice-Hall.

Tyler, L. E. (1976). The intelligence we test—An evolving concept. In L. B. Resnick (Ed.), *The nature of intelligence* (pp. 13–26). Hillsdale, NJ: Lawrence Erlbaum Associates, Inc.

Tyler, L. E. (1978). My life as a psychologist. In T. S. Krawiec (Ed.), *The psychologists* (Vol. 3, pp. 289–362). Brandon, VT: Clinical Psychology Publishing.

Tyler, L. E. (1978). Toward a new design for universal education. In J. C. Flanagan (Ed.), *Perspectives on improving education: Project TALENT's young adults look back* (pp. 57–68). New York: Praeger.

Tyler, L. E. (1981). More stately mansions— Psychology extends its boundaries. *Annual Review of Psychology, 32,* 1–20.

Tyler, L. E. (1984). What tests don't measure. *Journal of Counseling and Human Development, 63,* 48–50.

Tyler, L. E., & Goodenough, F. (1959). *Developmental psychology.* New York: Appleton–Century–Crofts.

Tyler, L. E., & Sundberg, N. (1962). *Clinical psychology: An introduction to research and practice.* New York: Appleton–Century–Crofts.

Tyler, L. E., & Sundberg, N. D. (1970). Awareness of action possibilities of Indian, Dutch, and American adolescents. *Journal of Cross-Cultural Psychology, 1,* 153–157.

Tyler, L. E., & Sundberg, N. D. (1970). Values of Indian and American adolescents. *Journal of Personality and Social Psychology, 16,* 374–397.

Tyler, L. E., Sundberg, N. D., & Poole, M. E. (1984). Decade differences in rural adolescents' views of life possibilities. *Journal of Youth and Adolescence, 12,* 45–46.

Tyler, L. E., Sundberg, N. D., Rohila, P. K., & Greene, M. M. (1968). Patterns of choices in Dutch, American, and Indian adolescents. *Journal of Counseling Psychology, 15*(6) 522–529.

Tyler, L. E., Sundberg, N. D., & Taplin, J. (1973). *Clinical psychology: Expanding horizons.* Englewood Cliffs, NJ: Prentice-Hall.

Tyler, L. E., Sundberg, N. D., & Taplin, J. (1983). *Introduction to clinical psychology: Perspectives, issues, and contributions to human service.* Englewood Cliffs, NJ: Prentice-Hall.

CHAPTER 5

Anne Anastasi

Anne Anastasi

When I am asked to talk or write about my own life history, my immediate reaction is to resist. In reading B. F. Skinner's (1983) article in the March 1983 *American Psychologist*, I found a partial explanation for my resistance. Skinner wrote: "Aging scholars come into possession of a unique stock-in-trade—their memories. They learn that they can hold a restless audience with personal reminiscences. . . . The trouble is that it takes you backward. You begin to live your life in the wrong direction" (p. 243). *That* is what I do not like to do. Skinner also referred to the name dropping that occurs when we reminisce about contacts with well-known psychologists who are no longer living. Because I have been around a long time—both in psychology and in the American Psychological Association (APA)—I am often perceived as a resource for such reminiscences. The multiplicity of biographical summaries I have consequently had to provide, ranging from a short paragraph to a whole chapter, adds a measure of boredom (my own and the reader's) to my other reasons for resistance.

In the effort at least to minimize duplication, I shall not at this time try to give any overall autobiographical sketch.[1] Instead, I

---

[1] For more comprehensive and systematic coverage, see Lindzey (1980, pp. 1–37); a more condensed summary of career development is given in articles in the *American Psychologist* ("Distinguished Scientific Award," 1982; "American Psychological Foundation," 1985); information about the context and climate in which I worked over 5 decades can be found in a volume of my selected papers, especially in chapter 1 (Anastasi, 1982a).

have identified a major theme that seemed to emerge as I looked over my career experiences. Loosely expressed, it can be called "Chance Encounters and Locus of Control." As I examined the list of suggested topics sent to the participants in this symposium, I realized more and more that chance encounters had played a significant role in shaping my life path. I had recently read a provocative article on this topic by Albert Bandura (1982), which strengthened my hypothesis and provided an enlightening discussion of this etiological mechanism. Also relevant is a short comment by Norman Munn (1983) in the *American Psychologist*: Munn described a chance encounter that had a pronounced effect on his own life (see also Munn, 1980). Munn's encounter was with a book in a store window, rather than with a person. Bandura, however, used the term *chance encounter* to refer not only to people but also to inanimate objects and even to any kind of life event.

Let me illustrate with some chance encounters in my own life. One of the suggested questions sent to the symposium participants reads: "Job entry and how first and subsequent positions were obtained?" My first full-time position was obtained on a spring day in 1930 in New York City as I was crossing Broadway westward at 119th Street, on my way from the Columbia Graduate Psychology Department to Barnard College. Harry L. Hollingworth, then chairman of the Barnard Psychology Department, was crossing the street in the opposite direction, and we met midway on a pedestrian safety zone. Holly (as he was generally known among the students) asked me whether I had made any plans for the fall. Upon my replying in the negative, he offered me an instructorship at Barnard, and I accepted. This was the total transaction, except for a printed, one-page letter of appointment received several months later from the corporate secretary of the university. I am still convinced that the chance encounter in the middle of the street contributed substantially to my receiving the offer. Holly disliked writing letters or phoning people—there was no department secretary at Barnard in those years—and he always tried to follow the simplest procedures in carrying out administrative functions. To be sure, these simple hiring procedures were more common in the 1930s than they are in the 1980s. Such mechanisms as search committees, recruiting through classified ads in the *APA Monitor*, campus visits, and departmental voting were quite unknown.

The Barnard incident was probably more dramatic in its fortuitousness than other chance encounters through which I obtained jobs. Nevertheless, it is a fact that I never applied for any job I obtained; conversely, I never obtained any job for which I applied. In one or two instances, I was actually offered a job after applying, but upon learning more about the nature of the job, I decided I was not the right person for it.

Other chance events had an even more far-reaching influence in directing the course of my life. Take, for example, the possible conflict between family and career roles. Shortly after my marriage, I developed a cervical cancer. The radium and deep X-ray treatment I received proved most effective in bringing about a rapid and permanent recovery, with a minimum of discomfort and little or no disruption of my activities. Because I was hospitalized over the Christmas and New Year holidays, I missed only two classes at Barnard. An inevitable side effect, however, was complete reproductive sterility. Having accepted this fact as given, I simply concentrated with renewed vigor on my work. The possible role conflict was obviously resolved, and the decision was taken out of my hands.

Calamities have played a significant role in shaping my life. When I was approximately 1 year old, my father died. As a result, the family structure in which I grew up was quite atypical. My grandmother ruled the household and was responsible for my upbringing, which included regularly scheduled academic lessons over several years. My mother was the wage earner who left for the office each morning and whose safe return was eagerly awaited each evening. Her younger brother, my uncle, was a charming dilettante interested in poetry, music, parties, and the company of fair ladies, with whom he was very popular. He did have jobs, but it was difficult for him to hold on to money. He had a generous nature and enjoyed giving things away. Both my mother and my uncle had received an excellent education, with emphasis on the classics and the humanities, but they lacked marketable skills.

When my mother faced the necessity of earning a living to support a family of four, she had several traditional alternatives available to her—from learning secretarial skills to remarriage. She chose none of these, but decided first that business is where the money is and second that bookkeeping is what makes business run. Accordingly, she borrowed some books from the public library and taught herself bookkeeping and, in due course, accounting. She found a job in a small piano manufacturing company and soon became its general manager. Then she opened her own piano factory, of which she was president and my uncle was vice president. One of his first contributions was to choose a name for the corporation. Drawing upon his classic education, he called it the Ebe Piano Company. Ebe (commonly spelled *Hebe* in the English transliteration) was the Greek goddess of youth, cupbearer of the gods, and hence was associated with joy, feasting, and gladness. She is the sort of goddess who would appeal especially to my uncle.

My mother subsequently held several other jobs, but always as some variant of business manager. As a by-product of these experiences, she developed an unswerving determination that I should receive the best possible education so that I could always earn my living without the uncertainties and stresses that she had endured.

My early familial experiences, in combination with a considerable degree of isolation from external contacts, probably account for my ignorance about the sex-role stereotypes of our culture. I can confidently report that I was unaware of these stereotypes until I entered Barnard College. It seems ironic that a college whose dean, Virginia C. Gildersleeve, was a vigorous exponent of educational and vocational equality for the sexes, should be where I first learned about sex-role stereotypes. Let me emphasize, however, that I did *not* learn about them from the faculty. At that time, the Barnard faculty included several internationally eminent scientists and scholars, most of whom taught also in the Columbia Graduate School. No, I learned about sex-role stereotypes from my fellow students, and I learned even more about them from the recurrent alumnae demands that Barnard give more attention to the "special educational needs of WOMEN!" Although my relations with my Barnard professors were exhilarating and gratifying, I found my contacts with fellow students far less enjoyable. This was my first experience in a sex-segregated group, and I felt alien and uncomfortable. I did not fully achieve rapport with fellow students until I crossed the street to attend coeducational graduate classes, which I began to do in my junior year.

Let me turn to my last example of chance events. If we define such events as unplanned and unanticipated occurrences, my election to offices in professional societies fits the definition very well indeed. In 1947, I was elected president of the Eastern Psychological Association. To say I was surprised is an understatement. Astonishment bordering on shock describes my feeling more accurately. Let me explain that my surprise did not arise from my being a woman— two women had preceded me in that office (Margaret Floy Washburn and Edna Heidbreder). What caused my surprise was that I was only an assistant professor. By the time I was elected president of APA in 1971, that particular deficiency had been corrected: I had then been a full professor for 20 years. Nevertheless, election to association offices of any sort was an event I had never considered, anticipated, aspired to, or in any way thought about. I certainly had done nothing to work toward it or—heaven forbid—to campaign for it. I am not taking any credit, however, for the latter restraint. At that time, it simply was not done. Campaigning was generally regarded with disfavor; reactions ranged from considering it in bad taste to considering it as downright unprofessional. These attitudes have certainly changed!

As I look over the examples I have cited, it seems that my life has been a journey in a rudderless boat tossed and buffeted by the waves of chance, with no control on my part. How can I reconcile that impression with the observation that, as assessed by any locus-of-control instrument I have seen, I would clearly score close to the extreme of internal control. I have a strong sense of exercising control over my life, and I fight hard for what I want.

Some provocative ideas about the resolution of this apparent dilemma can be found in the previously mentioned article by Bandura (1982) on chance encounters. Bandura described several influences that foster the unity evident in many lives, despite the "branching power of chance encounters" (p. 747). The selection of environments within which chance encounters occur, as well as the individual's value system, enduring interests, and gradually accumulating knowledge and skills within a limited area, all contribute to moving her or him in a controllable and predictable direction. There are many alternative routes to the same broadly defined goal. It is the branching into these alternative routes that is often the result of chance encounters. Another important variable pertains to individual differences in the *reaction* to chance events. Response to a misfortune can vary from self-pity, depression, and even suicide to enhanced motivation and a determination to show the world that it can't keep you down. Looking at individual responses from a slightly different angle, we can recognize the influence of *cognitive appraisal*, defined by Lazarus and DeLongis (1983) as "the way a person construes the significance of an encounter for his or her well-being, that is, as irrelevant, benign, harmful, threatening, or challenging" (p. 249).

If I look for the unifying, guiding goal in my own development, I can best describe it as a desire to understand the world around me; to use tough-minded rational procedures; to debunk weak, sloppy generalizations; to fight charlatanism; and to correct popular misconceptions. This is a broadly defined goal. It obviously permits much branching on the way, through chance encounters. It enabled me to change my field of specialization from mathematics to psychology after I learned that mathematics could be used in psychology. The latter field appealed to me because it was a newer specialty, still in a formative stage, and because of its empirical, experimental approach. I could thus enjoy the best of two possible worlds. I should add that taking Hollingworth's courses in psychology during my sophomore year was what finally induced me to change my major. His approach to science and his vigorous debunking of slipshod thinking struck responsive chords in my feelings, which I could not resist.

Closely associated with my basic goal was my strong task orientation and subject-matter immersion. I was not primarily career oriented or job oriented. Nor did I plan my life with regard to such goals as economic growth, the attainment of status and prestige, or winning the acceptance and approval of my fellow humans. I wanted only to pursue the tasks I had chosen for myself. In this connection, let me leave one thought with you. Perhaps the implications of task orientation versus self-orientation can be better understood in the light of some research on test anxiety. Factor analyses of the behavior classified under test anxiety have generally revealed two factors: an emotionality factor, with accompanying physiological reactions, and a cognitive or worry factor (see Anastasi, 1982b, pp. 36–38). The cognitive factor includes negative self-oriented thoughts such as expectation of doing poorly, concerns about the consequences of failure, and urgency to perform well. These thoughts draw attention away from the task-oriented behavior required by the test and thereby disrupt performance. When individuals focus attention on themselves as test takers, they have little attention to spare for the content of the test. I suggest that something of the sort may occur in conducting one's life through a basically self-oriented approach.

ACKNOWLEDGMENTS

This chapter was presented at the symposium entitled "Eminent Women in Psychology: Personal and Historical Reflections" (A. N. O'Connell, Chair), which was conducted at the annual convention of the American Psychological Association, Anaheim, CA, August 1983.

REFERENCES

American Psychological Foundation Awards for 1984. (1985). *American Psychologist*, *40*, 340–341.
Anastasi, A. (1982a). *Contributions to differential psychology: Selected papers*. New York: Praeger.

Anastasi, A. (1982b). *Psychological testing* (5th ed.). New York: Macmillan.
Bandura, A. (1982). The psychology of chance encounters and life paths. *American Psychologist, 37,* 747–755.
Distinguished Scientific Award for the Applications of Psychology: 1981. (1982). *American Psychologist, 37,* 52–59.
Lazarus, R. S., & DeLongis, A. (1983). Psychological stress and coping in aging. *American Psychologist, 38,* 245–254.
Lindzey, G. (Ed.). (1980). *A history of psychology in autobiography* (Vol. 7). San Francisco: Freeman.
Munn, N. L. (1980). *Being and becoming: An autobiography.* Adelaide, South Australia: Adelaide University Press.
Munn, N. L. (1983). More on chance encounters and life paths. *American Psychologist, 38,* 351–352.
Skinner, B. F. (1983). Intellectual self-management in old age. *American Psychologist, 38,* 239–244.

REPRESENTATIVE PUBLICATIONS

Anastasi, A. (1930). A group factor in immediate memory. *Archives of Psychology.* No. 120, pp. 1–61.
Anastasi, A. (1936). The influence of specific experience upon mental organization. *Genetic Psychology Monographs; 18*(4), 245–355.
Anastasi, A. (1948). The nature of psychological "traits." *Psychological Review, 55* 127–138.
Anastasi, A. (1956). Intelligence and family size. *Psychological Bulletin, 53,* 187–209.
Anastasi, A. (1958). *Differential psychology* (3rd ed.). New York: Macmillan.
Anastasi, A. (1958). Heredity, environment, and the question "How?" *Psychological Review, 65,* 197–208.
Anastasi, A. (Ed.). (1965). *Individual differences.* New York: Wiley.
Anastasi, A. (Ed.). *Testing problems in perspective.* Washington, DC: American Council on Education.
Anastasi, A. (1967). Psychology, psychologists, and psychological testing. *American Psychologist, 22,* 297–306.
Anastasi, A. (1970). On the formation of psychological traits. *American Psychologist, 25,* 899–910.
Anastasi, A. (1972). The cultivation of diversity. *American Psychologist, 27,* 1091–1099.
Anastasi, A. (1972). Reminiscences of a differential psychologist. In T. S. Krawiec (Ed.), *The psychologists* (pp. 3–37). New York: Oxford University Press.
Anastasi, A. (1979). *Fields of applied psychology* (2nd ed.). New York: McGraw-Hill.
Anastasi, A. (1981). Coaching, test sophistication, and developed abilities. *American Psychologist, 36,* 1086–1093.
Anastasi, A. (1981). Sex differences: Historical perspectives and methodological implications. *Developmental Review, 1,* 187–206.
Anastasi, A. (1983). Evolving trait concepts. *American Psychologist, 38,* 175–184.
Anastasi, A. (1983). Psychological testing. In C. E. Walker (Ed.), *Handbook of clinical psychology: Theory, research, and practice* (Vol. 1, pp. 420–444). Homewood, IL: Dow-Jones Irwin.

Anastasi, A. (1983). What do intelligence tests measure? In S. B. Anderson & J. S. Helmick (Eds.), *On educational testing: Intelligence, performance standards, test anxiety, and latent traits* (pp. 5–28). San Francisco: Jossey-Bass.

Anastasi, A. (1984). Aptitude and achievement tests: The curious case of the indestructible strawperson. In B. S. Plake (Ed.), *Social and technical issues in testing: Implications for test construction and usage* (pp. 129–140). Hillsdale, NJ: Lawrence Erlbaum Associates, Inc.

Anastasi, A. (1984). Traits revisited—With some current implications. In D. P. Rogers (Ed.), *Foundations of psychology: Some personal views* (pp. 185–206). New York: Praeger.

Anastasi, A. (1985). Psychological testing: Basic concepts and common misconceptions. In A. M. Rogers & C. J. Scheirer (Eds.), *The G. Stanley Hall Lecture Series* (Vol. 5, pp. 87–120). Washington, DC: American Psychological Association.

Anastasi, A. (1985). Reciprocal relations between cognitive and affective development—With implications for sex differences. In T. B. Sonderegger & R. A. Dienstbier (Eds.), *Nebraska Symposium on Motivation: Vol. 32. Psychology and gender* (pp. 3–35). Lincoln: University of Nebraska Press.

Anastasi, A. (1985). Some emerging trends in psychological measurement: A fifty-year perspective. *Applied Psychological Measurement, 9*, 121–138.

Anastasi, A. (1986). Evolving concepts of test validation. *Annual Review of Psychology, 37*, 1–15.

Anastasi, A. (1986). Experiential structuring of psychological traits. *Developmental Review, 6*, 181–202.

Anastasi, A. (1986). Intelligence as a quality of behavior, In R. J. Sternberg & D. K. Detterman (Eds.), *What is intelligence? Contemporary viewpoints on its nature and definition* (pp. 19–21). Norwood, NJ: Ablex.

Anastasi, A. (1988). *Psychological testing* (6th ed.). New York: Macmillan.

Anastasi, A., & Cordova, F. A. (1953). Some effects of bilingualism upon the intelligence test performance of Puerto Rican children in New York City. *Journal of Educational Psychology, 44*, 1–19.

Anastasi, A., & Foley, J. P., Jr. (1938). A study of animal drawings by Indian children of the North Pacific Coast. *Journal of Social Psychology, 9*, 363–374.

Anastasi, A., & Foley, J. P., Jr. (1944). An experimental study of the drawing behavior of adult psychotics in comparison with that of a normal control group. *Journal of Experimental Psychology, 34*, 169–194.

Anastasi, A., Fuller, J. L., Scott, J. P., & Schmitt, J. R. (1955). A factor analysis of the performance of dogs on certain learning tests. *Zoologica, 40*(3), 33–46.

Anastasi, A., & Levee, R. F. (1959). Intellectual defect and musical talent. *American Journal of Mental Deficiency, 64*, 695–703.

Anastasi, A., & Schaefer, C. E. (1969). Biographical correlates of artistic and literary creativity in adolescent girls. *Journal of Applied Psychology, 53*, 267–273.

CHAPTER 6

Marie Skodak Crissey

Marie Skodak Crissey

An invitation to contribute to a volume on senior women—no matter how eminent—is a kind of dubious honor. If one is still on this side of senility, one doesn't really feel *that* old to merit reverence due to longevity. If one has slipped to the *other* side of senility, there is the risk of maundering reminiscences, which are of no interest to anyone. But perhaps a glance back at earlier paths, at the barriers now leveled, at the roads still to be traveled, may be of some value or interest to those whose "senior" years will be in the 21st century. It just may even be that the reinvention of some wheels can be forestalled.

FAMILY BACKGROUND
AND EARLY YEARS

My parents' accented English clearly identified them both as Hungarians and as recent immigrants. However, we did not live in the usual ethnic enclave, nor did most of our social contacts originate there. My parents' education and sociocultural backgrounds were distinctly "middle class" and "above" that of most of their unskilled and uneducated compatriots. Doing well in school and participating in "American" community activities were the channels to acceptance by the community's established middle class. This direction toward academic excellence and toward college and professional careers came both from family precedents and from the expectations of the families (both WASP and others) with whom our family associated. Specific careers were not identified. It was expected that college would develop this.

How, then, did I get involved in psychology? I graduated from a good, but not extraordinary public high school without ever having heard the word *psychology*. There were no psychology courses or "adjustment programs" or counselors. You took commercial or industrial courses, or a general program, or the classical precollege Latin, sciences, math, and English. In the late 1920s, high school girls studying the precollege program by and large did go on to college—and not for an MRS, but for career preparation. Of the dozen or so in my intimate group, none married early, some not at all, and those who did married late in life, in their 50s and 60s.

Choice of college was dictated by finances. A large state university offered the widest choice of career preparation at modest cost. In high school, there was no guidance with regard to possible alternatives.

In 1927, I entered Ohio State University as a chemistry major. Soon finding that the mathematics and precision of analytical chemistry were beyond me, I drifted into history, which was interesting but not absorbing. The financial debacle, which for our family began while I was a sophomore and escalated into the Great Depression, soon revised my life style. From an elegant dormitory, I moved into a co-op house with gas grate stove and shared—everything. I also got a job, a good one, waitress at the faculty club. It meant scheduling classes around meal service, mad dashes between classes—but also 35¢ an hour and discount meals. According to custom, we were assigned tables, and faculty, following well-worn paths, habitually occupied the same tables—even the same chairs. You learned who wanted coffee now, who hated dressing on the salad. As newcomer (I learned later), I drew what were regarded as "difficult" tables—the psychologists! Not knowing what psychologists were, I wasn't bothered by their idiosyncrasies (I thought the athletic department had much worse manners). As I served and cleared plates, I began to hear fascinating bits of conversation. They must have been impressed by my attentiveness to their coffee cups and water glasses.

And so, I enrolled in my first psychology class with Dr. A. Sophie Rogers. She was one of those unique people with MD and PhD and joint appointments in medicine and liberal arts. I suppose being condemned to teach huge introductory classes was a kind of discrimination. We just thought we were fortunate. She was a terrific teacher. Her teaching assistant—Ruth—was a meticulous reader of exams—it was a great semester.

From then on I took all the courses available, with the exception of experimental psychology and statistics. My encounter with chemistry had left permanent scars. I took courses with Harold Burtt for industrial psychology, Robert Williams for physiological psychology, all the educational psychology and most of all the clinical, abnormal, and retardation psychology courses. Within the boundaries of an undergraduate major and a master's degree, not only was it possible to get a wide academic exposure, but practicums were available at institutions for the retarded, for the mentally ill, and for delinquent adolescents; at social service centers; at special education classes; and at a private school for the gifted. Comparable programs may exist today, but I do not know of any. With today's focus on a less strenuous life, such intensive programs have no doubt gone out of style.

In the meantime, the Great Depression deepened. Jobs in 1931 simply did not exist. Well prepared as I was to be a school psychologist, complete with teacher certificate and all that experience, such positions had simply vanished. So I escaped to Europe for a year on a fellowship that broadened my cultural horizons but did little for my professional competencies.

A CAREER BEGINS

Some 50 resumes and applications later in 1932, I found a summer job at the Rome New York State School as examiner for the colonies—a decentralized homelike program for the mentally retarded. The concept has reemerged in community living programs, but minus some of the advantages of the earlier model. I also was awarded the then most prestigious assistantship in clinical psychology, with the presumption that I would go on for a PhD at Ohio State. How many remember 1933–34? University salaries were cut 30%, and the encouragement given everyone was "If you find another job—go get it." The general depression and demoralization extended to all aspects of life. Interdepartmental and intradepartmental hostilities escalated. Promising candidates were mercilessly failed. I was one of several caught in the cross fire—and had no stomach for failure at that point. So when a modest announcement offering summer employment in Iowa appeared on the bulletin board, I was one of the fortunate three who were accepted.

The summer of 1933 in Iowa was one of relentless heat and dust. It was the dust-bowl era, when farms literally blew away into the next county. A comb placed on the dresser overnight left its pattern in fine dust. Dust was in teeth, eyes, on the road—everywhere. There were spectacular sunsets—unmatched since and gladly missed.

How do I describe that summer, which in retrospect was a turning point in my career? I was paid $30 a month, plus room and board in the state institutions. On those occasions when we went to the headquarters at Iowa City, other equally nonaffluent graduate students invited us to share their pads—literally on the floor! There were three of us—all women—with MAs—plus training, one each from Minnesota, Pennsylvania, and Ohio. Our task was to give psychological examinations to residents in two state institutions for dependent children, in two large institutions for the mentally retarded, and, if time permitted, in two institutions for delinquent adolescents. Because this involved some 4,000 residents, *not* counting the delinquents, in a 3-month period by three people, it was clear that there was to be no dilly-dallying. Nor were we to use shortcuts (not yet devised in the early 1930s). The routine program was the Stanford–Binet Scale of Intelligence in its classical entirety, a brief spelling–reading–arithmetic test for school enrollees, and the Kuhlmann–Binet for toddlers or severely retarded. A brief summary and comments were included on the protocols. Tests were double-scored and were entered in the files and records. Records of the examinees were reviewed both to gather case data and to learn whether earlier tests had been given. We had no clerical help. We were *it*.

In most institutions, we began work after breakfast, about 7:30, and continued until lunch (no coffee breaks in those days). Because most residents had duties around meal times, we couldn't start again until about 1:00, and we stopped about 4:30. That gave some time for the clerical jobs before supper. After supper, the children in all the institutions and the non-employed older residents had free time on the playground or at baseball games. We were expected to participate, and naturally we did. In the process we got to know the children outside the testing situation. Although the staff called us "the brain testers," we were more widely known as "the brain sisters." We played jacks, hide and seek, baseball, volley ball, whatever, and problems of rapport just didn't seem to arise.

The fun and games, plus the heroic effort to test everyone on the institution rosters, had a serious scientific purpose. The Iowa Child Welfare Research Station, a quasi-independent unit of the State University of Iowa, had been engaged in research on mental and physical development of children for some years. Harold Skeels, in the course of developing training and research opportunities for graduate students and locating naive research participants, had established relationships with first one and then with the remaining institutions. By utilizing the resources of the station and the institutions, for something under $1,000, approximately 1,500 residents were given psychological examinations—establishing the data base for a number of subsequent dissertations.

At that time, major responsibility for adoptions of children removed from their parents in Iowa was with the state. Placements were being made basically by political appointees untainted by training or sophistication. It so happened that one child placed for adoption proved to be rather markedly retarded and was refused admission by the school when he came of kindergarten age. The irate adoptive parents threatened suit for misrepresentation. At that point, the authorities learned from Skeels that there were indeed ways to determine a child's mental status and that similar fiascos could be avoided through the use of psychological tests. After the requisite maneuvering, a procedure was established by the Iowa State Board of Control: Preplacement evaluation would be conducted for all infants and children considered for adoptive placement, and the preadoption evaluation of all children would follow at least 1 year of residence in the adoptive home. A position was subsequently created to implement the preadoption as well as the institutional resident evaluation programs.

In the meantime, the summer had passed. I returned to Ohio State University and became increasingly disenchanted with academia. In 1934, when the "real world" of Iowa became available, I went—dust, mud roads, and institution meals notwithstanding.

Any work can be routine if viewed that way. It was my assignment to see that new admissions to the institutions were given psychological evaluations and to reevaluate residents at least every 2 years (1 year for younger children). Later, many of the retests were done by graduate students working on dissertations. Because each child and each situation was unique, the days were never routine or dull.

A significant aspect of the job was the preadoption examination. This involved a careful study of the rather meager family background records and home visitor reports, followed by a visit to the adoptive home. These homes were all over the state and ranged from substantial estates to meager farm tenant cottages. It was a highly emotional time for the families—newly washed farm coveralls, freshly scrubbed linoleum floors, the fragrance of Fels Naptha soap competing with that of home-baked bread. The children were polished and combed, the toys were placed on discrete display. Although this was an examination of the child, it was the family that would pass or fail. Skeels and I made these examinations, and our styles were much the same. Most tests were given on the floor, the child's natural turf. The parents—cautioned to be noninvolved—usually framed the doorway. In running commentaries, we explained the test, interpreted the results, included suggestions for future activities, and gave indications of how the results were going—not a white-coated clinical approach, but homey, reassuring and comfortable. Getting agreement for repeat examinations for research—nothing to do with the adoption—was no problem.

At this point, I must digress a bit and weave in a little history. Imagine the task of assessment in the early 1900s, when there were no benchmarks of what a normal 2-year-old child might be expected to do or what an 8-year-old child might reasonably be able to know. Early in this century, at the Vineland Training School in New Jersey, Henry Goddard was trying to find some assessment technique to aid in the identification and classification of mental deficiency. From a trip to Europe, he brought back a newly devised, small series of test items designed by Alfred Binet and his associate, Henry Simon. In the New Jersey research center was Elizabeth Kite, fluent in French and a trained historian cum social worker. She had been doing home visitations for admissions to Vineland, saw immediately the usefulness of this scale, and persuaded the initially not so enthusiastic Henry Goddard to standardize it on American subjects. This appeared as the 1911 Goddard–Binet Scale—copies of which, incidentally, were found in the Iowa institution files that summer of 1933.

The rest is testing history, but with some neglected ramifications. There is not really space here to review the social climate and philosophies of the 1910–1940 period, but it should be recalled that there were anxieties about the influence of dysgenic racial and ethnic mixtures on "solid American stock." The inferiority of some social classes and ethnic groups was not disputed. Mendelian laws of heredity were applied to many characteristics, and family studies of Nams and Jukes set the stage for an ambitious study in New Jersey of a family whose alias was the Kallikaks. Kite and her associates not only visited and tested this family and its numerous members, but in a related study interviewed several hundred other dwellers of the remote Pineland areas of New Jersey. The data were overwhelming, and out of the studies came the conclusion that mental retardation—in instances in which a physiological or medical basis could not be established—was largely familial, hereditary, and irremediable. It was an inevitable consequence that prevention (lacking birth control pills) could be achieved only by social separation and/or constant supervision. Associated with this was concern for the protection of the less competent from exploitation by the evils of society.

At the same time these studies were being conducted, Lewis Terman and his associates standardized and expanded the Binet series. The IQ, or the ratio between mental age and life age, and the tests on which it was based became standard tools of psychological research. Repeated tests of the same individuals or tests of comparable groups indicated little change in rate of mental growth over the school years. From this it was a natural step to conclude that, once a proper test had been made, the lifetime rate of development and eventual intellectual status could be predicted—with consequences for guidance, education and career planning, and so on.

All this was significant for me because Goddard and his clinic associate, Francis Maxfield, were my chief mentors at Ohio State. So it was with this frame of reference that I came to Iowa. (Skeel's background had been in animal husbandry, with *its* emphasis on genetic breeding outcomes.)

As we read the natural family histories of the children placed for adoption, many could well have been those of the Kallikaks. The progeny of social incompetents, residents of county homes, school drop-outs, the great majority of the children did not sound like promising adoptees for substantial middle-class and farm homes. With heavy hearts, we went on the first home visits equipped with a short, well-planned speech: We would offer to exchange the retarded child for perhaps another, more promising model. We never had occasion, however, to use the speech—not with children placed during infancy. No adoptees were retarded; indeed, more were above average than were merely average.

Concurrently, there was research going on at the Iowa Child Welfare Research Station. Beth Wellman and corps of graduate students were finding that the IQ was indeed not fixed at birth (Wellman, 1932), that mental development *was* influenced by environmental opportunity (Wellman, 1932–1933, 1934–1935), that the longer a child remained in deprived and stultifying circumstances, the more the child's mental development was stunted (Skeels & Fillmore, 1937), that remedial preschools offering less than 100 reasonably consecutive days were of little benefit (Skeels, Updegraff, Wellman, & Williams, 1935), and so forth. Some of these findings have not really been implemented to this day. Under the stimulating leadership of George Stoddard, the Station experienced its finest hours (Stoddard, 1939). The challenge to accepted beliefs rocked the psychological and educational world, and the literature was filled with acrimonious attacks, which even publication of raw data could not still.

Meanwhile, preadoption tests, and subsequent retests of the same children, were accumulating in the files. It was apparent that they should be pulled together and should be evaluated and published. Skeels, by then involved in administrative responsibilities, had no time for this. I could not bear to turn over the data—and "my children"—to anyone else, so I returned to academia, this time to the University of Iowa. My dissertation was on the preadoption and postadoption examinations. There were follow-up studies of the same group of adoptees, into adulthood, and contacts with some continue to this day.

The question could be raised as to why I did not remain with a research facility and continue on a full-time basis with what has remained a side interest for nearly half a century. In 1938–39, jobs were still scarce, research was not regarded as meriting a full-time position, liaison between the state and the university was precarious, and the Station did not offer a haven for its graduates, who were supposed to go out into the real world and spread the gospel of proper child care and development. And so I too went forth.

OUT OF ACADEMIA
AND INTO THE REAL WORLD

I was fortunate when a former classmate invited me to join the Flint, Child Guidance Center staff as assistant director. As an auto manufacturing center, Flint, Michigan had particular difficulty with employment of young people. A small group of forward-looking community leaders wished to extend the services of the Guidance Center to the normal high school population, particularly in the area of vocational and educational guidance. To demonstrate the feasibility and value of an exemplary guidance program, a grant was secured, and liaison with the University of Michigan was arranged. It was my responsibility to take over the day-to-day operation of the child guidance/mental health aspects of the Center, to supervise the social workers and psychologists, and to provide consultation to the local schools. Parallel with this was the experimental high school guidance project with two full-time counselors, a research psychologist, and a secretary. An entering ninth grade was divided into experimental and control halves; the two groups remained in one high school, with the same classes and teachers, and received the same periodic aptitude, achievement, interest, and personality tests. My relationship was primarily in the evaluation and research aspects and later in the extension of education and skills to counselors in the entire high school system.

Although the study and later evaluation were disrupted by the onset of World War II in 1941–42, the results clearly indicated the value of the focused guidance program in the experimental group. On the whole, the experimental group had fewer drop-outs, somewhat better grades, more appropriate and realistic post–high-school plans, greater participation in school and (later) in community activities, ultimately somewhat higher income, and generally better feelings about their school experiences. Later follow-up studies conducted by counselors indicated that some of the benefits were visible in the experimental group several years into adulthood.

Although the school guidance project was terminated, the community functions of the Guidance Center increased during the war years. Those were exciting times. World War II took the men for military service or war industries. I became director of the Guidance Center in 1942, I think the only woman administrator of a guidance or mental health center at that time. Attention was focused on day care, on career counseling, on the effect of war on family disruptions. The war ended. Mental health facilities became psychiatric centers under state auspices, and the role of psychology was diminished, except in the Veterans Administration, which blossomed under federal funding. The comrades-in-arms network came on the scene with its consequences. A returned-from-service psychiatrist became director of the Guidance Center, and I began private practice, again one of two psychologists in private practice in the state and the only woman.

As part-time lecturer and instructor at the University of Michigan from 1942 to 1957, I again tested academia and considered affiliation only to learn that "because I was—unfortunately—a woman," the appointment went to a man. At that time, the only woman on the faculty was the head of the women's physical education department. From 1978 to 1983 the dean of that school was a woman, Dr. Joan Stark.

A SCHOOL PSYCHOLOGIST AT LAST

The last segment of my varied career covered some 20 years. Nearly a quarter century after I had prepared to be a school psychologist, I finally became one. In 1949, the Dearborn schools, under the leadership of a forward-looking superintendent, hired two school social workers. To "help out" in getting the program started, I began on a part-time basis—and stayed 20 years.

Although there is much to be said for educational and vocational planning, in truth many life choices are fortuitous. My University of Michigan teaching had developed from out of the Flint Guidance Project attempts to extend counselor skills among high school teachers and administrators. When the state of Michigan Department of Education authorized school social work programs, the certification for these positions required dual training in professional education and social case work. Since there had been no previous training program in universities offering a combined curriculum, those aspirants who were teachers needed to take courses in social work, interviewing, and related areas. Social workers, on the other hand, needed courses in pedagogy, school organization, educational psychology, and so forth. I was one of the few who had a background in both fields as well as research and clinical experience in child and adolescent development, testing, and related areas. For the 15 years after the programs were initiated, I taught courses at various centers around the state under the auspices of the University of Michigan. Most of the enrollees were teachers and school administrators who aspired to become counselors or school social workers.

In Dearborn, with its rapidly growing school population and quite diverse ethnic composition, psychologists were soon brought onto the social-work team. Responsibility for special education of the mentally handicapped and of the learning disabled was included in the Psychological Services Department. My fortunate contacts with universities made it possible to have internships for school psychologists, field-work placements for school social workers, and student-teacherships in special education. Case conferences, with invited psychiatric consultants, provided in-service development for Dearborn staff, teachers, and administrators as well as for workers from nearby school systems. Various innovations became models for other schools in providing psychological and educational services to students with special needs.

When I began at Dearborn, special education classes for the mentally retarded had become the classical dumping rooms supervised by well-meaning but fragile, elderly ladies. After their retirement outstanding teachers were recruited, the admission procedures were clarified, and the program was expanded. Children were admitted at a young age, before years of failure could set in. Preemployment was given by trained teacher-counselors; this was followed by supervised work placements. A modified, integrated program preceded what is currently described as mainstreaming.

The parents of retarded children were assisted in forming a local chapter of the association for Retarded Children (ARC) and in establishing a program under private management. The Dearborn schools were among the first to establish classes for trainable students. State and federal support of special education for learning-handicapped students was just becoming possible when I retired.

Nor were the gifted overlooked. Whenever finances and administration cooperation permitted, various programs were started. Unfortunately, these found less support during the egalitarian 1960s than they deserved.

IN RETROSPECT

In reviewing what has been a busy life, I find it difficult to pick out the most important or most significant part. During my entire professional career, I wore several hats simultaneously. Few who knew me in one capacity were aware that I functioned with equal effort in other fields. I was known by some colleagues as a school administrator active on state committees and boards, as someone involved in developing training programs, articulating policies, influencing practices in education and special services. As a psychologist, I was a member of the Miami Conference on Graduate Education in Psychology, of the Thayer Conference on School Psychology, and of the Northwestern University Conference on Counseling. I was a member of many American Psychological Association (APA) committees related to mental retardation and school services. At the national level, I was president of Division 13 (Consulting) and of Division 33 (Mental Retardation) of the APA. I was APA Council Representative for several divisions over a span of some dozen years.

At the state level, I was president of the Michigan Psychological Association, member of the committee that established state certification, and member of the first certifying board.

For 10 years, I was a member of the board of directors of the American Board of Professional Psychology and had particular responsibility for developing standards and procedures for the recognition of school psychologists.

Through all the years of university teaching and school administration, I was also involved in private practice. Much of the work was with adoption agencies, but I also provided services to the blind and to the vocational rehabilitation of the physically impaired.

Research and publishing, unfortunately, became neglected areas deferred to a future of leisure and contemplation. I am still waiting for that leisure time.

This review by no means lists all my activities in national, state, and local matters. Perhaps it gives a flavor of what happened to a female professional who had a reputation as a "red-tape cutter" and who looked first at what was needed and found the possible route rather than worry about "what *they* would think" or agonize about obstacles.

My major contribution to research and theory occurred early in my career. The concept that intelligence was not solely the product of genetic heredity was revolutionary in the 1930s. Strenuously resisted by some research centers in the 1930s and 1940s, the evidence for the effectiveness of environmental impact was congenial to the spirit of the 1960s and 1970s. It was, in fact, the scientific underpinning of much of the civil rights, egalitarian, mainstreaming—Great Society—movements. It can be anticipated that, although the pendulum swings from "all nature" to "all nurture," it will some day settle to a more reasonable "interaction of both."

On a personal note, recognition in the form of the 1968 Joseph P. Kennedy International Award, which Harold Skeels and I were honored to receive at an impressive ceremony in Chicago, was the pinnacle of the many awards I have been fortunate to have received.

In 1969, there were changes in the Dearborn schools and in my family circumstances, and the daily 150-mile commute seemed ever longer. I decided it was time for me to smell the flowers, to relieve the pressure from too many hats. So I retired.

In 1966, I had married Orlo L. Crissey, widower of my dear friend, Iowa classmate, and long-time colleague in psychological activities. Instantly, I acquired children and grandchildren. I entered a life enriched by travel, gardens, and community activities.

Not surprisingly, I continued private practice of sorts for a few years. APA and American Association on Mental Deficiency committee work and convention responsibilities continue. Two major research projects still await, neatly boxed and accumulating related references. A renewed interest has been the exploration of some history, specifically of the period before and around the coming of the Binet test, the Kallikaks, and the nature–nurture controversy of the 1930s and 1940s. There are few of us left from that period, which was a most exciting one for applied psychology.

I have been fortunate enough to have had excellent secretarial help. For some 40 years at the Guidance Center and later in private practice, I truly had a "secretary" who not only managed the professional duties but was invaluable in the extra assistance a "wife" manages for a professional. At the Dearborn schools there was a succession of gifted, conscientious secretarial assistants who helped juggle the various responsibilities. Nor could any of this have been possible without the competence, cooperation, and support of all those on the various staffs and in the many organizations to which I belonged.

How can one possibly cover the experiences and observations of a half century of work in a field that has always been exciting, challenging, and fun? There is no way to acknowledge the influence of those who molded my thinking, whittled my prejudices, honed my insights, softened my attitudes. Some were the helplessly retarded, from whom I learned compassion; some were my critics, from whom I learned self-assurance. My professional life has been spent mostly among men—men were my peers.

There have been—and always will be—barriers to advancement. They may arise because a person is a woman or because she or he has a foreign name or a different philosophy of life or whatever. Life has a way of evening things out. In retrospect, what is remembered are the successes, the challenges that have been met. The inevitable disappointments, small heartaches, fade like old photographs. And that's probably the way it should be.

REFERENCES

Skeels, H. M., & Fillmore, E. A. (1937). Mental development of children from under-privileged homes. *Journal of Genetic Psychology, 50*, 427–439.

Skeels, H. M., Updegraff, R., Wellman, B. L., & Williams, H. M. (1935). A study of environmental stimulation. *University of Iowa Studies in Child Welfare, 15* (4), 191.

Stoddard, G. D. (1939, January) The IQ: Its ups and downs. *The Educational Record Supplement*, pp. 44–57.

Wellman, B. L. (1932). Some new bases for interpretations of the IQ. *Pedagogical Seminar and Journal of Genetic Psychology, 41*, 116–126.

Wellman, B. L. (1932–1933). The effect of preschool attendance upon the IQ. *Journal of Experimental Education, 1*, 48–69.

Wellman, B. L. (1934–1935). Growth in intelligence under differing school environments. *Journal of Experimental Education, 3*, 59–83.

REPRESENTATIVE PUBLICATIONS

Crissey, M. S. (1975). Mental retardation—Past, present and future. *American Psychologist, 30*, 800–808.

Crissey, M. S. (1977). Prevention in retrospect: Adoption follow-up. In G. Albee &

J. Joffe (Eds.), *Primary prevention of psychopathology: Vol. 1. The issues* (pp. 187–202). Hanover, NH: University Press of New England.

Crissey, M. S. (1982). Vignettes in mental retardation—Once upon a time. *Education and Training of the Mentally Retarded,17,* 183–184.

Crissey, M. S. (1982). Vignettes in mental retardation—There was a little school house. *Education and Training of the Mentally Retarded, 17,* 305–306.

Crissey, M. S. (1983). School psychology: Reminiscences of earlier times. *Journal of School Psychology, 21,* 163–177.

Crissey, M. S. (1983). Vignettes in mental retardation—The searchlight of science. *Education and Training of the Mentally Retarded, 18,* 59–61.

Crissey, M. S. (1983). Vignettes in mental retardation—Charts and tests and consequences. *Education and Training of the Mentally Retarded, 18,* 117–119.

Crissey, M. S., & Rosen, M. (1986). *Institutions for the mentally retarded: A changing role in changing times.* Austin, TX: Pro-Ed.

Crissey, O. L., & Skodak, M. (1942). Stated vocational aims and Strong Interest Test scores of high school senior girls. *Journal of Applied Psychology, 26*(1), 64–74.

Crissey, M. S. (1967). Adult status of individuals who experienced early intervention. In B. W. Richards (Ed.) Proceedings of the First Congress of the International Association for the Scientific Study of Mental Deficiency, Montpelier, France. Michael Jackson Pub. Co.

Scholl, G. T., Bauman, M. K., & Crissey, M. S. (1969). *A study of the vocational success of groups of the visually handicapped.* Ann Arbor: University of Michigan School of Education.

Skeels, H. M., & Skodak. M. (1965). Techniques for a high yield follow-up study in the field. *Public Health Reports, 80,* 249–257.

Skodak, M. (1938). Girls on parole—And after. *Journal of Juvenile Research, 22,* 145–161.

Skodak, M. (1938). The mental development of adopted children whose true mothers are feebleminded. *Child Development, 9,* 303–308.

Skodak, M. (1939). Children in foster homes: A study in mental development. University of Iowa, *Studies in Child Welfare, 16,* 156.

Skodak, M. (1939). Two little boys. *National Parent Teacher, 33*(10), 9–12.

Skodak, M. (1943). Intellectual growth of children in foster homes. In R. G. Barker, J. S. Kounin, & H. F. Wright (Eds.), *Child behavior and development* (pp. 259–278). McGraw-Hill.

Skodak, M. (1950). Child dependency. In D. H. Fryer & E. R. Henry (Eds.), *Handbook of applied psychology* (Vol. 2, pp. 538–546). New York: Holt Rinehart.

Skodak, M. (1950). Mental growth of adopted children in the same family. *Journal of Genetic Psychology, 77,* 3–9.

Skodak, M. (1967). *A follow-up and comparison of graduates from two types of high school programs for the mentally handicapped* (Final report of U.W. HEW, Office of Education, Project No. 6–80680, Grant No. 3–7–068680–0106). Dearborn, MI: Dearborn Public Schools Press.

Skodak, M., & Skeels, H. M. (1945). A follow-up study of children in adoptive homes. *Journal of Genetic Psychology, 66,* 21–58.

Skodak, M., & Skeels, H. M. (1949). A final follow-up study of one hundred adopted children. *Journal of Genetic Psychology, 75,* 85–125.

Wellman, B. L., Skeels, H. M., & Skodak, M. (1940). Review of McNemar's critical examination of Iowa studies. *Psychological Bulletin, 37,* 93–111.

CHAPTER 7

Erika Fromm

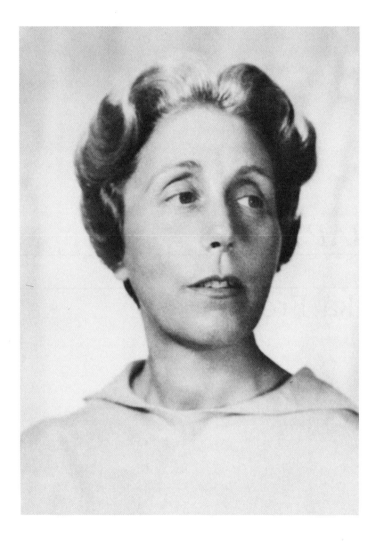

Erika Fromm

I was the oldest of eight children, born in 1910 into an orthodox Jewish family that had a good deal of intellectual and artistic interests. My mother died in the great influenza epidemic that swept the world after World War I, when I was 8 years old, and my father, a physician, was left with three small children. He remarried my mother's younger sister 1 ½ years later and in quick succession had another five children with her. From the age of 11 years on, I helped take care of my younger siblings and started to mother them.

In our whole family, the attitude prevailed that men are superior to women, intellectually and in all other respects. However, my father also enjoyed and encouraged the lively curiosity of his eldest daughter.

From the age of 7 or 8 years on, there was no doubt in my mind that I wanted to have a profession *and* to be a wife and a mother. I also wanted to be someone who helps people who suffer. In adolescence, I added that I also wanted to be a professor.

When I was 17 or 18 years old, the Nazis began to gain great influence, and it became clear that, being a Jew, I either would get a PhD very fast or I would not be able to become a professional at all. I got a PhD in psychology in December 1933, just before I was 23 years old. Two weeks later, I left Germany because the Nazis had attained full power there.

I went to Holland, a country in an economic depression, and got a position as research assistant in the Psychology Laboratory (run by a psychiatrist!) of the Psychiatric Clinic of the University of Amsterdam. The pay was 25 guilders ($15) a month, but in buying power it was probably the equivalent of $25. My room—in an attic—cost 15 guilders, so I had 10 guilders a month on which to live . . . and I starved. But I loved Holland and its deeply democratic, warm people; I also loved my work.

At the end of 1934, I wrote to my teacher, Max Wertheimer, and to Wolfgang Köhler, both Gestalt theorists who had emigrated to the United States in 1933, and asked them for help in finding me a job there. Both wrote back that there were no jobs for psychologists in the United States, that the depression there was as bad as it was in Holland. Köhler added a piece of well-meant advice: "Give up being a psychologist, learn to be a farmer, go to Israel and cultivate the land." I was deeply hurt. How could anyone ask me to give up psychology, the field I loved and to which I was already so deeply committed? I hung on in the Netherlands. Half a year later, I acquired a better job, one that allowed me to create the first Psychology Laboratory in Dutch State Hospitals.

I became engaged to Paul Fromm in 1936, a man deeply interested in contemporary music. He still lived in Germany. The Nazis did not allow him to get out of Germany for more than 2 weeks at a time until the middle of 1938, by which time they had taken away, bit by bit, the family business and all the money his family owned. He felt that war was coming and that my beloved Holland would not be able to stay out of it. So I pulled up my roots again and went with him to the United States. He was right, the Nazis did overrun Holland. Only 25% of the total Jewish population in Holland survived (only 3% of those who were put into concentration camps survived). We would surely not have been among the survivors. I am glad we came to the United States. This country has been very good to us. But it is hard to emigrate twice. And you never, never can forget how many of your friends, family, colleagues, and patients have perished in the Holocaust.

All my professional role models have been male. I had three: As a child, I had my father, a devoted general practitioner-internist who would also sit for hours and *listen* to his patient's problems. I think I have internalized his devotion to wanting to help the suffering human being, and this is what made me become a *clinical* psychologist.

In high school, my role model was a young poet and university graduate student from whom I took language lessons in contemporary Hebrew. He was a most inspiring teacher—and now at 84 years of age, he still teaches (at Boston University). When I was 15 years old, I fell madly in love with him, but he did not notice. He had a desk in the public library at which he sat for many hours every day and studied. To see him more than once a week (at my lessons), I managed also to get myself a desk in that same library facing his desk from the other end of the room. But I had to do something to deserve that desk. I could not just stare at my idol. So I came to write my first scientific paper. Because I loved the man—albeit in unrequited puppy love—I internalized his utter devotion to and real passion for scientific pursuits and research.

At the University of Frankfurt, this ego ideal was reinforced through my identifying with my great teacher, Max Wertheimer, the "Father of Gestalt Theory" from whom I also learned that scientific research could be fun if one is flexible, versatile, and creative. Wertheimer was a highly inventive experimental psychologist. He was a rebel (against association theory and other cognitive theories of his time) and a pioneer. Since mid-adolescence, I too had already been a rebel—against orthodoxy. I identified with Wertheimer's joy in pioneering—and still do.

In Holland, in my early 20s, I made friends with a wonderful woman 16 years my senior; she became a role model to me in all other aspects of life. She was a wife and mother of three children, a former social worker who was deeply interested in the visual arts. She was a joyous, wonderful, giving human being. When I was too proud to admit to anyone that I was starving and desperate, she rescued me by insisting that I come and live with her family, giving me, the refugee, a home and making me a real part of her life. As a person, she has remained my ego ideal for half a century now. She had a great ability to give of herself and to inspire others to do their best and give their best. In my own psychoanalysis, I recognized that there were great similarities of personality between her and the beloved mother I had lost as a child.

I like being a woman. But it has clearly hindered me in my profession on at least two occasions; in a more pervasive and *partially* self-induced way, it has hindered me all my life (I always step back in favor of men and never can assert myself against them).

In the 1940s, I wanted to get an MD in addition to my PhD and applied for admittance as a student to a medical school at which I already was a research associate. I was told they could not take me because they had a *numerus clausus* for women (only 4% women per class). Fifteen years later, a full professorship that had been promised to me at a well-known university was delayed for 9 years, mainly due to my sex and partly due to the fact that I am passionately a clinician. Finally, I was given the professorship after the women's liberation movement showed that, among the 1,000 tenured professors at my university, there were only 26 tenured women. Even then, of course, I got a much lower salary than male professors did.

Because I am a married woman with a family, I have always worked longer hours than a man would work. A married woman, and even more so, a woman with a child still at home, never is the full master of her time. She does not have uninterrupted times for research and writing. As soon as my husband or my daughter would come home, I have always had the feeling that I had to stop my work, at least for some time, even if I was in the middle of trying to formulate a "great thought." Please understand, I always *wanted* to be with my child (who is the best thing I ever produced), I wanted to be with my husband, and I wanted to be there for both of them.

Let me say to those of you who have or contemplate having children: Don't rob yourself of the joy of having children and of being with your children. It is not an either-or: children *or* a career. They can be combined. It takes some juggling, but it is possible, and why settle for the joys of one when it is possible to have both?

INTEREST IN PSYCHOANALYSIS

At 15 years of age, I literally "discovered" psychoanalysis: I was asked to dust every book in my parents' library, and I found hidden behind a row of other books several of Freud's writings, which my parents clearly did not want their children to see. This, of course, aroused my curiosity. Secretly, I read all I could find.

In the late 1940s and early 1950s I took my psychoanalytic training at the Chicago Institute for Psychoanalysis. On the day we were to be graduated, however, the very powerful American Psychoanalytic Association insisted on its union rule that only MDs could be psychoanalysts. I kept fighting for psychologists to be admitted to psychoanalytic training institutes and to be able to become full psychoanalysts. Yet for a quarter of a century, my and other psychologists' efforts were crowned by dismally little success. So we, the psychologists, finally decided that we must develop our own psychoanalytic society and our own psychoanalytic training institutes. This is how first Psychologists Interested in the Study of Psychoanalysis (PISP) and then the APA Division for Psychoanalysis (Division 39) came into being.

In the late 1950s Thomas M. French asked me to write a book with him on dream interpretation. The book was originally published in 1964, went out of print in 1968, and was republished in 1986 (French & Fromm, 1964/1986) as a "modern classic of psychoanalysis" by International Universities Press. In the book *(Dream Interpretation: A New Approach)*, French and I departed from Freud (1900/1953) in some ways. Like Freud, we conceived of the dream as an expression of conflict. But unlike Freud, we thought the conflict is a *focal* conflict, a conflict in which the patient is involved in his present life, here and now, and for which the *ego* seeks to find a solution here and now. Freud felt the dream is the expression of an unresolved childhood struggle between id wishes and the superego, whereas we place much greater emphasis on seeing the dream as a product of *ego functioning* and on its being an attempt to find a solution for a here-and-now conflict. We *do* not deny that here-and-now conflicts may have their roots in old, unsolved conflicts. But our emphasis is on the current conflict situation and on the ego's attempt to find solutions. We also feel that, when interpreting a dream, one must not rest until one has been able to account for every bit of the dream content and every association in the sense of all of them forming *one consistent whole.*

In the 1950s, I also became more and more aware that psychoanalysis, which takes so long, is really a therapy that only the rich can afford. My social conscience revolted against that, particularly after the American Psychoanalytic Association had denigrated and practically suppressed Franz Alexander and Tom French's (1946) book on short-term psychoanalytic psychotherapy, *Psychoanalytic Therapy: Principles and Applications.* In this book, Alexander and French advocated that many patients can be helped psychoanalytically within a few hours and that in many cases it is not necessary for them to have to reexperience the origins of their difficulties in a *long*-term transference analysis. There are ways of doing this in a shorter time span. One way, I found, is through hypnosis.

INTEREST IN HYPNOSIS

Since 1960, I have been deeply interested in hypnosis and hypnoanalysis, a field in which, ever since, I have pioneered a good deal. Freud said that the dream is the "Royal Road to the Unconscious." I consider hypnosis another royal road to the unconscious, a road that goes down to the unconscious more steeply and much faster than psychoanalysis does, but which—when handled by fully trained experts who do not pierce defenses at inappropriate times and who handle hypnosis in a permissive, not an authoritarian, way—is safe, much faster than psychoanalysis, and very effective.

I became fascinated with the field of hypnosis. Whole new worlds of phenomena, research, and therapeutic possibilities opened up to me. Since 1960, I have done a good deal of experimental, theoretical, and clinical research in the field (Brown & Fromm, 1987; Fromm 1965a, 1970, 1976, 1977a, 1977b, 1979; Fromm et al., 1981; Fromm & Eisen, 1982; Fromm & Shor, 1979; Fromm, Skinner, Lombard, & Kahn, in press; Lombard, Kahn, & Fromm, in press; Gruenewald, Fromm, & Oberlander, 1979) and have been able to develop further the field of hypnoanalysis (Brown & Fromm, 1986; Eisen & Fromm, 1983; Fromm, 1965b, 1968, 1972, 1978–1979, 1979, 1981, 1984a, 1984b; Fromm & Gardner, 1979; Fromm & Hurt, 1980). The area of hypnoanalysis was opened up by Gill and Brenman (1959). I have also done a great deal of teaching of clinical as well as experimental hypnosis, both at the University of Chicago and in continuing education workshops all across the United States and in Europe. As the clinical editor of the *International Journal of Clinical and Experimental Hypnosis*, I attempt to help authors write good and scientifically responsible articles in the area of hypnosis.

RESEARCH IN HYPNOSIS
AND HYPNOANALYSIS

In my research, I began to explore imagery, and primary process and secondary process in hypnosis. Hypnosis is a regression in the service of the ego (Fromm, 1965b; Gill & Brenman, 1959). In the deeply hypnotized adult, the typically strong increase in imagery over that found in the waking state is the result of the mobility and fluidity of psychic energies and of affect (Brown & Fromm, 1986).

Strong increase in imagery—thinking in pictorial form rather than in words—is one of the outstanding characteristics of the hypnotic state, just as it is one of the outstanding characteristics of the nocturnal dream. This is related to the increase in primary process in hypnosis, and in dreaming, over that found in the waking state (Fromm, 1978–1979). Still, imagery and primary process are not the same. Imagery is the form of thinking and experiencing in which, in hypnosis, primary process expresses itself.

The hypnoanalyst's role is that of a "benign guide" (Eisen & Fromm, 1983) who gives the patient the open-ended suggestion that "some" imagery will come up in the patient's mind that has "some" relation to the patient's psychic dilemmas. Then the hypnoanalyst helps the patient to understand (e.g., by means of free association) the imagery that has arisen in the trance and to connect it to the patient's conflict. That is, we help the patient interpret imagery in hypnoanalysis pretty much the same way we help the patient interpret dream imagery in psychoanalysis.

Another major area of my hypnoanalytic research has been that of the modes of ego functioning. The psychoanalytic theory of activity and passivity of the ego was initiated by Rapaport (Gill, 1967, pp. 530–568) and was extended by me (Fromm, 1972) and by my student Donald Stolar (Stolar & Fromm, 1974). The concept of ego receptivity, an important and exciting concept, was later added to Rapaport's scheme by Deikman (1971) and was developed by me with regard to the role it plays in hypnosis and in creativity (Fromm, 1976, 1977b, 1979). The ego is active or autonomous when the individual can make an ego-syntonic *choice*; it is passive or lacks autonomy when the individual is overwhelmed by instinctual drives (Rapaport, 1967, pp. 530–568), by demands coming from the environment (Fromm, 1972), or by the superego (Stolar & Fromm, 1974).

Essentially the issue of activity and passivity of the ego is tied to the concept of coping or failing to cope. There are two forms of coping: sovereign or masterful coping and protective or defensive coping. In both, the ego is active and maintains autonomy.

When the patient submits to ego-dystonic demands coming from the instincts, from the external world, or from the superego, the ego is passive. In these cases, the patient either goes along with the demands even though he or she does not want to, or the patient feels overwhelmed and feels that there is no choice but to submit. Both responses are forms of ego passivity. Ego passivity of the latter type occurs characteristically in psychoses, in panic, in catastrophic reactions, in brainwashing, and in heterohypnosis (when an authoritarian hypnotist forces a patient into doing, feeling, or experiencing something that the patient definitely does not want to experience; Fromm, 1972). This ego passivity is usually accompanied by unpleasant affect.

However, not all states in which active control and voluntarism are relinquished are states of ego passivity; many states are characterized by ego receptivity (Fromm, 1977a, 1977b). In ego receptivity, critical judgment, strict adherence to reality orientation, and active goal-directed thinking are held to a minimum, and the individual allows unconscious and preconscious material to float freely into the mind. There is an openness to experience, which William James (1935) would have characterized as watching the stream of consciousness flow by. Ego receptivity is the prevailing state in heterohypnosis; it also occurs a good deal in self-hypnosis (Fromm et al., in press). In heterohypnosis, the patient opens up to the hypnotist and is more receptive to the therapist's suggestions than the patient would be in the waking state. Hypnotic suggestibility really is nothing else but heightened ego receptivity (Fromm, 1979).

Ego receptivity implies that the "gates" to primary process thoughts and images have opened more widely than they do in the waking state. Ego receptivity generally is an ego syntonic state.

In the active ego mode, the organism is ready and able to manipulate the environment. The receptive mode is organized around intake from the environment rather than around manipulation of the environment. In the receptive mode, one *allows* things to happen; one does not *make them* happen. The barriers between conscious awareness and the unconscious and preconscious are lowered. This leads to a greater availability of unconscious material.

CLINICAL WORK
IN HYPNOANALYSIS

Hypnoanalysis in many instances has certain advantages over psychoanalysis. In the field of clinical practice, not only, as already mentioned, does it shorten the time the patient has to stay in treatment, but it also allows hypnoanalysts to do things that in ordinary psychoanalysis cannot be done. Working with hypnosis, one has numerous techniques at one's disposal by means of which one can help the patient to remember and bring up into conscious awareness events, dreams, and feelings that have been forgotten or to produce a real dream during the therapy session. For instance, the hypnoanalyst can give the patient the posthypnotic suggestion that, the next time the patient comes in and sits or lies down on the couch on which he or she usually lies, the patient will remember the forgotten dream of the night before, and this usually is what happens. But if the patient seats him- or herself somewhere else, the hypnoanalyst knows that the patient needs to keep the dream repressed, and the hypnoanalyst respects that need for a while.

In addition, the hypnoanalyst can tell a patient to dream about the particular problem he or she is currently struggling with, or the hypnoanalyst can suggest that the patient will dream consecutive dreams dealing with the same problem and that in these dreams the patient will find better and better solutions.

In hypnoanalysis, as in psychoanalysis, dreams are, of course, mainly used as uncovering techniques. Two other uncovering techniques—hypermnesia and age regression—are unique to hypnosis and can only be used in the hypnotic state.

Since about 1975, I have also begun to work with hypnoanalysis of borderline and narcissistic patients and with patients suffering from posttraumatic stress disorders (PTSD)s—particularly incest victims, female and male (Brown & Fromm, 1986).

Hypnoanalysis with neurotic or psychosomatic problems usually takes somewhere between 3 months and 1 year. But hypnoanalysis with patients arrested at or regressed to pre-oedipal levels—the severely narcissistic, the borderlines, and psychotic patients—takes much longer.

The hypnoanalytic methods to be employed in the therapy of borderline and narcissistic patients are: being a good, empathic, mothering, and proudly mirroring figure for the patient; working toward object constancy; working toward internalization of the "good" love object; integrating love objects and hate objects solidly; achieving separate self-constancy and object constancy; gaining control of splitting as a defense; aiding in the development of structure and realistic evaluation of the self and of others; ego building; and enhancing the patient's control over affect. All these methods I have taken over from the psychoanalytic work of Mahler, Pine and Bergman, Kernberg, Kohut, Masterson, Gerald Adler, and other object relationship theorists and self theorists. The hypnotic techniques I have integrated for these purposes with the above-named psychoanalytic methods are: extensive imagery and fantasy production, free association, nonverbal communication (e.g., the hypnoanalyst's putting her hand on the patient's arm reassuringly when the patient becomes too overwhelmed by affect, indicating—nonverbally—her empathic presence and support), automatic drawing or writing, hypermnesia and age regression, hypnotic and posthypnotic suggestions, and ego strengthening (see Brown & Fromm, 1986, chaps. 8 and 9).

The treatment of PTSD is technically one of the most difficult types of hypnoanalysis to be undertaken. Treatment necessitates handling the material that comes up even much more symbolically than is done in many other kinds of cases. Imagery, hypermnesia and age regression, the use of screen memories (through which much of the affect initially connected with the trauma is worked through, as opposed to early uncovering of the original trauma), employing hypnotic drawings and anagrams, and the building in of delays are all techniques and parameters that can purposefully be employed to have the repressed material unfold *at the patient's own speed*. Even when the hypnoanalyst for a very long time is aware of the trauma that the patient has gone through—and frequently this trauma becomes clear to the hypnoanalyst from material the patient brings up in initial sessions of hypnosis—the hypnoanalyst must not overwhelm the patient by confronting her or him with "the truth" or pushing her or him to become aware of the full truth.

In cases of repressed traumatic experiences, hypnoanalysis usually proceeds, I have found, from the screen memory or the disguised presentation (e.g., in automatic drawings or writings) to the uncovering. If there is a danger of fragmenting under the impact of having to face the original trauma in all its starkness—that is, if or when the patient's ego is not strong enough to withstand such disclosure—the material perhaps had better be worked out on the screen memory only. After the material has been uncovered and worked through, there follows a phase of liberation, increased creativity, autonomy, real growth, and integration. This holds for Vietnam War veterans as well as for victims of incest (see chaps. 8 and 9 in Brown & Fromm, 1986).

CONCLUSION

I have pioneered quite a bit in my professional life, taken on joyfully many a challenge, and explored novel things. In the last 25 years, I think my colleagues and I have succeeded in demystifying hypnosis, in taking it out of the realm of sensationalism, and in putting it on a sound, calm, scientific keel.

For the last 20 years, I have fought equally hard for the survival of clinical psychology within the programs of our good universities. In many universities, other factions of the psychology departments have tried to kill clinical psychology. The battles goes on.

Now I am at an advanced age, but nonetheless I hope to continue to investigate new things and to fight for what I believe in for some time to come. I also fervently hope that I have strengthened in you—or aroused in you—the pioneering spirit. Psychologist-psychoanalysts, who have so much more research training than MDs, should do more psychoanalytic research and should pioneer in finding new ways of integrating psychoanalytic theory with hypnosis or in finding other methods of helping those who suffer emotional pain. Psychologists should also extend the frontiers of psychoanalytic theory, open a few windows, let in a lot of fresh air.

I am professor emeritus now, but I continue to work 7 days a week, often until 2:00 a.m., out of sheer passion and joy in being a psychologist. I hope I have instilled in my bright and inquisitive students a sense of excitement and enthusiasm for pioneering investigative work as well as deep empathy for the suffering patient.[1]

---

[1]Parts of this chapter are from a paper the author gave in response to receiving the 1985 Award of the Division of Psychoanalysis (Division 39) of the American Psychological Association. It was published in *Psychoanalytic Psychology*, 1987, 4, under the title "Psychoanalysis and Hypnoanalysis: A Personal History and a Challenge."

REFERENCES

Alexander, F., & French, T. M. (1946). *Psychoanalytic therapy: Principles and applications*. New York: Ronald.

Brown, D. P., & Fromm, E. (1986). *Hypnotherapy and hypnoanalysis*. Hillsdale, NJ: Lawrence Erlbaum Associates, Inc.

Brown, D. P., & Fromm, E. (1987). *Hypnosis and behavioral medicine*. Hillsdale, NJ: Lawrence Erlbaum Associates, Inc.

Deikman, A. (1971). Bimodal consciousness, *Archives of General Psychiatry, 25*, 481–489.

Eisen, M., & Fromm, E. (1983). The clinical use of self-hypnosis in hypnotherapy: Tapping the functions of imagery and adaptive regression. *International Journal of Clinical and Experimental Hypnosis, 31*, 243–255.

French, T. M. & Fromm, E. (1986). *Dream interpretation: A new approach* (2nd ed.). New York: International Universities Press. (Original work published 1964).

Freud, S. (1953). The interpretation of dreams. In J. Strachey (Ed. & Trans.). *The standard edition of the complete psychological works of Sigmund Freud* (Vols. 4 & 5). London: Hogarth. (Original work published 1900).

Fromm, E. (1965a). Hypnoanalysis: Theory and two case excerpts. *Psychotherapy: Theory, Research and Practice, 2*, 127–133.

Fromm, E. (1965b). Spontaneous autohypnotic age-regression in a nocturnal dream. *International Journal of Clinical and Experimental Hypnosis, 13*, 119–131.

Fromm, E. (1968). Transference and countertransference in hypnoanalysis. *International Journal of Clinical and Experimental Hypnosis 16*, 77–84.

Fromm, E. (1970). Age regression with unexpected reappearance of a repressed childhood language. *International Journal of Clinical and Experimental Hypnosis 18*, 79–88.

Fromm, E. (1972). Ego activity and ego passivity in hypnosis. *International Journal of Clinical and Experimental Hypnosis, 20*, 238–251.

Fromm, E. (1976). Altered states of consciousness and ego psychology. *Social Service Review, 50*, 557–569.

Fromm, E. (1977a). Altered states of consciousness and hypnosis: A discussion. *International Journal of Clinical and Experimental Hypnosis, 25*, 325–334.

Fromm, E. (1977b). An ego psychological theory of altered states of consciousness. *International Journal of Clinical and Experimental Hypnosis, 25*, 372–387.

Fromm, E. (1978–1979). Primary and secondary process in waking and in altered states of consciousness. *Journal of Altered States of Consciousness 4*, 115–128.

Fromm, E. (1979). The nature of hypnosis and other altered states of consciousness: An ego-psychological theory. In E. Fromm & R. E. Shor (Eds.), *Hypnosis:*

Developments in research and new perspectives (2nd ed., pp. 81–103). New York: Aldine.

Fromm, E. (1981). Ego-psychological parameters of hypnosis and their clinical applications. In H. J. Wain (Ed.), *Clinical and theoretical aspects of hypnosis* (pp. 33–53). Miami, FL: Symposia Specialists Medical Books.

Fromm, E. (1984a). Hypnoanalysis—With particular emphasis on the borderline patient. *Psychoanalytic Psychology, 1*, 61–76.

Fromm, E. (1984b). Theory and practice of hypnoanalysis. In W. C. Wester II & A. Smith (Eds.), *Clinical hypnosis: A multidisciplinary approach* (pp. 142–154). New York: Lippincott.

Fromm, E., Brown, D. P., Hurt, S. W., Oberlander, J. Z., Boxer, A. M., & Pfeifer, G. (1981). The phenomena and characteristics of self-hypnosis. *International Journal of Clinical and Experimental Hypnosis, 29*, 189–246.

Fromm, E., & Eisen, M. R. (1982). Self-hypnosis as a therapeutic aid in the mourning process. *American Journal of Clinical Hypnosis, 25*, 3–14.

Fromm, E., & Gardner, G. G. (1979). Ego psychology and hypnoanalysis: An integration of theory and technique. *Bulletin of the Menninger Clinic, 43*, 413–423.

Fromm, E., & Hurt, S. W. (1980). Ego-psychological parameters of hypnosis and altered states of consciousness. In G. D. Burrows & L. Dennerstein (Eds.), *Handbook of hypnosis and psychosomatic medicine* (pp. 13–27). New York: Elsevier/North Holland Biomedical Press.

Fromm, E., & Shor, R. E. (Eds.). (1979). *Hypnosis: Developments in research and new perspectives* (2nd ed.). New York: Aldine.

Fromm, E., Skinner, S., Lombard, L., & Kahn, S. (in press). The modes of ego functioning in self-hypnosis. *Imagery, Cognition, & Personality*.

Gill, M. M., & Brenman, M. (1959). *Hypnosis and related states: Psychoanalytic studies in regression*. New York: International Universities Press.

Gruenewald, D., Fromm, E., & Oberlander, M. I. (1979). Hypnosis and adaptive regression: An ego-psychological inquiry. In E. Fromm & R. E. Shor (Eds.), *Hypnosis: Developments in research and new perspectives* (2nd ed., pp. 619–635). New York: Aldine.

James, W. (1935). *The varieties of religious experience*. New York: Longman, Green.

Lombard, L., Kahn, S., & Fromm, E. (in press). The role of imagery in self-hypnosis: Its relationship to personality characteristic and gender. *International Journal of Clinical and Experimental Hypnosis*.

Rapaport, D. (1967). Some metapyschological considerations concerning activity and passivity. In M. M. Gill (Ed.), *The collected papers of David Rapaport* (pp. 530–568). New York: Basic.

Stolar, D., & Fromm, E. (1974). Activity and passivity of the ego in relation to the superego. *International Review of Psychoanalysis, 1*, 297–311.

REPRESENTATIVE PUBLICATIONS

Brosin, H. W., & Fromm, E. (1942). Some principles of Gestalt psychology in the Rorschach experiment. *Rorschach Research Exchange, 6*, 1–15.

Fromm, E. (1946). Study of a case of pseudo deaf-muteness—"Psychic deafness." *Journal of Nervous and Mental Disease, 103*, 37–59.

Fromm, E. (1958). The psychoanalytic interpretation of dreams and projective techniques. *American Journal of Orthopsychiatry, 28*, 67–72.

Fromm, E. (1960). Projective aspects of intelligence testing. In A. I. Rabin & M.

Haworth (Eds.), *Projective techniques with children* (pp. 225–236). New York: Grune & Stratton.

Fromm, E. (1965). Awareness versus consciousness. *Psychological Reports, 16,* 711–712.

Fromm, E. (1967). [Modern theories and practices of hypnotherapy]. *Seishin-shintai igaku, 7,* 147–161.

Fromm, E. (1968). Dissociative and integrative processes in hypnoanalysis. *American Journal of Clinical Hypnosis, 10,* 174–177.

Fromm, E. (1969). The manifest and the latent content of two paintings by Hieronymus Bosch: A psychoanalytic contribution to the study of creativity. *American Imago, 26,* 145–166.

Fromm, E. (1975). Selfhypnosis: A new area of research. *Psychotherapy: Theory, Research and Practice, 12,* 295–301.

Fromm, E. (1980). Values in hypnotherapy. *Psychotherapy: Theory, Research and Practice, 17,* 425–430.

Fromm, E. (1981). How to write a clinical paper: A brief communication. *International Journal of Clinical and Experimental Hypnosis, 29,* 5–9.

Fromm, E. (1982). Auto-hypnose [Autohypnosis]. *Dth: Kwartaalschrift voor Directieve Therapie en Hypnose, 2,* 100–118.

Fromm, E. (1987). Significant developments in clinical hypnosis during the past 25 years. *International Journal of Clinical and Experimental Hypnosis, 35,* 215–230.

Fromm, E., & French, T. M. (1962). Formation and evaluation of hypotheses in dream interpretation. *Journal of Psychology, 54,* 271–283.

Fromm, E., Hartman, L. D., & Marschak, M. (1957). Children's intelligence tests as a measure of dynamic personality functioning. *American Journal of Orthopsychiatry, 27,* 134–144.

Fromm, E., Oberlander, M. I., & Gruenewald, D. (1970). Perceptual and cognitive processes in different states of consciousness: The waking state and hypnosis. *Journal of Projective Techniques and Personality Assessment, 5,* 375–387.

Oppenheimer, E. [Fromm, E.]. (1934). *Optische versuche über ruhe und bewegung* [Optical experiments on induced movement]. *Psychologische Forschung, 20,* 1–46.

Oppenheimer, E. [Fromm, E.], & Speijer, N. (1937). *Resultaten van de Rorschach test in een geval van dementia paralytica voor en na bahandeling met malaria* [Results of the Rorschach test in a case of dementia paralytica before and after malaria treatment]. *Psychiatrische en Neurologische Bladen* (No. 3).

Stolar, D., & Fromm, E. (1974). Activity and passivity of the ego in relation to the superego. *International Review of Psycho-Analysis, 1,* 297–311.

Wilson, A., & Fromm, E. (1982). Aftermath of the concentration camp: The second generation. *Journal of the American Academy of Psychoanalysis, 10*(2), 289–313.

CHAPTER 8

Lillian E. Troll

Lillian E. Troll

I know now, but did not always know, that being female made a difference in my development as a psychologist, just as it had in my general life development. Most of my life, however, I thought that ability and chance between them were the major explanations of what happened—if I thought about it at all, that is. Only after my "consciousness was raised" in the feminist surge of the late 1960s and early 1970s did I start to give weight to gender effects. Reading *The Feminine Mystique* by Betty Friedan (1963), which I did in 1970, worked like a kaleidoscopic shift, putting all the pieces together into a new pattern. Because I am writing this in 1987, I am reporting from this new perspective, elaborated on, of course, by the events and interpretations of the intervening 15 years.

I was born in Chicago in 1915, aborting my mother's college career. Both my parents were immigrants from Russia, from where they came separately and alone while in their early teens. When I look at my grandchildren of that age and try to imagine them taking off across the world that way, it is not easy. Both my mother (Bertha Holland) and father (Morris Ellman) were already, by 14 and 15 years of age, avid intellectuals, motivated to come to America because that was where they could continue their education. Once here, it took hard work and enormous self-discipline to accumulate the necessary money. They met at Michigan Agricultural College (now Michigan State University), where my father was a senior agriculture student (he was a disciple of Tolstoy) and my mother a freshman home economics student. They married with an agreement that my father would support my mother through the rest of college, whereupon my mother transferred to the University of Chicago while my father accepted a job in Canada to train *stetl* Jews in farming and supervise them on ranches in Saskatchewan and Alberta. But I intervened. By this time, my mother's five siblings and their mother had been brought over by their combined effort and were living in Chicago. My mother stayed with them until I was 6 months old, then traveled with me by train to join my father in Winnipeg.

We moved a lot during my childhood, from Winnipeg to a farm near Madison, Wisconsin, back to Winnipeg, to Montreal, to Winnipeg, to Regina, and finally, in 1929, back to Chicago. I went to many schools over the first eight grades, starting at the age of 7 (in 1923) in Winnipeg and finishing high school (in 1933) in Chicago. Partly because I was repeatedly a new girl in town, school was the place to make friends. I was a good student, and the hours at school were the best part of each day.

EDUCATION

Hyde Park High School, at that time, was one of the best in the city, partly because the Depression kept many brilliant students and teachers in the public schools. A generation later, many of those students would have been in independent schools and many of the teachers would have had other options, perhaps teaching in colleges. I thus had knowledgeable and inspring teachers and challenging classmates. To approximate the same quality of education a generation later, we had to send our children to private schools, and it saddens me that my grandchildren's experiences of school are often mediocre and unexciting.

When I graduated high school in 1933 at the height of the Depression, I almost automatically continued on to the University of Chicago. I could afford to because we lived two blocks from campus. Anyway, there weren't any other options. With scholarships and other financial aid, I probably earned as much while I was at the university as I would have been able to in any job then available. Graduate school followed undergraduate. The university was my home. In fact it was my family's home. One of my aunts, my mother, my father, my sister Vera, and at least seven of my cousins (not to mention two of my nephews) all attended. My mother completed her degree when we moved back to Chicago, when I was in my early teens and my sister was about 10. She graduated as a social worker in 1932 and went on to a notable career that lasted until she finally retired at the age of 80. My father accommodated to the exigencies of the Depression by getting a master's degree in social work, abandoning agriculture to becoming the director of one of the newly created Social Security offices in Chicago. Obviously, my family valued education, intelligence, and achievement—probably more for men than for women, but still also for women. Just marrying an intelligent, educated, achieving man was not enough. (It was for many of my friends, though, and still is for a few of them.)

Both Hyde Park High School and the University of Chicago treated us women students as seriously as our male classmates. After all, the job market was bleak for all of us, and our mentors did not have to play Solomon. I have been told recently that the University of Chicago has, from its beginning in the 1890s, led the academic world in its proportion and recognition of women students. This did not apply, however, to women faculty members or even to graduate students. I think women were supposed to disappear after the BA or BS—or, the equivalent of disappearance—to go into home economics or education.

The first time I was aware that I was affected by sex bias was when I applied for admission to the University of Chicago Medical School in 1937. I had pursued a double major: pre-med and psychology. I chose pre-med because I had to struggle to do even moderately well in it and thus felt that I was learning a lot, and I chose psychology because it provided easy relief from the rigors of pre-med. The quotas set for women and Jews for medical school admission were four, I think, and I was fifth or sixth. It is true that I could have gone to a different medical school (I was accepted at others), but I interpreted this rejection as a sign and turned to graduate work in psychology instead. At the back of my mind was also the thought that if I had to work as hard in medical school as I had in pre-med, I wouldn't have the energy left to charm a prospective husband.

Unfortunately, the area of psychology that most interested me—developmental psychology—had been shunted to home economics because its major professor (in my mind the most scholarly psychologist on the faculty), was a woman. Years later, I recalled Helen Koch's rage over that action. Students of home economics were considered second class, of inferior ability compared to psychologists, and lower in scientific motivation. Their primary goals were marriage and raising children instead of teaching and research. It goes without saying that they were all women. It was my proud belief that I was not like them, that their primary goals were my secondary goals. This does not mean, though, that I and my "scientific" friends did not also want to get married and raise children. I remember spending hours in Harper Library debating favorite names for our future children between bouts of study, even though most of us weren't anywhere close to finding a father for these children. Luckily, the Committee on Human Development was formed during my graduate years, so that I could get a respectable degree.

Did my interest in child psychology stem from being a woman? I did not think so, at least at that time. I looked at that area as the most challenging possible. What could be more important than learning how to change the behavior of human beings during their formative years? It was clear that this was the most effective way to improve the world, an ultimate goal for most of us at that time. On the other hand, I sure did love working with the 2- and 3-year-olds in the nursery school. Incidentally, I learned that changing behavior was both more difficult and more interesting than changing diapers.

As it turned out, I did not get my degree then. After passing prelims and moving well along on my dissertation (a factor study of music ability tests—Thurstone was on my committee), I was invited by Marion Richardson, my statistics professor, to take the civil service exam for test constructor and come to work for the test-construction office he had been asked to create in the War Department. So, on July 1, 1941, with no thought of being involved in a war, I and my new husband, Hans Troll, moved to Washington, DC. The job gave us an income that enabled marriage, and as Hans was a musician, he could live in Washington as well as anywhere. We felt proud to belong to the elite group that created all the Army selection and placement tests. In fact, we kept reassuring ourselves how elite we were by taking every new test ourselves.

I don't think being a woman had anything to do with not finishing my dissertation then. All of us on the staff of the Personnel Research Section at that time were ABDs, having come to Washington with the firm belief that we would complete our dissertations there. None of us did. But all the men—most of us *were* men, of course—finished right after the war ended in 1945 and went on to brilliant careers. Only three or four of the six or seven women (some came later, some left sooner) ever did, several of us not until we had given birth to and raised children. It is interesting that none of us—men or women—had children during the war years. I myself took 25 years to finish my PhD (in 1967).

SUBURBIA

In 1945, the end of the war brought an end to our office and the demand for our professional services. I was at the critical age of 29. Even then, everybody said that one must have one's first child before 30—or else! (I have been trying to counter that myth for many years.) Months before V–J Day, we knew our office was disbanding; we began writing the history of our achievements. Ruth Churchill, my immediate superior, had a desk facing mine, and we kept moving our desks closer together to accommodate our expanding middles. We had a joint shower early in November. Her son, Tom, was born later that month, and my daughter, Kitty, a month later. We had both worked until near the births, of course. Having a child was as much an achievement to us as any test we constructed. The fact that Ruth got pregnant a month sooner that I was a part of her acknowledged superiority to me—after all, she had been hired to our office 6 months before I was, which gave her a higher rank. High achievement motivated people remain highly motivated in everything they do, as I have tried to demonstrate in my more recent work (e.g., Troll & Schwartz, 1984).

What I haven't mentioned is that I left our War Department office for a year in 1942 to join my husband in Boston, where he had gone to get a master's degree in musicology at the Harvard Graduate School. He wanted to further the musical career started in Vienna but interrupted by Hitler. During that time, I taught at Pine Manor Junior College in Wellesley and became convinced that I was not made to be a college teacher, even at what amounted to a finishing school. At the time, I was positive, in fact, that women's voices could not inspire students the way men's did. This may have had a lot to do with my change in career focus later on to clinical work with children.

The year to become a homemaker was 1945. Like thousands of other women workers of the war years, I turned to raising children (Kathren in 1945, Jeanne in 1947, and Gregory in 1949) and moving the vacuum cleaner around. (It rarely got put away because those were the years when I dropped one activity to react to a crisis somewhere else.) My friends and I joined women's clubs, the PTA, and community improvement activities. My name was posted as "address unknown" by the American Psychological Association (APA) because I considered professional identity irrelevant. As my children were growing up, they had no idea I had ever worked as a psychologist—or probably that I had ever worked outside the home arena. I learned how to strip wallpaper, to make brick-and-board bookcases, and to cook gourmet, but the only psychological work I did was to run a small and unsuccessful nursery school in a New Jersey town where children had all the room to play and mothers were home all day. The only customers we got were severe problems, and not enough of them. As my husband earned progressively more money—he had left music for engineering by then—we moved from an apartment in Queens, New York, to a "development house" on Long Island to two houses in Mahwah, New Jersey, to an enormous brick house on a hill in Waban, Massachusetts.

RETURNING

A series of chance events led to my getting "back in" the workforce. One spring morning, after I had been weeding crabgrass on my hilltop aerie, I jumped up, retrieved my hat and gloves from the attic (still, in 1955, *de rigeur* for formal occasions like job inquiries), and went to see Edward Landy, head of the school psychology unit in the Newton (MA) Public Schools. I had met him once at a party and asked if I could talk to him about volunteering in his office. He had said to call him. That morning, he didn't come through right away because he didn't believe in volunteers, but he did call in September, 6 months later. One of the staff psychologists got burned smoking in bed, and it was the beginning of the school year, when lots of diagnostic testing had to be done. I accepted because the job was defined as a 2-week stint and because I could work when my children were in school and be home when they were there (the office and all the schools I had to visit were close to home). Even though I desperately wanted to work again, I didn't feel that it would be appropriately feminine to hold a full-time, permanent job. That was definitely not the thing to do if you were a married woman in the mid-1950s. I was the first of our suburban crowd to go back to work, and everyone wanted to know why I had done so. I had to justify it somehow, so I found myself saying it seemed important not to waste my education. It took almost 10 years for most of the other women I knew then in Newton to follow me as "returnees."

The woman I replaced took many months to recover and then decided to go back to school to finish her PhD. Significantly, she was not married. So, I ended up staying at that job for 6 years. I acquired tenure but was being paid only at the BA level. (I had skipped the master's because it was not a serious degree for those of us headed for a doctorate). Again, it did not seem appropriately feminine to hold a 9-to-5 job and get paid as much as I was worth. The Newton situation was good, therefore, because that made the job *not serious, not threatening to my gender identity.*

Then the situation changed drastically. My husband developed job problems and did not earn enough to support the family. What I earned became important, particularly a year or so later when he decided to end our marriage. This too jolted me into confronting all the feminist issues that later became familiar to many women of my age cohort. Because I no longer had to be a dutiful wife, I was freed to deviate from the women-at-home restrictions I and my friends had imposed upon ourselves.

Finishing my PhD would both enable me to earn more money and give me the credentials to investigate some of the puzzling theoretical questions that had confronted me in my years of clinical work, particularly those questions related to family dynamics. What I was observing was completely different from what the books said. Most obviously, parents were not so much creating the problems of their children as they were all jointly sharing those problems. Because Ed Landy had raised the usually pedestrain job of school psychologist from test giving and guidance to working with parents, children, teachers, and the community, and because I differed from most of my colleagues in Newton in being older and a parent myself, I was in a position to see transmission patterns of behavior across nuclear households in extended families.

My first step in this direction was unsuccessful. I moved to Palo Alto in 1963 because my sister and her family lived there and I hoped she would help me cope with my teenagers while I went back to school. After checking out Stanford and Berkeley, though, it appeared that I would do better by returning to the University of Chicago. I was told I was too old to be accepted at Stanford and I would have to start graduate work over at Berkeley. Fortunately, the Committee on Human Development at Chicago not only welcomed me back but even offered to support me if I returned to campus. I waited until Jeannie was graduated from high school in 1965, had my derelict Rambler station wagon reconditioned, and, disregarding the garage owner's warning, drove across the mountains to Chicago and to a finally successful achievement of the title "doctor." This was 1967.

It would certainly have been more expeditious to complete my original dissertation, but it no longer interested me. I found I had a passionate desire to know more about family behavior, partly due to my clinical experiences and partly due to my personal ones. My new dissertation, accordingly, was on personality similarities between college students and their parents (Troll, 1967; Troll, Neugarten, & Kraines, 1969). Bernice Neugarten was the committee chair, and Ruth Kraines was also a member of the committee. Ruth had returned a few years before me, and Bernice had maintained an amost continuous presence at the university, completing her doctorate years before. The three of us had been together in graduate school in 1940.

I came back to campus at the height of the student movement, which was being studied by Neugarten and Richard Flacks—the Youth and Social Change Project. They asked me to administer that research in exchange for using the data I acquired for my own research. I had originally planned to study high school seniors and their parents, using interviews and a variety of personality tests, but now ended up studying college-age men and women and their parents, devising a coding scheme applied to open-ended (and some structured) interview data. My background in test construction gave me confidence to do so, but I still insisted—as did my committee—that these data be subjected to rigorous multivariate procedures. Happily for my hypotheses, these older—and more adventurous—respondents showed substantial confirmation of intrafamily similarities that belied the prevalent promulgations about a generation gap.

It was by chance that at the time I applied for readmission to the University of Chicago, a young graduate student in the School of Education had just completed a study of the frequency with which graduate students completed their PhDs. Because that percentage was very small, which alarmed university officials about the success rate of the programs, I was able to return with astonishingly minimal demands for updating. It was by chance that there was a push to encourage graduate students in gerontology just when I was returning and that I could attend classes taught by Robert Havighurst and be Neugarten's teaching assistant in adult development. It was by chance that universities started searching for gerontologists to teach when I was ready to teach (well, not to teach exactly, because I was still sure my voice was a disability). So I became a life-span developmentalist. It occurs to me that I have moved away from aiming to improve human life via optimal child raising to trying to understand the course of human life, a much more limited goal.

ACADEMIA

Because I believed I would make a terrible teacher, I was delighted to be able to join the faculty of the Merrill-Palmer Institute in Detroit, where I was assured of no class large enough to lecture to and plenty of research time and facilities. But chance again! The institute came on hard times in a couple of years and disbanded its research component; in 1970, I joined the psychology faculty at Wayne State University, just a few blocks away. And here necessity led to my finding out that I too could lecture to large classes and often enough could get recognition for good teaching. The Detroit years, between 1967 and 1975, were highly productive. I not only learned to love teaching and even lecturing in public, but I wrote and published a lot and joined with some friends in organizing citywide efforts for child care and help for the old. After my dissertation research, my next major work was a decade review of research on later-life family relationships (Troll, 1971), to which I have returned twice since (Troll, 1986; Troll, Miller, & Atchley, 1979). I developed my understanding and delineation of adult development in my first book (Troll, 1975/1985), standing firmly on the shoulders of Neugarten, and, with Joan and Kenneth Israel (Troll, Israel, & Israel, 1977), edited a volume that explored the state of the art in thinking about older women.

When I accepted an offer to go to Rutgers University in 1975, as chair of the University College Psychology Department, I continued working on adult development and aging (Troll, 1982), on family issues (Troll, 1986; Troll et al., 1979), particularly in the later years, and on the state of older women (Troll, 1985, 1987). In fact, my retirement in July 1986 has not changed my interests much either, even though it has transferred the scene of activities from New Jersey to California. The first year of retirement was taken up with too much teaching, which I have promised myself to end. I am hoping, as soon as I have caught up with commitments for chapters in various volumes, to publish the findings from analyses of the hundreds of three-generation families (all adults) whose interviews I have been collecting for many years.

I haven't given a lot of consideration to the effect of my being a woman on my academic career, either its content or its process. During my student years, it mattered whether our companions were of our own sex or of the opposite sex, but it did not mold the topics we discussed or the seriousness of our discussions. Later, however, after most of us were married, that changed. After the dating and mating years, men lunched or talked informally with men, women with women. One of my male colleagues once commented that he would have enjoyed intellectual discussions at lunch with women, but he was scared to try because these would have been viewed as sexual overtures. Further, the discussions among my academic colleagues rarely dealt with ideas or experiences on the job. I discovered, when I occasionally joined all-male lunch groups, that they talked about academic policy, grantsmanship, gossip, and money. Academic women's lunch discussions were about home, family, children, and parents.

That meant that we women—and there was always just a handful of us compared to the much larger numbers of men—did not usually discover the important bits of information that would have helped us professionally: the character of the new dean, what grants were coming up, what the chances were for tenure and promotion, and so forth.

A word about mentors. Not all my mentors have been women, but those who were have been strategic, starting with Helen Koch at the University of Chicago and Bernice Neugarten, who picked up her mantle when she retired from the university. Among the men were Andrew Brown, long ago at the Institute for Juvenile Research in Chicago (and a teacher at the university); Samuel Beck, under whom I did a clinical internship at Michael Reese Hospital; and Marion Richardson, my statistics professor at the university who later enticed me to Washington. In Detroit, there were Irving Sigel and Eli Saltz. About 8 years ago, I joined Margaret Bacon, the eminent anthropologist, and a few other prominent women academicians in deliberately forming an "old-girls network." Our mission was to help other women in academia, but we also intended to help our male students and junior colleagues. This effort unfortunately faded away, partly due to Margaret's illness.

Mentors are not necessarily role models, but in my case I wanted to be a scholar like Helen Koch and Bernice Neugarten and later like Jessie Bernard. In fact, almost all my role models, starting with my mother, have been women, women who did not lose their sensitivity and warmth as they increased their knowledge and skill and power.

It still surprises me, finally, that my interests and passions have turned out to be so sex-stereotyped, so affiliative and oriented toward affiliation: family relations and family transmission of culture and values (e.g., Troll & Bengtson, 1979), life-span development (e.g., Troll, 1982), sex differences and sex roles (e.g., Troll & Parron, 1981). And my favorite kind of research is person-to-person interviewing and observation. It is true that I know men who share these interests—Vern Bengtson, for one—but a look around classrooms or APA sessions shows the ratios to be unequal. There is one big advantage to this. I have had little problem integrating my own family involvement with my professional interests. My years as a daughter, a sister, a wife, a mother, and a grandmother have given me insights I could not have gotten from reading or laboratory experiments. Like most mothers, I was the one to take the children to the doctor or the dentist, to be with them when they were in the hospital, to arrange their birthday parties, and to chaperone their teenage gatherings. When my husband was no longer able to support them, I knew without thinking that I had to earn enough to do so. Even after they became adults, I was there when they (and my grandchildren) needed me. I was the caretaker of my mother when she got old and needed help. And it is against the standard of these immediacies that I have evaluated and reexamined a lot of the assumptions that pervade standard family psychology and sociology (Troll, 1980, 1987; cf. Troll et al., 1979; Troll & Smith, 1976).

REFERENCES

Friedan, B. (1963). *The feminine mystique.* New York: Norton.

Troll, L. (1967). *Personality similarities between family members. Multivariate analysis of personality ratings of college students and their parents.* Unpublished doctoral dissertation, University of Chicago, Chicago.

Troll, L. (1971). The family in the second half of life: A decade review. *Journal of Marriage and the Family, 33,* 263–290.

Troll, L. (1982). *Continuations: Adult development and aging.* Monterey, CA: Brooks/Cole.

Troll, L. (1985). *Development in early and middle adulthood: The best is yet to be—Maybe.* Monterey, CA: Brooks/Cole. (Original work published 1975).

Troll, L. (1985). Old age. In C. Tavris (Ed.), *Everywoman's emotional well-being* (pp. 258–280). Garden City, NY: Doubleday.

Troll, L. (Ed.). (1986). *Family issues in current gerontology.* New York: Springer.

Troll. L. (1987). Mother–daughter relationships through the life span. In S. Oskamp (Ed.), *Applied social psychology annual* (Vol. 7, pp. 294–306). Newbury Park, CA: Sage.

Troll, L. & Bengtson, V. (1979). Generations in the family. In W. Burr, R. Hill, F. Nye, & L. Reiss (Eds.), *Contemporary theories about the family* (Vol. 1, pp. 127–161). New York: Free Press.

Troll, L., Israel, J., & Israel, K. (Eds.). (1977). *Looking ahead: A woman's guide to the problems and joys of growing older.* Englewood Cliffs, NJ: Prentice-Hall.

Troll, L., Miller, S., & Atchley, R. (1979). *Families of later life.* Belmont, CA: Wadsworth.

Troll, L., Neugarten, B., & Kraines, R. (1969). Similarities in values and other personality characteristics in college students and their parents. *Merrill–Palmer Quarterly, 14,* 323–336.

Troll, L., & Parron, E. (1981). The double shift: Age changes in sex roles amid changing sex roles. in J. Birren & C. Eisdorfer (Eds.), *Annual review of gerontology and geriatrics* (pp. 118–143). New York: Springer.

Troll, L., & Schwartz, L. (1984). A three-generational analysis of change in women's motivaton and power. In L. Stamm & C. Ryff (Eds.), *Social power and influence of women: AAAS Symposium* (pp. 81–98). Boulder, CO: Westview Press and AAAS.

Troll, L., & Smith, J. (1967). Attachment through the life span: Some questions about dyadic bonds among adults. *Human Development, 19,* 156–170.

REPRESENTATIVE PUBLICATIONS

Alington, D., & Troll, L. (1984). Social change and equality: The roles of women and economics. In G. Baruch & J. Brooks/Gunn (Eds.), *Between youth and old age: Women and change.* New York: Plenum.

Bengtson, V., & Troll, L. (1978). Youth and their parents: Feedback and intergenerational influence in socialization. In R. Lerner & G. Spanier, (Eds.), *Child influences on marital and family interactions.* NY: Academic Press.

Fields, T., Huston, A., Quay, H. C., Troll, L., & Finley, G. (Eds.) (1982). *Review of human development.* New York: Wiley.

Freedman, D. K., Troll, L., Mills, A. B., & Baken, P. (1965). Acute organic disorder accompanied by mental symptoms. Intensive treatment in general hospitals for patients who suffer from Acute Brain Syndrome. Unpublished manuscript, Department of Mental Hygiene, Sacramento, CA.

Personnel Research Section, The Adjutant General's Office (1944–1945). War Department. *Statistical Manual (Vols. I & II).* Washington, D.C.: U.S. Government Printing Office. Perspectives on treating older women. Bio-Monitoring Applications, (cassette recording) 1977.

Schlossberg, N. (Coordinator), Hagestad, G., Siegler, I., & Troll, L. (1985). *The adult years: Continuity and change.* International Universities Consortium, College Park, MD.

Schlossberg, N., Troll, L., & Liebowitz, S. (1977). *Perspectives on counseling.* Melbourne, FL.: Krieger.

Seltzer, M., & Troll, L. (1982). Shifting public attitudes toward filial responsibility. In L. Troll (Ed.), *Elders and their families: Generations.* San Francisco, CA: Western Gerontological Society.

Troll, L. (1969). Issues in the study of the family: A review of Gerald Handel's Psychological interior of the family. *Merrill-Palmer Quarterly, 15,* 221–226.

Troll, L. (1970). Issues in the study of generations. *Aging and Human Development, 1*(3), 200–218.

Troll, L. (1971). Eating and aging. *Journal of the American Dietetic Association, 59*(5), 456–459.

Troll, L. (1971). Family of later life. A decade review. In C. Broderick, (Ed.), *A decade of family research and action.* National Council on Family Relations.

Troll, L. (1971). The family in the second half of life: A decade review. *Journal of Marriage and the Family, 33*(2), 263–290.

Troll, L. (1972). The "generation gap" in later life. *Sociological Focus, 21*(3), 347–351.

Troll, L. (1972). Parent–child conflict and the generation gap. *Family Coordinator, 21*(3), 347–351.

Troll, L. (1973). The onus of developmental tasks and other comments. *Aging and Human Development.*

Troll, L. (1976). The effect of changing sex roles on the family of later life. Ford Foundation Conference.

Troll, L. (1980). Grandparenting. In L. Poon (Ed.), *Aging in the 1980s.* Washington, DC: American Psychological Association.

Troll, L. (1980). Intergenerational relations in later life. In N. Datan & N. Lohmann (Eds.), *Transitions of aging.* New York: Academic Press, 1980.

Troll, L. (Ed.). (1980). Interpersonal relations section. In L. Poon (Ed.), *Aging in the 1980s.* Washington, DC. American Psychological Association.

Troll, L. (Ed.). (1981). Household, family, and kin. In Prospect Associates: National research plan on aging. Potomac, MD.

Troll, L. (Ed.). (1982). *Elders and their families: Generations.* San Francisco, CA: Western Gerontological Society.

Troll, L. (1982). Family life in middle and old age: The generation gap. In F. Berardo (Ed.), *The Annals of the American Academy of Political and Social Science.* Philadelphia, PA.

Troll, L. (1982). Introduction. In L. Troll (Ed.), *Elders and their families: Generations.* San Francisco, CA: Western Gerontological Society.

Troll, L. (1983). Grandparents: The family watchdogs. In T. Brubaker (Ed.), *Family relationships in later life.* Beverly Hills, CA: Sage.

Troll, L. (1985). *Development in early and middle adulthood* (2nd ed.). Monterey, CA: Brooks/Cole.

Troll, L. (1985). Old age. In C. Tavris (Ed.), *Everywoman's emotional well-being.* New York: Doubleday.

Troll, L. (1985). On the timing of grandparenting. In V. Bengtson & J. Robertson (Eds.), *Grandparenthood.* Beverly Hills, CA: Sage.

Troll, L. (Ed.). (1986). *Family issues in current gerontology.* New York: Springer, 1986.

Troll, L., & Bengtson, V. (1979). Generations in the family. In W. Burr, R. Hill, F. Nye, & I. Reiss (Eds.), *Contemporary theories about the family: Vol. 1.* New York: Free Press.

Troll, L., Israel, J., & Israel, K. (Eds.). (1977). *Looking ahead: A Woman's Guide to the problems and joys of growing older.* Englewood Cliffs, NJ: Prentice-Hall.

Troll, L., Miller, S., & Atchley, R. (1979). *Families of later life.* Belmont, CA: Wadsworth.

Troll, L., Neugarten, B., & Kraines, R. (1969). Similarities in values and other personality characteristics in college students and their parents. *Merrill-Palmer Quarterly, 15,* 323–336.

Troll, L., & Parron, E. (1981). The double shift: Age changes in sex roles amid changing sex roles. In J. Birren & C. Eisdorfer (Eds.), *Annual Review of Gerontology and Geriatrics.*

Troll, L., & Schwartz, L. A. (1984). A three-generational analysis of change in women's motivation and power. In L. S. Stam & C. D. Ryff (Eds.), *Social power and influence of women. AAAS Symposium volume.* Boulder, CO: Westview Press and AAAS.

Troll, L. & Stapley, J. (1985). Elders and the extended family system: Health, family salience, and affect. In J. Munnich & E. Olbricht (Eds.), *Life-span and change in a gerontological perspective.* New York: Academic Press.

Troll, L., & Turner, J. (1978). Overcoming age-sex discrimination. Washington, DC: U.S. House of Representatives Select Committee on Aging Compendium.

Troll, L., & Turner, B. (1979). Sex differences in problems of later life. In V. Franks & E. Gomberg (Eds.), *Gender and disordered behavior.* New York: Bruner-Mazel.

CHAPTER 9

Olga E. de Cillis Engelhardt

Olga E. de Cillis Engelhardt

I was born in New York City August 26, 1917. My early years lacked the influence of grandparents, for both maternal and paternal grandparents died shortly before I was born. My parents had five children—four daughters and one son. I was the fourth daughter, born 5 years after the third offspring. My brother was the last child, born five years later. My parents did not attend college, were self-educated and desirous of fostering the educational development and opportunities of their five children. They offered both encouragement and support. My oldest sister, Grace, due to financial reverses brought on by the depression, did not attend college. As finances improved, Kae, the next oldest, obtained her undergraduate degree from New York University. Irma, the third sibling, and I attended Hunter College. My brother studied chemical engineering at Columbia University. He was inducted into the Air Corp at the end of his sophomore year. After participating in World War II, he re-entered Columbia, obtained his undergraduate degree, and continued toward his master's degree. I was the only one who chose to go on for the doctoral degree. I had full blessings from both mother and father. Both parents had created an environment where intellectual pursuits were fostered. I recall a very pleasant childhood full of interesting experiences. I have many memories of family trips to museums, zoos, botanical gardens, libraries, and theaters, such as the Civic Repertory Theatre for performances, featuring Eve Le Gallienne, Jules Garfield, and Joseph Schildkraut, among others.

During adolescence, I was very much influenced by my father, who was an avid reader, and by two older sisters who were pursu-

121

ing careers in public administration and in the education of handicapped children, respectively. I too wanted to prepare myself for a career but early on did not have a specific goal or exposure to the field of psychology.

After graduating from Evander Childs High school as valedictorian of my class, I enrolled at Hunter College while the economy was still in the throes of the Depression. Finances were tight during the first 2 years of college. I supplemented my allowance by working as a part-time salesperson at R. H. Macy's in the sweater department. Meanwhile, search continued for possible career opportunities. In my sophomore year, I decided to major in sociology and to minor in psychology. At that point, I had aspirations of becoming a social worker and emulating the career choice of one of my older sisters. In 1936, Hunter did not offer a program in social work. However, a major in sociology had become available shortly before I became interested in it. The faculty in the department had been recycled from other disciplines. I can remember spending an entire year learning about the water system and sewage purification methods in New York City. I became disenchanted with lack of theory and dullness of content.

Psychology was far more interesting than the study of sewage systems. The psychology professor who had a marked influence on the future course of my career was Dr. Bernard Riess, who taught social psychology. One day in class, stimulated by a question I had asked, he commented that he believed many allergies were psychosomatic in origin and that neurotics were more prone to allergic reactions, but he did not know of any research that could support that statement. After class, I approached him with the suggestion that it might be possible to test the hypothesis if I could get permission to use children in the allergy clinic of New York Hospital as subjects. In my junior year, I was a volunteer worker at New York Hospital (part of Cornell Medical School). The hospital was just a short walk from college at 68th Street, and I worked there three afternoons a week and on Saturdays as an aide in the Department of Pediatrics.

The medical director of the department agreed to the study. Children who came to the Pediatrics Clinic were tested using the Pintner-Forlano Study of Personality—a paper-and-pencil test designed for children.

The research design was simple and in the tradition of research papers of its kind during that period. The design lacked our current design sophistication, but that was 48 years ago when almost all graduate schools used Henry Garrett's book, *Statistics in Psy-*

chology and Education (1938), prior to the advent of texts such as those written by Fred Kerlinger (1973), William Hays (1973), and Jerome Myers (1979), and Winer (1971). Dr. Riess suggested that the paper be read at a regional psychological meeting. The paper was submitted and was accepted for reading at the Eastern Psychological Association (EPA) meeting in Philadelphia in 1939. I was an undergraduate and very flattered to find Ross Stagner in the audience. He commented very favorably on our reported results—children with known allergies did indeed test as more neurotic on the Pintner–Forlano Personality test than a matched group of nonallergic children. At the time, I felt I had indeed found a discipline I wanted to pursue, although I was also drawn to the study of political science. One of the courses I enrolled in that same year was International Relations with Dr. Elizabeth Linsky—a brilliant and insightful political scientist. She selected me to attend a collegiate international relations conference conducted on the campus of Bryn Mawr. It was my second opportunity to interact with students attending different colleges and universities, and I found the interchange of ideas very stimulating.

In addition to the opportunity to do research, attending college at Hunter College provided the exhilaration of being part of an exciting city. The main campus of Hunter was, and is, at 68th Street. At the time I was a student, enrollment pressure was great, and the need for additional classroom space forced the administration to seek space in another building. That year, the space was located at 2 Park Avenue. I had a class in the main building at 68th Street at 3:50 p.m., and the next class was at 4:10 p.m. at 2 Park Avenue (32nd Street). The schedule allowed 20 min between classes to commute via subway between 68th Street and 32nd Street. With only 20 min between classes, it was necessary to leave the building at 68th with alacrity, take the Lexington Avenue subway to 33rd Street, walk a half block to 2 Park Avenue, and ride the elevator up to the 32nd floor. One afternoon, students piled into the elevator, packed tighter than sardines, and the elevator stopped midway between the 31st and 32nd floors. Space was nonexistent, bodies were packed, arms held books, and there was no space to move. We were confined in close quarters for 45 min. Finally the rescue squad arrived and extricated students through the opening in the top of the elevator. To this day, I do not enter an elevator until I am sure it has a means of egress.

At Hunter, Dr. Riess was my mentor. After reading the research paper at the EPA, I prepared it for publication with his assistance and guidance. It was accepted by the *Journal of Abnormal and*

Social Psychology and was published during my first year of graduate study (Riess & de Cillis, 1940).

At the suggestion of Dr. Riess, I went on to graduate school in psychology at Columbia University, his alma mater. Mentors can be and are very helpful!

Intrigued by Dr. Riess's recounting in class of his experiences in the animal laboratory, I intended to explore the realm of comparative psychology. Dr. Carl Warden, of animal motivation fame, was director of the animal laboratory. He allowed me, as a research student, to conduct an experiment in the animal laboratory for my master's thesis. Norman Maier's (1939) book, *Studies of Abnormal Behavior in the Rat* (1939), had just been published. Could similar results be obtained in some other animal species? I obtained approval from Dr. Warden to conduct an experiment in the animal laboratory for my master's thesis, replicating and extending Maier's experiment using guinea pigs.

Maier used a discrimination task involving a jumping method previously developed by Lashley (1912). The equipment consisted of a jumping stand and a feeding platform. The task for the animal was to jump from the stand to the feeding platform to obtain food. After the animal learned to jump from the stand to the feeding platform, the discrimination task was introduced. A screen with two doors was placed on the feeding platform. One door was black with a white circle and was lightly held in place; the other was white with a black circle and was tightly fastened. The task was to discriminate between the two patterns. When the rat jumped to the black door with the white circle, the door opened and food was available; when the rat jumped to the white door with the black circle, the door remained closed, resulting in a bump to the nose and drop into a net below. After about 70 to 80 trials, rats learned to discriminate between the patterns and consistently jumped to the pattern that was rewarded. The procedure was then altered: Jumping to the black door with the white circle was no longer rewarded positively with food but negatively with a bump to the nose and a drop into the net. After a few trials, rats developed resistance and would not jump; they remained motionless on the jumping stand. To overcome this resistance, Maier used a loud blast of compressed air to force the animal to jump. The discrimination task was made insolvable, and the lack of solution led to nervousness. Maier's rats, when so thwarted, showed a variety of neurotic behaviors—they refused food, developed convulsions and tics, and, in the passive phase, rolled up into balls. Maier attributed the "neurotic" behavior to frustration.

Shortly after Maier's book appeared, Clifford Morgan attempted to replicate the experiment while he was on the faculty at the University of Rochester. He subsequently was offered an assistant professorship in the Department of Psychology at Harvard. I traveled to Cambridge to consult with him about the research I was doing. He predicted that, although it would be possible to demonstrate discrimination learning in the guinea pig, no "neurotic" behavior would be manifested when the animals were thwarted—unless the behavior was triggered by high-frequency sounds!

Using the same Lashley jumping method and procedure Maier had employed on rats, I began my experiment using guinea pigs. The first task was to acquaint the animals with the jumping stand and the feeding platform by placing the stand and platform close together so that the animal could walk from one to the other to obtain food. In later trials, the jumping stand was moved away from the feeding platform. The animal had to jump to the feeding platform to obtain food. Then, in order to replicate Maier's experiment, it was essential that the pigs jump a distance of 12 to 18 in. Faculty and graduate students were convinced that pigs could not jump that distance. Bets were rampant up and down Schermerhorn Hall (the building housing the Psychology Laboratory). The bets concerned the jumping prowess of guinea pigs, and wagers were based on the fact that guinea pigs had no tail, hence no leverage, and, unlike their fellow rodents, the rats, could not jump. However, pigs could be taught to jump by the simple but tedious expedient of moving the jumping stand away from the feeding platform very gradually over many training sessions.

After the guinea pigs learned to jump from the stand to the feeding platform, discrimination learning was started. Two differently patterned doors were placed on a screen on the feeding platform. The black-with-white-circle door was lightly fastened, and the white-with-black-circle door was tightly fastened. Guinea pigs learned to discriminate between the patterns. The pigs jumped to the black door, the door opened, and the animal was rewarded with food. When, however, the pigs jumped to the tightly fastened white door, they bumped their noses and fell several feet into a net. The pigs did learn to discriminate between the two patterns and were ready for the next phase of the experiment. After learning to jump to the black door to obtain food, the door was locked in subsequent trials. When the problem was made unsolvable—neither door would open, and the animals bumped their noses and fell into the net—resistance did occur. A loud blast of air was used to overcome the resistance. However, when jumping to either door did not result in a reward, guinea pigs, unlike Maier's rats, did not display "neurotic" behavior, even when high-frequency air blasts were used to nudge them on the jumping stand. There were no convulsions or tics. They were not the least bit perturbed when they were thwarted, when they bumped their noses against the locked compartment door and fell into the net. They remained the same plodding, unruffled critters. The "neurotic" behavior was not produced or elicited either by the sound of the hissing air blast used to "encourage" the pig to jump or by the frustrating nature of the task. The negative results of the experiment were dutifully written, and the master's thesis (de Cillis, 1940) is on file at Columbia University.

Having become familiar with chimpanzees, rats, guinea pigs, and chickens, I found the prospect of working with two-legged critters more appealing. The shift in emphasis also meant a shift in locale from the second-floor animal laboratory of Schermerhorn Hall to the third-floor human experimental lab.

I was enrolled in Professor Robert S. Woodworth's Experimental Psychology class in the fall of 1941. The text for the course was one he had written (Woodworth, 1939). My laboratory partners were Fred Frick, who later became affiliated with the Lincoln Laboratory at Massachusetts Institute of Technology after a 3-year appointment at Harvard, and Irving Janis, who joined the Yale faculty after obtaining his degree from Columbia and who became permanently attached to that institution. The other occupants on the third floor were Fred Keller, William Schoenfeld, Albert Poffenberger, Elizabeth Hurlock (the only woman faculty member), and John Volkmann. When World War II was declared, Frick and Janis enlisted in the Armed Services. They resumed their graduate studies several years later.

There were many experiments in progress on the third floor—some with humans, some with animals. It was about that time that Keller became interested in B. F. Skinner's reinforcement theory. The first Skinner box off the premises of Harvard was given to Keller. Thus, Skinner boxes were introduced to the third floor the year before commercially sold Skinner box pellets were available. It was not unusual to find graduate students mixing bran mash, rolling the mash into long narrow rolls, and then cutting them into pellets to be placed in the magazine of the Skinner box. As interesting as reinforcement theory was, I decided to devote myself to research on human topics, specifically, to small-scale intensive psychophysical experimentation—many observations on a few well-trained subjects, subjects who had served in a variety of psychophysical experiments and who were skilled in making judgments.

Under the sponsorship of Woodworth and Volkmann, I undertook my dissertation research in the area of cutaneous sensitivity. Only three subjects were employed, but hundreds of judgments were recorded. The purpose of the study was to determine absolute thresholds for tactual movement. The stimulus was a fine stream of air under pressure moving across a cutaneous area. In accordance with quantum theory as first proposed by von Békésy (1930) and Volkmann (1941) and verified by Stevens, Morgan, and Volkmann (1941), the plotted psychophysical judgments should be rectilinear rather than sigmoidal.

Stevens et al. (1941) confirmed von Békésy's hypothesis for both pitch and loudness discrimination. The hypothesis was further confirmed for pitch by Flynn (1943), for olfactory thresholds by Jerome (1942), for tactual movement by de Cillis (1944) and visual size by Volkmann (1946).

My coursework at Columbia was completed. It was during this period of collecting data for my dissertation that I was sponsored by Keller for membership in the Society of Sigma Xi, and Volkmann suggested I become a member of the American Psychological Association (APA). I attended my first APA meeting in Chicago in 1940 prior to becoming a member.

Because all my course work was completed, my dissertation topic approved, and data collection underway, I accepted a position with the Psychological Corporation doing market research under the supervision of Philip Corby. The curriculum in graduate school offered only one course in the applied area, Applied Psychology (taught by Albert Poffenberger). I wanted to know what the world of applied psychology was like in practice. It was my first experience with market research. I learned the gamut—from questionnaire design, sampling, and interviewing to use of IBM cards and IBM sorters. I wrote drafts of reports for clients like Coca-Cola and many other companies interested in market research. I worked at Psychological Corporation during the day and ran subjects in the Columbia lab at night. While at Psychological Corporation, I managed to collect all the data necessary for writing my dissertation. After 6 months, I received a phone call from Professor Keller, who had heard that there was a vacancy in the Psychology Department of the University of Connecticut. A friend with whom he had gone to graduate school at Harvard needed a replacement for a departing faculty member. Professor Keller asked if I would like to try my hand at teaching. He strongly urged that I investigate the position by getting in touch with the department chair at the University of Connecticut, Weston A. Bousfield, his former classmate at Harvard.

I did not know where Storrs, CT, was but found after I visited there that I liked what I saw and so did they. The position of instructor entailed teaching courses in experimental psychology, introductory psychology, applied psychology, and industrial psychology. The position had opened when Leonard Ferguson accepted a research position with an insurance company. Although there were intrinsic rewards involved in teaching, the extrinsic rewards were better for Ferguson at the Metropolitan Life Insurance Company in New York. A lot of activity went on as I tried to whip the experimental psychology laboratory into shape—designing the curriculum, constructing equipment, deciding on the array of experiments to be conducted by students, outlining the experiments, and so forth. At the same time, I conducted library research in the area of industrial psychology, becoming immersed in time and motion study, selection and placement, and Taylor–Russell tables. I spent my nights and weekends alternately upgrading my skills in the applied area, keeping up with the literature in the experimental area, and writing my dissertation on cutaneous sensitivity. After a 1 1/2 years at the University of Connecticut, I completed my dissertation and received my PhD from Columbia in 1944.

Shortly thereafter, Vincent Nowlis decided to leave the University of Connecticut to join Alfred Kinsey as an interviewer in the early stages of the research on sexual behavior in the male human. I was asked to take over the area of social psychology. Although I had never taught social psychology, I had studied with both Otto Klineberg and Gardner Murphy at Columbia and looked forward to developing my own course.

In 1946 I was elevated in rank to assistant professor. A year later, I was tenured. I did not realize until several years later how rapidly I had advanced! The department continued to grow, and a graduate program in clinical psychology was developed by Sol Garfield. It was during this period that Charles Osgood, then at the University of Connecticut, started writing his book, *Methods and Theory in Experimental Psychology* (1953). When Osgood left before completing his book in order to avail himself of an excellent research opportunity at the University of Illinois at Champaign Urbana, I was asked to teach the graduate seminar in General Psychology. As director of the experimental psychology laboratory, I had, of course, kept up with the literature and could fill this void. I had joined the faculty at the University of Connecticut in January 1943. I had progressed from instructor to assistant professor, was tenured, and had earned a sabbatic leave. I applied for one, and it was granted on the stipulation that I use the leave to develop the curriculum in industrial psychology. Meanwhile, in 1949, I had become engaged to George J. Engelhardt, a colleague who had received an AB from Harvard and a PhD from Yale. My fiancé obtained a position at Loyola University in Chicago in the Department of English in the area of medieval and comparative literature. I had an opportunity to work at several places to acquire additional experience in the area of industrial psychology. I selected the Industrial Relations Center at the University of Chicago as the place that would afford the greatest potential for my growth in this area. While visiting with my sister Irma, now Mrs. Talmadge Phillips, my fiancé and I were married at Fort Monroe, Virginia.

The University of Chicago affiliation was a very rich experience that allowed me to be involved in many applied projects. I was able to interact with company personnel and prepare programs and projects to suit their needs. This new world of developing programs for diverse companies was sufficiently challenging to induce me to stay at the University of Chicago and forego teaching and my tenured position at the University of Connecticut. I was a research associate in the Industrial Relations Center from 1950 to 1952 and an assistant professor and director of the Human Relations Project from 1952 to 1955. Here I developed training programs for companies like Weyerhauser Timber, Campbell Soup, Wierton Steel, and other national and multinational companies. One of the most exciting and challenging assignments involved leading a seminar for senior executives in the national offices of the Campbell Soup Company in Camden, NJ, one of the companies for whom I had designed many training programs. The participants consisted of the president of the company and his staff: the vice-presidents of purchasing, marketing, production, and so forth. The participants were very bright and articulate; they raised some interesting and insightful questions despite their not being familiar with psychological terminology. The 5 years I spent working on projects for diverse companies gave me the background and hands-on experience that I had been seeking. One of the companies wanted a very special project conducted that demanded a great deal of confidentiality, and hence the company could not go through regular university channels. The president of the company suggested that the project be conducted as a consulting project that I would design and direct. I resigned from the University of Chicago to conduct a market research study of food preferences. The project provided me with the opportunity to start my own consulting firm. In 1956, when the survey analysis was 1 month away from being completed, I discovered that I was pregnant. The pregnancy occurred after being married for 7 years.

By mutual consent, my husband and I agreed that having a family would not be compatible with traveling around the country consulting and making presentations to client companies. So I voluntarily exited the consulting field to indulge in parenting.

The experience of having one child, John (in 1957), led to the desire to have another, and soon the family was increased by the birth of James in 1959. During child rearing, my husband and I supervised the design and construction of a house on a heavily wooded lot. We did this to provide the children with the opportunity to appreciate the wonders of nature. Growing up in this environment enabled them to distinguish and recognize white oak, shagbark hickory, sugar maple, red oak, linden, and ironwood trees; they were able to feed squirrels and raccoons, and so forth. With the help of a novice architect, I became the general contractor for the homebuilding venture. It was fun selecting the kind of brick I wanted, designing a kitchen, having a second-floor living room that jutted right out into an oak tree. All the glassed area gave one the feeling of living in a tree house. Life with my family seemed to be full of the kinds of things that parents customarily are involved in: visits to museums and zoos, swimming, tennis, and piano lessons; visits to historical sites; gymnastics; Cub Scouts and Boy Scouts; car pooling; and travel. Every summer, the family traveled to different states; this we alternated with similar travel in Eastern and Western Canada, including the Maritimes. This provided an opportunity not only to become familiar with the country but also to collect Indian and Alaskan art, thereby increasing our collection of folk art, primitive art, and artifacts. However, during this time, I also kept up with the field of psychology. In 1965, when my younger son, James, was about to enter first grade, George and I mutually decided that I would return to my professional activities. It was agreed that teaching would be less disruptive to family living than consulting with its inevitable travel. I joined the faculty of Valparaiso University as a visiting lecturer teaching social psychology. The field of social psychology had changed so dramatically since the time I had last taught it at the University of Connecticut that a redesign of the entire course was imperative. Teaching was exciting, but driving 100 mi (round trip) was somewhat time consuming, and I looked for a teaching position closer to home.

North Central College, an old, established liberal arts school that wanted my expertise in industrial and social psychology, offered me a full professorship. In my last academic position, I held the rank of assistant professor. Acceptance of this offer enabled me to skip the rank of associate professor. A few years later, I became department chair, changed the curriculum, added to staff, and built a well-rounded set of offerings that included comparative psychology (with a well-equipped animal laboratory), laboratory courses in experimental psychology; heavy emphasis on statistics and quantitative methodology; and developmental, social, and clinical psychology and a healthy complement of applied courses such as consumer, personnel, and industrial/organizational psychology. Basic and very fundamental core courses were not slighted to emphasize the clinical area or the other applied fields. Later I was also asked to chair the Division of Social and Behavioral Sciences—a division consisting of the Sociology/Anthropology, Physical Education, Education, Psychology, and Political Science departments. Once again my skills as a psychologist and administrator were tapped. A knowledge of group dynamics was a distinct asset in dealing with the varied problems of this diverse group.

During my 17-year stay at North Central College as a tenured full professor, I was given two professional term leaves (6 months each). Due to family responsibilities, I spent both leaves at Northwestern University as a visiting scholar. It was during this postdoctoral period that I learned to use mainframe computers to do research and multivariate statistics.

While at North Central College, I was the psychological consultant to the Lilly project—a Lilly Foundation-supported study of values. Research conducted during this period resulted in five social psychology papers that were presented at Psychonomic Society meetings. The papers were "Choice Dilemma Decisions and the F Scale"; "The Relationship Between Flexibility of Closure, Field Independence, Rigidity, Intelligence and Creativity"; "More on the Protestant Ethic: Rigidity, Intolerance of Ambiguity and Dogmatism"; "Intolerance of Ambiguity Revisited: Authoritarianism and Locus of Control"; What Can Attitudes, Interests and Personality Measures Tell Us About Student Retention: A Discriminate Analysis."

The press of administrative work made it difficult to find the time, however, to prepare the articles for publication. While at North Central, I fostered undergraduate internships and the installation of a chapter of Psi Chi to stimulate student interest in research. I was the recipient of the first Clarence F. Dissinger Memorial Fund Faculty Award for Distinguished Teaching. During this same period I was selected by the Lilly Foundation for a postdoctoral fellowship in Illuminative Evaluation. Later I accepted a postdoctoral fellowship in Evaluation Research at Northwestern University.

In the next episode of my career, I was invited to apply for an opening at Northeastern Illinois University as the director of the Division of Business and Management. My position at North Central College was as far as one could go up the academic ladder; there was only one rung left—dean of the faculty—and that position was very amply filled. The opportunities for a new and challenging position were exciting. The move, if it was effected, would mean leaving a tenured full professorship in psychology to become a nontenured full professor in management. I applied, was interviewed, and offered the position despite the fact that business schools are notoriously dominated by men. I applied for early retirement at North Central College, and it was approved. The rank of professor emeritus was conferred June 1981.

At Northeastern Illinois University, my colleagues now are faculty members in finance, accounting, business law, marketing, and management. My past background in industrial/organizational, consumer, and personnel psychology, as well as my consulting experience in personnel, training, market research, and marketing has made dealing with management and marketing curricula and specialists in these areas relatively easy. The areas of finance, accounting, and business law presented some problems but none that were insurmountable.

Both prior administrative experience and a knowledge of group dynamics were invaluable in restructuring the curriculum in five disciplines. Through group discussion with specialists in five departmental areas and through smaller group discussions with knowledgeable faculty within each area of specialization, it was possible to overhaul the curriculum of the division. In the world of the Division of Business and Management, there is no animal laboratory, no laboratory experimentation, no sociopsychological research. There is, instead, a rather pragmatic view of the world. But there are compensating factors. It has been a rewarding experience to see the group change from one that was fractionated to one that is cohesive and shares common goals.

In the position of director of the Division of Business and Management, I aspired to make the division an autonomous college. The curriculum was expanded, faculty size was increased, requirements for majors in business were made more stringent. Then innumerable forms were filled out for the Board of Governors of Northeastern Illinois University. Many questions were also answered for the Illinois Board of Higher Education before this group would grant collegiate status. It was also necessary to justify five BS degree programs in accounting, finance, management, marketing, and general business administration.

Collegiate status was granted June 1983, 2 years after I joined the institution. On July 1, 1983, I was appointed dean of the College of Business and Management, a position I still hold.

During my college and university years, I encountered very few women in psychology, and, of those, most were in the fields of clinical and developmental psychology. For me there were no women role models in experimental, comparative, or social psychology. While at the University of Connecticut, I was the only women member of the department for the first 5 years of my affiliation. However, I joined the Connecticut Valley Association of Psychologists, and it was at meetings of this group that I met Marion A. Bills—my first encounter with a woman actively engaged in the field of industrial/organizational psychology. She was employed as a personnel researcher by Aetna Life Insurance Company in Hartford. She was indeed an impressive role model!

I have often been asked what strategies I used to establish myself as a competent professional in fields dominated by men. Very simply put, I have always sought to guide myself by the same standards applied to my male colleagues—never expecting any accommodation because I was a woman. Overall, my professional life has been marked by flexibility—a willingness to tackle any task thrust upon me, to learn about new fields within and outside of psychology. My professional life has been marked by a readiness to accept change and to take risks, to welcome promotions and their concomitant responsibilities, and to forego tenure for challenging new experiences. If there had not been a family, the career path upward might have been more direct, and progress up the academic ladder faster. Very likely, publications might have been more numerous. Women who choose to step out of the professional role in order to raise a family must be prepared to find it more difficult to resume where they left off. They might find, as I did, that you start out again at a somewhat lower rung on the ladder and need to climb back up. Having a family and not losing a beat may suit some women, but affairs such as these are individual matters. I found that I could integrate work into the total fabric of living—a feat that could not have been accomplished without the aid of a very understanding husband.

REFERENCES

de Cillis, O. E. (1940). *Abnormal behavior in the guinea pig*. Unpublished manuscript, Columbia University, Psychology Library, New York.

de Cillis, O. E. (1944). Absolute thresholds for the perception of tactual movements. *Archives of Psychology* (No. 294). New York.

Flynn, B. M. (1943). Pitch discrimination: The form of the psychometric function and simple reaction time to liminal differences. *Archives of Psychology* (No. 280). New York.

Garrett, H. E. (1938). *Statistics in psychology and education* (2nd ed.). New York: Longmans, Green.

Hays, W. L. (1973). *Statistics.* New York Holt, Rinehart & Winston.

Jerome, E. A. (1942). Olfactory thresholds measured in terms of stimulus pressure and volume. *Archives of Psychology* (No. 274). New York.

Kerlinger, F. N. (1973). *Foundations of behavioral research: Educational, psychological and sociological inquiry* (2nd ed.). New York: Holt, Rinehart & Winston.

Lashley, K. S. (1912). Visual discrimination of size and form in the albino rat. *Journal of Animal Behavior, 2,* 310–331.

Maier, N. R. F. (1939). *Studies of abnormal behavior in the rat.* New York: Harper and Brothers.

Myers, J. L. (1979). *Fundamentals of experimental design* (3rd ed.). Boston, MA: Allyn & Bacon.

Osgood, C. E. (1953). *Methods and theory in experimental psychology.* New York: Oxford University Press.

Riess, B. S., & de Cillis, O. E. (1940). Personality differences in allergic and non-allergic children. *Journal of Abnormal and Social Psychology, 35,* 104–113.

Stevens, S. S., Morgan, C. T., & Volkmann, J. (1941). Theory of the neural quantum in the discrimination of loudness and pitch. *American Journal of Psychology, 54,* 315–335.

Volkmann, J. (1941). Quantum theory in psychology. *Transactions of the New York Academy of Science* (Series II), *3*(8), 213–217.

von Békésy, G. (1930). Uber das Fechnérsche Gesetz und Seine Bedentung für die Theorie der Akustischen Beobachtungsfehlr und die Theorie des Hörens. *Annalen der Physik, 73,* 329–359.

Volkmann, J. (1946). Evidence for the quantal discrimination of visual size. *American Psychologist, 1,* 271.

Winer, B. F. (1971). *Statistical principles in experimental design* (2nd ed.). New York: McGraw-Hill.

Woodworth, R. S. (1939). *Experimental psychology.* New York: Henry Holt.

REPRESENTATIVE PUBLICATIONS

Bousfield, W. A., Orbison, W. D., & de Cillis, O. E. (1945). *Group demonstrations and exercises in psychology.* Ann Arbor, MI: Edwards Brothers.

de Cillis, O. E., & Orbison, W. D., (1950). A comparison of the Terman–Miles Attitude Interest Analysis Test and the Mf scale of the Minnesota Multiphasic Personality Inventory. *Journal of Applied Psychology, 34,* 338–342.

Engelhardt, O. de Cillis, (1950). The Minnesota Clerical Test: Sex differences and norms for college groups. *Journal of Applied Psychology, 34,* 412–414.

Engelhardt, O. de Cillis, (1979). Trends in undergraduate education and training in industrial organizational psychology. *Industrial Organizational Psychologist, 16*(1), 2–3.

Engelhardt, O. E. (1986). [Review of *None of the above: Behind the myth of scholastic aptitude*]. *Journal of College Admissions* (No. 110), 38–39.

CHAPTER 10

Patricia Cain Smith

Patricia Cain Smith

My first vivid memories are happy ones—of looking out the front windows across the plains to the snow-covered mountains along the horizon and of cheerfully pulling books to the floor from tall white bookcases in the living room. That first home was in the village of Choteau, Montana. I was an only child, born in 1917.

Retrospective reports are necessarily distorted. Nevertheless, I clearly remember occasions on which my parents articulated their values and illustrated them by their actions. They were Western liberals. Their values included responsibility for the effects of one's behavior on others, for the completion of tasks undertaken, for accuracy; I learned to respect facts; to enjoy acquiring new ideas; and not to be afraid physically or intellectually. There was no attempt to instill "feminine" virtues or to discourage reasonable risk taking. At home, I enjoyed "play school," which gave me an advantage in both reading and arithmetic.

My father's changes of job and fortune necessitated numerous moves. I became used to the stresses of being the new kid on the block and to the vagaries of different school systems in different cities, but home was emotionally secure. I played word games and discussed books with Mother. I played card games and learned about gambling odds and "lightning calculation" from Father. I was given violin lessons. Mother taught me to swim and to ride a horse; no one, however, taught me to cook, sew, set a table, or dust a house. I was programmed to pursue a career.

The last family move was to my father's hometown, Falls City,

Nebraska (population 5,700), in 1927. The school system was extremely authoritarian—we were not allowed to talk even between classes, at our lockers—but excellent academically, I received as much individual attention as I wanted or needed. I loved school and was valedictorian of my small class.

A busy adolescence abruptly became adulthood, however, when I was 15 years old. My father killed himself. A combination of the Great Depression and business judgments that had been more humane than economically sound brought about his last business failure.

My father had been a very warm, humorous, generous, and joyful person, and I had adored him. His death effectively completed my vocational programming. I never questioned that I must work for a secure living and that meaningful work for me would involve both people and numbers. I decided to become a psychometric statistician—not too far from my eventual role.

In 1935 I entered the University of Nebraska; I majored in mathematics and psychology. J. P. Guilford, a pioneer researcher in scaling, psychometrics, and experimental psychology, was my principal mentor; his influence has remained very important throughout my life. He taught several of my courses, including psychophysics, scaling, psychometrics, and factor analysis. He directed my honors thesis on sex differences in color preferences. There I first experienced "the joy of insight," when the facts came together into an orderly whole.

After one graduate semester at Northwestern University, I spent a year at Bryn Mawr College with Harry Helson, working on perception of color. There I learned the importance of adaptation level and frame of reference in judgments, not only of color and brightness but also of persons. Nevertheless, I did not really want my doctorate in laboratory experimental psychology, and so I transferred to Cornell University.

Graduate training at Cornell was flexible. I found a highly compatible and competent chair of my graduate committee in T. A. Ryan (known to everyone as "Art"), who represented industrial and business psychology. He was interested both in problems of effort and fatigue and in statistics. I elected one minor in experimental psychology with Harry P. Weld and split the other between psychobiology with Howard S. Liddell and neurology with James Papez.

My early biases, established at Nebraska, were strengthened at Cornell. I became convinced that verbal reports could be quite reliable indices of feelings, *if* the right questions were asked. Despite the search for "universal laws" that applied to all people, I was certain that wherever anything of any real importance was being investigated, there were individual differences. This was true even for physiological and neurological reactions to stress. Liddell, in his pioneer experiments on "conditioned neuroses" in animals, Papez, in his explorations of the neurology of the stress circuit, and John Lacey (still a graduate student then), in his studies of physiological reactions under stress, all pointed to the same generalization—that both situational and individual factors entered into an individual's reactions. I began to realize that there were not only multiple causes, but also multiple effects, in even the "purest" situation. Further, I became convinced that we must be meticulous not only in our manipulation of experimental variables but also in our measurement of outcomes.

Art Ryan's interest in fatigue led to my interest in industrial monotony. I started from a rather sanctimonious "Florence Nightingale" point of view, envisioning myself as somehow finding and curing the factors that caused people to suffer monotony and boredom in what I assumed were tedious and repetitive jobs.

The research I wanted to do required close observation and questioning of many workers performing short-cycled tasks. My fiancé, Olin Smith, introduced me to the owner of a small garment factory. The owner approved my research proposal. I learned a great deal from the resulting dissertation. First, my being able to do the field study at all was a function as much of chance opportunity as of careful planning. Second, contrary to the literature, workers' verbal reports of feeling did not correspond to their overt behavior. They paced their work according to what they *intended* to do each day. These goals, rather than the workers' subjective feelings, determined their output. But the workers could express those feelings clearly. Feelings of monotony were not frequent; when they did occur, they proved to be a function of factors both in the situation and in the individual.

Olie and I were married in March, and I completed my dissertation in September, 1942. Pearl Harbor had decided the immediate careers of young men and, for that matter, of young women just completing their degrees. Olie prepared for army life, and I started hunting for a job. Again, it was not a matter of choice.

I wanted to work in the "real world" and sought a job in industry. The Cornell Psychology Department had not yet placed a student directly into such a setting. My resume looked pretty good to our inexperienced eyes—excellent academic record, evidence of drive (7 years from high school to PhD), honors, junior Phi Beta Kappa, high test scores (and all that), strong recommendations not only from professors but also from part-time employers and even from a union representative, good statistical background, and an applied dissertation topic. But, although I sent out 250 letters of inquiry, I received only 3 encouraging replies. I gratefully accepted the one offer that resulted and started work at Aetna Life and Affiliated Companies 2 days after my final oral examinations.

My 18 months as an intern at Aetna shaped much of my later professional behavior. True, I learned personnel techniques. But I also had a role model to follow, Dr. Marion Bills—a woman, a pioneer industrial psychologist, an officer of the company, and my supervisor. Miss Bills taught me how and when to support, oppose, or advocate changes in company policy, how to be seen as a professional person rather than as a female subordinate, and when to stand firmly on principle or (temporarily) to compromise.

Then opportunity knocked again. My resume was still on file at Cornell. A young industrial engineer, Kurt Salmon, was looking for someone to head a new personnel section of his consulting firm, which then specialized in a "woman's industry," the garment industry. He offered me the opportunity to build a new program at three times my salary at Aetna. I grabbed the chance.

Learning to consult is a sink-or-swim process, even with the best of supervision. My first assignment was to translate into dollars and cents the savings that might be expected from enlightened personnel practices. When I protested that I knew nothing about accounting, Kurt Salmon simply handed me a couple of accounting books. In the next few weeks, I produced the basis of a talk on "Personnel Activities That Pay," which outlines some of the substantial savings to be expected from apparently small increases in productivity, attendance, and job tenure. That talk, with variations, saw me through many engineers' and businessmen's luncheons. My healthy respect for the economic soundness of what I was doing stood me in very good stead through many later battles to keep criterion data clean and to stick to sound policies. I learned that the best way to defend a policy was to prove that it saved money. Nothing brings out the humanitarian in a manager as rapidly as the realization that humane actions are economically profitable as well.

In consulting, I learned how to diagnose organizational problems. The administrator in the front office often did not know what was going on in the factory, but the switchboard operator and the nightwatchman often did, and much could be learned in the "ladies room." Checking out such leads helped me avoid some nasty surprises and formed the basis for my gradual acquisition of a semiclinical skill in "smelling" the morale in an organization.

I learned much about selling ideas, too, mostly by imitation of my boss and of other skillful persuaders, from plant nurses to engineers. At first, most of my consulting work involved direct application of textbook principles and techniques. I supervised the introduction of nearly a hundred new personnel departments in the years 1944 to 1948. We systematized selection, placement, training, incentives, job evaluation, counseling, and supervisory methods; we validated tests; and we did research on special organizational problems.

The number of clients expanded rapidly, largely through referrals. By the end of my second year with Kurt Salmon Associates, I supervised a small staff of consultants. Less and less I did the work I liked—research, and work with individual employees or supervisors—and more and more I was an administrator, estimating and "selling" new consulting jobs, troubleshooting, and writing reports, always under pressure of time. In 1 year, I flew over 100,000 mi, and in DC-3s; the only woman who had logged more miles that year was Eleanor Roosevelt. To the air travel should be added thousands of miles by train, bus, rented car, and even, in one case, the back of a mail truck. Although I had my moments of pleasure in playing the lady executive, wearing designer suits and talking to powerful people, mostly I was feeling little joy of accomplishment and was constantly straightening out tangled and frustrating but basically uninteresting situations. Moreover, my personal situation had changed.

My husband was discharged from the Army in 1946. When, after a year at Vanderbilt University, he decided that he too might find the doctoral program at Cornell suited to his needs, we moved to Ithaca, NY. Flying in and out of Ithaca every week proved very impractical. So, in 1948 I decided that it was time for me to settle down. I continued as research director with Kurt Salmon Associates on a consulting basis, part-time. To get myself out of bed in the mornings that first year and to help finances, I accepted two part-time teaching jobs, one at Ithaca College and the other at Wells College. The following summer, I was asked to teach at Cornell a special session, mostly for returning veterans, on the fields of psychology and industrial psychology.

That temporary summer appointment at Cornell was extended through the academic year, and my period of attempted domesticity was terminated. My status rose from assistant professor in 1949 to associate professor in 1954 and finally to full professor in 1963. Therein lies a small tale. It was only after the fact, and from persons in other departments, that I learned that I was the first woman to be granted tenure in the endowed schools at Cornell, the first to be accepted as a member of the graduate faculty from those schools, and later, the first to be promoted to full professor; I also learned that the Psychology Department had faced considerable opposition in proposing these changes. When I found out about the novelty of each of these events, I felt that it was about time! I certainly was under no misapprehension that I was the greatest female scholar to have hit those schools at Cornell in its almost 100 years.

Actually, sex discrimination was very far from my mind at that time, because I was concerned merely with doing as good a job as I knew how, until I could get back into industry. In the course of my teaching, I undertook many research projects with students but prepared no articles for publication. I worked hard, trying to handle my multiple roles, but made no attempt to set priorities among them. Olie and I had bought an 1830 farm house 7 mi out of town and were starting its renovation. He, meanwhile, had completed all the work for his doctorate except the writing the of his dissertation, and he was earning his way doing contract research. His interests had turned to what is usually called "applied experimental psychology," and he worked on a wide variety of perceptual problems for pilots, both Air Force and Navy. He also started a prize-winning Christmas-tree plantation on our farm. I participated in many of the experiments and also in the marketing of the Christmas trees. We ran a neat little study on color preference for trees and validated the results of the scaling in a controlled study of sales. We also established a small consulting firm that undertook several industrial interventions and evaluations.

I thoroughly enjoyed all aspects of research—the interaction with advanced undergraduate and graduate students, the tricks of seizing opportunity and convincing management to cooperate in projects, the compulsive attention to detail and flexibility of planning that kept the data clean even through natural disasters, strikes, unexpected layoffs, and the myriad of other problems that beset field investigators. In addition to conducting field studies, we ran several projects on rating and scaling. I saw no necessity, however, to write the results for publication. I disliked writing and avoided it skillfully. My short-term goals were to do my day-to-day job, but in the long term I wanted to go back to the real world where I could hear the sound of machinery and help people produce things.

A colleague had to warn me explicitly that I was facing Cornell's policy of "up and out" after 7 years. With a publication score of zero, I would certainly be "out." I had to reassess my goals realistically. Again, there was no real choice. If we wanted to stay at Cornell at all, I had to play the academic game "for keeps." I started to write, much as I hated it.

In 1953 I published the first article on monotony based on my dissertation (11 years afterward—Smith, 1953) and, although it took all summer, completed a chapter in a survey book (Smith, 1954). With Art Ryan, I started work on a textbook. He had to push me, gently and tactfully but constantly, to keep me at it. We finally published it in 1954 (Ryan & Smith, 1954). That same year, I completed a research report with Olie on the use of photographs for spatial adjustments (Smith & Smith, 1954). After that, writing became somewhat less painful, but almost always I wrote only when I felt an obligation to a co-author. Nonetheless, I completed a good deal of research, at least a third of which I managed to publish.

Rather than following a grand research plan, I merely bore in mind several problems needing research and watched for opportunities to study them.

A few unifying beliefs have guided my professional pursuits. First, measurement must be accurate. Measurement is at the heart of replicable and generalizable research. This emphasis on appropriate measures started at Nebraska with Guilford and was reinforced throughout my experimental training. Ryan's concern with validation of verbal report against behavior and (vice versa) and his statistical sophistication alerted me to the crucial criterion problem. When I began to try to solve problems arising in industry, I found that I needed hard facts, which meant clean measurement.

My concern with criteria has manifested itself in two ways. One is by my continued attention to criterion measures in all my research. The other is by my preparation of the chapter on criteria (Smith, 1976) in the classic and widely referenced *Handbook of Industrial and Organizational Psychology* (Dunnette, 1976). For almost all of my academic life, I taught courses in psychophysics and scaling. In these courses, I required students to complete measurement projects. As a result, most of my publications have a strong quantitative flavor. But I have neither the ability nor the interest to be a creative theoretician in measurement. For me, measurement is crucial, but only as a means to an end.

Second, research should be both relevant and general. I feel that in psychology, as in all sciences, there should be some contact with practical issues, but that one-shot studies that do not generalize beyond one particular situation should not clutter the body of scientific knowledge.

A related belief was that there should be a two-way flow of information and theory between the so-called applied fields and the general, traditionally experimental field of psychology. Therefore, a psychologist should try to achieve competence in both the general field and in his or her specialty.

Again, I had no choice. I had to keep up to date on problems of general psychology. I taught a variety of courses in industrial and general psychology, psychophysics, scaling, measurement and research methods. I was a member of many widely varied graduate committees. I was actively engaged in research with Olie on his research grants. (This work resulted in 29 joint publications, including a monograph on perceptual development—Smith & Smith, 1966.)

We also spent a stimulating year (1955–1956) in experimental psychology at the University of Louvain (in Belgium). There we worked with Professor Albert Michotte, who became a close friend and father figure. Research there resulted in our one purely qualitative publication (Smith & Smith, 1961, published, surprisingly, by the *Journal of Experimental Psychology*) plus several quantitative articles.

Reading kept me informed about the published research in my specialty. Consulting helped to keep me in contact with the "real world." I tried to spend at least half of my research time on the immediate practical problems of the organizations with which I dealt.

I found both sets of knowledge—general and industrial—useful and mutually supportive. Linked to that interaction of applied and "pure" was that of individual differences and experimental psychology. Many of my joint studies with Olie attempted to incorporate what Cronbach (1957) labeled *the two disciplines of scientific psychology*. We investigated simultaneously the effects of both experimental treatments and individual differences in various aspects of the perception of space and distance. Further, almost all of my research from doctoral dissertation to present has shown that both sets of variables are operating in any phenomenon that I have found to be psychologically interesting. Moreover, most problems have proved, therefore, to be multivariate.

A third belief was that preferences and satisfactions are an important area for research. What makes a job pleasant or unpleasant for a particular worker? Concern with this question led to my initial choice of monotony as a topic for my dissertation. The results of that research broadened my interests to the more general problem of satisfaction with various facets of the job. Eventually, I wanted to investigate the complex manner in which multiple factors interact to lead to satisfactions and behaviors of various kinds.

But we know too little about the effects of the task itself. Art Ryan had called my attention to the work of Baldamus (1951), which outlined factors in the task that pull the worker toward completion and that may lead to pleasant feelings. A student and I performed a field experiment (Smith & Lem, 1955) that showed surprisingly strong and rapid effects of manipulating the size of the batch of work. This and other studies indicate the importance of the design of tasks for greater employee satisfaction. I have worked in this area whenever opportunity has arisen.

Improved measurement of job satisfaction remained "on hold" for years. Numerous proposals for grant support were rejected either as "too applied" or "too theoretical." I was overjoyed, therefore, when I was asked to consult on a project studying the impact of policy concerning retirement age. Obviously, the project would have to assess the effects, in a large national sample, on satisfaction both for retirees and present employees. Thus began the work on the Job Descriptive Index (JDI) and on the parallel Retirement Descriptive Index.

My graduate assistants in psychology and I had a much larger role than expected on that project. We secured company cooperation and did the field research for much of the national sample as well as all of the quantitative and much of the qualitative design and analysis.

The data were rich in information, and each graduate assistant could stake out claims on sections of the data bank. They learned that research can be hilariously funny, utterly maddening, joyfully insightful, stiflingly tedious, socially rewarding, yet endlessly lonely. It seems more than coincidental that from our research team, Lorne Kendall, Chuck Hulin, and Ed Locke all developed into highly productive researchers.

By now I had come to realize that "publish or perish" has a second, less cynical meaning. If you do not publish your research, the *ideas* will perish, together with all the work that was invested in acquiring them. So we soon started publishing on parts of the data and presented a symposium at the meeting of the American Psychological Association in 1961. This drew a large crowd and many requests for reprints. Nevertheless, a series on the development of the JDI was rejected in several versions for journal publication. We finally published a book on the theory and development. A second volume was to summarize Lorne Kendall's analyses of the impact of community and organizational factors. Because of his untimely death, it was never completed.

The work on Behaviorally Anchored Rating Scales (BARS) also

began when opportunity knocked. My graduate seminar on interviewing had convinced me that even interviewers with much experience and training rely on global, first impressions that are usually both unreliable and invalid. To improve judgments, the rater has to be almost coerced into repeatedly observing and rating, as independently as possible, on several discriminably different dimensions. I recognized that what went on in the interview also happened in evaluations of on-the-job performance. I wanted to tie all such judgments to observations of actual behavior.

About 1958 I started working as a consultant for the National League for Nursing. We needed to compare the effectiveness of various programs for improving nursing practices and to validate tests against on-the-job behavior. But we needed measures of performance that were comparable from hospital to hospital and rater to rater.

We worked out a method (eventually called BARS) that presented graphic rating forms on which head nurses could record and scale the behaviors they observed; they could then discuss the behaviors with the nurses. We gathered data on hundreds of head nurses. Lorne Kendall assisted in the computations and pointed out some innovative features of the method. The resulting article (Smith & Kendall, 1963) became a citation classic partly because the procedures proved useful in many situations and partly, I'm afraid, because some aspects of scale construction seemed to make easy thesis topics.

About that time, Olie and I reached a real decision point in our lives. The principal lines of our research had been established during our 18 years at Cornell. Life there was pleasant in many ways. We had close friends. I enjoyed playing in weekly sessions of a departmental string quartet. And we loved the physical setting of our restored old farmhouse and the beautiful glacial country of the Finger Lakes.

But the job situation became less satisfying. The students were excellent, but I was heavily overloaded, particularly with graduate committees. The priorities of the College of Arts and Sciences did not include any expansion for the Psychology Department, and especially not in an applied field of psychology. Moreover, the year-by-year support of Olie's research by grants was uncertain.

When rumors arose that we could be moved from Cornell, several alternatives quickly appeared. After an extremely painful period of decision making, we decided to join the new and rapidly expanding graduate faculty in the Department of Psychology at Bowling Green State University. We moved in 1966.

A major attraction there was Dr. Robert Guion. Another appealing feature was the promise of an expanding staff and high status for our field. Psychology had top priority in the plans for the growing university. Olie had a professorship in his own right.

It was a wrenching change, but in almost all aspects the move has been a happy one. The faculty grew steadily. They have proved to be stimulating and supportive, as have the students. The first two doctorates in industrial/organizational psychology were awarded to Sheldon Zedeck and Frank Landy, both of whom have become well known in the field. A stream of excellent students has followed.

My research continued in much the same lines as before. My goal of a standardized measure of aspects of job satisfaction had largely been achieved. The book on the JDI (Smith, Kendall, & Hulin, 1969) was well received. Other investigators have reported that the JDI has become by far the most frequently used instrument in published research on job satisfaction (O'Connor, Peters, & Gordon, 1978; Yeager, 1981).

Our current research on satisfaction is financed through a fund resulting from the continuing sale of the JDI by Bowling Green State University, to which we donated the copyright when the book (*The Measurement of Satisfaction in Work and Retirement*) went out of print (Smith, Kendall, & Hulin, 1969, 1975). We have completed a revision and updating of the JDI using more advanced psychometric methods (Smith et al., 1987).

The JDI quite satisfactorily diagnoses satisfaction with five of the principal aspects of the job (work, pay, promotion, supervision, and co-workers). But, no combination of items from the JDI can capture all of the feelings a person has about his or her job. We need a separate global measure.

Therefore, in 1977 Gail Ironson (then a postdoctoral student) and I started construction of a scale of Satisfaction with the Job in General (JIG). We have since completed the scale, with much assistance and collaboration from Gail Ironson's students at the University of South Florida and from mine at Bowling Green (Ironson et al., 1987).

Further, I have been collaborating with Bonnie Sandman, Bill Balzer, Gail Ironson, and others on measures of job stress. My retirement in 1980 has not interrupted these research activities. I continue to be active in both consulting and editorial work for journals.

Despite my aversion to writing, I have been forced to do a good deal of it through the years. To date, it has added up to 2 books, 11 chapters in books (mostly theoretical or integrative in nature), 59 articles in psychological journals (54 of which were reports of empirical research and 9 of which were considered of sufficiently wide interest to be reprinted in books of undergraduate readings), 24 papers presented at professional meetings, 11 symposium presentations (formal discussions at meetings), 24 published reviews of books, 3 invited addresses at national or international meetings, plus discussion hours and the usual miscellaneous invited talks to professional and university groups. Many or most of these publications have several coauthors, usually students.

I start a research project not by choice but because scientific curiosity, the desire to solve a problem, or the hope of clarifying an issue forces me to do research and to think. That part is truly pleasurable. Then the demands of the job or my obligations to my collaborators force me to summarize the results for publication. Seeing that part completed is at least mildly gratifying to me. I hope that you will be one of those who actually enjoy the process!

This autobiography has forced me to evaluate what I have learned so far. Perhaps I have written too much today about industrial/organizational psychology and too little about women. In truth, I have never thought of myself as a woman psychologist, but rather as a psychologist who happened to be a woman. In retrospect, that happenstance seems to have been a disadvantage both in reducing job alternatives and in adding to my work load. I felt that I had to take on almost any duty to prove my worth. At one time, I actually believed that the world is run by obligations, not by joy. Because we are often on the defensive, women are, I believe, particularly likely to allow themselves to be trapped into such beliefs.

But there were advantages, too, to being a woman. It seemed as if employees, including managers, talked more readily to me. My male colleagues often gave me opportunities and recognition because they themselves were feminists. I was highly visible. For years I was perhaps the only woman in academic industrial/organizational psychology. As long as I did a reasonably competent job, this visibility was an advantage.

I have watched many closed doors crack open for women. Those slight openings have led some of us to expect more cracks and wider openings, which have not always come about. But a large part of our inability to push those doors open more widely lies in our own attitudes and fears. As we learn to approach our work less defensively, our gender will, I hope, become less apparent. It will be less salient to others as well as to ourselves. Of course we must fight against injustice, not only for women but for all human beings. But we must also presume the male world to be innocent until proven guilty. We must try not to be paranoid, demanding, abrasive, or petty. Otherwise, we are asking for discrimination. It becomes a self-fulfilling prophecy.

How would I do it all differently? What advice can I give to the young woman—or man—entering my field? Most of the advice sounds like pious platitudes. Work hard. Don't quit just because you fail the first time. Set priorities and schedule your time to reach your goals. Be considerate of others and of yourself and your body, if only because they will repay you in kind.

Apply some marketing principles to the convincing of both clients and colleagues of the worth of your ideas. Don't bother to attack prevalent theories. Instead present your own insights and evidence positively. As Thomas Kuhn and other philosophers of science have agreed strongly, "Old theories never die; rather, they are displaced by better ones." If you like some aspects of a neglected theory or concept, resurrect it. Give the authors due credit. But, cynically, give the old wine a bright new bottle and a new, catchy label.

And remember that psychology can be great fun. Almost any task I have undertaken has proved interesting, once I became committed to it. To paraphrase an old song, "When I'm not with the work I love, I love the work I'm with." Work is often frustrating, but it is also full of laughs. Research, particularly, must necessarily be lonely much of the time. It is incredibly time consuming. At the end of a study, however, there is frequently the "joy of insight." That joy is particularly great if it can be shared. And even if some old doors remain closed, others crack open. Watch for those openings and be ready to enter.

REFERENCES

Baldamus, W. (1951). Incentives and work analysis. *University of Birmingham Studies in Economic and Society* (Monograph No. A1).

Cronbach, L. J. (1957). The two disciplines of scientific psychology. *American Psychologist, 12,* 671–684.

Dunnette, M. D. (Ed.). (1976). *Handbook of industrial and organizational psychology.* Chicago: Rand McNally.

Ironson, G. H., Smith, P. C., Brannick, M. T., Gibson, W. M., Paul, K. B., & Miank, D. C. (1987). *Construction of a "Job in General" scale: A comparison of global, composite, and specific measures.* Unpublished manuscript, Bowling Green State University, Department of Psychology, Bowling Green, OH.

O'Connor, E. J., Peters, L. H., & Gordon, S. M. (1978). The measurement of job satisfaction: Current practices and future considerations. *Journal of Management, 4,* 17–26.

Ryan, T. A., & Smith, P. C. (1954). *Principles of industrial psychology.* New York: Ronald.

Smith, O. W., & Smith, P. C. (1954). *The use of photographs as a basis for behavorial adjustments to space and distance.* Washington, DC: Bolling Air Force Base, Audio-Visual Aids Division, Human Resources Research Laboratories.

Smith, O. W., & Smith, P. C. (1966). Developmental studies of spatial judgments by children and adults. *Perceptual and Motor Skills,* (Monograph Supp. 1–V), *22,* 3–73.

Smith, P. C. (1953). The curve of output as a criterion of boredom. *Journal of Applied Psychology, 37,* 69–74.

Smith, P. C. (1954). Industrial psychology: Selection and placement of workers. In F. L. Marcuse (Ed.), *Areas of psychology* (pp. 36–80). New York: Harper.

Smith, P. C. (1976). Behaviors, results, and organizational effectiveness: The problem of criteria. In M. D. Dunnette (Ed.), *Handbook of industrial and organizational psychology* (pp. 745–775). Chicago: Rand McNally.

Smith, P. C., Balzer, W. K., Brannick, M. T., Chi, W., Eggleston, S., Gibson, W. M., Johnson, B., Josephson, H., Paul, K. B., Reilley, C., & Whalen, M. (1987). The revised JDI: A facelift for an old friend. *The Industrial Organizational Psychologist 24*(4), 31–33.

Smith, P. C., & Kendall, L. M. (1963). Retranslation of expectations: An approach to the construction of unambiguous anchors for rating scales. *Journal of Applied Psychology, 47,* 149–155.

Smith, P. C., Kendall, L. M., & Hulin, C. L. (1969). *The measurement of satisfaction in work and retirement.* Chicago: Rand McNally.

Smith, P. C., Kendall, L. M., & Hulin, C. L. (1975). *The Job Descriptive Index.* Bowling Green, OH: Bowling Green State University, Department of Psychology.

Smith, P. C., & Lem, C. (1955). Positive aspects of motivation in repetitive work: Effects of lot size upon spacing of voluntary work stoppages. *Journal of Applied Psychology, 39,* 330–333.

Smith, P. C., & Smith, O. W. (1961). Veridical perceptions of cylindricality: A problem of depth perception and object identification. *Journal of Experimental Psychology, 62,* 145–152.

Yeager, S. J. (1981). Dimensionality of the Job Descriptive Index. *Academy of Management Journal, 24,* 205–212.

REPRESENTATIVE PUBLICATIONS

Guilford, J. P., & Smith, P. C. (1959). A system of color preferences. *American Journal of Psychology, 72,* 487–502.

Hulin, C. L., & Smith, P. C. (1965). A linear model of job satisfaction. *Journal of Applied Psychology, 49,* 209–216.

Ironson, G. H., & Smith, P. C. (1981). Anchors away—The stability of meaning when their location is changed. *Personnel Psychology, 34,* 249–262.

Johnson, S. M., Smith, P. C., & Tucker, S. M. (1982). Response format of the Job Descriptive Index: Assessment of reliability and validity by the multitrait, multimethod matrix. *Journal of Applied Pschology, 67,* 500–505.

Lawrence, L. C., & Smith, P. C. (1955). Group decision and employee participation. *Journal of Applied Psychology, 39,* 334–337.

Locke, E. A., Smith, P. C., Kendall, L. M., Hulin, C. L., & Miller, A. M. (1964). Convergent and discriminant validity for areas and rating methods of job satisfaction. *Journal of Applied Psychology, 48,* 313–319.

Ryan T. A., & Smith, P. C. (1954). *Principles of industrial psychology.* New York: Ronald.

Smith, O. W., & Smith, P. C. (1957). Interaction of the effects of cues involved in judgments of curvature. *American Journal of Psychology, 70,* 361–375.

Smith, O. W., Smith, P. C., & Hubbard, D. (1958). Perceived distance as a function of the method of representing perspective. *American Journal of Psychology, 71,* 662–674.

Smith, P. C. (1955). The prediction of individual differences in susceptibility to industrial monotony. *Journal of Applied Psychology, 39,* 322–329.

Smith, P. C. (1965). Probleme der motivation in berufsleben [Problems of motivation at work]. In H. Thomae (Ed.), *Die Motivation menschlichen Handelns* [Motivation in human enterprises], (pp. 285–287). Cologne, West Germany: Kiepenheuer and Witsch.

Smith, P. C. (1967). The development of a method of measurement of job satisfaction: The Cornell Studies. In E. A. Fleishman (Ed.), *Studies in personnel and industrial psychology* (rev. ed., pp. 343–349). Homewood, IL: Dorsey.

Smith, P. C. (1985, August). *Global measures: Do we need them?* Invited address presented at the meeting of the American Psychological Association, Washington, DC.

Smith, P. C., & Cranny, C. J. (1968). The psychology of men at work. *Annual Review of Psychology, 19,* 467–497.

Smith, P. C., & Curnow, R. (1966). The "arousal hypothesis" and the effects of music on purchasing behvior. *Journal of Applied Psychology, 50,* 255–256.

Smith, P. C., & Gold, R. A. (1956). Prediction of success from examination of performance during the training period. *Journal of Applied Psychology, 40,* 83–86.

Smith, P. C., Mitchel, J., & Rollo, J. (1974). Influence of varying sources of information on judments of interviews. *Psychological Reports, 34,* 683–688.

Smith, P. C., & Smith, O. W. (1961). Ball throwing responses to photographically portrayed targets. *Journal of Experimental Psychology, 62,* 223–233.

Taylor, J. G., & Smith, P. C. (1957). An investigation of the shape of learning curves for industrial motor tasks. *Journal of Applied Psychology, 40,* 142–149.

Wijting, J., & Smith, P. C. (1969). Interacting effects of motivation, ability, and noise on activation and performance in a memorizing task. *Organizational Behavior and Human Performance, 4,* 353–364.

Wollack, S., Goodale, J. G., Wijting, J. P., & Smith, P. C. (1971). Development of the Survey of Work Values. *Journal of Applied Psychology, 55,* 331–338.

Wollack, S. W., Wijting, J., Goodale, J., & Smith, P. C. (1970). Weighting agreement responses by item scale values. *Journal of Applied Psychology, 54,* 174–175.

Zedeck, S., Cranny, C. J., Vale, C. A., & Smith, P. C. (1971). Comparison of "joint moderators" in three prediction techniques. *Journal of Applied Psychology, 55,* 234–240.

Zedeck, S., & Smith, P. C. (1968). The psychophysical determination of equitable payment: A methodological study. *Journal of Applied Psychology, 52,* 343–347.

CHAPTER 11

Jane Loevinger

Jane Loevinger

Being invited to contribute to this volume on "eminent women" has given me occasion to reflect on my life as a whole. If there is a single theme, it is iconoclasm. I have never been a True Believer in any cause, although I have often been accused of it, always by people unsympathetic to the cause they think I believe in. This skeptical attitude, even toward ideas in the fields that most interest me (e.g., psychometrics, psychoanalysis, and the women's movement), would have made me a chronic outsider even if being a woman had not already marked me. There is no niche to be filled by a Socratic woman. A woman, even more than a man, had better be a conformist if she wants to get ahead in the world.

When I was graduated with an undergraduate degree from the University of Minnesota in 1937, I was first offered an assistantship at the Institute of Child Welfare there, but then the offer was withdrawn. I do not think that my being a woman was a factor, for Florence Goodenough was the leading spirit there. Far more important at that time were the facts that I was a Jew and that I was considered to have radical political sympathies. I had also applied for an assistantship in the Psychology Department, and as graduation approached, Richard Elliott, the department head, pointed out to me that their best graduate students were women, some of whom were Jewish, and the department found it almost impossible to find jobs for them. The only academic openings available were in small denominational colleges in rural Minnesota. Such schools would not consider hiring either a Jew or a woman, he pointed out. He continued, "I wouldn't want you to become a clerk in a dime store."

By the way, I do not think he personally was prejudiced against either women or Jews. Finally, he recommended that I marry a psychologist—presumably a solution to my professional aspirations. Quite apart from my being 19 years old, very immature, and not interested in getting married, I was as outraged by the suggestion as a young woman would be today. I hope young women today find a more direct expression of their outrage than I did.

I seriously considered applying for a job as a proofreader at the University of Minnesota Press, whose editor, Margaret Harding, was a friend of mine. (That was a lowly job, but those were Depression days, Yuppies had not been invented, and I would not have qualified if they had.) Mrs. Harding refused to permit me to apply. "It's not for you," she said.

At the last minute, one of the men assistants in psychology moved up to another job, and I was given an assistantship for one graduate year on the unusual condition that I go elsewhere at the end of the year. The following year, I accepted a teaching assistantship at the University of California, which at that time meant only Berkeley. During my career there, I was never aware of prejudice against Jews, women, or sympathizers with left-wing movements.

These episodes are hardly fascinating, but they may give some perspective on today's hard times. Breaking into the academic world is extraordinarily difficult today, and, seeing people at the peak of their careers, one may think they moved into high positions without all the setbacks and discouragements assailing the young today. Those whose careers go back before World War II knew hard times indeed. Even men who later achieved international recognition often went from one postdoctoral assistantship to another until the war finally opened up jobs. The Depression and a variety of seldom-challenged prejudices, not only against women but against Jews, Blacks, and people who openly cohabited without benefit of marriage license, were all problems. The obstacles for Blacks were far the worst. At Minnesota during the early 1930s, they not only could not live on campus, but there was no housing in any part of town anywhere near campus where they were permitted to live.

During World War II, being a woman was an advantage. Even though I had not completed a PhD thesis, I was offered several relatively good jobs—academic and nonacademic—that would normally have gone to a person with a PhD and probably to a man. Employers preferred women because there was no danger that a change in eligibility for the draft would mean searching for a replacement.

For me, however, the advantage was short-lived. I was an instructor for a year at Stanford, then for a little more than a year at Berkeley. Then I quit in order to finish my dissertation (Loevinger, 1947)—financially, the best investment I ever made. By then I was married to Sam I. Weissman, who had come to Berkeley as a postdoctoral fellow in chemistry. Before I finished my thesis, he left to work at a site known officially as "Box 16613, Santa Fe, New Mexico." That was Los Alamos, one of the home bases of the atomic bomb. I spent the remainder of the war years there.

It is difficult today to justify the reasoning behind "the bomb," as it is sometimes called today. Suffice it to say that it was generally believed by the scientists taking part in the project that Hitler's Germany was working on an atomic bomb, and it was "them" or "us." Very few scientists refused to work on the project, and it was unthinkable that a Jewish scientist would refuse.

One aspect of my experience there was unique in my life, although not unique for other women. The pressure on women to get some sort of job was intense, and so I proceeded to do so, although after the usual PhD thesis hassle, I would have been better off taking a vacation, something no one did at Los Alamos. I worked briefly and ineffectually at a computer lab, but then I developed a protracted illness. By the time I recovered, I was about 5 months pregnant, and the doctor advised me not to go back to work. I know what it is to feel the sting of disapproval of working women who think someone who does not have a regular job "isn't doing anything." The peculiar circumstances of life at that time in that place gave me the opportunity to enjoy a few months with my first child, Judith, uninterrupted by professional concerns.

After the war, my husband, although many years past his PhD, found himself at the bottom of the academic ladder in the Department of Chemistry at Washington University in St. Louis. The situation for women had suddenly changed. Men denied adequate opportunity first by the Depression and then by the demands of war were scrambling to resume their careers. The pressure on women to retire from competition and just to be good housewives was immense. This is the era that my friend (and Berkeley teaching assistant) Betty Friedan (1963) has recorded eloquently in *The Feminine Mystique*.

For a number of years, the only opportunities I had to work as a psychologist were as part-time substitute teacher or as night school teacher or as research assistant on Air Force projects at Washington University. These were unrewarding positions, and I soon abandoned them to follow my own star—to a considerable extent at my own and my family's expense.

In thinking about what being a woman does to one's career, one must separate intrinsic from extrinsic complications. There are difficulties ineluctably intrinsic to a woman's situation. Small children need and want mothering or at least parenting (a word that hardly existed when my children were small). Also, on more than one occasion I was asked to apply for positions in distant cities to which I could not move without breaking up my family.

The extrinsic difficulties included not only prejudice on the part of department heads and other employers, who are or at least used to be comfortable with their "old-boy network," but also the widespread social pressures, from women as well as men, to be a "good wife and mother," that is, to be subservient and self-effacing.

I have my own private honor roll of those who encouraged my career during the dark days after the war. Leaving out the members of my family, I want to mention my former teachers and colleagues at Berkeley and most especially Egon Brunswik. Second, I want to mention the American Association of University Women (AAUW), who awarded me the Margaret Justin Fellowship for the year 1955–1956. It was a small amount of money, but it was worth a great deal in the way of validating my aspirations and my continuing interest in psychology. Finally, I must thank the National Institute of Mental Health, which for many years provided for my salary and research funds.

During my tenure as AAUW fellow, I was invited to make occasional appearances before AAUW meetings as a guest speaker. I accepted an invitation to speak at a meeting in Little Rock, Arkansas, probably a regional meeting, as I rode back on the train with a woman from the St. Louis chapter. My reception by the group there was initially warm, but at some time during my talk I felt a pall descending, and from then on the audience was icy. On the way back on the train, I asked my friend about this. She told me I had lost the audience when I remarked that discrimination against women in the professions is a lot like discrimination against Blacks—Negroes, as we then used to say. That was something the women of Little Rock did not want to hear.

Little Rock had at that time become a national code word for segregation, so I should have known what to expect. The reason that I did not involves the history of the AAUW. Originally they had had, *de facto* though never *de jure*, segregated White chapters in many communities. In some places, Black women joined the national but not the local chapter; perhaps elsewhere they had their own chapters. In 1949 a national AAUW convention had reaffirmed that the only requirement for membership would be graduation from an approved institution. In St. Louis, this resulted in a split.

One group remained affiliated with the national organization, to which I owed my fellowship, but the other, segregated faction, which called itself the College Club, managed to keep the assets of the local chapter, including all local AAUW archives and, I think, a building. As I was invited to a meeting of a group affiliated with the national AAUW, I simply assumed that they would be people championing equal rights and equal recognition for Blacks as well as women. It is easy to pass judgment on Southerners at this distance. The minutes of the 1949 convention reveal, not objections to Black members, but concern over local laws and customs that forbade public meetings of Blacks and Whites.

During the period when I was employed as an assistant on Air Force projects (where, as I explained to my incredulous son, Michael, I was a test pilot), my major interest was in psychometric methods (Loevinger, 1954; Loevinger, Gleser, & DuBois, 1953), an interest that is also reflected in my later work (Loevinger, 1957, completed largely during AAUW tenure).

Women as subjects for psychological research are so prominent now that it is hard to remember that up to the early 1950s, almost every paper in a psychological journal described its subjects as "native-born White American males." My own experiences and those of my friends, particularly of two dear friends who became victims of postpartum psychoses, led me to an interest in motherhood as an experience and to the traits of women as pertinent to the tasks of family life. Thus, when I left the Air Force project, I set out to study women and, in particular, mothers, by means of psychological tests. As it turned out, several other psychologists were doing similar research at the same time, including Robert and Pauline Sears, Joe Shoben, Dick Bell and Earl Schaefer, among others, but it was still a relatively novel endeavor. My studies were supported by a series of grants from the National Institute of Mental Health (Loevinger, 1957; Loevinger, Sweet, Ossorio, & LaPerriere, 1962; Loevinger & Wessler, 1970; Loevinger, Wessler, & Redmore, 1970). Local sponsors were, variously, Jewish Hospital, the Department of Child Psychiatry of the Washington University School of Medicine, and the Social Science Institute of Washington University, which no longer exists.

The study of women's attitudes toward problems of family life gradually broadened to include personality more generally and especially what I came to call ego development (Loevinger, 1966, 1976; Loevinger & Wessler, 1970). How the study of ego development grew out of the study of mothers' attitudes I have recounted several times recently (Loevinger, 1979, 1984, 1987).

For many years I harbored the dream that someone would be

favorably impressed by my research and by the recognition I had received outside St. Louis and would therefore ask me to bring my research project to their department or offer me a position, but that did not happen. Every position I obtained in St. Louis was obtained at my request, with the exception of my most recent one—as William Stuckenberg Professor of Human Values and Moral Development. It was other women who goaded me into asking that I be granted tenure at Washington University. Finally, in 1971, 25 years after I arrived in St. Louis, I became professor of psychology, again on my initiative. I think I was the first woman full professor in the department, except for one woman who was for many years an associate professor and who was promoted to full professor a year before she became emerita. I was not turned down for positions in the psychology department prior to that—I was never permitted to apply.

The atmosphere both in the Department of Psychology and in the Washington University administration is now different from the one that prevailed after World War II. At that time, Blacks were not even admitted to the University as students, much less as faculty. The postwar faculty and administration, under the leadership of Arthur Holly Compton as chancellor, began immediately to remedy that disgraceful situation. Women were never totally and conspicuously excluded from faculty as Blacks were, so it took longer for the subtle discrimination against them to be recognized.

At present I believe the commitment of Washington University to affirmative action is genuine and not just compliance with the law. How much of that change was brought about by change in the people at the top, how much by changing laws, and how much by civil rights and women's movements are hard to say.

If I seem to overemphasize the relation between discrimination against women and against Blacks, let us not forget their ironic connection. Howard Smith, a Representative from Virginia, wanted to make the Civil Rights Act of 1964 so ridiculous that it could not possibly be passed. To do so, he added sex to Title VII, Equal Employment Opportunity, which forbade discrimination on the basis of race, color, and national origin. Employees of educational institutions were exempt from the original act but were, I believe, included in an executive order a short while later. It was at that point that women began suing universities to rectify sex discrimination of long standing. The universities were threatened with cutoff of all federal funds, which would have been fatal for some institutions and for an enormous number of projects in most others. Institutions immediately began to look around for ways to be fairer to women.

In the wake of that movement, I finally achieved a regular faculty position, although I personally never threatened to sue. Perhaps it was only a coincidence that I became a full professor with tenure 1 week after I wrote to the administration that my next letter would go to the local chapter of the American Association of University Professors.

Has it been a disadvantage to my career to be a woman? Yes. Some of the disadvantages are intrinsic to the two-career family, and no laws can entirely change that. Partly I was just born too soon. I am grateful to the women's movement for making respectable many of my idiosyncrasies, which seemed for many years egocentric, selfish, or freakish. I may be all those things, but much of the problem was simply that I would not give up my career as a psychologist. Has it been an advantage? Yes, that too. Women bring to psychology experiences of half the species, experiences that men cannot totally share. Moreover, I was free to follow my own star early in my career, at a point when a man might have felt compelled to do what was popular or socially approved or what would gain support from colleagues. Life would have been easier if we had been wealthier, but it would have been much harder if my salary had been needed for survival.

To a large extent, my circumstances are unique, just as everyone's are, and so generalizations fail. I had more inclination to work alone than some women do. Those with a talent for administration, for example, cannot exercise that talent in the splendid isolation that I endured. On the other hand, a highly efficient woman could have made much better use of her time than I did, lacking the discipline of a regular job.

Being a woman has given me an advantage in a way that Else Frenkel-Brunswik first called to my attention. I have had the privilege of associating informally with some of the most distinguished scientists of our time by virtue not of my merits as a scientist but of being married to a well-known scientist. I am not in the least intimidated when the stimulus-response behaviorists or the Skinnerians claim that they and they alone know what True Science is, because I know how far removed their approach to science is from that of eminent physicists, chemists, biologists, and mathematicians whose conversations I have been privileged to listen in on.

Returning to the theme of iconoclasm, no one has ever refuted in print my demonstration that there is no noncircular definition of test reliability (Loevinger, 1947, 1957, 1965), but that proof has not made me popular among psychometricians. (I have never quite rid myself of the thought that if the same papers had been written by a man, they might have been taken more seriously.) By bad luck, I arrived with an interest in psychoanalysis at a university the psychologists of which were mostly behaviorists and the psychiatry department of which included some men who seem determined to stamp out psychoanalysis. I never accepted some of the dogmas of psychoanalysis, such as the idea of cathexis or psychic energy, and this did not make me particularly popular among local psychoanalysts either.

I have a great deal to thank the women's movement for, but I am also not always popular with some members of that group. With regard to women's attempts to change the way people use language, I am of two minds. In the final revision of my book on ego development (Loevinger, 1976), undertaken at the behest of the editor, I found that eliminating sexist language was in most instances a boon. For example, in place of the trite word "man," I substituted variously "individual," "person," "human being," and so on according to context. The meaning was clarified, and the style was noticeably improved. But ideology and high principles are no, excuse for bad writing. I am appalled at the barbarisms (e.g., "s/he" or "him/her") that some feminists, not always women, inject into their writing. Such barbarisms can make a text almost unreadable.

I am deeply committed to the liberation of women, although not to everything done under that banner. I try always to keep women's issues in perspective. We are not the only oppressed group in this world; I hope I never forget the others. There are countries where, if a woman is seduced or even raped by a man, she is forever disgraced and cast out from society, even from her own family, while the man goes unpunished. There are countries where little girls are taken from their beds in the middle of the night and are brutally circumcised. I have no solutions to such problems, no suggestions for what we can do about them. But we should not forget that they are the real issues in the liberation of women. They cast a shadow over issues like the use of "he" as a generic pronoun and whether women are admitted to the Men's Bar and Grill.

Having begun my career in the shadow of "the bomb," I am ending it in the shadow of the "Star Wars" boycott. Many physicists, engineers, computer scientists, and other professional experts are refusing to accept grants, contracts, or employment related to the Strategic Defense Initiative (SDI or "Star Wars") because they consider its aims impossible to achieve and its pursuit destructive of the best interests of the country. My interest as a psychologist lies in the moral dilemma posed for scientists who see money flow easily to projects of which they cannot approve and money simultaneously dry up for alternative research. Moral dilemmas are of course the core of contemporary research in moral development by Kohlberg and many others, and moral development is a part of or closely related to the field of ego development, in which I have been working for many years.

What my students, Michiel Westenberg and Kathryn Hemker, and I are working on is ways to tap, by means of paper-and pencil tests, people's thinking about such moral dilemmas of professional life. There have been many times when I have thought, and more times when I have been aware that others were thinking, how can one justify working in psychology when the overriding and fateful things are taking place in physics and chemistry and biology? I do not apologize to my current subjects for my interest in the psychological aspects of nuclear war. For, as I explain to them, if nuclear war comes, it will have been made by people; if it is averted, it will have been averted by people. People, even scientists, are finally recognizing that not every problem has a high-tech fix. Psychology may assume new importance in this posttechnological age.

REFERENCES

Friedan, B. (1963). *The feminine mystique.* New York: Norton.

Loevinger, J. (1947). A systematic approach to the construction and evaluation of tests of ability. *Psychological Monographs, 61* (Whole No. 285).

Loevinger, J. (1954). The attenuation paradox in test theory. *Psychological Bulletin, 51,* 493–504.

Loevinger, J. (1957). Objective tests as instruments of psychological theory. *Psychological Reports, 3,* 635–694.

Loevinger, J. (1965). Person and population as psychometric concepts. *Psychological Review, 72,* 143–155.

Loevinger, J. (1966). The meaning and measurement of ego development. *American Psychologist, 21,* 195–206.

Loevinger, J. (1976). *Ego development: Conceptions and theories.* San Francisco: Jossey-Bass.

Loevinger, J. (1979). *Scientific ways in the study of ego development.* Worcester, MA: Clark University Press.

Loevinger, J. (1984). On the self and predicting behavior. In R. A. Zucker, J. Aronoff, & A. I. Rabin (Eds.), *Personality and the prediction of behavior* (pp. 43–68). Orlando, FL: Academic.

Loevinger, J. (1987). *Paradigms of personality.* New York: Freeman.

Loevinger, J., Gleser, G. C., & DuBois, P. H. (1953). Maximizing the discriminating power of a multiple-score test. *Psychometrika, 18,* 309–317.

Loevinger, J., Sweet, B., Ossorio, A. G., & LaPerriere, K. (1962). Measuring personality patterns of women. *Genetic Psychology Monographs, 65,* 53–136.

Loevinger, J., & Wessler, R. (1970). *Measuring ego development: 1. Construction and use of a sentence completion test.* San Francisco: Jossey-Bass.

Loevinger, J., Wessler, R., & Redmore, C. (1970). *Measuring ego development: 2. Scoring manual for women and girls.* San Francisco: Jossey-Bass.

REPRESENTATIVE PUBLICATIONS

Loevinger, J. (1938). "Reasoning" in maze-bright and maze-dull rats. *Journal of Comparative Psychology, 26,* 413–426.

Loevinger, J. (1940). Intelligence as related to socioeconomic factors. *Yearbook, National Society for the Study of Education, 39* (Pt. 1), 159–210.

Loevinger, J. (1951). Intelligence. In H. Helson (Ed.), *Theoretical foundations of psychology* (pp. 557–601). New York: Van Nostrand.

Loevinger, J. (1959). Theory and techniques of assessment. *Annual Review of Psychology, 10,* 287–316.

Loevinger, J. (1965). Measurement in clinical research, In B. B. Wolman (Ed.), *Handbook of clinical psychology* (pp. 78–94). New York: McGraw-Hill.

Loevinger, J. (1966). Psychological tests in the conceptual framework of psychology. In K. R. Hammond (Ed.), *The psychology of Egon Brunswik* (pp. 107–148). New York: Holt, Rinehart & Winston.

Loevinger, J. (1979). Construct validity of the Sentence Completion Test of ego development *Applied Psychological Measurement, 3,* 281–311.

Loevinger, J. (1983). On ego development and the structure of personality. *Developmental Review, 3,* 339–350.

Loevinger, J. (1985). Revision of the Sentence Completion Test for ego development. *Journal of Personality and Social Psychology, 48,* 420–427.

Loevinger, J. (1986). On Kohlberg's contribution to ego development. In S. Modgil & C. Modgil (Eds.), *Lawrence Kohlberg: Consensus and controversy* (pp. 183–193). Lewes, Sussex, England: Falmer.

Loevinger, J. (1986). On the structure of personality. In D. J. Bearison & H. Zimiles (Eds.), *Thought and emotion: Developmental perspectives* (pp. 65–74). Hillsdale, NJ: Lawrence Erlbaum Associates, Inc.

Loevinger, J., Cohn, L. D., Redmore, C. D., Bonneville, L. P., Streich, D. D., & Sargent, M. (1985). Ego development in college. *Journal of Personality and Social Psychology, 48,* 947–962.

Loevinger, J., & Knoll, E. (1983). Personality: Stages, traits, and the self. *Annual Review of Psychology, 34,* 195–222.

CHAPTER 12

Frances K. Graham

Frances K. Graham

My decision to become a psychologist was made in 1936, my sophomore, undergraduate year and happened because Pennsylvania State University had a requirement that liberal arts students take introductory psychology. I knew little about psychology but thought it relied mainly on common sense and would not be an efficient use of time. Fortunately, I was unable to persuade my adviser that another course in mathematics would be a good substitute. Before the semester ended, I had been converted. I announced my decision to my parents and asked permission to finish my undergraduate degree early so that the money for my final undergraduate year could finance the first graduate year. We were still in the Great Depression of the 1930s, and my father had borrowed money for my education from his sister—a biology teacher whose education he had helped support. He felt strongly that women should be well-educated and that they ought to be capable of earning a living should the need arise.

My conversion to psychology was not, of course, independent of my background and the attitudes about women and work that I had held up to this point. I was a first child, born August 1, 1918 in Canastota, New York, and my only sibling, a brother, was born 4 years later. Both our parents were college-educated and placed a high value on education, as had the preceding generation. Their marriage was a model of equality within a framework that preserved traditional sex roles. My mother, trained as a librarian, became a self-taught accountant during the Depression in order to assist my

father, an engineer and inventor. Later they executed a formal partnership to operate as dealers in heavy-construction equipment.

My preadolescent years were lived between World War I and the
Depression; a period of optimism and affluence in the United States.
I was taught in the Prospect Park, Pennsylvania, public schools that
we had saved democracy, that there would never be another war,
and that women had the vote. I know I expected no barriers in life
and felt that, if anything, women were the favored sex.

With adolescence and the onset of the Depression, I learned of
associated disadvantages. One was the discovery that if funds were
insufficient to send two children to college, the male child took
priority because he would later be financially responsible for a family. A second disadvantage was that girls and women were more
restricted in where they could go and with whom, and, it seemed
clear, their position in life was unduly dependent on an appropriate
marriage. Although women were to be cherished and protected,
these benefits had to be earned; I received a good deal of direct and
indirect instruction in womanly behavior. There was nothing
unusual in this, but it is odd to look back and realize how pervasive
the sex-typing was and how much has changed in recent decades.

I believe that I tried, unconsciously, to chart a compromise course
by avoiding the most flagrantly sex-typed activities. I did not like
sewing, cooking, and most homemaking activities—nor did my
mother—but I was also uninterested in typically male activities such
as carpentry, mechanics, and science. Lack of interest in the latter
probably derived from my first course in general science; the course
seemed to consist of boys and the male teacher talking about
airplanes and automobiles about which I knew little and cared not
at all. Fortunately, sports were heavily encouraged by my father
and did not usually involve direct competition with males.
Schoolwork, in general, and mathematics, in particular, were also
safe areas; excelling in school was not considered masculine. There
was also no reason to avoid social life, and I did not. It was important, however, to obey the cultural stricture against getting too emotionally involved too young, and I certainly did not find that easy.

So I went off to college in 1935, fond of boys, learning, sports,
and clothes, in that order, and I planned to be an accountant. It was
the best way I knew to make a living from mathematics: Teaching
seemed too typically woman's work, and I had no understanding
of academic life or of the possibilities afforded by mathematics or
science to make new discoveries. The required psychology course
intervened. It was my first experience with teaching that viewed
a field of knowledge as developing, as involving not only what was

already known, but also what needed to be found out. The teacher, an assistant professor of clinical psychology named Fred Brown, had a temporary appointment, and I have not seen him since, but I wish he could know the impact his teaching had.

Psychology also had the advantage that people, not machines, were its basic subject matter, and psychology should, therefore, be a field in which women would be welcome. In fact, I believed it would allow me to have the two things I thought essential—an interesting career and a family. I literally thought that I could set up a rat laboratory in the basement of a future home and live the non-career aspects of my life on the floors above. As a result I immediately changed to a psychology major and enrolled heavily in science courses I had previously avoided. I took physics and chemistry with the engineers, biology and genetics in liberal arts, and human anatomy dissection with the physical education majors. I expected and found these courses to be valuable tools in understanding the more complex science of psychology.

The next step was graduate school. I was accepted by the two schools to which I applied, but neither offered financial support, although it might be thought that graduation at 19 years at the top of the liberal arts roster would warrant some aid. Fortunately, Pennsylvania State University had the enlightened policy of 1-year graduate fellowships that could be used anywhere, and so with Penn State's assistance, I entered Yale in the fall of 1938.

A setback came when the chair of the Psychology Department, during an entry interview, warned me that it might not be possible for a woman PhD in psychology to find employment. However, everything else was encouraging. There were some women students and several women adjunct faculty, and there was a continual ferment about ideas and research. Formal requirements were minimal. Certainly none were needed to motivate students: The usual working day was 14 hours and we received the equivalent of daily seminars in the debates among faculty and students that went on in the offices and corridors.

Unfortunately, financial matters still had to be considered. I had small jobs unrelated to psychology, but, without a fellowship for the second year, they would not cover expenses. So I again applied to graduate schools, and this time a women's college, Bryn Mawr, offered support. However, Yale also found a small fellowship designated for women, and I was able to continue there.

My personal life also took a fortunate turn. In 1939 I became engaged to a fellow graduate student, David Graham, and we were married 6 months before Pearl Harbor. Planning for marriage led to a reassessment of career options. I still wanted to be an experimental psychologist, but the rat laboratory in the basement was ill-suited to apartment living, and an academic appointment would be difficult with my choices geographically restricted. A shift to clinical psychology would clearly offer more opportunities, but Yale did not have any explicitly clinical training: There was only one formal course; in addition, a group of students organized a seminar on projective techniques, and we also made monthly trips to New York for a seminar on the Rorschach test. The most valuable experience came through two 3-year apprenticeships, one with Pauline Sears in a child psychiatric clinic and one with Dorothy Marquis in pediatric psychology. I also assisted in a continuation of Marquis's pioneering studies of neonate conditioning (Marquis, 1931). An interest in infancy had been part of the reason for selecting Yale and was to prove a lifelong interest.

I thus acquired credentials in child clinical psychology, respectable for the times, although my primary training was in experimental psychology and my thesis (F. K. Graham, 1943) was a rat learning study done under the joint supervision of Clark Hull and Donald Marquis. Psychology was less specialized then, and it was assumed that if students were taught general principles, they could always acquire the knowledge needed for a specific problem. Under Hull's influence, the Yale Institute of Human Relations, which housed the departments of psychology, sociology, and cultural anthropology in a wing of the medical school, envisioned a grand unifying theory. Learning theory blended with psychoanalytic concepts—as in the work of Robert Sears, Hobart Mowrer, and Neal Miller—might connect personality dynamics, motivation, and development with physiology and with social, economic, and even cultural behavior.

In the intellectual atmosphere that prevailed, women participated on an equal basis with men. However, there was one curious exception that reduced the opportunities for women students to benefit from the interdisciplinary environment: A continuing Monday night seminar for the whole institute was closed to women on the familiar grounds that their presence would inhibit certain kinds of discussion. It is odd that no one, including me, appeared to be disturbed by this prohibition, but I heard some years later that an invited outside speaker, either Margaret Mead or Ruth Benedict, insisted on the presence of women; this apparently ended the exclusion permanently.

In all other respects, the graduate psychology program at Yale was very supportive of women students. Faculty and students had a strong sense of in-group identification and common purpose, and there were many two-career marriages: Dorothy and Don Marquis, Catherine and Walter Miles, and Pat and Bob Sears among the faculty; Judson and Julie Brown, Bob and Libby French, Al and Isabelle Liberman, Helen and Vincent Nowliss, John and Bea Whiting, and several others, among the students. Although the wife's career was often determined by the husband's position, all of these women were or became successful in their professions. However, the Depression, together with graduate school, had altered my views about the position of women. Working women were unpopular during the Depression—they were seen as taking jobs away from male heads of families. Although still confident that ample opportunities were available for women, I no longer saw the sex as favored. "Different but equal" was more apt. Nonetheless, some uneasiness about women's worth and proper role seeped in with the psychoanalytic concepts I had acquired during graduate school.

My confidence was further strained when, in the spring of 1942, I had to consider what to do after graduation. My husband, then finishing his second year of medical school, wanted to transfer to a larger clinical center, so that locating in any of several cities was possible. I really did not know how to go about looking for a job—academic positions were not advertised, and, in any case, applications were normally by invitation—but I consulted with the faculty, who consulted with the Yale network and, through Carlyle Jacobsen, constructed a position for me in St. Louis. I would work halftime in the city Child Guidance Clinic and halftime in a nontenure-track position in neuropsychiatry at Washington University. The work was entirely clinical, and it was not what I desired, but it would keep me in psychology, and it would let me earn a living.

In fact, the clinical work was extremely interesting, and I never regretted having had the experience, but I wanted some released time for research, and that was not viewed sympathetically. It was suggested that I conduct research on patients—a sensible plan—but even patient research required time, and time was in short supply. However, I recruited an older MA psychologist, Barbara Kendall, and a young finishing school volunteer, Ruth Dawson Bioletti, and we managed to develop a memory-for-designs test for brain damage that is still in use (F. K. Graham & Kendall, 1960).

I did not lack role models in St. Louis. One was Margaret Gildea, the psychiatrist wife of the department chair, and an attractive, forceful, and sophisticated woman with two teenage children. Through her I was introduced to Karen Horney's writings and the feminist ideas they advocated (Horney, 1939). I admired Margaret, especially when she intervened in psychiatric staff conferences to take issue with the generally prevailing view that male illnesses were the fault of mother or wife and that female illnesses were due to narcissism, hostility, or hypochondriasis.

Another important model was Gerty Cori, who, with her husband Carl, won the Nobel prize in medicine and physiology 6 months after Washington University finally gave her tenure. The most important person, however, was Helen Tredway Graham, my mother-in-law, a full professor and a distinguished neurophysiologist (e.g., Gasser & H. T. Graham, 1933) who had been active in the suffrage movement and who remained active in community affairs. Helen Graham had boundless energy and pursued her research as long as she lived, receiving at age 75 a 5-year federal grant that was renewed at age 80.

We remained in St. Louis, except for two brief interruptions, until 1957. The first interruption was occasioned by my husband's being called to active duty in the Army Medical Service. This was in 1945, some months after our first child was born. Because Dave was initially stationed in Pennsylvania, I lived nearby with my parents until our second child was born and Dave had been sent overseas. In 1946, with Helen Graham's encouragement, I returned to St. Louis to work. This time I negotiated with the medical school in advance to free a half day of my half-time position for research. I also acquired a research assistant. Bob Sears wrote of a promising student, Bettye Caldwell, and the medical school agreed to support her while she obtained the PhD. Her later innovative work in preschool education of Little Rock minorities has made her one of the university's most distinguished alumna.

Barbara Kendall and I continued our collaboration, but this period in St. Louis lasted less than 2 years because Dave had returned and had accepted a 3-year fellowship in psychosomatic medicine at Cornell Medical School in New York City. Finding a position for me was only one problem. Finding a place to live was a Herculean task in those early postwar days. I had spent weeks in St. Louis trying to rent, and when I finally succeeded by paying an exorbitant price for the landlady's furniture, she put a for-sale sign on the house within a month. This time we were luckier. Through a relative, we acquired a huge, rent-controlled apartment on Riverside Drive, and, somewhat by accident, I obtained an instructorship at Barnard, my first tenure-track appointment. I had telephoned Dick Youtz, the Department of Psychology chair, about the possibility of teaching an introductory psychology section, and it transpired that he needed a full-time replacement who could also teach experimental and developmental courses. That we were both Yale graduates was not a hindrance.

This was unbelievable good fortune, but the first year I could barely stay ahead of the students. By the second year, I was able to offer individual research opportunities to a few of the honors students, three of whom co-authored a paper with me (F. K. Graham, Charwat, Honig, & Weltz, 1951). Wanda Charwat Bronson, Alice Honig, and Paula Weltz, as well as two others—Frances Fuchs Schachter and Vera John-Steiner—continued on to graduate school, and all established successful careers in psychology. This was my first and, with one exception, my only experience with undergraduate teaching, and it was one of the most rewarding periods in my career.

The Barnard position was full-time, but I found that, with the academic holidays and summer break, no more hours were required than had been spent on my half-time position in St. Louis. I had arranged in advance not to carry faculty responsibilities beyond teaching and to be on campus only mornings and two afternoons a week. The children were in nursery school in the mornings and were supervised by a housekeeper on the two afternoons. I have always had household help, but at that time it posed several problems. One was financial. My instructor's salary did not cover the costs of working and replacing myself in the home, so that my job actually drained our resources, a situation in which many working women found themselves.

A second problem was the guilt I felt about leaving the children. Cultural attitudes were opposed to women's working during child-rearing years, and these attitudes were reinforced by psychological theory, especially within developmental psychology. I disagreed with the theory and tried to encourage students and daughters to be more liberated than I was. I also tried to choose housekeepers for their warmth and liking of children. Because this seemed to be negatively correlated with cleaning skills but positively with cooking, we usually ate well in the midst of disorder. The worst problem was turnover. Although I never missed a class, I had close calls. One Monday morning, when a newly hired housekeeper failed to appear, I had a full day of teaching ahead, Dave had already left for the hospital, the live-in student had classes, and the children had chicken pox. But my mother was able to arrive from Philadelphia by noon, and in the meantime my laundress, having appeared unexpectedly, was pressed into babysitting.

I would have liked to remain at Barnard, where I had been promoted to assistant professor, but Dave had an offer from Washington University, and so, in 1951, we returned again to St. Louis. With financial security about to begin, this was an opportune time to enlarge the family, and I also needed time to examine the work situation. I strongly wished to continue research and teaching rather than resume clinical work, and Bob Sears had given me an important idea. He had described the newly established National Institute of Mental Health (NIMH) and had suggested that I apply for a research grant that could include my salary to conduct the research.

I had been stimulated by Hebb's (1949) book, *The Organization of Behavior*, and wanted to investigate the consequences of brain damage on early cognitive development. Bettye Caldwell arranged a meeting with Alexis Hartmann, the Department of Pediatrics chair, and it transpired that he had funds to initiate a study relating newborn blood oxygenation to obstetrical variables. A young woman pediatrician, Miriam Pennoyer, would be responsible for this aspect of the work, and my role would be to develop measures of neonatal behavioral functioning and to organize a follow-up study.

I began work on the anoxia research in July 1953 with an appointment as a research associate in pediatrics and in psychiatry. I continued to work half-time due to the new baby, who was born in 1952, and did not take a full-time position until she reached school age. My first major task was preparation of a grant application to carry us past the 16-month start-up period, so I applied to the National Institutes of Health, with Pennoyer and Hartmann as co-investigators. We were funded for 7 years by the Neurological Institute, but not before a site visit to find out why salaries of the two women investigators would be paid by the grant. I observed the same concern later, as a study section member. People seemed not to be generally aware that educational institutions, like private research organizations, may have professional positions the salaries for which came only through outside funding. Needless to add, many of these positions were held by women.

The work progressed well. Two years later, I applied for an additional grant to support validation of tests for brain injury in preschool children. The proposed research would tap processes that had proved to be sensitive to injury in adult research, and several tests were analogues of those used in Lukas Teuber's research on World War II veterans (e.g., Semnes, Weinstein, Ghent, & Teuber, 1960). It was very fortunate, therefore, that Teuber site-visited me in connection with the grant. He was interested in the research, invited me to visit his laboratory, introduced me to other neuropsychologists, and from then until his death was very generous in encouraging my work. I began to receive other invitations to speak and to attend conferences, and I participated regularly in scientific society meetings. In the relative isolation of my medical school position, it was particularly important to me to maintain a close identification with psychology and to have the stimulation provided by national contacts.

There was one major drawback to my broadened participation. To my surprise, I was anxious about speaking before groups of largely male scientists. It was a surprise because I had been active in theatricals and public speaking, and I was always comfortable in the classroom, whether as student or teacher. I also liked chairing a session: Putting speakers at ease and stimulating discussion were the familiar aspects of the "good hostess" role. So the psychodynamics of my discomfiture were not obscure: a classic role conflict. I tried many devices to overcome the problem and eventually learned that the best way was to speak without notes, thus forcing myself to concentrate on the message rather than the delivery. Or perhaps it was overcome when the momentum of the women's movement made role conflicts obsolete.

The anoxia project made it possible to enlarge the research team. At different times, Bettye Caldwell, Ruth Matarazzo, Claire Ernhart, and several women students were collaborators. I was not aware that I was developing a female research group. It happened because, like me, they had no place in the regular academic system, and medical schools could at least provide appointments, space, and, sometimes, salaries.

The acquisition of federal grants set the pattern I have followed ever since. This was fortunate because another move was imminent. Dave was enthusiastic about an offer from the University of Wisconsin. Although I was initially reluctant, I acquiesced when the offer was repeated in 1957 and the new dean of the medical school treated me as a welcome asset. He offered me a position in the newly formed Department of Pediatrics, and I was able to transfer the preschool brain-injury grant to Wisconsin and retain direction of, and salary from, the anoxia grant that remained in St. Louis. Claire Ernhart, who supervised the St. Louis work, was also paid from both grants, and, for several years, she commuted bimonthly between Madison and St. Louis. In 1962 and 1963, we published final reports on these projects, which included a 3-year followup of the anoxic newborns (F. K. Graham, Ernhart, Thurston, & Craft, 1962). Other investigators retested the children at age 7 (Corah, Anthony, Painter, Stern, & Thurston, 1965).

I had the same position title in Wisconsin that I had held in St.

Louis (i.e., research associate). An assistant professorship on the tenure track had been offered, but, now 15 years post-PhD, the prospect of being an assistant professor was no longer appealing. Several years later, I joined the Department of Psychology as a lecturer with voting rights and the privilege of supervising doctoral theses. It was not until 1964, 22 years post-PhD, that I became, almost accidentally, a tenured associate professor. This came about because the NIMH began a Research Scientist Award program that paid most of the salary of research investigators for 5-year renewable periods. I wanted to relieve my regular grants of providing my salary and also to have more flexibility in pursuing new research lines and engaging in other professional activities, including some teaching. I applied for and received an award and, to meet an unanticipated condition of the award, the university gave me tenure. Four years later I was promoted to full professor, and a year after that I was invited to join the Department of Psychology in the same capacity. It was agreed that I would serve half my time in the Department of Psychology and half in the Department of Pediatrics, would have a position on the executive committees of each department, and would teach one graduate course or seminar in psychology each year. Altogether, it was a very agreeable arrangement.

As a result of the Research Scientist Award, I could make the shift to the psychophysiological research for which I had been preparing. The anoxia and brain-injury studies (F. K. Graham, Ernhart, Craft, & Berman, 1963; F. K. Graham et al., 1962; Ernhart, F. K. Graham, Eichman, Marshall, & Thurston, 1963) had suggested that the pattern typically seen after injury to the adult brain was not the pattern observed after early injury. Cognitive deficits appeared to be greater the earlier the injury, whereas perceptomotor impairment showed the opposite relationship. It seemed unlikely, therefore, that perceptual impairment could explain cognitive impairment. An attentional deficit appeared to be a promising candidate, and I wanted to investigate the attentional process using psychophysiological techniques. These are particularly well suited for work with infants but are also useful across the life span. My husband had introduced me to electrophysiological recording—and I overcame my resistance to learning about electronics—in the course of our collaboration on psychosomatic studies (e.g., D. T. Graham, Kabler, & F. K. Graham, 1962).

I found psychophysiology fascinating and, on alternate years, taught the graduate level psychophysiology laboratory course that Peter Lang had begun for clinical students and that we expanded to include students from all areas of psychology and from outside the department. With the aid of psychophysiologists in the medical school, including my husband in the Department of Medicine, Bob Roessler and Norman Greenfield in the Department of Psychiatry, Lewis Leavitt in the Department of Pediatrics, and, later, many other faculty, we developed an outstanding graduate program. Training in psychophysiology had been mainly postdoctoral up to that point, and we took pride in the program and in the fact that, in the ensuing years, Wisconsin provided four presidents of the Society for Psychophysiological Research.

The application of psychophysiological methods to cognitive issues proved as fruitful as I had hoped. My initial research was on the cardiac component of orienting, a form of passive attention, and a 1966 paper with Rachel Clifton (F. K. Graham & Clifton, 1966) became a Citation Classic. Later I studied the startle reflex, an automatic interruption of processing, and the phenomenon of "prepulse inhibition"—the reflex inhibition of a startle by any brief change in stimulation shortly preceding a startle-eliciting stimulus (e.g., F. K. Graham, 1979). The latter phenomenon is robust in adults of many species but does not appear to be fully mature until near adolescence, a surprising lag given its origin in the midbrain. The lag also contrasts with the ability of even 4-month-old infants to orient and to show low-level filtering effects of attending to interesting stimuli (Anthony & F. K. Graham, 1983). Because cardiac changes, startle blink, and brain potentials can be measured without the need for a subject to cooperate or even to be awake, the methods are powerful not only for studying infants, but also for studying psychopathology. We found, for example, that an anencephalic infant, born without forebrain, was actually precocious in discriminating small differences in stimulation (F. K. Graham, Leavitt, Strock, & Brown, 1978).

The research still continues and has been continuously funded by federal agencies. With support from the William T. Grant Foundation, the laboratory was computerized in the early 1970s, and, when I look now at the racks upon racks of electronics, I am amazed at what has been wrought. I wish my general science teacher, who had so little interest in teaching high school girls, could see it. The Research Scientist Award has also been renewed regularly, and, in 1980, the University of Wisconsin conferred an endowed Hilldale Research Professorship on me. It provided a nonlapsing, nonrestricted $10,000 a year for my research. The psychophysiological aspects of the research were recognized in 1981 by a Distinguished Contributions Award from the Society for Psychophysiological Research (Lang, 1982), the first time a woman had been so honored;

the developmental aspects were recognized, in 1982, by the G. Stanley Hall medal from the American Psychological Association Division on Developmental Psychology (Clifton, 1982). I was very much moved when my alma mater, Pennsylvania State University, gave me a Distinguished Alumna Award the following year.

We remained at the University of Wisconsin for 29 busy, satisfying years. Many students, fellows, and visitors shared in my research. At first, there were only women: Phyllis Berman, my first PhD student; Lorna Benjamin, my first postdoctoral fellow; Rachel Clifton, who declined an assistant professorship to apply for an NIMH postdoctoral fellowship with me; Kathleen Berg, half of the only two-career marriage born in my laboratory; Gunilla Bohlin of the University of Uppsala, my first foreign visitor. David Grant asked how I located such outstanding students and, I can add, students who became such outstanding and dedicated scientists. The answer was, of course, very simple—I was selecting from the infrequently tapped pool of women applicants. Later, I also had excellent male students and fellows.

Another result of the Research Scientist Award was that I could participate more in scientific societies, in reviewing for journals, and in consulting for federal agencies. I had served since 1957 as a consultant to the Collaborative Project on Perinatal Complications, which the Neurological Institute organized among some 14 universities and hospitals. I later enjoyed a 4-year term on the study section (now, the peer review panel), evaluating grant applications in experimental psychology. From 1977 to 1981 (and as chair from 1979 to 1981), I was privileged to serve on the six-person Board of Scientific Counselors, which reviews in-house laboratories of the NIMH. The most exciting experience was a 2-year term on President Carter's congressionally mandated Commission for the Study of the Ethics of Medicine and Biomedical and Behavioral Research. Among the issues on which the commission made reports to Congress were a definition of death, the distribution of health care, genetics engineering, and the use of human subjects in research. In contrast to earlier years when I was often the only woman on a board, the President's commission had an even division of men and women and minority members drawn from both sexes.

In the meantime, our children launched their professional careers: Our son, Andrew, is now a research chemist in industry; the younger daughter, Mary, is a lawyer; and the older daughter, Norma, is a psychologist—a full professor at Columbia University. Norma's election to the Society for Experimental Psychologists made us the first parent–child dyad in the society's 82-year history.

The lives of our daughters reflect how much times have changed. Norma, who has commuted for 7 years between New York and Oregon while having and raising three children, objects to the current idea that women cannot "have it all," that is, both career and family. She believes that children enrich careers as well as lives of mother and father when both act as parents: The cost is taken from other activities. I think I agree with that. Over the years, I have often wished for more energy and more time. On the other hand, there have been energy and time even for some things other than career and family. When young, we enjoyed an active social life and a fair number of vigorous activities—tennis, ice skating, canoeing, camping. Now my interests are archaeology and bird watching, and travel is the major excitement: I have twice organized yachting trips to rarely visited places in the Aegean; on a recent trip, we rented a 16th-century farmhouse in Provence.

Then, 2 years ago, my husband and I decided that it was time to try something new, preferably in a milder climate. I let a few people know of the decision. The most attractive offer came from the University of Delaware, to which we moved in July of 1986. Dave retired and is an adjunct professor of psychology, participating in the training of clinical students. The University of Wisconsin released my laboratory equipment, and I was able to transfer my Research Scientist Award and research grants from the NIMH and from the National Institute of Child Health and Human Development. Thus my work is much the same as before, but, for the first time since the days at Barnard, I am full-time at an academic department of psychology. One of the most rewarding features of the move is the opportunity of being in a strong cognitive program and of collaborating with a young clinical psychophysiologist, Robert Simons, who happens also to be my son-in-law. I am pleased that the University of Wisconsin Department of Psychology has put my picture in their gallery of such distinguished former colleagues as Harry Harlow and David Grant and hope that my picture will not long be the only one of a woman to be hung there.

I will try to summarize my account in terms of two issues we were asked to address—coping strategies and support factors. It is not easy to separate strategy from luck, and I had a great deal of the latter. I do think one conscious attitude was an advantage: having a clear idea of my priorities. Family and research came first, and anything else could be sacrificed, if necessary, including paid work. That might be translated as willingness to work within the system, but I mean something more positive. Knowing what you want and what losses you can accept makes it easier to negotiate and refuse options. Other than that somewhat hardheaded view, I guess my main operating principle was, and is, that I find research the most exciting activity imaginable.

It should be obvious from this account that I had more than my fair share of support—parents who valued education and careers for women and a husband who had the same values. I had adequate financial security, and I was not taught to place a high value on financial success. I have also had a great deal of support from women of all ages. I did not realize until I prepared this report just how heavily I had relied on women and in how much of my research another woman had been the critical factor making it possible. But then I think of how much help I have had from male professors, colleagues, and just friends, and it is too difficult to draw a balance sheet.

I can say without any conflict that the women's movement had a major impact on me. I am sure that many gratifying invitations and elections never would have included me otherwise. More important, it has helped resolve my own ambivalence about an appropriate female role, and it has given me the sense of a common bond among women that would have been unthinkable in the excluding cliques I knew in adolescence.

It is also obvious that I owe much to the fact that medical schools have a flexible system that can accommodate nonstandard careers—part-time work or work in only one sector of the research-teaching–service triad. Finally, what would I have done without the federal grant system? I hope that I would have found some other means to do research. According to former student Phyllis Berman, I was given to such homilies as "If in a desert, study cacti," but the grant system keeps the cacti blooming.

ACKNOWLEDGMENTS

Preparation of this autobiography was supported by a Research Scientist award MH 21762.

REFERENCES

Anthony, B. J., & Graham, F. K. (1983). Evidence for sensory-selective set in young infants. *Science, 220,* 742–744.

Clifton, R. K. (1982, Fall) G. Stanley Hall Award presentation to Frances K. Graham. *Newsletter of the American Psychological Association Division on Development Psychology,* pp. 8–9.

Corah, N. L., Anthony, E. J., Painter, P., Stern, J. A., & Thurston, D. (1965). Effect of perinatal anoxia after seven years. *Psychological Monographs, 79*, 1–34.

Ernhart, C. B., Graham, F. K., Eichman, P. L., Marshall, J. M., & Thurston, D. (1963). Brain-Injury in the preschool child: Some developmental considerations. II. Comparisons of brain-injured and normal children. *Psychological Monographs, 77*, 17–33.

Gasser, H. S., & Graham, H. T. (1933). Potentials produced in the spinal cord by stimulation of the dorsal roots. *American Journal of Physiology, 103*, 303–320.

Graham, D. T., Kabler, J. D., & Graham, F. K (1962). Physiological responses to the suggestion of attitudes specific for hives and hypertension. *Psychosomatic Medicine, 24*, 159–169.

Graham, F. K. (1943). Conditioned inhibition and conditioned excitation in transfer of discrimination. *Journal of Experimental Psychology, 33*, 351–368.

Graham, F. K. (1978). Commentary on Graham and Clifton's "heart rate change as a component of the orienting response." *Current Contents, 21*, 16.

Graham, F. K. (1979). Distinguishing among orienting, defense, and startle reflexes. In H. D. Kimmel, E. H. van Olst, & J. F. Orlebeke (Eds.), *The orienting reflex in humans* (pp. 137–166). An international conference sponsored by the North Atlantic Treaty Organization. Hillsdale, NJ: Lawrence Erlbaum Associates, Inc.

Graham, F. K., Charwat, W., Honig, A., & Weltz, P. (1951). Aggression as a function of the attack and the attacker. *Journal of Abnormal and Social Psychology, 46*, 512–520.

Graham, F. K., & Clifton, R. K. (1966). Heart rate change as a component of the orienting response. *Psychological Bulletin, 65*, 305–320.

Graham, F. K., Ernhart, C. B., Craft, M., & Berman, P. W. (1963). Brain injury in the preschool child: Some developmental considerations. I. Performance of normal children. *Psychological Monographs, 77*, 1–16.

Graham, F. K., Ernhart, C. B., Thurston, D., & Craft, M. (1962). Development three years after perinatal anoxia and other potentially damaging newborn experiences. *Psychological Monographs, 76*, 1–53.

Graham, F. K., & Kendall, B. S. (1960). Memory-for-Designs Test: Revised general manual. *Perceptual and Motor Skills, 2-VII* (Monograph Suppl.), 147–188.

Graham, F. K., Leavitt, L. A., Strock, B. D., & Brown, J. W. (1978). Precocious cardiac orienting in a human, anencephalic infant. *Science, 199*, 322–324.

Hebb, D. O. (1949). *The organization of behavior.* New York: Wiley.

Horney, K. (1939). *New ways in psychoanalysis.* New York: Norton.

Lang, P. J. (1982). SPR Award, 1981, for distinguished contributions to psychophysiology: Frances Keesler Graham. *Psychophysiology, 19*, 121–123.

Marquis, D. P. (1931). Can conditioned responses be established in the newborn infant? *Journal of Genetic Psychology, 39*, 479–492.

Semnes, J., Weinstein, S., Ghent, L., & Teuber, H.-L. (1960). *Somatosensory changes after penetrating brain wounds in man.* Cambridge, MA: Harvard University Press.

REPRESENTATIVE PUBLICATIONS

Balaban, M. T., Anthony, B. J., & Graham, F. K. (1985). Modality-repetition and attentional effects on reflex blinking in infants and adults. *Infant Behavior and Development, 8*, 443–457.

Berman, P. W., Graham, F. K., Eichman, P. L., & Waisman, H. A. (1961). Psychological and neurological status of diet-treated phenylketonuric children and their siblings. *Pediatrics, 28*, 924–934.

Berman, P. W., Waisman, H. A., & Graham, F. K. (1966). Intelligence in treated phenylketonuric children: A developmental study. *Child Development, 37,* 731–747.

Bohlin, G., Graham, F. K., Silverstein, L. D., & Hackley, S. A. (1981). Cardiac orienting and startle blink modification in novel and signal situations. *Psychophysiology, 18,* 603–611.

Chase, W. G., Graham, F. K., & Graham, D. T. (1968). Components of heart rate response in anticipation of reaction time and exercise tasks. *Journal of Experimental Psychology, 76,* 642–648.

Graham, F. K. (1956). Behavioral differences between normal and traumatized newborns. I. The test procedures. *Psychological Monographs, 70,* 1–16.

Graham, F. K. (1973). Habituation and dishabituation of responses innervated by the autonomic nervous system. In H. V. S. Peeke & M. J. Herz (Eds.), *Habituation: Behavioral studies and physiological substrates* (pp. 163–218). New York: Academic.

Graham, F. K. (1975). The more or less startling effects of weak prestimulation. *Psychophysiology, 12,* 238–248.

Graham, F. K. (1980). Control of reflex blink excitability. In R. F. Thompson, L. H. Hicks, & V. B. Shvyrkov (Eds.), *Neural mechanisms of goal-directed behavior and learning* (pp. 511–519). (Proceedings of the first Soviet-American Symposium, National Academy of Sciences.) New York: Academic Press.

Graham, F. K. (1987). Sokolov registered, model evicted. In P. K. Ackles, J. R. Jennings, & M. G. H. Coles (Eds.), *Advances in psychophysiology* (Vol. 2, pp. 207–227). Greenwich, CT: JAI.

Graham, F. K., Anthony, B. J., & Zeigler, B. L. (1983). The orienting response and developmental processes. In D. Siddle (Ed.), *Orienting and habituation: Perspectives in human reserach* (pp. 371–430). Sussex, England: Wiley.

Graham, F. K., Ernhart, C. B., Eichman, P. L., Marshall, J. M., & Thurston, D. (1963). Brain-injury in the preschool chold. II. Comparisons of brain-injured and normal children. *Psychological Monographs, 77,* 17–33.

Graham, F. K., & Jackson, J. C. (1970). Arousal systems and infant heart rate responses. In L. P. Lipsitt & H. W. Reese (Eds.), *Advances in child development and behavior* (Vol. 5, pp. 59–117). New York: Academic Press.

Graham, F. K., & Kendall, B. S. (1946). Performance of brain-damaged cases on a memory-for-designs test. *Journal of Abnormal and Social Psychology, 41,* 303–314.

Graham, F. K., & Kunish, N. O. (1965). Physiological responses of unhypnotized subjects to attitude suggestions. *Psychosomatic Medicine, 27,* 317–329.

Graham, F. K., & Murray, G. M. (1977). Discordant effects of weak prestimulation on magnitude and latency of the reflex blink. *Physiological Psychology, 5,* 108–114.

Graham, F. K., Putnam, L. E., & Leavitt, L. A. (1975). Lead stimulation effects on human cardiac orienting and blink reflexes. *Journal of Experimental Psychology: Human Perception and Performance, 1,* 161–169.

Graham, F. K., Strock, B. D., & Zeigler, B. L. (1981). Excitatory and inhibitory influences on reflex responsiveness. In W. A. Collins (Ed.), *Minnesota Symposium on child psychology: Vol. 14. Aspects of the development of competence* (pp. 1–38). Hillsdale, NJ: Lawrence Erlbaum Associates, Inc.

Hackley, S. A., & Graham, F. K (1983). Early selective attention effects on cutaneous and acoustic blink reflexes. *Physiological Psychology, 11,* 235–242.

Headrick, M. W., & Graham, F. K. (1969). Multiple component heart rate response conditioned under paced respiration. *Journal of Experimental Psychology, 79,* 486–494.

Jackson, J. C., Kantowitz, S. R., & Graham, F. K. (1971). Can newborns show cardiac orienting? *Child Development, 42,* 107–121.

Leavitt, L. A., Brown, J. W., Morse, P. A., & Graham, F. K. (1976). Cardiac orienting and auditory discrimination in 6-week-old infants. *Developmental Psychology, 12,* 514–523.

Putnam, L. E., Ross, L. E., & Graham, F. K. (1974). Cardiac orienting during "good" and "poor" differential eyelid conditioning. *Journal of Experimental Psychology, 102,* 563–573.

Silverstein, L. D., Graham, F. K., & Calloway, J. M. (1980). Preconditioning and excitablity of the human orbicularis oculi reflex as a function of state. *Electroencephalography and Clinical Neurophysiology, 48,* 406–417.

Weisbard, C., & Graham, F. K. (1971). Heart rate change as a component of the orienting response in monkeys. *Journal of Comparative and Physiological Psychology, 76,* 74–83.

CHAPTER 13

Janet Taylor Spence

Janet Taylor Spence

Shortly after I received my PhD, one of my mother's acquaintances chirped happily about this accomplishment: "Helen, I don't see how you hatched her!" The remark amused us all, and it became a frequently repeated family favorite. Her surprise, however, was quite misplaced.

As did her mother before her, my mother graduated (in 1916) from Vassar College. She then went on to Columbia University to earn a master's degree in economics and later to work (in some low capacity) in the office of the president of Columbia, Nicholas Murray Butler. She never admitted to having had any career ambitions, but graduate school and New York City were clearly more exciting than returning to her hometown of Toledo, Ohio, and her family was willing to indulge her. In New York, she met John C. Taylor, the man who was to become her husband.

My father, born and reared in Massachusetts, had left school and joined the Canadian Army when World War I broke out, drawn jointly, like many young men, by patriotism and the promise of adventure. (His parents came to the United States from England as young adults but retained strong ties to their families there and to relatives in Canada.) On one of othe few occasions I remember him talking about his army experiences overseas, he told amusing but revealing anecdotes about his self-appointed role as "guard house lawyer," trying to get his fellows out of trouble and narrowly avoiding getting himself into it. His military duties came to an end when he was seriously wounded. He met my mother in New York, where he was working as a reporter. My mother returned to Toledo, my father followed and started a manufacturing business, they married, and, in 1923, I was born. The family was complete with the birth of my sister in 1927.

This embrace of conventionality was not to last too long. Reflecting the concern with the underdog that first became evident in his army days, my father became interested in the writings of the British socialists and in the emerging Socialist Party in this country. During the 1930s, following the start of the Great Depression in 1929, my father became very active in the Socialist Party, running for governor at one point. He also gave up his business career and threw in his lot with the emerging labor movement, becoming the business manager of several labor unions associated with the American Federation of Labor. One of these was the local teacher's unions, which led to his election to the school board for several terms.

I have sometimes described the political atmosphere in my home during the 1930s as Republican-Socialist. The Republican half, represented by my mother, was much diluted by her sympathy for the problems of the economically deprived and belief in human rights; equally important, she found the U.S. and British Socialist leaders who came to dinner when they were in town charming and articulate; soon she too became politically involved. Hard economic times plus, she later confessed, boredom, led her to go to work, first as the executive secretary of the local League of Women Voters and subsequently as a manager of several local "good government" election campaigns. These led to her appointment by a reform-minded judge of the Court of Domestic Relations as head of a public social agency that was in the process of evolving into what is now Aid to Families and Dependent Children. For the first time, staff members were about to become civil service employees who were required to have social work credentials. My mother set about learning to administer a fair-size social service agency, putting together a professional staff, and earning a second master's degree, this time in social work.

As children and teenagers, my sister and I were fully exposed to all these activities, and in various ways we took part in them. But, although both of us remain interested and reasonably well-informed about politics and, I hope, sensitive to the kinds of social issues that concerned both my parents, neither of us became the kind of activists they were.

Perhaps it was due to my exposure to the human suffering so common during the Depression and my parents' concern with it that as a young adolescent I decided I wanted to become a psychologist. Prior to World War II, psychologists were few in number, and the general public knew little about the discipline. My ignorance was just as profound. All I knew was that psychology was "about people." And at that point, I had no ambitions about having a career. Life's scenario was clear: I would, as a matter of course, go to college; then after working a couple of years (presumably doing whatever it was that psychologists did), I would retire to marriage and motherhood to live, in the words of fairy tales, "happily ever after." Prescient I was not. Children were never to be, and my retirement is still in the future. (The former, but not the latter, is a matter of regret.)

In 1941 I entered Oberlin College eager to begin my study of psychology. My first disappointment was the discovery that first-year students were not permitted to take psychology courses, a common restriction at the time that disappeared after World War II. But there was more disappointment to come. The Oberlin Department of Psychology was behavioristic and experimental in orientation, whereas I expected humanism. Courses in experimental psychology left me particularly puzzled and discontented. Psychology was not my favorite subject (that was history), but still it was a psychologist I wanted to be. It was not until I took a course in history and systems in the second semester of my senior year that I began dimly to understand and appreciate the nature of psychology as a scientific discipline. The course was taught by Raymond L. Stetson, well known for his work in phonetics and an impressive scholar. Stetson, who had come out of retirement to teach, had studied with William James at Harvard at the turn of the century, and his firsthand familiarity with James and other pioneers in psychology made history come alive.

Stetson's recall from retirement was a consequence of World War II. Pearl Harbor and the entry of the United States into the war happened in the December of my first year; the Japanese surrender in August 1945 came after my graduation the previous June. As more and more faculty members (almost all of whom were male) were called into military service or went to work for war-related federal agencies, it became necessary to call upon retired professors to take their place. The exodus of male students to the military was even greater. One consequence was that during my senior year, I was appointed as the department assistant, a post that up to then had been held by a male graduate student. However, we did not become a predominantly female student body. At Oberlin, as at many colleges and universities, male civilians were replaced by military units composed of young men who were sent to college for a year or two before going to officer training schools or to specialized training programs. In some ways, day-to-day college life went on quite ordinarily, but the war was never far from our consciousness, if for no other reason than the casualty lists that so often contained the names of friends and relatives.

In the fall of 1945, I entered the graduate program at Yale University as a clinical student. Then as now, the Department of Psychology at Yale was a distinguished one, its most famous member at the time being Clark L. Hull, whose most influential book, *Principles of Behavior: An Introduction to Behavior Theory* (1943), had only recently been published. Until the late 1950s, the topic that dominated American psychology was learning, and Hull was one of the preeminent learning theorists of his era. His theories were attractive to a number of Yale faculty and graduate students, among them Kenneth W. Spence, who later bcame my husband. Their collaboration went on for many years after Spence left Yale, and his contributions were such that during its heyday, the theory became identified as Hull–Spence theory.

Hull's influence was not confined to experimental psychologists. A group of Yale faculty and students attempted in the 1930s and 1940s to integrate Hullian learning theory with other disciplines such as anthropology and psychoanalysis. Among the group were Neal Miller, whose specialty was then animal learning and motivation; the psychoanalytically oriented clinician, John Dollard; developmental psychologist Robert Sears; and anthropologist John W. M. Whiting. One of the most impressive and influential products of these efforts was the book *Personality and Psychotherapy: An Analysis in Terms of Learning, Thinking, and Culture* (Dollard & Miller, 1950).

Although I was to become caught up in these efforts to apply learning theory principles to clinically relevant phenomena, it was not at Yale. The war, which had just ended, had seriously disrupted the graduate program, and the war's effects were still very much in evidence. Faculty members such as Miller were still in uniform, and others such as Carl Hovland, chair of the department, were too busy in Washington, DC, to be able to attend to the program. Hull was not well and was likely to appear only to teach his seminar. (My exposure to Hull was confined to a single lecture he gave in a newly instituted, brutally demanding proseminar, which has continued to serve me as a model of how not to train graduate students.) At that time, clinical courses were few and as a first-year student, my only exposure was work with Catherine Cox Miles. This was largely confined to the Stanford–Binet Scale of Intelligence, developed by Lewis Terman of Stanford University with whom Miles has worked. One of their best known collaborations is their study of genius. Although I did not discover it until much later, she and Terman had also developed the first tests of masculinity–femininity, and she was the author of a chapter on "Sex in Social Psychology" in the 1935 *Handbook of Social Psychology* (Miles, 1935). The next chapter on gender in subsequent editions of the *Handbook* was not to appear until half a century later and was written by myself, Kay Deaux of Purdue University, and my Texas colleague, Robert Helmreich (Spence, Deaux, & Helmreich, 1985).

With its lack of an appealing curriculum and its nonsupportive atmosphere, the Yale of 1945–1946 was not for me. The entry-level degree for clinicians at that time was a master's degree plus internship. Not yet ready to face going elsewhere to pursue a doctorate, I applied, successfully, to the New York State Rotating Internship Training Program, one of the few internships in the country. Early in the fall, I learned from a friend at Yale that she had just been appointed to a well-organized (and well-paying) clinical training program the Veterans Administration had just instituted in a local (and probably newly opened) Veterans Administration hospital. This was part of a massive national program, as it turned out, aimed at stimulating graduate schools to develop clinical faculties and helping to train the large number of graduate clinical and counseling psychologists who were needed to attend to the needs of the returning veterans. (It was the Veterans Administration that required the doctorate for its professional staff, a standard that was soon adopted by others.) This accident of timing would have been bad luck for me had I not made the crucial discovery in the course of my internship year that my interests lay not in clinical practice but in the puzzles that human behavior presented.

The psychology staff at two of the three insitutions at which I served in the New York State Rotating Program consisted of a single master's-level person, but at Letchworth Village, a state school for the retarded, the two-person staff was headed by Thomas McCullough, a Yale PhD in experimental psychology. I leaned much from McCullough about how to observe and how to ask questions that needed answering. It was McCullough who suggested that I would enjoy studying with his fellow student at Yale, Kenneth Spence and that I should apply to the University of Iowa for my PhD. It was excellent advice.

In the 1940s, psychologists and philosophers of science actively collaborated to establish the epistemological foundations of psychology. One of these partnerships was between Spence and the philosopher Gustav Bergmann, who was also at Iowa (e.g., Bergmann & K. W. Spence, 1941). In Spence's course on learning, which I took during my first semester at Iowa, we were first introduced to some of these philosophical writings. They came as something of a revelation, giving me for the first time a firm, coherent sense of psychology as a discipline. And like others before me, I felt the pull of the potential integrating power of Hull–Spence learning theory.

The Yale–Iowa connection was not limited to Spence. Judson Brown, who had been a student of Neal Miller, was on the faculty. Robert Sears and John Whiting were at the Child Welfare Research Station, a graduate program in child development that was administratively separate from the Department of Psychology but housed in the same building and with strong links to it. Under the leadership of I. E. Farber, the department made it possible for students to emphasize clinical research rather than practice, and this was the direction I chose to follow.

Whereas some, like Dollard and Miller, elected to analyze real-life, clinically relevant phenomena in terms of behavioral principles discovered in the laboratory, I attempted to bring clinically relevant phenomena into the laboratory. Anxiety was a pivotal concept in psychodynamic theories. In my dissertation, supervised by Spence and conducted in his laboratory, I elected to investigate whether one of the components of anxiety as a dispositional characteristic was "drive" (the "energetic" component of the Hullian motivational complex). Quite simply, I investigated whether chronically anxious individuals would classically condition more rapidly than less anxious individuals. As it turned out, they did (Taylor, 1951), but before I could do the study, I had to find a way to assess anxiety as a personality characteristic. As I could not find a satisfactory self-report instrument, I devised one, which I titled the Manifest Anxiety Scale.

The oral examination at which I defended my dissertation had an important outcome. A fellow student who was doing a study with the Manifest Anxiety Scale and a different type of learning task was finding that highly anxious individuals performed worse than individuals who were not very anxious. Expecting questions about the discrepancy between my findings and his, I went into my oral examination with a half-formed theory about the conditions under which anxiety or drive level would either facilitate or interfere with performance. With the help of some judicious questions from Kenneth, I came out with a fully formed "drive theory" that would be the major subject of my research for the next decade (e.g., Taylor,

1956). The same zeitgeist that had led me to this work on anxiety made it attractive to others, and for some years, the literature was full of studies related to manifest anxiety and drive theory. The Manifest Anxiety Scale also turned out to be a popular success. In fact, the article (Taylor, 1953) in which I described the scale is one of the most highly cited in the psychological literature. By now, however, the Manifest Anxiety Scale has been largely replaced by other, more systematically devised instruments, the development of which it helped to stimulate.

After getting my PhD, I joined the psychology faculty at Northwestern University. The relatively small size of psychology faculties and the commensurately small number of new PhDs who graduated each year made recruiting in those days a rather casual affair. The chair of the Northwestern department, Robert Seashore, was visiting his family in Iowa City (his father, a well-known psychologist, had been the dean of liberal arts at Iowa for many years before his retirement) and dropped by the department to see who might be available for an opening at Northwestern. My name was on the list of new PhDs, and Seashore (he later told me) allowed as how having a woman on the faculty was a novel and interesting idea. I was invited for an interview and shortly thereafter was offered the job. Happily, I did not learn until much later that some members had been strongly opposed to having a woman as a colleague. To their credit, however, everyone behaved well once the deed was done. Early on I did observe a certain amount of testing: Was I to be the department playgirl, one of the boys, or the prim, disapproving schoolteacher who blanched at swear words and dirty jokes? But soon they settled down to accepting me simply as a colleague who happened to be female, and I became a full-fledged member of a warm, closely knit department. Promotion, however, was slow.

One profitable collaboration in which I engaged while at Northwestern was the writing of an introductory statistics text, co-authored with the experimentalists Benton Underwood and Carl Duncan and with John Cotton, the statistician of the crew (Underwood, Duncan, Taylor, & Cotton, 1954). In my first year there, I had been assigned the undergraduate statistics course, and much to my surprise, I enjoyed teaching it so much that I have done so voluntarily ever since. I also took over the major responsibility for subsequent revisions, along with Cotton (who is now at the University of California at Santa Barbara). The fourth edition was published several years ago (Spence, Cotton, Underwood, & Duncan, 1982), and the fifth is currently underway.

The Northwestern years came to an end in 1960 when, after marrying Kenneth Spence, I moved back to Iowa City. Nepotism rules prevented my appointment in the Department of Psychology there, so I went to work as a research psychologist at the Iowa City Veterans Administration Hospital. I missed teaching and working with students, but the psychology trainees were quite tolerant in listening to me talk on and on about the work I was doing. I was also able to collaborate in research with faculty members in the department, including, in addition to my husband, Leonard Goodstein, who is curently the Executive Officer of the American Psychological Association (APA), and Rudolph Schulz, now dean of the Graduate School at Iowa.

While at Northwestern, I had developed an interest in schizophrenia and motivational theories about the disorder. However, except by working with graduate students on their master's theses and doctoral dissertations, I had not had the opportunity to engage in research in this area. Being on the staff of a VA hospital and having access to psychiatric patients in other nearby VA hospitals gave me that chance. Typically, the design of these studies involved determining whether various kinds of performance feedback or reinforcers had differential effects on the performance of schizophrenics and nonschizophrenics. I began to recognize that the reinforcers had far more complex properties than had been assumed, which made the implications of the results for hypotheses about schizophrenia difficult to determine. I therefore started to try to understand the effects of the experimental manipulations themselves. This pursuit, however, was disrupted when we moved to Texas.

During the early 1960s, colleges and universities expanded rapidly as the flood of babies born immediately after World War II began to reach college age. The country was economically prosperous, and the federal government, spurred on by competitiveness with the Soviet Union, was pouring large sums into the support of undergraduate and graduate education and scientific research. One of the institutions that was making a great leap forward was the University of Texas at Austin, and the Department of Psychology was one of the departments into which heavy resources were to be poured. In 1964, Gardner Lindzey, then at the University of Minnesota, accepted the department chairmanship and persuaded Kenneth to move to Texas with him. In the next few years, other major senior appointments and many junior appointments followed.

As an aside, the temperature when we moved to Austin in mid-August was as usual in the 90s. Although air-conditioning was everywhere, my husband very shortly announced that we would not be spending much of our summers in Texas. I was delighted. Like many men devoted to their professions, Kenneth had always been reluctant to take more than brief vacations, although we did spend a couple weeks each year at my family's summer place on Cape Cod. Although I have always had more than a dash of workaholism as well, I believe firmly in the benefits of the lengthy, largely nonworking summer vacations that academic schedules permit to rejuvenate one's energy and enthusiasm. Texas heat created a new believer, and from then on, Cape Cod saw more of us. And still does of me.

At Texas, nepotism rules again prevented me from becoming a member of the Department of Psychology. I was given a research associate appointment and was stationed at the Austin State School, an institution for the retarded. Then, after a year, I was appointed to the faculty of the Department of Educational Psychology in the College of Education at the University.

While at the State School, I discovered that some of the same questions about the functions and effects of reinforcers I had begun to study in Iowa City also cropped up in the developmental literature. I therefore continued pursuing these problems, but with a change to retarded and normal children as subjects. After moving to the Department of Educational Psychology, it seemed appropriate to keep on with this line of research, as one of my teaching assignments was a course in child development.

Unfortunately, the decade that had started so brightly did not end well. A few months after having been diagnosed as having cancer, my husband died. As I was struggling to adjust to my loss, the country was beginning to be torn apart by the war in Vietnam. The high tide of growth and federal support of higher education had been reached and was starting to ebb.

Within the university, Lindzey (who is presently director of the Center for Advanced Studies in the Behavioral Sciences in Palo Alto, California) moved up the administrative ladder to become academic vice-president, and I moved to the Department of Psychology to take his place as chair. The position, which I held for 4 years, was demanding and time-consuming, not calculated to stimulate one's research career. I began to run out of intellectual steam, and, with the emergence of cognitive theories inspired by computer models, so too did the learning theory approach to many phenomena that had been so popular in American psychology.

I began a second, quite different research career almost by happenstance. I was reading about a study of interpersonal attraction by my colleagues Robert Helmreich and Elliot Aronson (Helmreich,

Aronson, & LeFan, 1970) in which they demonstrated, among other things, that their college student subjects found a competent, academically successful target figure more likable than an incompetent one. Doubtless sensitized by the women's movement that was beginning to emerge, it struck me that their target figures were men doing stereotypically masculine things. What about competent women, I asked myself? Would they be as well-liked as less competent women, particularly if their academic and extracurricular interests were in areas dominated by men? Next day, I proposed to Helmreich that it might be fun to find out. As we thought about the question, it grew more complex, and we decided that it would be important to include in our increasingly elaborate design a measure of our subjects' attitudes toward men's and women's roles. Unable to find an appropriate instrument of recent vintage, we devised one. The result was the Attitudes Toward Women Scale (Spence & Helmreich, 1972b), an instrument that many investigators have also found to be useful. Our experimental study (Spence & Helmreich, 1972a) had an unexpected outcome: Even our conservative subjects not only preferred more competent to less competent women but rated highest the woman who was competent in stereotypically masculine areas. That counterintuitive outcome intrigued me and led to further studies that in turn stimulated still more. I had stumbled into a new and highly fascinating area of research.

One of these studies led to the development of another self-report instrument, the Personal Attributes Questionnaire (Spence, Helmreich, & Stapp, 1975), a measure of instrumental and expressive personality characteristics that many theorists have implied constitute the core of masculinity and femininity. Research initially stimulated by this instrument and the theories to which it has been related has led us in a number of theoretical and empirical directions, such as the development of a novel theory of gender identity (Spence, 1985), the study of achievement motives and of sex differences in achievement (Spence & Helmreich, 1983), and, most recently, investigations of the personality factors related to physical aggression in dating couples. Although these studies are in many ways radically different from my earlier research, they continue to reflect my abiding interest in personality characteristics and in the motivational wellsprings of behavior. They also reveal what seems to be a penchant for developing assessment instruments, first exhibited when I put together the Manifest Anxiety Scale for my dissertation.

At the same time that gender-relevant topics were becoming the subject of my research (and, simultaneously, of many other social and behavioral scientists), I began to receive invitations to give talks at other universities so that I could "serve as a role model" for their women students. The implication, I think unintended, was that whether one had something worth listening to was relatively unimportant; it was enough to be a woman. It seemed only fair that in return I should talk about gender research, although at first, my hosts seemed taken aback. Happily, this kind of invitation soon disappeared, and I am now asked to speak about this gender research.

For the same reasons, I also began to receive a rash of invitations to become a member of various kinds of committees and boards. At first, like other women in the same position, I felt obligated to accept commitments that I might otherwise have refused when it looked as though acceptance might break new ground and make it easier for women to participate in these professional activities in the future.

Editorial duties were also making my life busier. Lindzey became editor of *Contemporary Psychology*, the book review journal published by APA, and I agreed to become his associate editor. Subsequently I succeeded Lindzey as editor, serving from 1974 to 1979. My first involvement in the governmental affairs of APA came in 1970, with my election to the Board of Scientific Affairs. Since that time, I have continuously served APA in various capacities, including a 3-year term as a member of the APA Board of Directors (1976 to 1978). In 1984, I was President of APA, an office that meant a second term on the board as president-elect, president, and past-president.

APA is unusual in having had two women as presidents in its early years, Mary Calkins in 1905 and Margaret Floyd Washburn in 1921. A long hiatus followed, but in modern, postfeminist times, there have been five women presidents: Anne Anastasi, Florence L. Denmark, Leona E. Tyler, Bonnie R. Strickland, and myself; all are represented in this volume!

At one time, when APA was small, and its function little more than to foster scientific communication by publishing journals and holding conventions, the presidency was largely honorific. Now, with over 70,000 members APA provides a wide array of services to the profession and to the public, and the presidental office comes close to demanding all one's time and energies. The experience is still too recent for me to summarize it succinctly. I can only comment, as at least some of my predecessors have, that I wouldn't have missed it for the world, but I was glad when it was over!

In this brief account of a career, I have tried to put my own activities into context by conveying some sense of place, time, and people. Many other individuals—mentors, colleagues, collaborators—from whom I profited were undeservedly left unmentioned because there was no room in my allotted space. The narrative form also made it difficult to say much about graduate students. In this final commentary, I seize the opportunity to acknowledge them collectively. Sharing my ideas with students, helping them to shape their own, engaging in the intellectual give-and-take inside and outside the classroom—have all contributed to my own thinking and provided other benefits. The debt between student and teacher often goes in both directions.

REFERENCES

Bergmann, G., & Spence, K. W. (1941). Operationism and theory in psychology. *Psychological Review, 48,* 1–14.

Dollard, J., & Miller, N. E. (1950). *Personality and psychotherapy: An analysis in terms of learning, thinking, and culture.* New York: McGraw-Hill.

Helmreich, R. L., Aronson, E., & LeFan, J. (1970). To err is humanizing—sometimes: Effects of self-esteem, competence and a pratfall on interpersonal attraction. *Journal of Personality and Social Psychology, 16,* 259–264.

Hull, C. L. (1943). *Principles of behavior: An introduction to behavior theory.* New York: Appleton–Century–Crofts.

Miles, C. C. (1935). Sex in social psychology. In C. Murchison (Ed.) *Handbook of social Psychology* (pp. 106–131). Worcester, MA: Clark University Press.

Spence, J. T. (1985). Gender identification and its implications for masculinity and femininity. In T. B. Sonderegger (Ed.), *Nebraska Symposium on Motivation and Achievement: Vol. 32. Psychology and Gender* (pp. 59–95). Lincoln: University of Nebraska Press.

Spence, J. T., Cotton, J. W., Underwood, B. J., & Duncan, C. P. (1982). *Elementary statistics* (4th ed.). Englewood Cliifs, NJ: Prentice-Hall.

Spence, J. T., Deaux, K., & Helmreich, R. L. (1985). Sex roles in contemporary American society. In G. Lindzey & E. Aronson (Eds.), *Handbook of social psychology* (3rd ed., pp. 149–178). Reading, MA: Addison-Wesley.

Spence, J. T., & Helmreich, R. L. (1972a). The Attitudes Toward Women Scale: An objective instrument to measure attitudes toward the rights and roles of women in contemporary society. *JSAS Catalog of Selected Documents in Psychology, 2,* 197–213.

Spence, J. T., & Helmreich, R. L. (1972b). Who likes competent women? Competence, sex-role congruence of interest, and subjects' attitudes toward women as determinants of interpersonal attraction. *Journal of Applied Social Psychology, 2,* 197–213.

Spence, J. T., & Helmreich, R. L. (1983). Achievement-related motives and behavior. In J. T. Spence (Ed.), *Achievement and achievement motives: Psychological and sociological approaches* (pp. 10–74). San Francisco: Freeman.

Spence, J. T., Helmreich, R. L., & Stapp, J. (1975). Ratings of self and peers on sex-role attributes and their relations to self-esteem and conceptions of masculinity and femininity. *Journal of Personality and Social Psychology, 32*, 29–39.

Taylor, J. A. (1951). The relationship of anxiety to the conditioned eyelid response. *Journal of Experimental Psychology, 41*, 81–92.

Taylor, J. A. (1953). A personality scale of manifest anxiety. *Journal of Abnormal and Social Psychology, 48*, 285–290.

Taylor, J. A. (1956). Drive theory and manifest anxiety. *Psychological Bulletin, 53*, 303–320.

Underwood, B. J., Duncan, C. P., Taylor, J. T., & Cotton, J. W. (1954). *Elementary statistics*. New York: Appleton-Century-Crofts.

REPRESENTATIVE PUBLICATIONS

Helmreich, R. L., Spence, J. T., Beane, W. E., Lucker, G. W., & Matthews, K. A. (1980). Making it in academic psychology: Demographic and personality correlates of attainment. *Journal of Personality and Social Psychology, 39*, 896–908.

Siem, F. L., & Spence, J. T. (1986). Gender-related traits and helping behaviors. *Journal of Personality and Social Psychology, 51*, 615–621.

Spence, J. T. (1964). Verbal discrimination performance under different verbal reinforcement combinations. *Journal of Experimental Psychology, 67*, 195–197.

Spence, J. T. (1970). The distracting effects of material reinforcers in the discrimination learning of lower- and middle-class children. *Child Development, 85*, 321–329.

Spence, J. T. (1970). Verbal reinforcement combinations and concept-identification learning: The role of nonreinforcement. *Journal of Experimental Psychology, 3*, 321–329.

Spence, J. T. (1985). Achievement American style: The rewards and costs of individualism. *American Psychologist, 40*, 1285–1295.

Spence, J. T., & Helmreich, R. L. (1978). *Masculinity and femininity: Their psychological dimensions, correlates and antecedents*. Austin: University of Texas Press.

Spence, J. T., Helmreich, R. L. (1980). Masculine instrumentality and feminine expressiveness: Their relationships with sex-role attitudes and behaviors. *Journal of Women Quarterly, 5*, 147–163.

Spence, J. T., Helmreich, R. L., & Pred, R. S. (1987). Impatience versus achievement strivings in the Type A pattern: Differential effects on students' health and academic achievement. *Journal of Applied Psychology, 72*, 340–346.

Spence, J. T., Lair, D. V., & Goodstein, L. D. (1963). Effects on different feedback conditions on verbal discrimination in schizophrenic and non-psychiatric subjects. *Journal of Verbal Learning and Verbal Behavior, 2*, 339–345.

Spence, J. T., & Spence, K. W. (1966). The motivational components of manifest anxiety: Drive and drive stimuli. In C. Spielberger (Ed.), *Anxiety and behavior* (pp. 291–326). Academic Press.

Taylor, J. A., & Spence, K. W. (1952). The relationship of anxiety level to performance in serial learning. *Journal of Experimental Psychology, 44*, 61–64.

CHAPTER 14

Dorothy Hansen Eichorn

Dorothy Hansen Eichorn

My recollections of childhood are of feeling highly valued; I suspect I was indulged. At my birth on November 18, 1924, Mother was 38, Father was 48, and they had been married over 13 years. My only living grandparent, my maternal grandmother, had recently moved to my parents' house. She was in ill health and died within a year. Mother's niece Helen, almost 14, was the other family member. Her mother died when Helen was 7, and my parents reared her from that time as their daughter. She was strongly attached to me and often took me along on her activities. With my arrival, a nursemaid was added to the household because Mother was manager of what for that day was a supermarket. It was part of a chain headquartered in Boston, and Mother made frequent trips there to attend meetings.

Upon the birth of my sister Laurel, March 1, 1926, Mother resigned. The officers of the company pleaded with her to stay, saying, "Line the shelves with babies, just come back after every one." However, except for occasional part-time work after Father's death in 1936, Mother was a housewife, and a patently contented one, until Laurel's last year in high school. How she came to a managerial position I do not know. She, two sisters, and two brothers were reared on a rather isolated hill farm in Berlin, Vermont. Girls fixed fences as well as food for the family and animals. Mother became an accomplished horsewoman early, driving buggies and work teams and riding both bareback and with saddle. Attendance at the town grammar school a good many miles away required real effort. Transport was by horse and "shanks mare," and the roads were unpaved and full of mud, snow, or ice much of the year. After eighth grade, Mother was tutored in commercial subjects by a family friend; Berlin had no high school. In 1910, a decade after Mother would have entered, only 15% of the U.S. population 14 to 17 years old was enrolled in secondary school. The proportion was undoubtedly less in rural areas.

Mother's first husband was an aspiring inventor who failed to earn an adequate living. She soon divorced him and supported herself and their son until she married my father. What jobs she held and whether she worked continuously after remarriage I do not know. This son was already at sea when I was born and died in a naval hospital when I was a child.

Father's parents and five older brothers were born in Denmark. They emigrated because Grandfather objected to the requirement that citizens register with the police whenever they moved. Father grew up in Troy, New York, and was graduated from the public schools there. He became an accountant for Swift meat packers and was transferred to Montpelier, Vermont, where he met Mother. Later he worked in the Vermont state offices, I believe as an auditor. By my birth, he was in the Mortgage and Loan Department of the National Life Insurance Company, which has its home office in Montpelier, and remained there to his death.

In addition to National Life (one of the oldest and largest life insurance companies in the nation), several other insurance companies, a number of banks, a printing firm, a few small factories, two hotels, many small businesses, and, of course, city, county, and state offices were included in Montpelier's economic base. My grade school and high school days coincided with the decade of the Great Depression, for I entered kindergarten in 1929, the year of the stock market crash, and, having skipped fourth grade, began my senior year in 1940, the last year of general depression. For Montpelier and many other areas of Vermont, economic disaster had already occurred. On November 3, 1927, the worst flood in the state's history rose suddenly, trapped people in their homes, and did over $100 million of damage (in the value of the time). Vermont refused federal aid, floated a bond issue, and set about cleaning and replacing.

Although we and many other families lost in bank failures any savings remaining after flood repairs, the effects of the Depression were muted by National's Life's policy of cutting wages by 50% but retaining essentially all its work force. Given a 30% decline in the cost of living and mother's Vermont-style skills in "making do," we children never felt deprived. Then just before Laurel began sixth grade and I the eighth, father died. Our only funds were the life insurance our parents managed to carry despite their Depression-reduced income. By renting one bedroom, selling Vermont woodcraft in our home, and working part-time occasionally, mother stretched the insurance until Laurel finished high school. Laurel and I did baby-sitting and odd jobs such as walking neighbors' dogs. After high school graduation, Helen worked as an accountant. She married an army officer in 1934 and moved from post to post. She gave us "luxuries" we might otherwise not have had.

Montpelier's population of 8,000 was spread over a wide area of hills and valleys, for most people lived in single-family houses with lawns and gardens. The city park was like a state forest, with hundreds of acres in which we hiked, climbed trees, watched birds, found wildflowers, skied, tobogganed, and snowshoed. We also hiked and biked the many roads leading from town into the countryside. Violence, particularly against children, was virtually unknown, so parents had few qualms about our going wherever our physical capabilities allowed. Soon after I could walk, I acquired a reputation for a wanderlust that prompted me to elude any humane restraints by untying knots and climbing fences. I was not running away. I simply had many places I wanted to go and intended to return before dark. But I was constantly being returned from far across town by mail carriers or older children. This result probably reinforced my behavior (I was never punished) and gave me confidence to journey forth in complete trust that the world would treat me well.

Except in the adult workplace, sex and, to a considerable extent, age distinctions were blurred. Girls and boys played together at school and in the neighborhood. For situations requiring many players, such as neighborhood games of touch football, the age range had to stretch. With the provision that I not cry, the two older boys next door let me join their activities and gave me free rein with their Lincoln Logs and erector sets. Fathers and mothers fished, golfed, rode, skied and swam, depending on their personal inclinations. Fathers (at least the ones I knew) did a lot of the child care and some cooking and housework. Mothers as well as fathers gardened, shoveled sidewalks, and put up storm windows. Although we addressed all adults outside the family as Mr. and Mrs., as adolescents we worked with them in community theater, band, church committees and suppers, and civic activities and competed with them in golf and tennis tournaments. Children often performed for civic, church, and fraternal organizations, visited their fathers' workplaces, and played around the statehouse and in the legislature's chambers when sessions were over. When the legislature was in session, we were welcome in the gallery. From there we saw some women, for Vermont has elected more women and fewer lawyers to its legislature than any other state.

Many other women were employed, but they were single, widowed, or had invalid husbands because the policy during the Depression was one income per family. The net effect was to save jobs for women who needed them, because in Montpelier women were in "traditional" occupations (e.g., nurse, teacher, bookkeeper), except for a few who owned or co-owned businesses. However, the feats of Amelia Earhart, Helen Wills, and "Babe" Didrickson were constantly in the news, and in children's books the bravery and accomplishments of Vermont's pioneer women were prominent. Women's opinions on family and public issues seemed respected equally with men's. Until I left Vermont, I never heard anyone say women were less intelligent than men or that boys should have preference for college in hard times.

Although neither of us knew where the money would come from, mother and I assumed I would go to college, so I took the college preparatory curriculum—Latin, French, chemistry, physics, math. The teacher and I were the only females in solid geometry and trigonometry, but no one remarked on this. Schoolwork had always been easy for me, except for music, in which I had absolutely no talent, so I had time to participate in many extracurricular and community activities. A boy and I were the first-string debating team, representing the school in competitions throughout the state. Girls' sports were intramural, but I was elected a cheerleader and accompanied the boys' teams around the state. Only a girl was elected secretary, but all other offices in classes and organizations were shared about equally, and I held most at one time or another.

My grades earned me a full-tuition scholarship to the local junior college, which I entered in September 1941. The previous summer I had had my first "adult" job in the office of the local newspaper, edited by a relatively young daughter of the owner, who had retired. During the college year, I was part-time secretary to the adjutant of the Vermont National Guard. At college I took mainly Spanish, political science, and economics, with shorthand as an "extra." In high school, I had 2 years of typing. These skills proved repeatedly useful, both in coursework and in supporting my education. Soon after the attack on Pearl Harbor, clerical skills were in high demand and short supply. In 1942, two college chums and I got summer jobs in Washington, DC. They returned to college in the fall, but

I had had three promotions and had become secretary to the associate director for personnel of a wartime agency. Living in a city on my own for the first time with money for clothes and travel and a supply of young officers was too tempting to a 17-year-old; I stayed.

About a year later I began to have doubts about the intellectual and economic prospects of being a "party girl" and decided to go back to school. Mother had recently become matron of the student hospital at Norwich University, which included during the war a U.S. Air Force Training Detachment (AFTD). When I arrived there I sensed that the improved financial situation was counterbalanced by the fact that Laurel had enrolled at the University of Vermont. Despite its title, this was a private university, not a state-supported one, and tuition had always been high. Laurel's only earnings would be from waitressing at the university. I became secretary to the commanding officer of the AFTD and worked just long enough to accumulate a minimal nest egg. In the summer of 1944, I entered the university as a sophomore. I, too, became a waitress.

Entertaining notions of going into the diplomatic corps in South America, I enrolled for second-year Spanish and planned a political science major. But two other courses proved to be turning points. The university required a laboratory science of all first-year students. Because of a lifelong aversion to gore and guts, I had avoided zoology, the only such course at junior college. Laurel advised against geology (she had barely passed); one roommate, a civil engineering major, advised against chemistry and physics. The other roommate, a premed, recommended zoology, so I enrolled. I also took Psychology 1 with John Metcalf, chair of the department. His lectures were scholarly, carefully marshaling the research evidence. The course had no laboratory but did incorporate minor experiments and participatory demonstrations. This was my first experience in which the research leading to the material being taught was emphasized. I always enjoyed learning simply for knowledge, but this subject piqued my curiosity in a different way. Metcalf and his wife, Ruth Clark, who also held a PhD in psychology, invited his A and B students to their home for buffet suppers and stimulating discussions. I earned an A + and Metcalf's encouragement to major in psychology.

Zoology was less tranquil, but the result was similar. With all men except the physically unfit off at war, most classes were predominantly female. Our first task in lab was to catch a frog from the tank and pith it. Almost universal shrieking resulted. I found such behavior more repugnant than the task, so I caught and pithed not only my own frog but those of most of the class. That a small wire properly placed could immediately still those twitchy animals aroused my curiosity about physiological processes and the physiological basis of behavior. Biological sciences became my minor and a lifelong interest.

One more event intervened before I changed majors. Several of the liveliest women on campus returned from Mexico full of tales about a fascinatingly different culture. I wrote the senora at whose home they stayed to request a room and set out by bus for Mexico City for the fall semester. The University of Mexico was on vacation, so I took Spanish at the workers' university, read widely in Mexican history and literature, and traveled around the country. My interest in human behavior broadened. When I returned to the University of Vermont in January 1945, I became a psychology major.

Metcalf assumed a mentor role, advising me not only on my major, but also on other courses and recreational reading. He urged me to take only the minimum hours required for the major and to devote other time to getting a broad background. He also invited me to do a senior honors thesis. Because memory and perception interested me most, he suggested that I read Bartlett's (1932) *Remembering: A Study in Experimental and Social Psychology*. My thesis experiment on delayed recall of nonrepresentative designs was an extension of research reported in that book. The courses I enjoyed most were the experimental psychology laboratory, Shakespeare, and genetics. Paul Moody, chair of zoology, taught by accident a lesson I appreciated later. Concentrating on the principle he was trying to convey, he often made arithmetic mistakes in genetic ratios but was completely unembarrassed. This was a reassuring memory when I began to teach.

The summer after my sophomore year, Laurel, two friends, and I worked in the Children's Unit at Rockland State Hospital in New York. While there, we attended some lectures in child psychology and psychiatry given by several psychiatrists and by Elaine Kinder, professor at Columbia, whom I also assisted with a research project. During school terms, my jobs included grading exams for Psychology 1, testing in a children's clinic, washing bottles in botany lab, and typing for Metcalf and other professors.

My summer job before my senior year had long-term effects. The Vermont Church Council sponsored a program in rural areas without ministers. Students were given brief, intensive training and then did 2-week stints in a series of communities. At each, we ran a church school weekday mornings and conducted service on Sunday. I learned about the openings from the university chaplain, who was adviser for the campus YWCA, of which I was president. Faculty included Dorothy Spoerl, professor of psychology at American University, who authored many of the children's materials for the Unitarian church, and two women with seminary degrees who were ordained ministers with churches in Vermont. Through Spoerl's lectures on cognitive and emotional development, I got my first inkling that some interesting research questions were developmental.

Early one morning in 1946, I arrived to prepare the school that was to house my program and found a young man already at work. A seminarian from Yale Divinity School, he was spending his second summer as a student minister in the adjacent town, suspected the school needed cleaning, and came to help. His name was Herman Eichorn; I called him Ike. He visited a few times during the next two weeks.

Throughout my senior year, I worked part-time in the council office, mainly on correspondence and scheduling. In the fall, Mother was found to have inoperable cancer and was hospitalized in Montpelier. Helen and her school-age son lived near Buffalo, New York; her husband was stationed in the Philippines. Laurel had married a returning veteran at the university, was graduated, had a job as a social worker, and was now pregnant. Neither sister was able to travel to Montpelier frequently, so late each afternoon I made the trip by train to see mother and returned on the night train. Women had to "sign in" by a certain hour and had limited "nights out"; the dean of women waived these rules for me.

Before Christmas, Ike, who had transferred to Union Theological Seminary for his last year, wrote to say he was visiting the council during the holiday and asked for a date. The fellow to whom I was "pinned" was going home for the vacation, so I said yes. After dinner and a movie, we returned to Laurel and Fred's house. About an hour later Ike proposed. I said I didn't want to marry because I was going to graduate school. He asked why I couldn't do both. After considering this alternative for an hour or so, I said yes. Heretofore I had managed to avoid, or at least escape from, entangling alliances. More startling to me than the precipitous engagement was my feeling that I would not behave in such a fashion before our June wedding date.

Despite a mild epidemic of marriages on campus and the fact that my three roommates were to be married after graduation, I had felt no pressure to marry. Our joking rationale for marriages at graduation was that we couldn't get organized in the morning without a roommate. I enjoyed dating, had a number of "steadies" of whom

I was fond, and assumed I probably would one day marry. I simply hadn't wanted to be fettered by having to make joint decisions.

In mid-January 1947, Mother died, and in late February, Laurel delivered. I settled Mother's business affairs. Many Friday afternoons as I sat in Metcalf's office for my thesis conference, I listened to hear if the planes were flying, because Ike and I took turns "weekending" in Burlington or New York. The severity of Vermont winters and the relatively primitive state of commercial flying made winter flights undependable. We were discussing our next steps, because each of us was about out of money. Ike's family could afford to support him, but they were Amish Mennonites—opposed to education beyond the eighth grade because it was "worldly." His father disowned him when he insisted on attending high school and college. Ike also had a war-occasioned "time-out." Their farm near Buffalo was considered essential employment, so when his father became seriously ill, Ike returned to manage the dairy. The ironic outcome was that he was able to save money for college and seminary.

The parish where Ike was a student minister offered him a full-time job that was to begin in 1947 after we were both graduated and married, and the American Board of Foreign Missions approached him about an overseas assignment. He had transferred to Union in the fall of 1946 after 2 years at Yale to take clinical pastoral training at Bellevue (a mental hospital). He wanted the additional 2 years of training required to be an accredited chaplain with his own training program. We decided to go to the parish, accumulate savings, and explore locations that would permit us to continue our educations together.

In June 1947, I was graduated *cum laude,* with honors in psychology. Ike was graduated about the same time. We then married and moved to the country. Laurel and I had rented our family home; in 1948 I had a chance to sell it, and Ike's father's estate had finally been settled. Ike's father had died intestate, and his having had a wife and 17 children, most of whom were married and had children, prolonged the legal machinations. By this time we knew that we could not survive another year in any parish. We genuinely liked the people, but were intellectually frustrated. If supplemented, our small inheritances were enough to see us through graduate work.

Few places had accredited clinical pastoral programs, whereas my possibilities for suitable graduate schools were more numerous. Ike was accepted for graduate study at Harvard Divinity School, with clinical training available through the nearby Episcopalian seminary. I was rejected by the Psychology Department at Harvard. A lengthy letter from Edwin Newman explained that my undergraduate record equaled or exceeded that of any applicant, but in their experience, women, particularly married women, dropped out of graduate school or later dropped out of the profession. The faculty could not afford to waste their time or the few openings they had. Years later Eddie and I became friends through activities of the American Psychological Association (APA). He nominated me for several roles, including, without my knowledge, president of a prestigious college. I never mentioned his rejection letter. I'm quite sure he had forgotten it.

I was admitted to summer school at Harvard and also got a part-time job testing at the Veterans Center there. I took advanced German, math, and History and Systems of Psychology. The latter was taught by Harry Helson, a well-known professor who was visiting. At the end of the course, he returned the customary postcard with an A and a complimentary note. No professor had added this touch in my undergraduate days. I resolved to use Helson's system if I had occasion to teach (research was my aim, not teaching).

I had also applied to Boston University for the 1948–1949 academic year and was promptly accepted. First semester I enrolled in advanced statistics, assuming the course I had at the University of Vermont met the prerequisite. I soon learned otherwise. The course was taught by John Alman, a statistician who headed the Boston University computing center. Fortunately, he spent much time in class deriving formulae, which only one man and I could follow. As had Moody at the University of Vermont, Alman sometimes got wound up in the long trail around the blackboard and made errors. I would shake my head gently. He would look at me and ask, "What's the problem?" I would point at the error, and he would correct it. These exchanges had two useful outcomes. First, I admitted my deficiencies in statistics and got references and help in correcting them. Second, I became his assistant for the second semester.

The other two courses I enjoyed were physiological psychology, which coalesced my interests in experimental psychology and zoology, and a seminar in experimental psychology taught by Ward Edwards, then a graduate student at Harvard. His fiancée, another graduate student at Harvard, was Skinner's assistant. She later dropped out, reinforcing the faculty's assertions. Ward was also a helpful adviser. I wanted a place with more opportunities in physiological psychology. Ward recommended Northwestern University due to the exciting work being done by Donald Lindsley on the reticular activating system. Two other places he suggested—the University of Chicago and the University of Rochester—also fit Ike's possible locations. The application form for Chicago was too lengthy; I discarded it. Rochester offered me a fellowship, and Northwestern offered a teaching assistantship. Then the clinical pastoral program at Rochester ended. Ike's alternative was the Training School for Boys at St. Charles, Illinois, so mine became Northwestern.

In June 1949, Ike received his STM and I received my MA. Before going to Illinois, we spent the summer at New Hampshire State Hospital, where Ike was in the clinical pastoral training program and I worked as a clinical psychologist.

Our living arrangements in Illinois were a bit unusual. Ike shared a room on the reformatory grounds; I had a room in a home in Evanston. We exchanged weekends, depending on his room mate's schedule. The next year we found an apartment in Evanston, and Ike commuted to his new job as chaplain at Elgin State Hospital. Anton Boisen, founder of clinical pastoral education and the former chaplain, lived on the grounds. He had worked with many of the early greats in psychiatry and psychology, such as McDougall at Harvard, and I loved to listen to his stories.

Several of the Northwestern graduate students, male and female, were married; there were also several single women. But, as at Boston University, the women were in social or clinical psychology. The students at Northwestern were a closely knit group. We also socialized periodically with the faculty. Each professor knew all the graduate students, and many took an interest in students other than those doing theses with them. In addition to physiological psychology, my favorite courses were in perception, learning, statistics, and endocrinology. I also learned Gilliland's infant test and worked for him occasionally testing infants. Other "outside" jobs included teaching introductory psychology at the Northwestern School of Nursing in Chicago and at the Latin American Institute. For 1949–1950, I was the teaching assistant for all beginning statistics (one of the professors was Janet Taylor, later Janet Taylor Spence).

Shortly after my arrival, one of the older male students warned me that Lindsley did not approve of women in graduate school. If this were the case, I saw only one possible evidence of it. While training me in the maintenance of the electroencephalograph (EEG), Lindsley gave me electrodes to repair. Handing me a very short piece of solder, he said, "Here, if you need more, you're no damn good." I had never seen a solder iron before, so I didn't expect to be good. I came to share his joy in gadgetry and was almost pleased when the EEG equipment acted up and we had to take amplifiers apart stage by stage and reassemble them. The department engineer also taught me to use the shop equipment. For 1950–1951, I was Lindsley's research and teaching assistant (he taught developmental as well as physiological psychology), and during that period he accepted another woman student. My thesis research—a study of photic driving and other physiological responses in infants— required two persons working constantly, and he was the other person (we had a sort of competition about who was best at soothing babies). Over the years, I have met many of his male and female students, and they all have reported similar kinds of support.

Just as I began to contemplate the postdoctoral job search in early 1951, two opportunities arose. Lindsley's undergraduate professor, Martin Reymert, known for research on the psychophysiology of emotion, was now at Mooseheart, Illinois, and was looking for a research associate. Don drove me down for an interview. Reymert offered me the job, expressing his delight at having "a daughter in science." To my surprise, I was also selected as director for an Air Force research contract in audiology at Northwestern. A fellow student who had experience on research grants from the U.S. Navy was the other final candidate, and I considered him better qualified. Then, in the spring of 1951, Ike was offered two chaplaincies in California. He very much wanted the one at Napa State Hospital. Reluctantly I agreed to go. Carl Seashore, chair of the Department of Psychology at Northwestern, knew Harold Jones, professor of psychology at University of California at Berkeley and director of the Institute of Child Welfare. Alman knew Herbert and Lois Hayden Meek Stolz and wrote to them. By coincidence, Herbert was the first director of the institute.

Literally upon our arrival at Napa in September 1951 (my PhD was awarded in late August), the superintendent followed his initial greeting by asking if I would teach in the evening at Napa Junior College. I interviewed and accepted. The director of the county Department of Social Welfare was in my class and offered a job as a social worker. With the understanding that I would leave immediately if I found more appropriate employment, I accepted. In October, I had an interview with Harold Jones. He wrote in November to offer a part-time research position at the institute to work with the physiological data from the Adolescent Growth Study (later Oakland Growth Study) and a lectureship in physiology to teach a developmental course. Thus began the 90-mi-a-day commute that I still make.

Ike was on call 24 hours a day, 7 days a week, so we lived on the hospital grounds, a location that proved helpful after Eric was born February 19, 1955. Household help was more plentiful in Napa, and Ike could make pediatrician visits, attend school events, and the like. His proximity also made it easier for me to go to grant review panels, committee meetings, and conventions. Had we lived at a midpoint, both of us would have been hampered. We never committed each other to social engagements without consultation. At first we socialized with both sets of colleagues and entertained his students. With two houses to manage (we built a country retreat) and increased work loads, we decided that he did his affairs and I did mine unless the other particularly wanted to attend. Ike's professional involvements were less demanding than mine, but he was our "community conscience"; those organizations got my money but not my time. I believed firmly in doing one's scientific civic duty, so I accepted many offices and other tasks, but I never sought them.

No one asked if I planned to retire or reduce my time during pregnancy or after delivery. When I inquired about sick leave during hospitalization, I was told by the chief secretary of the Department of Psychology, "Don't bother. You cover for the men when they get hurt playing with their kids; they can cover for you." One male colleague insisted on walking me each day during my pregnancy, Edward Tolman (the famous learning theorist) said complimentary things about my work and child, Warner Brown (an experimentalist who was everyone's favorite critic for papers in preparation) presented a blanket for the baby and gave me Granit's (1955) new book on the electrophysiology of perception. Mary and Harold Jones loaned an apartment in their house the last month, when I could not simultaneously fit behind the steering wheel and reach the pedals, and often had me for dinner when Ike was late. That was the extent of the "fuss."

Eric was born the Saturday of a 3-day weekend, and I returned to work Tuesday, given the fortuitous availability of a ride from Napa while I was not supposed to drive. Eric commuted to the institute with me (or sometimes with Ike) for preschool, but we retained our nursemaid to cover part-days, Eric's illnesses, and other emergencies. His primary school was nearby, and after school he went to a private home just off the hospital grounds. When about 10 years old, he announced he preferred to come home; with Ike's office so near, this was feasible. Having acquired a radio license, he soon was accepted as a volunteer in the hospital's internal broadcasting station and went there after school. A small private school existed in Napa during his fourth- and fifth-grade years, and Ike

drove him to and from the far end of town. About the time he returned to public school for sixth grade, we bought a house in the
suburbs. Most of the mothers of his playmates at the hospital were
psychiatrists, and the wives of couples with whom we socialized
were also professionals. He expressed amazement (and no envy)
when he discovered that some wives "stayed home all day."

During my early years at the institute, Jones, a secretary, and
I had offices within the Department of Psychology. The institute
building—with other offices, laboratory, and nursery school—was
on the other side of campus. I was invited to join the "brown bag"
group in the department faculty room, and my first close friendships were in that department. As I attended institute seminars and
social events, I came to know the many distinguished women
there—Mary Cover Jones, Nancy Bayley, Marjorie Honzik, and
Catherine Landreth (all developmental psychologists) and Elsa
Frenkel-Brunswik and Jean Macfarlane, whose specializations
were in personality. Nancy trained me in anthropometric techniques, including skeletal X-rays, and in her infant mental and
motor scales. I became her associate on the Berkeley Growth Study,
although I continued some work with the Oakland Growth Study
and replaced her as director of the Berkeley Study when she left
to head the developmental laboratory at the National Institutes of
Health. Bayley and, later, Honzik, had lectureships in psychology,
but only Macfarlane (psychology) and Landreth (home economics)
held professorships. Later, Mary Cover Jones became professor of
education. Olga Bridgeman, a PhD and MD, held a joint appointment in psychology and at the medical school and was the only
other woman in the "brown bag" group. One other woman was part-
time in clinical psychology.

For several years, the younger developmentalists in psychology
took turns going to San Francisco to teach nurses at the University of California Medical School, and I was included. I continued to
teach in physiology through 1958 and taught in anatomy from 1960
to 1963. From time to time I taught psychology—most often the
developmental psychology laboratory (my favorite course), but I also
taught adolescence and general developmental psychology. Other
teaching included a developmental psychology seminar at the
School of Social Welfare at Berkeley, summer session at the University of Minnesota, and many guest lectures for a variety of courses
and departments. I supervised the first honors student in psychology, had National Science Foundation students for laboratory from
1959 through 1967, and served as adviser for several group majors from 1954 to 1960. Only faculty may chair dissertations, but

I have served on thesis and examination committees for many graduate students in psychology, education, physical education, physiology, genetics, and even architecture. As my administrative load increased, I began to eliminate regular teaching and doing book reviews and to cut back on editing for journals, all activities in which I feel my contribution per unit time is less than in promoting group productivity through administration.

In 1960, the institute was renamed the Institute of Human Development, and the newly built Child Study Center expanded the nursery school to two units with increased laboratory facilities. Bayley returned in 1960, and she and I alternated as administrator of the center during 1960–1961. She retired, and John Clausen, professor of sociology, who was appointed director of the institute after Jones's retirement and death in 1960, named me administrator in 1962, a title I still hold. However, in 1975, Paul Mussen, then director of the institute, reinstituted the position of associate director and asked me to fill it. Only a faculty member may be director of research units, and I am the only person on a research appointment to serve as associate director of the institute. Jane Hunt was appointed co-administrator of the center and became the on-site person. I moved back to the institute offices, by now located in Tolman Hall. Meantime the institute's three longitudinal studies—the Berkeley and Oakland growth studies and the Guidance Study—had merged in 1967 into the Intergenerational Studies, and I had become principal investigator for this program, a role I continued through 1980. At that point, a large grant terminated, and we finished a book (Eichorn, Clausen, Haan, Honzik, & Mussen, 1981) reporting long-term results for which I authored one chapter, was first author for two, and served as chief editor. A new director, sociologist Guy Swanson, had ambitious plans for expanding institute activities toward which my efforts were needed, and I felt it was time to build a cadre of younger investigators to continue the Intergenerational Studies, although I continue to serve on steering committees for research planning.

My gradual move from psychophysiology to developmental psychology is apparent. It began in neurophysiological work with Lindsley, when I first saw that many issues could not be understood without knowledge of their development. At Berkeley, no appropriate laboratory existed. I met the electroencephalographer from Herrick Hospital in Berkeley, and we began joint research—he shocked the nurses by invading the sterility of the maternity floor to consult with me—that was terminated by his untimely death. In 1959, the psychologist at Sonoma State Hospital was organizing research facilities for a section for infants with Downs syndrome and asked me to consult on the physiological equipment and participate in the research, an activity I continued through 1967. In those days, one was one's own gadgeteer (a seductive pastime), miles of records were analyzed by "hand," and statistics were done on hand calculators. California required prior permission to buy any item classified as electronic. I spent hours driving not only between Berkeley or Napa and Sonoma but also to Oakland to buy four 60¢ connectors to make one piece of equipment do the work of two. The hospital psychologist left, and I inherited directing the project. A visitor, Donald Stedman, and I managed to get one behavioral paper written, Nancy Bayley got interested in the behavioral data and started to work with the technician and a graduate student, and I ceased laboratory research in psychophysiological psychology. I still feel guilty about piles of analyzed records and statistical analyses that never were written up for publication.

Data from several other kinds of experiments, as well as longitudinal analyses, remained unpublished, and I am often late with writing commitments, a result in part of administrative and professional activities. In addition, I revel in designing and executing research and in doing data analyses but loathe writing first drafts. I gladly give first authorship to anyone who will do that. "Polishing" a paper is rather fun. My direct contributions to women's programs are few. I think I aided the careers of several women, as well as of several men, and perhaps I helped pave the way. Years ago I was the only woman on a number of grant review and APA committees. After 2 years with a grant review group on which I was the first and then only female member, two of the remaining original men, long since close friends, told me that they all assumed women could do the work but feared loss of comradely interaction (which was exceptional). They added, "We didn't [lose the interaction]; it got better." Sex is an attribute Vermonters do not consider relevant in most activities. I think of a person as an experimental or educational psychologist or as an endocrinologist or whatever, not as a male nurse or a female physicist. The concept of role models is alien to a Vermonter; individualism and independence are expected, not just tolerated. Natural and economic environments are expected to be harsh; people are not. Obstacles are not to be deplored, but are fun to overcome. This sounds "preachy" and maudlin, but it is a heritage I think was a strength for me. My other strength was an obliging physiology, probably improved by a lot of outdoor exercise. I've always maintained that survival in graduate school and academia demanded more in the way of a strong back than a strong mind. It also helps to have a sense of humor, especially about one-self, and to pick ancestors, spouses, and children wisely.

Why does anyone take a road "less traveled"? Frost observed "that has made all the difference," but psychologists would hypothesize that some differences precede the choice. Yet research on retrospective data makes us question their validity. Personal histories are particularly suspect, for, we have learned, they are constantly being reconstructed. New generations cannot follow footsteps because the paths are always changing. The newcomers do have an inquiring spirit, however, and I wish those well who undertake to interpret our reflections. May these serve to direct them toward the broader goals of understanding individual differences and the development of vocational and other behaviors.

REFERENCES

Bartlett, F. (1932). *Remembering: A study in experimental and social psychology.* Cambridge: Cambridge University Press.

Eichorn, D., Clausen, J., Haan, N., Honzik, M., & Mussen, P. (Eds.). (1981). *Present and past in middle life.* New York: Academic Press.

Granit, R. (1955). *Receptors and sensory perception.* New Haven, CT: Yale University Press.

REPRESENTATIVE PUBLICATIONS

Brooks-Gunn, J., Petersen, A. C., & Eichorn, D. H. (Eds.). (1985). Time of maturation and psychosocial functioning in adolescence, Part I [Special issue]. *Journal of Youth and Adolescence, 14*(3).

Brooks-Gunn, J., Petersen, A. C., & Eichorn, D. H. (Eds.). (1985). Time of maturation and psychosocial functioning in adolescence, Part II [Special issue]. *Journal of Youth and Adolescence, 14*(4).

Clapp, W., & Eichorn, D. (1965). Some determinants of perceptual investigatory responses in children. *Journal of Experimental Child Psychology, 2,* 371–388.

Cronk, C., Roche, A., Kent, R., Berkeley, C., Reed, R., Valadian, I., Eichorn, D., & McCammon, R. (1982). Longitudinal trends and continuity in weight/stature from 3 months to 18 years. *Human Biology, 54,* 729–749.

Cronk, C., Roche, A., Kent, R., Eichorn, D., & McCammon, R. (1983). Longitudinal trends in subcutaneous fat thickness during adolescence. *American Journal of Physical Anthropology, 61,* 197–204.

Eckert, H., & Eichorn, D.(1974). Construct standards in skilled action. *Child Development, 45,* 439–445.

Eckert, H., & Eichorn, D. (1976). Reliability of reaction time. *Perceptual and Motor Skills, 43,* 1307–1310.

Eckert, H.,& Eichorn, D.(1978). Orientation in eye–hand coordination tasks. *Perceptual and Motor Skills, 47,* 259–263.

Eichorn, D. (1955). A comparison of laboratory determinations and Wetzel Grid estimates of basal metabolism among adolescents. *Journal of Pediatrics, 46,* 146–154.

Eichorn, D. (1963). Biological correlates of behavior. In H. Stevenson (Ed.), *Child psychology* [Yearbook of the National Society for Studies in Education, Pt. I] (pp. 4–61). Chicago: University of Chicago Press.

Eichorn, D. (1968). Adolescence. In D. Sills (Ed.), *International encyclopedia of the social sciences* (Vol. 1, pp. 84–96). McMillan & Free Press.

Eichorn, D. (1968). Biology of gestation and infancy. *Merill-Palmer Quarterly, 14,* 47–81.

Eichorn, D. (1968, January). Variations in growth rate. *Childhood Education, 44,* pp. 286–291.

Eichorn, D. (1970). Physiological development. In P. Mussen (Ed.), *Carmichael's manual of child psychology* (Vol. 1, pp. 157–283). New York: Wiley.

Eichorn, D. (1973). Intellectual change: A report from the Berkeley and Oakland longitudinal studies. In L. Jarvik, C. Eisdorfer, & J. Blum (Eds.), *Intellectual functioning in adults: Psychological and biological influences* (pp. 1–6). New York: Springer.

Eichorn, D. (1974). The Berkeley longitudinal studies: Continuities and correlates of behaviour. *Canadian Journal of Behavioural Sciences, 5* 297–320.

Eichorn, D. (1974). Biological, psychological and socio-cultural aspects of adolescence and youth. In J. Coleman R. Bremner, B. Clark, J. Davis, D. Eichorn, Z. Griliches, J. Kett, N. Ryder, Z. Doering, & J. Mays (Eds.), *Youth: Transition to adulthood* (pp. 91–111). Chicago: University of Chicago Press.

Eichorn, D. (1975). Asynchronizations in adolescent development. In S. Dragastin & G. Elder, Jr. (Eds.), *Adolescence in the life cycle* (pp. 81–96). New York: Halsted Press/Wiley.

Eichorn, D. (1978). Adulthood. In G. Balis, L. Wurmser, E. McDaniel, & R. Grenell (Eds.), *Dimensions of behavior* (pp. 495–530). Boston: Butterworth.

Eichorn, D. (1979). Physical development: Current foci of research. In J. Osofsky (Ed.), *Handbook of infant research* (pp. 253–282). New York: Wiley.

Eichorn, D. (1980). Biological development. In J. Adams (Ed.), *Understanding adolescence* (4th ed.). (pp. 54–77). Boston: Allyn & Bacon.

Eichorn, D., & Bayley, N. (1962). Growth in head circumference from birth through young adulthood. *Child Development, 33,* 257–271.

Eichorn, D., Clausen, J., Haan, N., Honzik, M., & Musen, P. (Eds.), (1981). *Present and past in middle life.* New York: Academic Press.

Eichorn, D., & Jones, H. (1952). Development of mental functions. *Review of Educational Research, 22,* 421–438.

Eichorn, D., & Jones, H. (1958). Maturation and behavior. In G. Seward & J. Seward (Eds.), *Current psychological issues* (pp. 211–248). New York: Holt.

Eichorn, D., & McKee, J., (1953). Oral temperature and subcutaneous fat during adolescence. *Child Development, 24,* 235–247.

Eichorn, D., & McKee, J. (1958). Physiological instability during adolescence. *Child Development, 29,* 255–268.

Eichorn, D., & VandenBos, G. (1985). Dissemination of scientific and professional knowledge: Journal publication within the APA. *American Psychologist, 40,* 1309–1316.

Honzik, M., Hunt, J., & Eichorn, D. (1976). Mental growth after age 18 years. *Compte-Rendu de la XIIIe Reunion des Equipes Chargees des Etudes sur la Croissance et le Developpement de l'Enfant Normal* (pp. 280–290). Rennes, France: Centre International de l'Enfance.

Hunt, J., & Eichorn, D. (1972). Maternal and child behaviors: A review of data from the Berkeley Growth Study. *Seminars in Psychiatry, 4,* 367–381.

Hunt, J., & Eichorn, D. (1979). Developmental testing of the infant and young child. In J. Howells (Ed.), *Modern perspectives in the psychiatry of infancy* (pp. 74–94). New York: Bruner/Mazel.

McCall, R., Eichorn, D., & Hogarty, P. (1977). Transitions in early mental development. *Monographs of the Society for Research in Child Development, 42*(3, Serial No. 171).

McKee, J., & Eichorn, D. (1953). Seasonal variations in physiological functions during adolescence. *Child Development, 24,* 225–247.

McKee, J., & Eichorn, D. (1955). The relation between metabolism and height and weight during adolescence. *Child Development, 26,* 205–212.

Mussen, P., Eichorn, D., & Honzik, M. (1982). Early adult antecedents of life satisfaction at age 70. *Journal of Gerontology, 3*(37), 316–322.

Mussen, P., Eichorn, D., Honzik, M., Bieber, S., & Meredith, W. (1980). Continuity and change in women's characteristics over four decades. *International Journal of Behavioral Development, 3,* 333–347.

Stedman, D., & Eichorn, D. (1964). A comparison of the growth and development of institutionalized and home-reared mongoloids during infancy and early childhood. *American Journal of Mental Deficiency, 69,* 391–401.

CHAPTER 15

Carolyn Robertson Payton

Carolyn Robertson Payton

I am a descendant of slaves on the maternal side of my family and of free Blacks on the paternal side. I credit some of the resilience I have felt as having been inherited from my slave grandfather, about whom the following story is recounted. He was originally named George Van Landinhan and was reared in North Carolina. It is reported that granddaddy either slapped or shot a White man and fled to Virginia, where he changed his name to George Flannagan. I have never been able to decide if his choice of Flannagan rather than Smith or Brown or Jones was indicative of cleverness or plain stupidity. That he was not apprehended does establish, at the minimum, that he had the ability to understand the workings of the slave owner's mind.

Granddaddy demonstrated his shrewdness in other ways. There were four children live-born to my grandfather and grandmother. There was one son and three daughters, one of whom was my mother. He recognized even in those days the need for adequate educational preparation for his children. The oldest, the son, was enrolled at Virginia Union University; the second oldest—my mother—was a graduate of Pratt Institute; and the third was trained as a musician and played the piano and organ at a local Baptist church. The youngest attended Virginia Sate College. Keep in mind that granddaddy was only 10 years old when the Emancipation Proclamation was signed, yet somehow he had learned that "a mind is a terrible thing to waste." It was only as I grew older that I came to recognize and appreciate the uniqueness of my family's educational background, especially because these events occurred less than 50 years after the end of the Civil War.

From my father's people I learned of the path that resulted in our coming to these shores. When several people were taken to be enslaved from the African village that was home to my ancestors, the king decreed that his son, Prince John, would accompany the travelers. This he was permitted to do, and the band wound up in South Carolina. There he, a free Black, was able to buy land and settle in Taylor, South Carolina. Prince John was my father's grandfather. Thus, I attribute to this side of my family the pool of courage I have often drawn upon when faced with events for which I have been unprepared or with events that I might have preferred to avoid. I also expect that this self-imposed exile from his native land may have contributed to the unswerving loyalty I hold for my family and friends and to my commitment to work for equality and justice—for Blacks in particular and oppressed people in general.

There you have my beginning as far back as I have been made aware. I was born in Norfolk, Virginia, in 1925—1 year and 9 months after my sister. My mother always maintained that my birth was due to her total ignorance of birth control procedures, for which I have been and will be eternally grateful. I know that she too was more than content at the results of her ignorance. My childhood years, spent during the Depression, were pleasant and relatively uneventful. I knew my dad would often be in search of work; he eventually secured a job as steward with the U.S. Geodetic and Coast Survey, which meant that he was away from us quite a lot. As daddy was a cook, and my mother a seamstress, there was no shortage of food or clothing

Although I was spared the distress of poverty, I experienced to the fullest the distress of my ethnicity. I have always been conscious of my Blackness and of the lack of status assigned to me as a consequence. My cues were the unpaved streets and sidewalks in my segregated neighborhood, the paucity of street lights, my elementary school with outdoor toilets—the same school that had been condemned for Whites preceding my mother's attendance there. The city zoo with polar bears and lions, swimming pool and skating rink, could be viewed only in passing, as it was off-limits to Blacks. Oceanview, with its ferris wheel and merry-go-round, was not accessible to us. We had only City Beach, with jellyfish and sinkholes. You can be sure that I grew up knowing that I was Black.

Ironically, although the establishment forced segregation down our throats at every turn, Blacks were nevertheless taught that America was the home of the free and the brave—the sweet land of liberty. I learned, as all children in public school, that I was an American and as such was guaranteed the pursuit of happiness, equality, and justice. I learned that lesson well and have continuously struggled to achieve these rights as a minority and as a woman.

It was a given in my family that I would go to college. My choice was Hampton Institute, as I had grown to know the campus through my visits to the library while spending summers with my great grandparents, who lived in Hampton. The ivy-covered buildings and its location on the water were especially appealing to me. My father had equally fond memories of Bennett College from his childhood years spent in Greensboro, North Carolina. Thus, in September 1941 my sister and I were dutifully enrolled at Bennett "where discriminating parents send their distinguished daughters." I did not know then nor even at the time of my graduation what a stroke of luck it was for me to have been educated at a women's college. I am convinced that my aspirations, attitudes, and expectations were affected by that experience. I had already internalized a sense of my capabilities as a women. My 4 years at Bennett further strengthened my sense of well-being. My role models and mentors were the women in the junior and senior classes who were pursuing studies to become physicians, biologists, physicists, musicians, and, of course, educators. My vision of what I could become was limited only by my imagination and aptitude. Given so many options, there is little wonder that I was unclear as to what I wanted to do with my life.

I was saved by my Blackness. By 1945, Virginia had been forced by the judicial system to implement the separate-but-equal doctrine within its educational institutions. If I elected to pursue graduate work in a discipline available to Whites at the White state schools but not available to Blacks at Virginia State College (the Black state school), the state would pay all expenses incurred at any school of my choice. I had taken a course in abnormal psychology as an elective and enjoyed it. Psychology was not offered at the graduate level as a major at Virginia State College but was at the University of Virginia. My course of study was decided. The University of Wisconsin at Madison was the school of choice because I knew other Bennett graduates in attendance.

I can still see the astonishment of Dr. Norman Cameron, chair of the Department of Psychology, when he read my transcript as I told him of my desire to become a psychologist. I may have had all of nine credits in psychology. My naïveté and my youth shielded me from dismay at beginning a graduate degree program in a field in which I had accrued nine credits. I was accepted and stayed there for 3 successive years until I earned the MS.

In this setting also, ethnicity was a more significant variable than was gender. There were other female students and staff but no other Blacks. I still have a very vivid memory of my loneliness as a graduate student. My situation was always heightened in the various lab courses in which I was enrolled, which typically required pairing off with a classmate. I was most uncomfortable at choosing any of my White classmates to team up with me and solved the issue by waiting until all selections had been made and gaining my partner by default, so to speak.

I came to Wisconsin with the intentions of being trained as a clinician. I had been attracted to this profession by my vision of helping to alleviate the psychological sufferings of individuals about whom I had read in case studies or encountered in life. I expect that my experiences as a Black may have contributed at some level to my ready identification with people under stress.

I also became interested in industrial psychology but did not pursue this interest, as I could not imagine an industry that would hire a Black psychologist. Note again that my avoidance of the field had nothing to do with my gender. Animal psychology was also fascinating as taught by Harry Harlow, renowned for his work with primates. In fact, Dr. Harlow was such an interesting instructor that I enrolled in as many of his courses as possible. Pragmatism again ruled the day with the realization that I would likely have more access to needy Blacks than rhesus monkeys. So I stuck with my initial choice and was graduated with the MS in clinical psychology.

As all graduate students, I wanted a research project that would change the world—Columbus discovering America, Newton and gravity, Einstein and relativity. I decided that with the newly developed Wechsler–Bellevue Test of Intelligence, I would demonstrate definitively and conclusively—putting to rest for all time—the myth of White intellectual superiority vis-à-vis Blacks. Here too you see that my focus was shaped by ethnicity rather than gender.

Anyway, in 1947 I began a comparative study of the intelligence of Black and White college students as measured by the Wechsler–Bellevue Test of Intelligence. The specific details are not at all clear to me now. I know that for the most part, my subjects were undergraduates and were matched for age, gender, college classification, and the like. I do recall my disappointment at my findings, so no doubt the Black subjects did not perform as well as the White subjects on this test of intelligence. However, I did not jump to the conclusion that Blacks were intellectually inferior to Whites but decided rather that the scale was not accurately measuring the true ability of Blacks.

Through the years, as I continued to use this instrument, I became even more suspicious of its ability to predict the academic achievement of Blacks. College students who might earn an IQ between 80 and 89 (low average) would often be among those graduating with honors. These same students were earning advanced degrees in all fields from prestigious graduate schools throughout the United States. I can only blame my youth for continuing to test while distrusting the results. Knowing that the test had been standardized on a sample of 1,081 adults drawn from New York City and surrounding areas, I insisted on applying the norms to a population not included in the sample. The original sample was unrepresentative of the total adult population in general and of Blacks in particular.

Much effort has been exerted to correct this specific limitation— and others—in the revisions of the scale. In fact, I served as a field supervisor for the standardization program of the 1976 revision of the Wechsler Adult Intelligence Scale. This entailed my selection of Black subjects based on age, gender, socioeconomic level, and the like. I then administered and scored the instrument. So, many years after my "failed" research, I was able to play a small part in the development and application of test norms for a highly respected and widely used test of intelligence.

But to come back to the University of Wisconsin, my thesis was approved in 1948, and I was awarded an MS in clinical psychology. For the first time I was faced with the reality of seeking a job. My only career option, as I saw it, was that of a college teacher. I also reasoned that the only college likely to employ me would be one of the colleges established for educating Blacks. This also limited my job search to the southern states, where the majority of such institutions were located.

I knew nothing of submitting resumes and cover letters to potential job sites. I had no idea as to what would be an appropriate salary; I had no dollar value to attach to my degree. I marvel at the wisdom of graduates today, who, even at the bachelor's level, expect to be employed at beginning salaries of $25,000 or more. In truth, I wondered if I might pay an employer to give me a chance to prove I deserved the job. I don't think I lacked self-confidence. I had experienced enough success to feel competent and capable. I simply did not have the sense of entitlement that I detect in the youth of today. Was this deficit due to my ethnicity or gender? I cannot answer.

The one resource that I found available, in my pursuit of employment, was the *Norfolk Journal and Guide*, a now defunct Black weekly newspaper. There in the classified section, I discovered that Livingstone College in Salisbury, North Carolina, was seeking to employ an instructor in psychology. I wrote them of my availability and was eventually hired.

I stayed at Livingstone for 5 years. I was the only psychologist on the faculty—a fact that afforded many opportunities for the honing of my skills. I taught introduction to psychology, child and adolescent psychology, abnormal psychology, and several education courses. I also established and maintained student personnel files that were used to help students make career choices or decisions about college majors. Additionally, I administered the psychological testing program.

Livingstone proved to be an excellent site for me as a beginning instructor. The faculty and staff were friendly, supportive, and encouraging. Also, the college had excellent tennis courts, so I was able to indulge in a favorite pastime of mine.

Although I was quite content to remain at Livingstone, my family was convinced that I should try to get a job nearer home. I applied to Norfolk State College but was not engaged. Then, in 1953, I responded to another job advertised in the *Norfolk Journal and Guide.* This was for a dean of women/psychology instructor at Elizabeth City State Teachers College in Elizabeth City, North Carolina. The administrative responsibilities appeared challenging, and, even more of an enticement, Elizabeth City was only a 40-min drive from Norfolk. My application for the position was accepted, and as far as I know this marked the only time that I have been hired solely because I was a woman.

Becoming a dean of women did indeed constitute a challenge, but quite different from what I had expected. Student personnel employees were hired to serve literally as substitute parental figures for the coeds. I was to chaperone school dances, escort the girls' basketball teams to all off-campus games, dole out permission for weekend or vacation trips, and ensure that our women always conducted themselves with proper decorum. I was the role model; thus, I had to be properly attired at all times, which often meant the wearing of hat and gloves. Attendance at chapel services or at any cultural programs held at the college was just short of mandatory for me.

All this was a bit of a strain for me. I was and am a very casual dresser. But, I did not flinch from the charge of my position. I donned hat and gloves and set about to become a model of propriety. Apparently I was successful at curbing my proclivities, as my contract continued to be renewed.

Other duties included supervising the three dormitory directresses and the dean of men. I coordinated all personnel sevices, activities, and records of the women students. I also supervised the dormitory program of women students and the extracurricular activities of off-campus students.

I stayed at ECTC, as we fondly spoke of the college, from September 1953 to May 1956. There were excellent tennis courts available as well as tournament-quality bridge players. I was content. Besides, I was only a 40-min drive from home.

As can be observed from my positions at Livingstone College and Elizabeth City, I was as involved in the field of student personnel as I was in psychology. To feel more comfortable in student personnel administration, I began study in the discipline. I started taking courses during summer at Columbia University Teachers College. I also began taking additional courses in psychology. I spent each summer in school—first because I liked school and second because it was fun to be in New York City. There were the outdoor concerts at Lewisohn Stadium, the Metropolitan Opera House, the Broadway theaters, the Apollo, and the night clubs. Many, many Blacks were enrolled at New York State University or at Columbia, so I was not lonely, as had been the case in Madison.

With all the pleasures associated with attending Columbia, little wonder that I discovered one day that I had acculumated more graduate credits than I could ever hope to transfer. Remember, I had not entered the university with the notion of getting the doctorate. A dim thought held by me was that I would eventually return to Madison to continue the study of psychology. However, I concluded it would be foolish to ignore the credits accumulated, so I applied and was accepted as a doctoral candidate at Teachers College. Dr. Esther Lloyd-Jones, a very eminent person in the student personnel field, was my adviser and a great support to me throughout my enrollment at Teachers College.

I left Elizabeth City in 1956. The previous summer, I had been invited to teach summer school at Virginia State College in Petersburg, Virginia. As a consequence, I was recruited to become an associate professor of psychology. I accepted the offer, as I was hopeful of eventually winding up at the Norfolk Division of Virginia State, where I could be reunited with the family. In spite of all my efforts, I was never to be invited to work in Norfolk. I consoled myself with thoughts of at least being able to resume my tennis and bridge playing. I was also only 45 minutes from home, which counted as another bonus.

Finally, I had landed in a real psychology department, even if only at the undergraduate level. My appointment called for me to teach half the time and serve as clinical counselor the other half. I did psychological testing and provided psychotherapy to students in my role as clinical counselor.

In 1958, I took a year's leave of absence from Virginia State in order to fulfill the residency requirement of Teachers College. I lived with an uncle in Corona, Long Island, commuted by subway to Columbia, and, to stretch my meager funds further, ate a lot of instant oatmeal and cream cheese sandwiches from Chock-Full-O-Nuts. Weekends were spent with two sisters who were graduates of Bennett College now living and working in New York.

Not only did I survive the ordeal of my diet and the rigor of graduate school that year—obtaining my EdD from Columbia in 1962—I obtained a lead to my next position.

A former student of mine from Virginia State had enrolled in the graduate program in psychology at Howard University. She informed me of an opening there and suggested that I apply. I did and was accepted. So, in 1959, I joined the faculty of the Howard University Psychology Department as assistant professor. There was no hesitation in accepting the appointment even though it meant I would be farther from home and my family. Perhaps I had finally individuated.

At Howard, my extensive exposure to the study of primate behavior was not to be wasted. On joining the Psychology Department, I inherited a primate laboratory. Dr. Leslie Hicks, professor of psychology at Howard, had also studied under Harlow and had established a primate laboratory at Howard. He accepted a postdoctorate fellowship my second year at the university, and his monkeys were up for grabs. Dr. Max Meenes, who then chaired the department, had decided to offer the monkeys to one of our neighboring universities when I agreed to undertake research utilizing the primates. I hoped that such research would result in a publication, which was essential for tenure.

I received a 3-year grant from the National Institute of Mental Health to explore the perception threshold of verticality in rhesus monkeys. We found that monkeys can make precise judgments of the visual vertical as exactly as human subjects do.

This research was to be the foundation for an exploration of perception in children. My interest in this area stemmed from reading the study of nursery school children conducted by Kenneth and Mamie Clark (1947). They discovered that 4-year-old Black nursery school children, when presented with dolls identical except for color, preferred the White doll. I wanted to determine the age at which children internalized the perceived social value ascribed to skin color. Understanding the determinants of a relativity simply perceptual phenomenon in an organism less complex than a human was thought to be a desirable first step.

This research was never undertaken, as the trajectory of my life changed. John F. Kennedy was elected president and made good on his campaign promise to estabish the Peace Corps.

My psychological specialty, more than gender, was the main factor in my getting involved with the agency. Dr. James Bayton, a renowned social psychologist at Howard, was initially invited to be the university representative to assist in the design of the selection procedures for service in the Peace Corps. He had neither the time nor the interest and strongly recommended me. He thought I would be most suitable, as I was considered to be a "soft" psychologist.

The Psychology Department at Howard has always held to a distinctively experimental orientation. Applied psychologists or clinical psychologists were generally merely tolerated by the pure psychologists on staff. Devising interview schedules or choosing psychological instruments to assess the potential for successful completion of an overseas tour by young Americans was not something of appeal to our experimentalists. I found these selection tasks most interesting and was pleased to be recommended. I became a field assessment officer (FAO) in June 1962 for trainees preparing to serve in Togo.

The FAO is responsible for the psychological evaluation and assessment of trainees at the training site. This entailed the preparation of comprehensive appraisals on each Peace Corps trainee based on psychological tests, personal interviews, clinical observations, faculty grades and assessments, peer reviews, and other pertinent information. All the data were used to derive the physical, mental, and technical qualifications of each trainee for success in the overseas assignment. Additionally, I prepared a resume on each trainee for the use of overseas personnel.

From September 1963 to December 1963, I was again invited to serve as an FAO for training being conducted in Washington. Then, in February 1964, I was asked to accompany the first group to be trained at the outward-bound Camp Crozier in Arecibo, Puerto Rico. As the FAO, I was also responsible for evaluating assessment under conditions presented by training and living at the camp with the objective of determining the feasibility of having continuous programs there. This assignment was completed in June 1964.

The enthusiasm, dedication, and commitment of the many young people with whom I became involved was contagious. I resigned from Howard University at the expiration of the leave of absence I had taken to accept the Puerto Rico assignment. I began to work full-time at the Peace Corps now as a field selection officer.

This position necessitated extensive overseas travel. My region of assignment was Latin America; thus, I had the opportunity to visit many of the countries there. Much enjoyment and enrichment was derived from this immersion in other cultures. Typically I would journey overseas to attend the end-of-service conferences held for debriefing purposes. The field selection officer would lead the discussion of the group of terminating volunteers and from the sessions attempt to measure the effectiveness of their training, selection procedures, site or job placement, and support obtained from overseas staff.

On many such trips, I was often surprised by the degree of hostility expressed by the volunteers toward the indigenous population. This was the very antithesis of the Peace Corps objective. Ideally, Peace Corps hoped to minimize the threats of war by building relationships between Americans and the people of the various countries in which volunteers served. Yet many of these volunteers were leaving their host countries with deeply felt bitterness and animosity toward the very people with whom they had lived and worked for 2 years. I was familiar with the characteristics of the typical Peace Corps trainee, the nature of their rigorous training programs, and the careful screening procedures used for selection. The one element that was unknown to me involved the overseas experience itself. What demands were being made of the volunteers that could so thoroughly exhaust their compassion and altruism?

I decided to ask for an overseas post to determine the conditions that would lead to a more satisfying experience for the volunteers. In November 1966, I set off to Barbados, the West Indies, to become deputy director for the eastern Caribbbean region. At that time, volunters were only stationed in Barbados and St. Lucia, but later programs were initiated in almost all the English-speaking islands of that region. I was named director for the post in September 1967. Even though women had been acceptable as volunteers since the first days of the Peace Corps, it appeared that Sargent Shriver was reluctant to appoint women to the overseas staff. There was only one other female country director during my tenure. As is often the case, once we were given the opportunity to demonstrate that women could be effective in running overseas programs, gender was dropped as a qualifier for these positions.

I returned to Washington, DC, in 1970, unsure of the direction in which I now wanted to aim my life. The Peace Corps had vitiated my interest in formalized teaching. It was also the time of the civil rights movement, with students demanding relevance from their professors. The turbulence of the campus was a far cry from the tranquility of the West Indies. The artificiality of the "us versus them" interactions between students and academicians was jarring to me after the egalitarian quality of Peace Corps life. Thus, I chose to leave the classroom for the more direct service unit of the Howard University Counseling Service. I became Director in 1970, with no thought of leaving before retirement.

This was not to be, as again Peace Corps lured me away. During the Republican administration, the Peace Corps lost its independence as an agency and, along with VISTA and the Foster Grand Parents program, was brought into the agency known as Action. President Carter appointed Sam Brown, known for his leadership role in the anti-Vietnam War movement, to the directorship of Action. After a search of many months for someone to take over the Peace Corps, my name was brought to the attention of Mr. Brown by a former eastern Caribbean female volunteer. He agreed to assess my qualifications and subsequenlty recommended me to President Carter, who then appointed me Peace Corps Director. In the long series of individuals named to head the agency, I was the first woman and Black so honored.

The relationship between the director of Action, Sam Brown, and the director of the Peace Corps was tenuous. This may have been linked to age differences (he was much younger than I), gender differences, or racial differences. Further, I could not help but be more knowledgeable about Peace Corps than he. We disagreed on a number of philosophical issues regarding Peace Corps programming and which countries deserved Peace Corps presence. Our quarrels were eventually made public, and President Carter asked for my resignation. Was I the culprit, most expendable, because I was a woman or because I was a Black?

There was an interim of nearly a year before the expiration of my leave of absence from Howard. So I was faced with unemployment at this juncture. As my departure from the Peace Corps was not without fanfare, my availability for employment was relatively well known. The president of a consultant firm who had known me when we both worked for the Peace Corps in the early 1960s invited me to join his firm as a vice-president. I was intrigued by the offer, as I had no experience working in the private sector, and readily accepted.

I was assigned to direct the company's contract with the National Institute on Drug Abuse to operate the Center for Multicultural

Awareness. The center would provide various services in the field of primary prevention of drug abuse for minority groups. Through this appointment, I was able to meet and develop lasting relationships with many individuals from the Asian-American, Native American, Pacific Islander, Hispanic-American, and Black-American populations. This appointment allowed me to become more knowledgeable and more appreciative of the true diversity of America. It certainly increased my sensitivity to individuals of varying backgrounds and life styles, which has made me a more effective therapist.

Writing this has caused me to reflect on my life. What stands out for me as landmarks is the influence of my family and my undergraduate days at a women's college. My family background was a prerequisite for my undergraduate days. I see nothing remarkable about my life. My innate curiosity led me to seek out a variety of educational experiences. The love and support of my family were a cushion that rendered my risk-taking behavior riskless. I worked most diligently to cleanse myself of bitterness and hatred resulting from the racism I experienced and to use my energies to bring about change.

I have been most fortunate at having my accomplishments recognized by my professional colleagues in the American Psychological Association. I encourage psychologists who are not affiliated to become affiliated. You will derive a multitude of benefits and satisfaction as a result of your involvement.

I am sure that readers are familiar with the many studies that have suggested that one of the major barriers to women's succeeding appears to be their fear of success. Such studies have indicated that women are socialized such that getting ahead is identified as a masculine trait to be avoided. Women seem to believe that if they are straight-A students or if they aspire to be the top student in class, their feminity is endangered, and all the rights and privileges associated with that role or status are also lost (Horner, 1972). Research on fear of success among Black female subjects has yielded contradictory results. It is not clear-cut that Black women are as anxious about striving for success as is true of Whites (Fleming, 1982; Mednick & Puryear, 1975). Certainly I was not conscious of such anxieties. I did feel the pressure of having to choose among the divergent ideas of the female role, one with which I was most comfortable. I chose to be a single woman, which allowed me the freedom to move wherever my fancy dictated. I am not sure how many of you are willing to make that sacrifice, but it may be called for.

I believe that women who have achieved have a tremendous responsiblity to reach out or back to help other women. If we do not, who will? Women have a major contribution to make to our society. We have always had the potential, but historically we have been led to believe that our view from the bridge was of little value. This is changing. More and more we are asking why must our perceptions be rejected, negated, disparaged. Carol Gilligan's (1982) recent work on conceptions of self and morality, the experiences of conflict and choice by men and women, addresses this point. She suggested that men and women do speak with different voices.

Consider, if you will, the impact on the goals and priorities of our nation were we to be directed by the voices that speak to the ethics of justice and care; that structure relationships based on the vision that women, men, Blacks, Whites—all people—are of equal worth; that, despite differences in power, try to ensure that fairness will prevail. Consider a nation in which everyone is given a response and everyone is included, a nation in which no one will be left alone or hurt. More and more women must join the chorus so that our different voices and different messages will be heard loudly and clearly.

REFERENCES

Clark, K., & Clark, M. P. (1947). Racial identification and preference in Negro children. In T. M. Newcomb & E.L. Hartley (Eds.), *Readings in social psychology* (pp. 169–178). New York: Holt.

Fleming, J. (1982). Fear of success in Black male and female graduate students: A pilot study. *Psychology of Women Quarterly, 6,* 327–341.

Gilligan, C. (1982). *In a different voice.* Cambridge. MA: Harvard University Press.

Horner, M. S. (1972). Toward an understanding of achievement-related conflicts in women. *Journal of Social Issues, 28,* 157–176.

Mednick, M. T. S., & Puryear, G. R. (1975). Motivational and personality factors related to career goals of Black college women. *Journal of Social and Behavioral Sciences, 21,* 1–30.

REPRESENTATIVE PUBLICATIONS

Payton, C. R. (1975). *Employment Qualification and Selection Procedures: Library of Congress* (Agreement No. A75–18). Washington, DC: Library of Congress.

Payton, C. R. (1981). Substance abuse and mental health: Special prevention strategies needed for ethnics of color (National Institute on Drug Abuse Public Health Report), *1,* 20–25.

Payton, C. R. (1984). Who must do the hard things? *American Psychologist, 39,* 391–397.

Payton, C. R. (1985). Addressing the special needs of minority women. In N. J. Evans (Ed.), *New directions for student services: No. 29. Facilitating the development of women*. San Francisco: Jossey-Bass.

Payton, C. R., & Blake, L. (1964). Difference limen for perception of the vertical in monkeys. *Journal of perceptual and Motor Skills*, 19, 455–461.

CHAPTER 16

Martha T. Mednick

Martha T. Mednick

FAMILY BACKGROUND AND EARLY YEARS

My parents were working-class immigrants, and my early years were very much dominated by education. There were various kinds of lessons and Yiddish school, and there was constant pressure to do well. My family had an almost mystical belief in the power of education to change the condition of life. It was also a strong value, a reverence for learning, and it was from them that I learned to love to learn, and to love and respect those who are learned.

Those were the years of the Depression. It was only through great sacrifice and very hard work on the part of both my parents that we were able to have a little more than what was freely available. Our house was full of books, and we all spent lots of time reading. I don't recall that any of my teachers in the early grades took a special interest in me. In fact, when all my girlfriends were sent to a special junior high school (new and experimental in those days) to rapidly advance through 2 years of work in 1, I stayed in the eight-grade school. In high school, I did excel, took the honors program, and was graduated with honors. However, I do not remember any special teachers. I continued my Yiddish/Hebrew schooling through high school, and, as I was going to school every day, my extracurricular life was curricular. Everyone always told me I was smart, but my reaction was to take it all for granted.

During late grade school and all through high school, I had a strong committed involvement in the Labor Zionist Youth Movement. I mention this because movement work of one sort or another has always been part of my life. My family members were movement people—my father a committed activist in the labor movement, my mother also an activist. To me it has always seemed entirely natural to get involved in causes that one believes in strongly.

EDUCATION

My undergraduate education was at the City College of New York (CCNY), then a free university. Although my parents were eager for me to be educated, their finances were such that if I had not had access to a free university, the likelihood of my having received a college education would have been very low. At the time I entered CCNY, women had not yet attained full citizenship in that venerable institution. It had been established as a men's school, and so it had remained until the early 1930s, when it was forced to admit a woman to its later formed College of Engineering. That woman found out that the charter did not exclude women, and she applied. Because she met all the qualifications, she could not be turned away. So the engineering school always had a few women . . . although very few. By 1946, there were, in addition to the College of Liberal Arts, a business college and a school of education. Both of these later-established units of the university admitted women. The College of Liberal Arts did not admit women until 1950.

I entered the College of Education in 1946. It had always seemed logical to go into teaching, and I assumed that would be my career. I entered college with a strong interest in science and thought I would pursue high school teaching. It is only in retrospect that I think of high school teaching as not a high enough aspiration. In my time, we revered our teachers. In my high school, just a run-of-the-mill New York City school, there were several teachers with doctorates; our principal had a PhD, and we were all in awe of this highly educated person. I am sure the presence of some of these people at the secondary level had to do with the Depression and the absence of jobs in that difficult time, but there they were—men as well as women—and they were part of my evaluation of what it took to be a teacher. Nevertheless, at CCNY, I soon decided that education was not for me. The reason was that the courses in education were almost all uninteresting, unchallenging, and a monumental waste of time. I decided that the reason for attending college did not include role-playing 6-year-olds and that I had to find something better. Soon I discovered that I could specialize in the College of Education, in psychological services, and I decided to give it a try.

Psychological services was a preprofessional program that existed side by side with the conventional liberal arts major (men only). I was able to take practical and theoretical psychology side by side, and I loved what I was learning and doing. Further, it fit my needs. I had to get out of school and become self-supporting, and school psychological services seemed a perfect answer. In my senior year, I applied to a new master's degree program in school psychology, was accepted, and was awarded a tuition scholarship. Psychology was one of the most popular and exciting majors at City College during those years. Once you took Gardner Murphy's course on personality, there was no turning back. He had a tremendous influence on a whole generation of social and personality psychologists. I think it made a difference because he attracted people who were thrilled to be in this major and to be learning what Murphy taught. It was as simple as that. He saw the future of the field and told us about it, and we decided to stay. It was also a lot of fun. I didn't know that it was a pioneering time, the beginning of enormous growth of the field, but that excitement became part of my motivation too. Still, the scholarship support was an important determinant of my continuing for the MS degree. Later, at Northwestern University, I received some scholarship support and then was in the Veteran's Administration Training Program, a training and economic bonanza for psychologists of that era. But that is getting ahead of the story. I obtained my master's degree in 1952 and joined my husband, Sarnoff Mednick, in Evanston, Illinois, where he was attending Northwestern. I took a job as a substitute teacher in elementary school while waiting for a school psychology job to come up. That was not too pleasant, and when the possibility of Veterans Administration support developed, I decided to apply for graduate school. I began studying for the doctorate in 1952 and obtained my degree in clinical psychology in 1955. At CCNY I had studied with the great, among them the eminent women Ruth Munroe and Florence Halpern. My strong background in psychodynamic theory, particularly in neo-Freudian theory, included knowledge of Karen Horney and Clara Thompson. So it never occurred to me that women did not belong in psychology.

The first year at Northwestern was horrendous, a brutal hurdle structured to weed us out. Fifty percent of the first-year class did not survive! We had a core curriculum, statistics, and B. J. Underwood's superb course in scientific method. The latter had a profound impact on me. Apart from learning about methods and the philosophy of science, I learned to think and write clearly and to be critical. That experience has continued to live within me and to affect my teaching, research, and writing to this day. By the end of the first year, having passed the examinations without having had a nervous breakdown, I had a good understanding of research methodology, a decent command of statistics, and good grounding in general psychology. My earlier training had provided me with knowledge in personality, especially in psychodynamics, and many testing skills, so I probably started at the Veterans Administration ahead of most. Northwestern had been very liberal about accepting my earlier graduate school credit and had admitted me as a post-master's student. So, by the time I entered my second year, I had only to complete a few courses, a qualifying exam, the clinical training requirement, and my dissertation.

Northwestern had a very small department, and the student culture was very strong, with a great deal of support from the "older" students. Each class developed close relationships. The faculty was quite supportive after the first-year hurdle was over; nevertheless, support was differential. I was not aware that being a woman made a difference. It did of course, but in a way, I am glad I did not recognize it. My level of stress was sufficient. As I have thought about those years, however, I recalled events that only seemed strange at the time, but that were clearly the result of bias. There was the head of the program telling us—and this has stuck in my mind clear as a bell—that the department did not mind admitting women even though they were not going to use their training. Now that is an amazing remark to hear during your orientation to graduate school. I remember thinking that the remark did not, of course, apply to me. My attribution was that I was different. I realize now that our class had a large proportion of women. Although it was to the credit of the department that it did not have a quota, as we know so many departments did even into the 1970s, the ratio probably made them just a bit nervous. It simply never occured to me that I would waste my training; I saw myself as having the right to it as long as I had the ability and the drive. Although there was little discrimination in the classroom, it is noteworthy that the students who became closely allied with the professors, especially those in tenured rank and with grants, were invariably men. Men were also the ones who were groomed and sent to the best places when they completed their work. Of course, there were also some men do didn't pass muster, but *none* of the women did.

In the clinical setting, sexism was more blatant and was expressed in many ways. In my first orientation there, we were asked not to wear tight sweaters because it was "seductive" to the male patients. Our supervisors were men, and I dare say that the problem was at least as much theirs as the patients'. But as young students, and in the ethos of the times, we readily accepted this as well-intentioned advice. Maybe it was. There were also many negative comments about professional women. A favorite used by male trainees was "castrating bitch." Of course, present company was always the exception. If they told you that you were very feminine in spite of being smart, it meant you were diffident about expressing your views, a little modest about your ideas, and not critical. So the real woman and the good student trainee image were a bit contradictory. I think this attitude in the clinic affected me in my supervisory relationships, which were very uneven and not all enjoyable. The few women who were on staff (I remember only two) were gossiped about, and the male trainees hated being supervised by them. But there was no expression of sisterhood or any special feelings of support from female psychologists in these settings, nor were these feelings expected.

Northwestern had one woman on the faculty; Janet Taylor (now Janet Talyor Spence), a young assistant professor. She was loved by all of us—a marvelous, dedicated teacher who was working in an area of psychology that was very exciting for us clinical trainees because we were committed to the idea of verifying clinical concepts in the experimental laboratory. Taylor's dissertation had been on the development of the Manifest Anxiety Scale, and she was continuing work on this and in the area of perceptual defense; these were the hot topics of the day, and students were attracted to her like flies. I will remind you that John Dollard and Neal Miller had just published *Personality and Psychotherapy: An Analysis in Terms of Learning, Thinking, and Culture* (1950), a translation of Freudian psychology into drive theory terms, and the Manifest Anxiety Scale had been devised as a measure of individual differences in drive level. This made possible the testing of a whole range of hypotheses about the effect of drive on various aspects of human behavior. My dissertation, under Taylor's direction, followed this developing tradition. I studied a phenomenon that had been observed in real life and that had been the subject of previous research—namely, the generalization and incubation of anxiety. I also looked at how individual differences in level of manifest anxiety affected incubation and generalization. Taylor was an adviser and a generally supportive person; I have adopted her as my model for how a dissertation adviser should be. I have always tried to emulate her. Real support for one's students is the lesson I learned, and that means that one is intimately involved with their work.

CAREER

There were probably at least three factors that complicated the search for my first job in 1955. One was that, after finishing my degree, I simply moved with my husband to Massachusetts and his first job at Harvard University. It never occurred to me to do otherwise. You must realize that I was already a bit weird for a woman of my generation. My college classmates had retired to have children, and my male peers had wives who were all PHTs (putting hubby through). They were marking time until hubby got his degree, and they could retire to suburban wifehood. In that context, it certainly never entered my mind for a moment not to go with him; that was not suggested, nor would I have done it. A second factor was the move to the Boston area, which was, and is, one of the most parochial professional areas in the country. At that time, Bostonians thought of the Midwest as barbaric, and many had never heard of Northwestern, so there was more than the usual amount of resistance. A third factor was that no one in the department or in my clinical placement offered to help in my job search. We all conspired in the view that, once having obtained one good job for a couple, obligations had been fulfilled. However, had my professors asked me, I certainly would have let it be known that I would be job hunting, but that did not happen. I think this was an instance in which my aspirations were simply not considered. Of course, as I have already noted, it never occurred to me that I would not use my training. Further, the basic circumstance of my life was that I had to work. The Harvard salary was so low that our combined income was one third of what we had been earning the previous year as graduate students! Clearly my status as a woman, and probably more as a wife, affected me negatively. However, because I didn't realize it was affecting me negatively, I did not attribute my adverse circumstances to that status.

The opportunity that finally came up was through my husband's Harvard connection. I mention this pointedly because it was to become a pattern. He had met Ogden Lindsley, an operant conditioner who was working with chronic schizophrenics; Lindsley hired me to be the laboratory clinician. The first study we did was an examination of the relationship between operant behavior of chronic schizophrenics and level of intelligence. I was able to apply some clinical concepts and skills to the studies being done in the laboratory. The chronic patients had been showing wide individual differences in operant conditioning, and we simply showed that one cause of these differences was intelligence level. Such an approach was outside the domain of the operant conditioner, so it was a good illustration of how two differing domains can result in a new way of approaching a problem. Lindsley was very open to this kind of new input, although I did not find that to be the case for other operant conditioners. I found working in this laboratory interesting and the affiliation with B. F. Skinner exciting, so I decided to extend the time there (as the lab has run out of funds) through a National Institute of Mental Health Postdoctoral Research Fellowship under the auspices of Skinner. The fellowship gave me the opportunity to do my own research and to continue in a quasi-student role. I was able to take advantage of Harvard's rich resources. One high spot was the Friday afternoon "pigeon lab" presided over by Skinner. There I was exposed to, among other events, the very earliest efforts to create programs for the teaching of mathematics. In 1956, the machines were very primitive, not computers, but the power of the approach was already apparent and the enthusiasm quite contagious. The research I did for my postdoctoral work, however, was on a clinical problem. It involved setting up a token economy with autistic children. It was very interesting but frustrating, and the outcome was too unclear to warrant publication. Nevertheless, my overall gain from the experience was enormous. I also kept my finger in the clinical area for some years by doing diagnostic testing, by supervising, and by teaching assessment courses, but my clinical days were really over. There is an irony here because the women in the field were more likely to become clinicians or child psychologists, and we were often told that we were good at that sort of thing. True or false, that had little to do with what happened to me.

The rest of my career history has to be divided into three parts: the "I will follow you anywhere and do whatever comes up" part, the postdivorce transition, and the years since arriving at Howard University. The first years, roughly from 1958 to 1964, coincided with having children and shifting to part-time work. My first daughter was born in 1957; the second was born in 1960. We were a typical academic family of the time, and we moved around quite a bit. We had moved from Harvard to Berkeley in 1958; in 1959, we moved to the University of Michigan, a home for us until 1967. In the early 1960s and mid-1960s for the first time I did some collaborative work with my husband, first on a personality textbook, *Research in Personality* (Mednick & Mednick, 1962), and then on the development of the Remote Associates Test (Mednick & Mednick, 1967), a measure of creative thinking. I must note here that a very important element in my career development was that I continued to publish—whether I worked full-time or part-time or not at all. Had I not done so, I believe my career as an academic would have been stymied.

After my marital status changed in 1964, I spent several years coming to terms with my professional identity and forging my own networks. This was not hard because I had become well acquainted with important members of the large community of psychologists in Ann Arbor. This was not due to my husband's connections, but rather because I was also affiliated with an important Michigan institution, the Institute of Social Research. Sarnoff Mednick and I had obtained a U.S. Office of Education grant that was administered by the Institute. The reason for this was that nepotism rules did not allow me to have an appointment in the Psychology Department. As principal investigator, and in order for me to be paid as a university employee, an appointment was necessary. So the Institute became the home of the grant, and also my home.

The end of the grant and my need to seek full-time work coincided. For a couple years, I worked fairly happily at the Institute, and as an adjunct professor at the University of Michigan School of Nursing. By 1967, however, I realized that soft money and part-time work, even if adding up to a full-time salary, was not what I wanted. I started to look for a tenure-track position. At this point, I had a few strikes against me—my checkered career path, little teaching experience, and, as I soon realized, discrimination. I reached out to various friends in the field; one of the people I talked with was Ted Newcomb. I had worked with him in the arrangements for the publication of the personality text, and he was a most helpful friend. He was the kind of person one could be very open with, and I asked him, rather naively I suppose, whether my being a woman would hamper my search. He was brutally frank as he told me of the realities of life, even at the University of Michigan in the radical 1960s. There was one tenured woman, Helen Peak, a social psychologist, in the department of more than 150 full-time faculty. To make matters worse, she was in an endowed chair reserved for a woman that had been cleverly nabbed by the enterprising head of the department in the early 1950s.

My search, also motivated by personal factors such as the desire to live in a more urban environment and a need for new vistas, did prove fruitful. It culminated in my move to Howard, which made the best offer in a big Eastern city. I came in as associate professor, was awarded tenure within a year, and attained the rank of full professor in 1971. Except for some years away on leave, I've been happily at Howard since 1968.

I need to include one other matter before getting on with the Howard years. During my last year or two in Ann Arbor, I became aware that there were several doctoral students doing their dissertations on women. Sandra Tangri was in the midst of her role-innovator study, Judith Bardwick was looking at women's fertility difficulties, and Matina Horner was studying sex differences in motivational conflict. Tangri was an office neighbor, and we spent many hours talking about her work. It was exciting, eye opening, and stimulating to talk with her and the others. A seminar that Bardwick ran one semester, which attracted several other faculty members and researchers, clinched it for me. I determined that women and achievement were going to be my next research area.

As soon as I was settled at Howard, I worked up a proposal for an issue of the *Journal of Social Issues*. I collaborated with Tangri on that issue, entitled "New Perspectives on Women" (Mednick & Tangri, 1972) and later expanded the issue into a book, *Women and Achievement: Motivational and Social Analysis* (Mednick, Tangri, & Hoffman, 1975). I was also able to obtain research funds, and during those years my graduate students at Howard did theses and dissertations that looked in various ways at race, class, and sex issues in the psychology of achievement. The feeling was that we were plowing new and different territory, and it was wonderfully exciting. I have never been bored with psychology, no matter what area I worked in, but working in the psychology of women added the element of passion. These were the years—perhaps the centerpiece of my life in psychology—when I worked with outstanding Black graduate students. Most of them have gone on to make important contributions to psychology, and, equally important, to serve as role models for a new generation. These include Gwendolyn Puryear Keita, Saundra Rice Murray, Peggy Carr, Cheryle Bailey, and Tom Robinson, as well as others. They have taught me while I have taught them.

About 1972, I began to get involved in organizational work on behalf of women in psychology. I chaired the Ad Hoc Committee on Women in Psychology of the American Psychological Association (APA), now the APA Continuing Committee on Women in Psychology. The committee's work focused on the status of women in the profession, and it was also a catalyst for the formation of the Division of the Psychology of Women (Division 35) within APA. My involvement with many aspects of the work of this group lasted for

7 or 8 years. These activities, whatever their larger significance may be, were very important for me. I felt a more complete professional by being engaged in this work. Also much to my surprise, it felt good to have a bit of influence and to be part of a movement for change. I also realized that I had organizational and leadership abilities, and the women's movement gave me the opportunity to find that out. It was also part of the excitement to work with the many women and the few men who were part of these efforts. They are too numerous to name, and it is hard to give appropriate credit to so many. Several stand out: Carolyn Sherif, who died in 1983, inspired me to think about a new psychology for women; and Barbara Wallston, also deceased (1987), worked with me in the trenches in a tireless and uniquely constructive fashion; Helen Astin talked me into taking on this work in the first place, and I owe her a debt of gratitude.

As the 1970s progressed, my interests and my activities gradually became more interdisciplinary. At conferences and other meetings, I began to meet and hear about the work of feminist scholars from many fields. The excitement of women's studies and my wish to try my hand at administration led me to accept a position as the director of the Department of Women's Studies at the University of Connecticut, where I spent 2 years helping to develop a fledgling program. Then I returned to Howard. In the University of Connecticut position, I learned about how a large state university operates and how meager resources could be stretched. I once again found out how important it is to construct a support network. Women came from the entire campus to assist in the development of the program. Because I worked alone, with one assistant, I needed the outside commitment, and fortunately I had it. We were able to persuade a doubting, at times hostile, academic community that women's scholarship was a legitimate field of study that belonged on a university campus.

SUPPORT

Although I've already discussed support indirectly, I will add a few comments. There were varying degrees of support in the academic environment. For example, in graduate school, the biggie professors had their "boys." Everyone knew who these "boys" were—they had every kind of support needed and were squired right into the best jobs that came up once their schoolwork was completed. For the rest of us, support varied; I recall taking this pretty much for granted and not feeling especially resentful or competitive.

As for role models, there were very few women in faculties at that time. There was also not much awareness about the situation. Nevertheless, there was an unspoken attraction to the few women who were around and a greater degree of comfort with them that I think mattered. A year at the University of Oregon, before the Northwestern years, had given me a chance to study with and get to know Leona Tyler, a great teacher and friend to her students. We have kept in touch over the years, and her sincere interest in former students' work is what has made that relationship important. Janet Taylor Spence, as I've said, showed me how to be a teacher in the best sense of the word. In reflecting on these women as role models, I can only say they certainly set high standards for me, but I think my real models were always my peers. In that connection, the fact that there was a significant number of women in our program was important.

IDENTITY AND COPING

In my earlier years as wife and young parent, my commitment was less to career than to family, although I never considered myself more a wife and mother than a psychologist. Probably I never considered it—I just did both to the extent I was able. Part-time work was a good solution; I was almost always fortunate to have work that engaged me and could be published. Although there was no question that I would pursue my work, my husband's career came first. Of course I followed him from job to job—one just did that.

I have always felt that academic life is ideally suited for a woman with a family—for a man too, if he is interested in a balanced life. In my own case, flexible scheduling made all the difference. Much of our work can also be done at home, and that helps too. My daughters never questioned the legitimacy of my work, and they did not expect me to stay at home any more than they expected their father to stay at home. I think it was also because they knew what I did, and I made them part of my work life as much as I could. I see the younger men on our faculty bringing children to work. For whatever the reason, it seems like a good idea. For women, especially, this means less of a split between home and work identities. I haven't got any advice for anyone in this era, however, for everything seems so different now. Also, I have to admit that what I did was pretty much ad hoc, and there certainly were times when things did not run smoothly, but this is true regardless of when and where mothers and fathers work. It is part of the tension of an involved, constructive life—an expected, not necessarily negative effect.

REFERENCES

Dollard, J., & Miller, N. E. (1950). *Personality and psychotherapy: An analysis in terms of learning, thinking, and culture.* New York: McGraw-Hill.

Mednick, M. T., & Tangri, S. S. (Eds.). (1972). New perspectives on women [Special issue]. *Journal of Social Issues, 28*(2).

Mednick, M. T., Tangri, S. S., & Hoffman, L. W. (1975). *Women and achievement: Motivational and social analysis.* New York: Hemisphere.

Mednick. S. A., & Mednick. M. T. (1962). *Research in personality.* New York: Holt, Rinehart & Winston.

Mednick. S. A., & Mednick, M. T. (1967). *The Remote Associates Test manual and test, Forms 1 and 2.* Boston: Houghton-Mifflin.

REPRESENTATIVE PUBLICATIONS

Mednick, M. T. (1963). Research creativity in psychology graduate students. *Journal of Consulting Psychology, 27,* 265–266.

Mednick, M. T. (1967). Mediated generalization and the incubation effect as a function of manifest anxiety. *Journal of Abnormal and Social Psychology, 55,* 315–321.

Mednick, M. T., (1978). Now we are four: What should we be when we grow up? *Psychology of Women Quarterly, 3,* 123–138.

Mednick, M. T. (1978). Psychology of women: Research issues and trends. *New York Academy of Science Annals, 309,* 77–92.

Mednick, M. T. (1979). The new psychology of women: A feminist analysis. In J. E. Gullahorn (Ed.), *Psychology of women in transition.* New York: Winston.

Mednick, M. T. (1982). Women and the psychology of achievement: Implications for personal and social change. In J. H. Bernadin (Ed.), *Women in the work force.* New York: Praeger.

Mednick, M. T. (1984). *Political Science Quarterly Review of the Managed Heart: The commercialization of human feeling* by A. R. Hothschild. Berkeley: University of California Press.

Mednick, M. T. (1984). The Society for the Study of Psychological Issues and Advocacy: A historical look. *Journal of Social Issues, 40*(3), 159–177.

Mednick, M. T. S. (1987). Single mothers: A review & critique. In J. Oskamp (Ed.), *Family processes and problems. Applied social psychology annual.* Beverly Hills, CA: Sage.

Mednick, M. T., & Lindsley, O. R. (1958). Some clinical correlates of operant behavior. *Journal of Abnormal and Social Psychology, 57,* 13–16.

Mednick, M. T., & Murray, S. A. (1977). Black women's achievement orientation: Motivational and cognitive factors. *Psychology of Women Quarterly, 1,* 229–246.

Mednick, M. T., & Weissman, H. J. (1975). Psychology of women: Selected topics. *Annual Review of Psychology.*

Murray, S. A., & Mednick, M. T. (1975). Perceiving the causes of achievement success and failure: Sex, race and motivational comparisons. *Journal of Consulting and Clinical Psychology, 43,* 881–885.

Puryear, G. R., & Mednick, M. T. (1974). Militancy, fear of success and affective attachment in Black college women. *Journal of Consulting and Clinical Psychology, 42,* 263–266.

Safir, M., Mednic, M. T., Israeli, D., & Bernard, J. (1985). *Women's worlds: From the new scholarship*, New York: Praeger.

Weston, P. J., & Mednick, M. T. (1970). Race, social class and the motive to avoid success in women. *Journal of Cross-Cultural Psychology*, *1*, 285–291.

CHAPTER 17

Martha E. Bernal

Martha E. Bernal

PREFACE

I am pleased and honored to have been invited to contribute my professional autobiography to Volume 2 of *Models of Achievement*. I know that this invitation was extended because I was believed to be the first Hispanic woman to receive the PhD in psychology and not because my objective record of achievement or my seniority in our profession equals that of the distinguished colleagues who are also contributing to this volume. In considering the invitation, I realized that some people would view this invitation as unmerited and offensive. Yet, if I refused, those who supported this award would be disappointed. I decided to accept this invitation because it seems important that the life experiences of female psychologists who are culturally diverse be represented among, and understood by, the members of the American Psychological Association (APA). I also want readers to know how difficult it was for me to earn a PhD and to become the first nationally visible Hispanic female psychologist, and perhaps to review their definition of merit. Psychologists need to know of the many reasons why there was no other like me prior to 1962 and why there have been precious few since then.

PROFESSIONAL AUTOBIOGRAPHY

In the era in which I attended graduate school, between 1952 and

1962, the number of women in graduate training in any area of U.S. psychology was still small compared to the number of men. But the number of Hispanic women was smaller still, as were the numbers of Hispanic men, or of any other ethnic minority group. Although the civil rights movement was about to begin, there was as yet no special consideration accorded groups of people, such as ethnic minorities and women, who had been deprived of their rights as citizens in various ways by White men.

My parents were young adults when they migrated to this country during the Mexican revolutionary era of the 1920s, when that whole country was in turmoil and people crossed the border as political refugees. My father, the second son of a printer, obtained a third-grade education in Mexico; my mother completed the sixth grade in a U.S. school during one of her family's migrations across the border. They met while attending English classes at night in preparation for their citizenship examinations. Both came from traditional Mexican families, although my father was more prone to adhere to the old European values. These values emphasized the family, modesty in dress and action, and a very strict morality that frowned on many things that young people take for granted now (including their right to date without a chaperone). They held the strong view that women stayed in their parents' home until they were married and that the woman's role was to take care of her husband, children, and home. Education and careers were for men only. Although my own background was very traditional, it was not necessarily typical of all Mexican Americans. Mexican-American families make a variety of acculturative adjustments to life in this country: monocultural Mexican, bicultural, or monocultural Anglo. These adjustments depend upon religious beliefs, generation born in the United States, educational and socioeconomic background, rural versus urban life experience, and strength of ethnic identity.

In 1937, when I began school in El Paso, Texas, the use of the Spanish language by Mexican children was punished in Texas schools. Because I did not speak English, I immediately learned that the dominant society disapproved of my language and heritage. My childhood social circle was composed of other Mexican-American children and a few Anglo children who attended the same school, but after the eighth grade, I had no Anglo friends. An invisible line divided the Mexican-American and Anglo-American people in that city, and that line became increasingly emphasized as we grew from children into adolescents and then into young adults. It was drawn by Anglos with generally superior socioeconomic and educational backgrounds, people who did not want their children to mix socially or intermarry with Mexican people. Many Mexican-American parents also frowned on intermarriage and regarded Anglos as "maleducados," referring not to their lack of education but to their perceived loose morals and lack of manners. Curiously, I can recall no discussion in my family about civil rights or discrimination, although all of us must have encountered some type of prejudice on a fairly frequent basis. I do remember, however, that we were grateful to be living in the United States instead of in Mexico, where other relatives lived in far more economically stressful circumstances than my immediate family experienced. Throughout my life, however critical I might be of this country, I have felt grateful for the opportunities of which I availed myself. They would most likely not have existed had I lived in Mexico.

Among my Mexican-American peers, there was much caring and a warm sense of belonging. I grew up in the same neighborhood and had the same dear friends until I left at the age of 21. I attended church, played, danced, sang, and shared my dreams, secrets, and experiences with friends with whom I still maintain contact. I shall always be grateful for the privilege of having been raised among them and having shared those vital years with them.

My immediate family was small, consisting of one sister who was 2 years older than I and another sister who was 13 years younger. Looking back on those years, I believe that my older sister, Cristina, tended to identify more strongly with her Mexican-oriented family and friends and to be more traditional in her values than I. Cristina married a fellow El Pasoan in her early 20s, while she was working as a legal secretary. He was in the military service, and they lived in various parts of the country, but never in El Paso. She must have found the sharp shift to living totally in the Anglo-American culture difficult. They have lived in San Diego for many years and have raised four children. My younger sister, Ysaura, became a bilingual education teacher and lives in Davis, California, with her two children. Our extended family was quite large, because grandparents on both sides had 13 children each, and about two thirds of these children survived to adulthood. This extended family, whom I saw frequently, was a source of support and comfort and gave me a strong sense of ethnic identity.

As I studied at El Paso High School and then at Texas Western College (now the University of Texas at El Paso), I experienced an emerging realization that my academic interests and personal ambitions would conflict in a profound way with my Mexican-American culture's expectations of me as a woman. Upon finishing high school, I literally had to conduct battle with my father about going to college. My sister Cristina already had agreed to go to business school instead of college, and it was difficult to break this precedent. My father's view was that, because we were women, we would be getting married, and a college education would be a waste. My mother was caring and supportive of my ambitions; however, I had to fight my own battles with dad. Some of my friends were not understanding, either; at this age, many of them were marrying and entering jobs, although a few, mostly men, planned to continue their schooling if their parents could afford the local college. I went to work for a year after high school, saved my salary, and announced I would be going to college. Eventually, my father gave in and assisted me financially even though, as little as it cost in those days to attend that particular public institution, I knew it was economically difficult for him to help. I believe it is the mix of traditional, culturally based views about the woman's role as a submissive, self-sacrificing "mamacita," the absence of a strong effort on the part of educational institutions to prepare Hispanic students properly for higher education, the negative social stereotypes of the Mexican woman that exist in the United States, and the lack of financial resources for education after high school that has kept disproportionate numbers of Hispanic women, relative to our Anglo counterparts, from getting a college education. Even when a student was able, teachers often advised against college preparation in high school and gave little encouragement for enrolling in difficult courses such as advanced mathematics. My Hispanic sisters and I were given such advice and little encouragement.

After entering college, the battle had to be fought again because I wanted to go to graduate school, and that meant moving to another geographical location. As I was completing college, I saw a notice on the Psychology Department bulletin board regarding a graduate assistantship at Louisiana State University at Baton Rouge, applied, and got the position. This time there resulted an extended struggle between my father and me. He literally felt he would be a failure as a father if he allowed me to go off. I suspect that he had no real sense of what kind of financial support this education would require and felt incapable of providing it, although he probably felt ashamed to admit to this feeling. Again I prevailed, and he personally drove me to Baton Rouge. He and Cristina helped me financially as best they could. Although I had federal training support for two of my graduate training years, I financed most of that education by working stints between periods of graduate study.

It would have been infinitely easier to have gone to business school, as my father suggested—to have stayed in El Paso, enjoyed my friends, kept peace with my father. I would have avoided the guilt I felt knowing that it was a heavy financial burden for him; I would have avoided the horrible homesickness that I experienced for years after leaving El Paso; I would have avoided the yearning for my ethnic ties and family that still haunts me. Call it stubbornness or wisdom, I felt that I must determine my own life, no matter what others thought was best for me. I also knew that the best place to invest my time, funds, and efforts was in my education.

Anglo friends used to ask me why I chose as I did, as they tried to understand why I was different from the popular stereotype of the Mexican-American woman. I always found it a difficult question and at times, in responding to it, found myself angry about the millions of Mexican-American women who had not "made it" in American society as well as aware of my loneliness for my ethnic sisters who were completely absent in the White world in which I had chosen to pursue my career. I only knew that I wanted to go to graduate school, although not necessarily for a PhD, at least initially. Mentors were rare in my educational background. There were no Hispanic teachers, male or female, anywhere in my education, either then or later. There were admirable teachers who challenged me to do my best, but I had no close relationships with any of them, and the only Hispanic woman I knew who had a career was a dear aunt Elvira who was a nurse in Mexico. I went to Baton Rouge by default, knowing nothing about any other training programs; the Louisiana State University notice was the only one I saw. Once there, I found that the "assistantship" was really a typing job that provided no psychological training.

I left Louisiana State after 1 year, worked full-time for 2 years, and then went to Syracuse University, where I earned a master's degree in special education in 1957. In 1959, I returned to graduate training in psychology at Indiana University. There is much to tell about the racism and sexism that pervaded these years of graduate school. I won't give details of how some professors (all my graduate professors were married men) chased my fellow female students and me around their labs and offices, or about how, for the female graduate student, the "research assistant" title was a euphemism for sexual service to professors. Based on discussions with fellow graduate students, I would guess that my experiences probably were fairly typical of those of other female graduate students of the era. I hasten to add that not all my professors were of this ilk, but there were enough for me to have formed the overall impression I have described.

Surprisingly, despite these experiences, my fellow female students never complained or expected things to be different. Our heroes were the successful and dedicated professors and psychologists with whom we studied and about whom we read. Graduate school was exciting, my fellow students cared for and helped one another, and I especially loved being at Indiana University in Bloomington. One of my models during those years at Indiana was my first dissertation adviser, a physiological psychologist, Roland C. Davis, who suffered a fatal heart attack before I completed the dissertation. Roland had done some pioneering work on the relation of stomach motility to hunger and on lie detection. Another model and mentor was Arnold Binder, now head of the social ecology program at the University of California at Irvine. Arnold became my adviser after Davis died; he valiantly struggled to teach me to write in scientific style. A very important person was Leon Levy, who was an inspiring and creative teacher. Later, when I was graduated, Leon cosigned a loan that provided me with funds on which to live until I was to receive my first paycheck. Leon now heads the Department of Psychology at the University of Maryland at Catonsville, Maryland. Harry Yamaguchi, knowing of my frantic desire to leave Bloomington at one point, took the trouble to tell me that the chances of ever completing my degree once I left the campus were only one in four. And so I stayed and finished, thanks to Harry, who recently retired from Indiana University.

Clinical psychology in 1962, when I took my PhD, was mired in psychodynamic theory, client-centered counseling, Sullivanian treatment, and projective tests. This combination of theory and treatment approaches had no appeal to me, and the effect of Levy's research course on projective testing was that I never again administered another projective test. Ferster and DeMyer (1961) and Lindsley (1956, 1960) were beginning to conduct operant-learning experiments with chronically psychotic adults and children. Their interesting point of view was supported by Indiana's hard-nosed empiricism and emphasis on learning theories. Contact with these people and their work, along with my training at Indiana, was to have a profound effect on my thinking as a clinician and behavioral scientist.

But that was not to happen until 2 years after leaving Bloomington because, still influenced by Davis, I first went to the University of California at Los Angeles (UCLA) as a U.S. Public Health Service postdoctoral research fellow in psychophysiology. After the postdoctoral training, I assumed my first teaching position as an assistant professor at the University of Arizona at Tucson, where I was further influenced by my colleagues, Roland Tharp and Ralph

Wetzel(1969).While in Arizona,I consulted at a mental health center and successfully worked with a maritally distressed husband and his chronically mentally ill wife using a behavioral approach. That was exciting: I instituted a series of programs prescribing how they were to change the behaviors that distressed one another. In my lectures, I discussed this innovative approach, and the students too found it exciting. Tucson, however, was very lonely, and a year later I returned to the Neuropsychiatric Institute at UCLA to find Ivar Lovaas (1967) beginning to teach language and socially appropriate behaviors to autistic children using operant-conditioning principles.

Although my first National Institute of Mental Health (NIMH) research grant in 1965 was awarded for studying psychophysiological orienting responses in autistic children (Bernal & Miller, 1970; Miller & Bernal, 1971), I was still interested primarily in learning theory applications to human problems, particularly to children. Before enrolling at Indiana, I had worked in an in-patient children's psychiatric hospital ward and had been appalled at the prevailing practices: Children had been locked up for years and were essentially raised by the lowest paid and least trained staff, parents were blamed for their children's tragedies, and there was no scientific basis for decisions about admission, release, or treatment. So when, at UCLA, a small boy who had a severe behavior problem was referred to my team, I took on the task of figuring out how to teach his parents to teach their child to behave appropriately. To achieve this goal, my students and I observed the child and his parents at home, in school, and in the clinic and made videotapes and reviewed them carefully. Then we devised lesson plans that were based on learning principles for the parents to follow (Bernal, Duryee, Pruitt, & Burns, 1968). That was the beginning of my career in applied clinical research, and I eventually gained a national reputation in the field of behavior modification by developing and assessing parent-training techniques for the treatment of conduct-problem children (Bernal, 1969, 1971, 1972a, 1972b). Other psychologists were thinking similarly during those years, although I didn't know about their work when I started mine in 1965. This parent-training work continued past 1971, when I moved to the University of Denver with a large grant in support of a major clinical research outcome study with the goal of assessing the efficacy of this approach (Bernal, 1983; Bernal, Klinnert, & Schultz, 1980; Bernal & North).

During this first part of my career, which ended with the publication of the outcome study (Bernal et al., 1980), my contribution, I believe, was that I approached children's psychological problems in a manner that was vastly different from the way things had been done. My work, and that of other pioneers in this field, eventually led to the adoption of a very different theory about human problems, namely, that children who had such problems were not internally ill or damaged but had learned their maladaptive behaviors. They could unlearn them and could be taught a more adaptive behavioral repertoire. The approach emphasized the teaching of behavioral principles to parents and other social agents in the child's life so as to teach the child more appropriate behaviors. The usefulness of the treatment was assessed on the basis of empiricism rather than clinical judgment. The results of my outcome study, however, raised serious questions about the efficacy of parent training as a treatment for all conduct-problem children, and in other publications I began to stress the importance of the several social systems in which the child operated as factors to be considered in assessment and treatment (Bernal & Klinnert, 1981).

In those days, I gave frequent workshops and lectures in different parts of the country to groups who were eager to know about these innovative behavioral approaches. But there also were groups of professionals who believed that applied behavioral approaches were unethical, if not heretical. I remember the day I presented my early work at the psychoanalytically oriented Reiss Davis Clinic in Los Angeles. At the end of my presentation, the whole audience walked out in total silence. I also recall one day in 1968 when I gave a colloquium at the UCLA Department of Psychiatry and was charged with using techniques reminiscent of the flogging of mentally ill people during the days before Phillipe Pinel. Behavioral treatments are widely used nowadays in many types of settings, but it was interesting to have been a part of a major advance in the treatment of human problems, an advance that initially met strong resistance from the prevailing mental health professional establishment.

A sharp change in my professional thinking occurred in 1979, during a sabbatical year. For many years, I had wanted to address the needs of Hispanic children in my role as a Hispanic psychologist, but I had to bring my other work to its conclusion first. Now I began to read in the fields of sociology, political science, history, and psychology about Mexican Americans and other minorities. It was the first time since I left El Paso that I freed myself to pursue such reading and thinking. And due to that opportunity, there resulted what is best understood as an acculturation conflict. I was shocked at what I learned had happened to Mexican Americans and to me. History is complex, so I will vastly simplify and personalize it for the sake of communicating my subjective experience. I was outraged at the knowledge that the land of my ancestors had been stolen by White settlers, that civilized Mexican people living in what had been Mexican territory had been reduced to laborers and servants for the White conquerors, that Texas laws resulted in my becoming ashamed of my native language and of the core of my Mexican identity because English-speaking people wanted to subjugate us. Remember, my basic education had taken place in Texas, and the history books there were notorious for their ethnocentrism and racial bias, so I had been provided a distorted view of historical events relating to Mexico.

I read the psychological literature in minority mental health and learned that my profession accorded emotionally disturbed White people its best services and resources and conducted its best research on them while neglecting or ignoring other groups. The psychological theory and body of knowledge that I had so enthusiastically studied and embraced were based almost exclusively on White middle-class subjects, mostly students. When minority people were compared with these White subjects, differences between the two groups were consistently found in favor of the Whites. My scientific colleagues interpreted these differences as due to intellectual, genetic, and cultural deficits in minority people.

Thus came I in direct and severe conflict with my profession and colleagues, and it was a jarring blow. It wasn't that I had been unaware of racism. What had escaped me was the pervasive manner in which racism affected minorities on a daily basis. I had been wearing blinders that protected me from seeing the surrounding evidence of a racism I abhorred. The search led to a still more painful revelation: All those years since becoming a graduate student, I had become White in my world view and perspectives, equally as ethnocentric as my White colleagues. In Spanish, the term is *vendida*—"bought by the White world." In this search, I learned that I even belittled members of my own ethnic group, as well as those of other ethnic groups, and realized that, if I did so, then there was reason to suspect that others around me also held such attitudes. Although the revelation stunned me, I knew that, since I had lived in a strictly White world for many years and had been raised in the same racist society, it would have been difficult to escape being exposed to and internalizing its perspectives about racial and ethnic minorities. Looking back over the years, I remembered that the first time I had seen another Hispanic psychologist was in 1972, when 25 of us—probably, at that time, all the existing Mexican-American psychologists who held a PhD in this country—gathered at the University of California at Riverside for a conference.

My first reaction to the encounter with these colleagues was one of utter amazement that they were equally as competent as Anglo psychologists.

Now I realized that my own life had been deeply and personally affected by racist America. Just as institutional racism operated to maintain unequal treatment of minority children in elementary schools, it also operated to restrict our access to undergraduate and graduate education. How else could the high minority school drop-out rates and the underrepresentation of minorities in higher education be understood? My own profession restricted ethnic minorities' access to graduate training and to service as professors on our faculties. It also graduated White behavioral scientists and practitioners who had been raised in a racist society, and many of these professionals devalued any but their own culture and language. These undereducated, culturally limited professionals looked at minorities at best with a paternalistic attitude and at worst with the view that minorities were intrinsically dumb, defective, violent, beyond help. I am not exaggerating; I am an enlightened professor of psychology. I have worked in White service settings and universities and have been educated in White schools and society. I have seen these racist phenomena firsthand. There exist psychologists and training programs that constitute exceptions to this charge, but the indifference of many of my professional colleagues to prevailing racist practices and their unwillingness to change those practices are appalling.

John Berry (1980), in writing about the varieties of adaptation to acculturation that immigrants experience, describes a three-phase course to acculturation: contact with the new host culture, conflict that is likely to result from that contact, and accommodation or adaptation to it. Accommodation may take many forms, from complete assimilation to biculturalism to rejection of the host culture. As a child, my first contact with the Anglo-American culture occurred upon entry into the school system, and conflict resulted from the beginning, although I accommodated by adhering to the social rules and conventions of the host culture and by achieving in the educational institutions. At the same time, due to my strong family ties, I maintained my identity as a Mexican American. Upon entering Anglo-American culture at the age of 21, my accommodation consisted of gradual assimilation (i.e., increasingly adopting the ways of the host culture as my own). And so I continued, except for visits with my family, until the upsetting realization that I've already described. Coming out of the life-consuming, busy years of climbing the academic ladder and building my career, I allowed myself inquiry into the culture of which I had become part and was shocked by what I learned and realized. Again I experienced conflict as a Mexican American in my host society. This time, however, it was to be much more difficult to arrive at a comfortable adaptation, possibly because my own ethnic identity and my loyalty to my ethnic group were at issue and because I had left the personal security and comfort provided by my family and my childhood friends. Furthermore, I was faced with coping on a daily basis with instances of the indifference to institutional racism that I have described, both in my immediate colleagues and across my profession.

After 1979, I wanted to conduct research that had bearing on central issues affecting ethnic minorities. For this reason, my previous research seemed dissatisfying, particularly because parent training was an intervention method developed for and assessed with middle-income White families and because I had found that efforts to use the approach with low-income minority families had been generally difficult and often ineffectual. It became necessary to change research fields, and I struggled for several years to carve out a new minority mental health research area for myself. As I tried unsuccessfully to generate grant funds for the work, I began to feel a sense of failure—the first in all my career. This experience led me to question my abilities and revived the old feelings of racial inferiority and second-class citizenship. The alienation I already felt among my colleagues was accentuated in this process. Coincident with these attempts was my resolution to try to make an impact on psychology at the broadest level possible so as to help make it more responsive to ethnic minority people. To achieve this goal, I embarked on social action research and writing (G. Bernal, M. E. Bernal, Martinez, Olmedo, & Santisteban, 1983; Bernal, 1980; Bernal, Barron, & Leary, 1983) that was to emphasize the status of psychological training in addressing the needs of minorities. I published a national survey of accredited clinical training programs on the preparation of psychologists to serve ethnic minority populations (Bernal & Padilla, 1982). For many years, I had served within the APA structure on various groups concerned with inclusion of minority perspectives within our national organization. I continued the work, this time as chair of the APA Committee on Ethnic Minority Human Resources Development. I also have served, since 1980, as a member of the board of directors of the newly formed National Hispanic Psychological Association and as the second president of the association from 1982 to 1984. In recent years, due to the efforts of many ethnic minority as well as dominant culture psychologists, our profession has become substantially more responsive and attentive to ethnic minority issues. I am proud to be a part of the group that has made that difference.

In 1984, while still at the University of Denver, I became project director of a new minority clinical training grant funded by NIMH. Most recently, I have been a senior postdoctoral Ford Foundation research fellow, retreading into still another research area: the development of ethnic identity in Mexican-American children. This research forms a background for work on a number of related topics: the measurement of ethnic identity in the developing child, the investigation of the mental health implications of children's ethnic identity, the socialization of ethnic minority children in U.S. society, and the influence on the ethnic minority child's sense of self resulting from the interaction of the child with the surrounding dominant society. This work currently is gaining momentum as I establish myself as a scholar in the field (Bernal, 1984, 1987; Van Parys & Bernal, 1985). This research shift has required extensive new learning from me in areas in which I was not trained.

In August 1986, I moved to Arizona State University from the University of Denver, where I had been on the faculty for 15 years. I am a professor in the Department of Psychology and an associate of the Hispanic Research Center, a campus multidisciplinary research unit. My very able collaborator on the ethnic identity research is another faculty member, George Knight, who has conducted cross-cultural developmental research (Knight & Kagan, 1977a, 1977b). The graduate students who work with us are Kurt Organista, Becky Maez, and Camille Garza. I highly value this partnership with George and our Mexican-American students. We are preparing grant proposals, submitting the first papers on the topic for publication, and have presented a research symposium on ethnic identity under Hispanic Research Center sponsorship. I am doing exciting, interesting things in an academic setting that values my individuality. My comfort as a bicultural Mexican-American psychologist has been vastly increased by coming to terms with sensitivities and feelings that were long suppressed and unrecognized. Finally, after all these years, there is a good fit between that identity and my professional work. In the years ahead, I have much to learn and many things left to accomplish.

REFERENCES

Bernal, G., Bernal, M. E., Martinez, A. C., Olmedo, E. L., & Santisteban, D. (1983). Hispanic mental health curriculum for psychology. In J. Chunn, J. P. Dunston,

& F. Ross-Sheriff (Eds.), *Mental health and people of color: Curriculum development and change.* Washington, DC: Howard University Press.

Bernal, M. E. (1969). Behavioral feedback in the modification of brat behaviors. *Journal of Nervous and Mental Diseases, 148,* 375–385.

Bernal, M.E. (1971). Training parents in child management. In R. Bradfield (Ed.), *Behavior modification of learning disabilities.* San Rafael, CA: Academic Press. Therapy Publications.

Bernal, M. E. (1972a). A behavioral prescripton for treating a child's eating problem. *Behavior Therapy and Experimental Psychiatry, 3,* 43–50.

Bernal, M. E. (1972b). The use of videotape feedback and operant learning principles in training parents in management of deviant children. *Advances in Behavior Therapy, 3,* 19–31.

Bernal, M. E. (1980). Hispanic issues in curriculum and training in psychology. *Hispanic Journal of Behavioral Sciences, 2,* 129–146.

Bernal, M. E. (1983). Consumer issues in parent training. In R. F. Dangel & R. A. Polster (Eds.), *Parent training: Foundations of research and practice* (pp. 477–503). New York: Guilford.

Bernal, M. E. (1984, August). *Racial attitude research on Hispanic children: Issues and directions.* Paper presented at the meeting of the American Psychological Association, Los Angeles.

Bernal, M. E. (1987, February). *The developing Mexican American child's understanding of ethnic identity.* Paper presented at the first symposium on Ethnic Identity: Conceptualization and Measurement of Mexican American Ethnic Identity in the Social Sciences, Tempe, AZ.

Bernal, M. E., Barron, B., & Leary, C. (1983). Use of application materials for recruitment of minority students in psychology. *Professional Psychology, 14,* 817–829.

Bernal, M. E., Duryee, J., Pruitt, H., & Burns, B. (1968). Behavior modification and the brat syndrome. *Journal of Consulting and Clinical Psychology, 32,* 447–455.

Bernal, M. E., & Klinnert, M. D. (1981, March). *Further insights on the results of a parent training outcome study.* Invited paper presented at the 13th Banff International Conference in Behavioral Sciences, Banff, Canada.

Bernal, M. E., Klinnert, M. D., & Schultz, L. A. (1980). Outcome evaluation of behavioral parent training and client centered parent counseling for children with conduct problems. *Journal of Applied Behavior Analysis, 13,* 127–141.

Bernal, M. E., & Miller, W. H. (1970). Electrodermal and cardiac responses of schizophrenic children to sensory stimuli. *Psychophysiology, 6,* 614–619.

Bernal, M. E., & North, J. A. (1978). Survey of parent training manuals. *Journal of Applied Behavior Analysis, 11,* 151–164.

Bernal, M. E., & Padilla, A. M. (1982). Survey of minority curricula and training in clinical psychology. *American Psychologist. 37,* 780–787.

Berry, J. W. (1980). Acculturation as varieties of adaptation. In A. M. Padilla (Ed.), *Acculturation: Theory, models, and some new findings.* Boulder, CO: Westview.

Ferster, C. B., & DeMyer, M. K. (1961). The development of performances in autistic children in an automatically controlled environment. *Journal of Chronic Diseases, 13,* 312–345.

Knight, G. P., & Kagan, S. (1977a). Acculturation of prosocial and competitive behaviors among second and third generation Mexican American children. *Journal of Crosscultural Psychology, 8,* 273–284.

Knight, G. P., & Kagan, S. (1977b). Development of prosocial and competitive behaviors in Anglo American and Mexican American children. *Child Development, 48,* 1385–1394.

Lindsley, O. R. (1956). Operant conditioning methods applied to research on chronic schizophrenics. *Psychiatric Research Reports, 5,* 118–153.

Lindsley, O. R. (1960). Characteristics of the behavior of chronic psychotics as revealed by free operant conditioning methods. *Diseases of the Nervous System, 21,* 66–78.

Lovaas, O. I. (1967). A behavior therapy approach to the treatment of childhood schizophrenia. In J. P. Hill (Ed.), *Minnesota Symposium on Child Psychology: Volume 1* (pp. 108–159). Minneapolis: University of Minnesota Press.

Miller, W. H., & Bernal, M. E. (1971). Measurement of the cardiac response in schizophrenic and normal children. *Psychophysiology, 8,* 533–537.

Tharp, R. G., & Wetzel, R. J. (1969). *Behavior modification in the natural environment.* New York: Academic.

Van Parys, M., & Bernal, M. E. (1985, August). *Ethnic identity of young Mexican American children.* Paper presented at the meeting of the American Psychological Association, Washington, DC.

REPRESENTATIVE PUBLICATIONS

Bernal, M. E. (1966). The report of being watched as a meaure of guilty behavior. In R. N. Haber (Ed.), *Research in motivation.* New York: Holt, Rinehart & Winston.

Bernal, M. E. (1979). Observer ethnicity effects on Chicano mothers and sons. *Hispanic Journal of Behavioral Sciences, 1,* 533–544.

Bernal, M. E., Delfini, L. F., North, J. A., & Kreutzer, S. L. (1976). Comparisons of boys' behaviors in homes and classrooms. In E. J. Mash, L. A. Hamerlynck, & L. C. Handy (Eds.), *Behavior modification and families.* New York: Brunner/Mazel.

Bernal, M. E., Gibson, D. M., Williams, E. E., & Pesses, D. I, (1971). A device for automatic audio tape recording. *Journal of Applied Behavior Analysis, 4,* 151–156.

Bernal, M. E., & Kreutzer, S. L. (1976). Relationship between excuses and dropout at a mental health center. *Journal of Consulting and Clinical Psychology, 44,* 494.

Bernal, M. E., North, J. A., & Kreutzer, S. L. (1974). Cross-validation of excuses and cooperation as possible measures for identification of clinical dropouts and continuers. *American Journal of Community Psychology, 2,* 151–163.

Bernal, M. E., & Schultz, L. (1985). How natural are naturalistic observations? *Special Education Technology, 7,* 27–34.

Thompson, R. J., & Bernal, M. E. (1982). Assessment of parent labeling of children referred for conduct problems. *Journal of Abnormal Child Psychology, 10,* 191–202.

CHAPTER 18

Florence L. Denmark

Florence L. Denmark

I was the second of two daughters who grew up in an extended Philadelphia family. My father was an attorney. My mother was a musician and had been studying for the concert stage. She gave up performing when she married. She gave music lessons until she had children, at which time she gave up teaching. I think she always felt frustrated in her ambition and didn't want her daughters to be frustrated in the same way. My grandparents, my two uncles (an attorney and a physician), and an aunt—all on my mother's side of the family—shared our large home. Our house was always a beehive of activity—with relatives, friends, patients, and clients dropping in.

I have to attribute a great deal of my motivation and desire to succeed to my mother. I suppose a clinician could interpret my mother's behavior as a projection of her own desires onto her daughters, and they would be right. I guess my mother was fortunate in that my sister and I were bright. If we hadn't been, it could have been a problem for her. We were encouraged to do well in school and were expected to get high grades.

Our father also expected a high level of performance. Although he was very proud of all that I accomplished, he never pushed me as my mother did. I resemble my father in terms of aptitudes, activities, and achievements, but my mother remained the driving force behind my accomplishments.

As a child, I loved to read. I always had my nose in a book, as did my father. When I was in first grade, I was skipped (advanced to the next highest grade). The principal put several of us in another classroom; I remember coming home at lunch time crying because I wasn't able to follow the class work. The class had been doing multiplication tables, and I couldn't immediately grasp the material. I didn't realize I had been skipped, My mother showed me how to multiply at lunch time, and I quickly caught up with the class. When I had a school assignment, I did it; I was afraid not to. My relationship with my mother was good, because I did as expected. According to my mother, I was a good child.

Another example of my mother's influence was her response to my sister's announcing she wanted to be a kindergarten teacher. My mother said to her, "Well, why not be a chemistry teacher," focusing her, at least educationally, on a higher level. My sister is now a medical doctor. For my mother, what I chose to do was less important than setting my goals high and achieving them. However, she did want me to study mathematics because I was good in math, although I never had that as my own career aspiration.

I didn't dare say, "I'm *not* going on to college." This was true of my sister too. I think I would have had a terrible life had I been a "B" rather than an "A" student, especially if I had the ability to do "A" work. It is one of the reasons I view my mother in a very positive way. She's been the real force behind my accomplishments.

However, there was one area in which my mother transmitted a traditional female viewpoint. Although achievement was crucial, my sister and I were still expected to be attractive and to attract men.

In my early school years, I did not have many friends, although this changed as I became older. However, I was very active in high school because I wanted to become a member of the National Honor Society. By adolescence, I knew to some extent the kinds of things I wanted and went after them. I was good at goal setting.

The way to become a member of the National Honor Society, at least in my high school, was by acquiring points. You had to have a certain amount of activity points; points were given for grades of As and Bs. I was successful, not only in being admitted to the National Honor Society, but in being admitted early in my high school career.

When I was in high school, I wasn't boy crazy—but I was definitely interested. I remember going roller-skating and ice-skating with a girlfriend to meet boys. I grew up in a time when boys weren't supposed to know that girls could think. Although everyone in school knew that I was bright, it was important not to demonstrate it by letting on how much you "knew." The attitude was that you didn't have to "brag" about it. When you were in the company of boys you talked about other things besides school and grades. However, I didn't concern myself to any great degree with whether I was scaring the boys away with my brains.

People in my high school class would call me "brains," "genius," and other similar names. I didn't enjoy it, but I didn't view it as negative either. It gave me a certain status that the others didn't have. I figured that my time, in terms of popularity, would come later—and it did. College was, as I had hoped, much different from high school. Intellect, rather than being a deficit, was a definite merit.

While in high school, I wrote a sports column for the school paper. Interested in sports from the perspectives of spectator and participant, I had an early career goal of being a sportswriter. If I were in school today, I might pursue this interest in sportswriting. However, in those years (the late 1940s) when I was a high school student, women did not get jobs as sportswriters, and I therefore discarded this first career aspiration. (I am still an avid sports fan.)

The career goal that did appear under my picture in the high school yearbook was physicist. My physics teacher had encouraged me in that direction. However, when a great uncle said to me, "You have to go to school at least 7 years to succeed with that degree," I felt, at the time, that 7 years of education and training were too much for me.

I was graduated from high school as class valedictorian, and by the time I entered the College for Women at the University of Pennsylvania, I had decided to major in history. History was interesting and fulfilling. After graduation, I planned to live in New York and work. In the 1950s, relatively few people in relation to the general population went to college; therefore, if you had a college degree, regardless of your major, you could get a job—never mind what kind of job.

My high school didn't offer a high school psychology course. The closest I had come to psychology prior to my university exposure was through one of my fellow students in high school. The day before taking the Scholastic Aptitude Test and the Achievement Examinations, this young man, who had been browsing through a psychology book, informed me, "Don't eat breakfast and don't eat lunch on the day of the test." He had read about a research study stating that hungry rats ran through their mazes faster than satiated rats; he assumed that this finding could be applied to humans taking aptitude tests. Fortunately, despite following this young man's advice, I did fine on my college entrance examinations.

In my sophomore year, I discovered psychology for the first time. My first course in psychology at the University of Pennsylvania was a laboratory course, and I loved it. However, I still loved history. I solved my dilemma by taking a double major. I was the first woman in the College for Women at the University of Pennsylvania to take a double major and was awarded honors in both disciplines.

My undergraduate research honors project in psychology had to do with leadership, an area on which I continued to work in graduate school, with my research results being published at a later date. The broader theme dealt with women leaders in comparison with men leaders. The results of this research indicated that women leaders were less authoritarian than men leaders and that women followers did *not* conform more than men followers to their leaders' positions. At the time, these findings were unexpected and contrary to the predicted outcome. Why did I carry out this particular study? It certainly foreshadowed my interest in social psychology and in the psychology of women. Probably I did this particular piece of research due to the "personal" perspective involved. Even as an undergraduate, I was active in campus organizations and played a leadership role in many of them. Therefore, I was interested in women as leaders.

I might also mention that, because I was a double honors major, I wrote my honors history thesis on Amelia Bloomer and the rise of Bloomerism. Once again, in retrospect, this would seem to point to my future scholarly interest. The undergraduate was parent to the professional—at least in my case.

However, while still an undergraduate and majoring in history and psychology, I was not committed to graduate work in either field. My entry into psychology was serendipitous. At that time, my best friend was a psychology major. We often talked about what we were going to do after graduation. Our "talks" would blossom into heated discussions as I tried to convince her that we should get our degrees and then move to New York and share an apartment. It was a very fashionable idea at the time, written up in magazines such as *Glamour*. Her response was always, "No, no. Let's do graduate work in psychology."

My friend wanted to be a clinical psychologist and felt that was what we both should do. I was always more interested in research. However, I was swayed by her argument. I remember talking to my adviser, Frank Irwin. He gave me the names of schools where I could acquire a major in clinical psychology—but with a research orientation. Another reason I didn't stay with history for graduate school was because I thought, "What am I going to do with a history major, besides teach?" I didn't want to teach. I felt psychology offered me many more options. My friend did not get admitted to graduate school. She went to New York to live and work; I continued with psychology.

I was accepted at Duke University, my first choice among the graduate schools to which I applied, and was granted a fellowship. However, when I was graduated from college in 1952, I did not go to Duke University. I became engaged. My first husband, a dental student, was going to be continuing his schooling at the University of Pennsylvania. Although I had wanted to do my graduate work at another university, I quickly applied to the University of Pennsylvania and was accepted with a teaching and research assistantship. I was 21 years old when I married for the first time in 1953.

Most female college students in the 1950s were admittedly at school to find husbands. The attitude about a college degree was that it was good contingency planning, in case, God forbid, one had to work. I joined my classmates by becoming engaged and later married. However, I was also an exception in that I went on to graduate school.

For many years, I went to college reunions and found that I was the only woman who had ever gone to graduate school and obtained a doctorate and a professional career. This changed later, when my classmates became "reentry" women.

I was fortunate in that my family never pressured me to get married, and this included my mother. I would have had trouble, however, if I had said I was getting married and was not pursuing a career. I was reared in a nontraditional home, with its emphasis on female achievement. But it also had some traditional components as well—it was important to be attractive, to have dates, to go to parties. Being a woman didn't hinder or help me in terms of my beliefs about myself. I felt I could do whatever I wanted to do.

In graduate school, as in undergraduate school, there were hardly any women on the faculty. Women as role models or mentors were scarce. At the University of Pennsylvania, there was one woman on the faculty in the 1950s, Dr. Mildred Loring Sylvester, a longtime tenured *assistant* professor of approximately 65 years of age. For many years, she had been in charge of the psychological clinic. One other woman was an associate (not an associate professor). She was Elizabeth Hurlock, author of well-known textbooks in child psychology. Why wasn't she on the full-time faculty? Eventually she was shunted to the School of Education.

In the 1950s, when I was a graduate student, there weren't many jobs for social psychologists or for academics in general. Therefore, in a sense, everyone in the nonprofessional fields in the doctoral program—male and female—was discriminated against. However, women faced additional barriers. For example, one of my friends was steered out of industrial psychology. She was emphatically told that it was not a field for a woman.

Another example of discrimination at the University of Pennsylvania was my failure to receive a promotion from graduate assistant to assistant instructor for 3 years, while some men were getting promoted after 1 year. The fellows who were promoted to assistant instructors, which meant they taught the classes rather than assisted the instructors, were more often than not sons of ministers. This form of discrimination was, of course, not directed only at women. However, I was told at the time that, although "they" wanted to promote me, they were afraid I could not conduct a class. I did have a great deal of stage fright. I assured the chair, however, that I could do it, and following promotion, I quickly overcame my stage fright—with no subsequent reappearance.

As part of my graduate clinical training, I was taking a course in projective techniques. I didn't have any trouble with the scoring, but when it came to the interpretations. I thought, "While I'm creating these wonderful stories, I don't know if they have a basis in fact." As I recall, I received comments from my instructor such as "You have the makings of a fine clinician," and I became a little frightened. I thought that if I were a creative writer, this way of working would be fine, but I felt I had no foundation for what I was saying. I didn't feel confident in what I was doing, even if I was good at it.

At that time, I was taking a research course in social psychology with Albert Pepitone and found it fascinating. In the clinical program, the only research I was exposed to was the conditioning of schizophrenics. I switched from clinical psychology into social psychology. I realized much later that I could have pursued both fields. However, I do not regret having left clinical psychology.

I received my PhD in 1958 and moved to New York. My first job in psychology in New York was obtained through Mary Reuder. Mary was at Queens College in charge of the evening session program. She learned through Frank Bakes, a professor at Pennsylvania, that I had just come to New York and asked me if I wanted to teach at Queens. I was delighted to accept her offer.

When I finished graduate school, I did not look for a full-time job. I had children and was involved with raising my family. If I were a man, I probably would have gone out looking for a full-time position. Therefore, one might say a barrier I encountered as a woman was the expectation of my involvement with child care. But it's not as if I were turned down. When I looked for a full-time position, I didn't have a problem in acquiring one, because in the 1960s, the job market was expanding. I had several offers. One offer was at Hunter College of the City University of New York, and one was at the Institute for Developmental Studies in New York. I chose to teach because the position at the institute was a structured position, 40 hr a week, and I felt the more flexible hours of the instructorship were better.

In the 1960s, when you had young children, it was not unusual to work part-time. It was not quite the right thing for a mother with children to work full-time; indeed, it was not quite the right thing to work at all. Working part-time was a compromise. Therefore, I taught at Queens College on a part-time basis and worked in the counseling center simultaneously. I was probably teaching 8 hr and counseling another 16 hr. Even though I was "part-time," a great deal of my time was invested in academia.

I had my three children after I earned my doctorate. One of the advantages of teaching, even when it is full-time, is that there is a certain amount of flexibility in your work hours. The biggest problem with the children was child care; I had to have full-time child care assistance. When the children were younger, I think they occasionally resented that I was working. I did hear a bit of "How come you're not home when I come home from school like so and so's mother is?" I think some of that was instilled in them by their father. But it didn't have any long-lasting negative effect on them.

At Queens College, I met Marcia Guttentag. We were in similar family situations—mother of young children and part-time instructor. While doing joint research, we began to talk and decided the only way to make any inroads in the field—and it was with academia that we were concerned—was either publish or perish. We published. I remember questioning myself back then as to whether I was getting on a treadmill. I could be involved with teaching in a more limited way. I decided, however, if I'm doing it, I'm going to do it all the way.

What spurred me to my accomplishments, such as getting a doctorate and working in the field? I just decided at one point that I was going to do it! I couldn't understand anyone who would get a doctorate and then not do anything with it. You might change your field of specialization later, but I thought if you get the PhD, you should use it in some way. If the job market is difficult, you could always get retrained in another aspect of psychology.

This attitude is reflected in my other activities as well, such as my organizational activities. When I get involved, I tend to be very active. You can go back and look at my high school yearbook and you'll see I was in numerous activities as well as being high school valedictorian. The same thing could be found in my college yearbook—lots and lots of activities. I continued that in my professional life. In other words, if I joined the American Psychological Association, I was going to be active in it. I've often thought if I had one special talent, it's generally that I'm electable!

After Sputnik and the increase in college enrollments, jobs at the beginning of the 1960s were plentiful. For a full-time teaching position, however, I had to look elsewhere. Mary Reuder had tried for several years to obtain a full-time position at Queens College for me. This position never did materialize. I hadn't been terribly concerned with it at the time—having three young children to raise—so I let it ride. When Mary knew a position at Hunter College was open, she suggested that I apply for it. In response to my application, I was invited for an interview.

A male faculty member on the interview committee knew I was married and asked me, "What does your husband do for a living?" At that time, you did not refuse to answer such questions. However, I recall asking myself, "Why is he asking me this?" The conclusion I came to was that this question was being asked in order to see how likely it was that my husband's company would relocate him. At that time, a great many companies were moving men around the country. I answered happily that my husband was a dentist, because I felt that this would demonstrate to the committee that I was a stable person and was not going to leave New York the following year. I learned that this information was used to place me at the lowest rank with the lowest salary available.

It was 1964. I had had my doctorate for 6 years. I had been published. I had been extremely active and supervised students in honors and independent research. I had taught several different courses. Despite all this, I was hired as an instructor. I have always thought that if I had it to do over again, I would have said my husband was a bedridden invalid.

I was assigned to Hunter College, City University of New York on the Bronx campus (now Lehman College). There I had the great fortune to meet Virginia Sexton. Virginia exposed me to organizations that I would otherwise have never known even existed and encouraged my involvement in them, Virginia would say, "I'm a member of _____, why don't you join? Why don't you join the New York Academy of Sciences or the New York State Psychological Association?" She saw to it that I became involved in some of the committees at the college. I became active as an adviser to Psi Chi. Her encouragement also led to my becoming president of the New York State Psychological Association.

Under Virginia's tutelage, I learned to seize the opportunity. For example, after I became president of the New York State Psychological Association, I was asked if I wanted to be nominated as a candidate for the American Psychological Association (APA) Council of Representatives. I of course said yes. If I had said no, I would probably have not been elected to the APA Council, nor would I have become president of the Division of the Psychology of Women (APA Division 35), nor would I have gotten into the governance structures of APA. I'm a risk taker. I feel competent in my ability, and I think I'm a good administrator. So I think I can do "it" and take a chance.

At the same time, my research continued. I began my research endeavors by doing traditional, experimental, social-psychological small-group studies. I'm not sure how I began specializing in the psychology of women. Long before the current women's movement, some of my early research was concerned with women in leadership and with reentry women students, The movement helped to foster my interest in the area, and teaching also contributed to my involvement. To my knowledge, I taught the first doctoral-level seminar in the United States in the psychology of women in 1971. Teaching "forced" me to stay immersed in reading in the field so I would remain up to date, and my research tended to shift in the direction of the psychology of women; much of my research in terms of focus and methodology remains that of a social psychologist. Involvement in establishing and shaping the psychology of women enabled me to become one of its pioneers.

I like what I do. Intellectual work and administrative/committee activities are absorbing—and stressful. I am a very strong person, but there are times when "overload" sets in. At those times, I think, "Gee, it would be nice to be a dependent individual." But it's not. It doesn't work that way.

I have to admit that the more I achieved professionally, the worse my first marriage became. My first husband felt threatened—a situation that has become all too familiar for many women—and a divorce followed.

I met my second husband, Robert Wesner, over a book. "Woman: Dependent or Independent Variable," (1975) co-edited and written by Rhoda Unger and myself, was signed up by Bob. At that time, he was an associate publisher with Aldine Publishing Company in Chicago. My second husband is tremendous. He pushes me. If I come home and I say, "Do you think I should run for vice-president of the

New York Academy of Sciences," he says, "Sure." My three children and my three stepchildren are also very proud of what I do. The support I receive from my husband and children is enormously important to me.

I feel that there were and still are barriers to women's achievement. I think that if I had not met certain career-wise women such as Mary Reuder and Virginia Sexton, I probably wouldn't have accomplished the things I did, perhaps not even acquired my first or second post-PhD jobs. I don't know. What I do know is that it was women as well as men who made things possible for me.

However, I've never had any one person as a role model. I've had many mentors, each serving different purposes. In social psychology, Albert Pepitone was a scholarly mentor. He helped me become involved in small groups and stay involved with them for some time. I was told by Al that, for years after I received my doctorate, I was held up as an example at the University of Pennsylvania, giving the admission committee a reason to take women into the psychology program. Mary Reuder nurtured me. She gave me a chance to get started. Through her, I was able to establish myself in a teaching position with a feeling of permanence that would not have been available through most adjunct positions. You felt as though you belonged. Virginia Sexton showed me the political ropes. The political mentor can be the most important because, unless you know those ropes, it sometimes doesn't make any difference how good you are—no one notices.

I feel it is important to serve as a role model for students. They can see, "Here's a woman who has made it and who has made it in research in the psychology of women." I want students to know that, if they want to do the same, there's nothing wrong with it and they can get ahead doing it.

I enjoy my contacts with students. This was one reason I never wanted to become a full-time administrator, even when I was head of the psychology doctoral program at the City University of New York Graduate School and wasn't required to teach. Whether I was head of the doctoral program or head of the Academic Skills Department for the high-risk student at Hunter College, I still taught a course in psychology. My decision not to become a full-time administrator was affirmed, when in 1987, I was the recipient of the first APA award for Distinguished Contributions to Education and Training in Psychology.

I think I'm different than my male colleagues. I tend to give more time to my students. However, I think this is generally more true of women than men. We're more willing to nurture. Whether we're socialized to do so is irrelevant. I think that some men are involved with teaching, research, whatever, and don't have much time for the students. But there are exceptions both ways. Nonetheless, I think it is important for students to feel someone cares and is concerned so that they will believe they can achieve and be successful.

To summarize, like most people, I was shaped by my childhood and my childhood environment. My mother's influence became a motivating force up to obtaining my doctorate; I emulated my father in many ways. My early career was influenced by Albert Pepitone, Mary Reuder, and Virginia Sexton. My husband, Robert Wesner, has always been a source of encouragement. Now that I am the Thomas Hunter Professor of the Social Sciences at Hunter College and at the City University of New York Graduate School and have held high offices in many professional and academic organizations, including the APA, it is time for me to give encouragement and assistance to others who seek my help, to be a role model and mentor. Those of us who have been successful have a responsibility to reach out to others.

REFERENCES

Unger, R., & Denmark, F.L. (1975). *Women: Dependent or independent variables?* New York: Psychological Dimensions.

REPRESENTATIVE PUBLICATIONS

Denmark, F. L. (1970, May/June). The effect of integration on academic achievement and self-concept. *Integrated Education: Race and Schools, 8*(3), 34–41.

Denmark, F. L. (Ed.). (1974). *Who discriminates against women.* Beverly Hills, CA: Sage.

Denmark, F. L. (Ed.). (1976). *Woman (Vol. 1).* New York: Psychological Dimensions.

Denmark, F. L. (1977). The psychology of women: An overview of an emerging field. *Personality and Social Psychology Bulletin, 3,* 356–367.

Denmark, F. L. (1977). Styles of leadership. *Psychology of Women Quarterly, 2*(2), 99–113.

Denmark, F. L. (1978). Psychological adjustment to motherhood. In B. B. Wolman (Ed.), *Psychological aspects of gynecology and obstetrics* (pp. 227–234). Oradell, NJ: Medical Economics.

Denmark, F. L. (1979). Women in psychology in the United States. In A. M. Briscoe & S. M. Pfafflin (Eds.), *Expanding the role or women in the sciences. Annals of the New York Academy of Sciences, 323,* 65–78.

Denmark, F. L. (1980). Psyche: From rocking the cradle to rocking the boat. *American Psychologist, 35,* 1057–1065.

Denmark, F. L. (Ed.). (1980). *Psychology: The leading edge into the unknown.* Annals of the New York Academy of Sciences. (Vol. 340). New York Academy of Sciences.

Denmark, F. L. (1983). Integrating the psychology of women into introductory psychology. In C. J. Schreier & A. Rogers (Eds.), *The G. Stanley Hall Lecture Series* (Vol. 3, pp. 33–75). Washington, DC: American Psychological Association.

Denmark, F.L. (1984). Women's worlds: Ghetto, refuge, or power base. In M. Safir, M.T. Mednick, D. Israeli , & J. Bernard (Eds.), *Women's worlds: From the scholarship*. New York: Praeger.

Denmark, F. L. (Ed.). (1985). *Social/ecological psychology and the psychology of women: Selected/revised papers. XXIII International Congress of Psychology* (Vol. 7). Amsterdam: North Holland.

Denmark, F. L., Baxter, B., & Shirk, E. J. (1976). The future goals of college women. In F. Denmark (Ed.), *Women* (Vol. 1, pp. 133–140). New York: Psychological Dimensions.

Denmark, F. L., & Block, J. (1980). *Psychodynamics of the psychology of women* (Pt. 1). *Weekly Psychology Update, 1*(7), 1–8.

Denmark, F. L., & Block, J. (1980). Psychodynamics of the psychology of women (Pt. 2). *Weekly Psychology Update, 1*(8), 1–8.

Denmark, F. L., & Diggory, J. (1966). Sex difference in attitudes towards leaders' display of authoritarian behavior. *Psychological Reports, 18*, 863–872.

Denmark, F. L., & Fernandez, L. C. (1985). Integrating information about the psychology of women into social psychology. In F. L. Denmark, (Ed.), *Social/ecological psychology and the psychology of women: Selected/revised papers. XXIII International Congress of Psychology* (Vol. 7, pp. 355–367). Amsterdam: North Holland.

Denmark, F. L., & Friedman, S. B. (1985). Social psychological aspects of rape. In S. Sunday & E. Tobach (Eds.), *Violence against women: A critique of the sociobiology of rape* (pp. 59–84). New York: Gordian.

Denmark, F. L., & Goodfield, H. M. (1978). A second look at adolescence theories. *Sex Roles: A Journal of Research, 4*(3), 375–379.

Denmark, F. L., & Guttentag, M. (1966). The effect of college attendance on mature women: Changes in self-concept and evaluation of student role. *Journal of Social Psychology, 69*, 155–158.

Denmark, F.L., & Guttentag, M. (1967). Dissonance in the self-concepts and educational concepts of colleges and non-college oriented women. *Journal of Counseling Psychology, 14*(2), 113–115.

Denmark, F. L., & Guttentag, M. (1969). Effect of integrated and non-integrated programs on cognitive change in pre-school children. *Perceptual and Motor Skills, 29*, 375–380.

Denmark, F., Murgatroyd, D., & Pepitone, A. (1965). Effect of differential valuation on group level of aspiration, decision time, and productivity. *Journal of Social Psychology, 67*, 201–209.

Denmark, F. L., & Ritter, B. (1972). Differential cognitive dissonance and decision latency. *Journal of Social Psychology, 86*, 69–74.

Denmark, F. L., & Rutschmann-Jaffe, R. (1979). The emerging female criminal. *International Journal of Group Tensions, 9*, 50–58.

Salzinger, K., & Denmark, F. L. (Eds.). (1978). *Psychology: The state of the art*. Annals of the New York Academy of Sciences. (Vol. 309). New York Academy of Sciences.

Denmark, F. L., Shaw, J.S., & Ciali, S. D. (1985). The relationship between sex roles, living arrangements, and the division of household responsibilities. *Sex Roles, 12*, 617–625.

Denmark, F. L., Shirk, E. J., & Baxter, B. (1972). *PROBE: A Program for Planning*

Ahead Educationally. Scottsville, NY: Transnational Programs Corporation. (Probe is a small group interactional experience resulting in behavioral changes.)

Denmark, F. L., Shirk, E. J., & Riley, R. T. (1972). The effect of ethnic and social class variables on semantic differential performance. *Journal of Social Psychology, 86,* 3–9.

Denmark, F. L., Tangri, S. S., & McCandless, S. (1979). Affiliation, achievement, and power. In J. Sherman & F. Denmark (Eds.), *The psychology of women: Future directions in research* (pp. 393–460). New York: Psychological Dimensions.

Denmark, F. L., & Trachtman, J. (1974). The psychologist as counselor in college "high risk programs." *Counseling Psychologist, 4*(2), 87–92.

Denmark, F. L., & Waters, J. (1977). Male and female in children's readers: A cross-cultural analysis. In Y. H. Poortinga (Ed.), *Basic problems in cross-cultural psychology* (pp. 190–197). Amsterdam: Swets & Zetlinger, B.V.

Denmark, F. L., Weinberg, N., & Block, J. (1982). Cross-national comparisons of women's life-styles in Israel, the USSR and USA. In L. L. Adler (Ed.), *Cross-cultural research at issue* (pp. 253–261). New York: Academic.

Guttentag, M., & Denmark, F. L. (1965). Psychiatric labelling: Role assignment based on the projective test performance of in-migrants. *International Journal of Social Psychiatry, 11*(2), 131–137.

Hunter College Women's Studies Collective. (1983). *Women's choices, women's realities.* New York: Oxford University Press.

Murgatroyd, D., Stuart, I., & Denmark, F. L. (1974). Perceptual style, locus of control, and personality variables in urban White college students. *Social Behavior and Personality, 2*(2), 204–211.

Riley, R. T., & Denmark, F. L. (1974). Field independence and measures of intelligence: Some reconsiderations. *Social Behavior and Personality, 2*(1), 25–29.

Russo, N. F., & Denmark, F. L. (1984). Women, psychology and public policy: Selected issues. *American Psychologist, 39,* 1161–1165.

Russo, N. F., & Denmark, F. L. (1987). Contributions of women to psychology. *Annual Review of Psychology, 38,* 279–298.

Sherman, J. A., & Denmark, F. L. (Eds.). (1979). *The Psychology of women: Future directions in research.* New York: Psychological Dimensions.

Starer, R., & Denmark, F. L. (1974). Discrimination against aspiring women. *International Journal of Group Tensions, 4,* 65–70.

Stuart, I., Murgatroyd, D., & Denmark, F. L. (1978). Perceptual style, locus of control and personality variables among East Indians and Blacks in Trinidad. *International Journal of Social Psychiatry, 24*(1), 26–32.

Trachtman, J., & Denmark, F. L. (1974). Self-esteem and other motivational variables: Some Black–White comparisons. *International Journal of Group Tensions, 4*(1). 136–143.

Waters, J., & Denmark, F. L. (1974). The beauty trap. *Journal of Clinical Issues in Psychology, 6*(1), 10–14.

Weinberg, N., & Denmark, F. L. (1978). Israeli women: The myth of sexual equality. *International Journal of Group Tensions, 8,* 112–119.

CHAPTER 19

Bonnie R. Strickland

Bonnie R. Strickland

My forebears on both my mother's and father's side first came to this country primarily from England and lived in the South for many generations. My father's mother traced her lineage to Richard Lee, who came to Virginia in 1641. Robert E. Lee was her distant relative, and both my father and my brother were named Roy Elkins to keep the R and E initials in the family. My paternal grandfather was a descendant of one of five Strickland brothers who came from England and settled all through the United States. My great-grandfather Strickland fought in the War Between the States, and my grandfather made his home in central Alabama. My father was born in 1910, the second of three boys, and was raised in Birmingham, Alabama.

My mother's family also had lived in the South, where I grew up hearing of the daring deeds of other "great grandfathers" and "great uncles" who had fought for the Confederacy. The family secret that I did not hear about for years is that my great-grandmother ran off with her sister's husband some time around 1880. The couple left Alabama with my grandmother, who was a young baby, and floated on a houseboat from Columbus, Georgia, as far as the river flowed, to the Gulf of Mexico. My great grandfather "doctored" folks along the way in exchange for food and supplies. The family disembarked at Apalachicola, Florida, where the Apalachicola River empties into the gulf. The couple became proprietors of a hotel that attracted visitors from the riverboats, lumbermen from the nearby swamps, and local fishermen. I am told that my grandmother, Rosalie Estelle

Lanier, eloped with a riverboat gambler by escaping over a porch roof to meet him. The marriage was short-lived, although my grandmother had one child who died very young. She subsequently married a local farmer who died a few years later, leaving her with four children. She then married a widower, Weldon Whitfield, whose previous wife, a part-Cherokee woman, had borne him three children. My mother was born during this third marriage and was the 12th living child of my grandmother. She grew up in Dalkeith, Florida, a community a few miles up the Apalachicola River, where my grandfather Whitfield ran a general store and my grandmother was the local postmistress. My grandfather also farmed, lumbered in the river swamp, and raised Tupelo honey, a honey that does not granulate and that is from Tupelo trees indigenous to that region. My mother, who was born in 1916, recalls that the family was fairly well off by the standards of that part of the panhandle of Florida and that she and her siblings had opportunities to travel and live for a time in cities such as Birmingham and New York. It was on a visit to Birmingham that my mother met my father, and they were married in 1934 after a 3-week courtship.

The marriage was at the height of the Great Depression, and my parents moved between Louisville, Kentucky, and Birmingham, Alabama, so that my father could find work on the L & N Railroad that ran between these two cities. I was born in Louisville on November 24, 1936, amd my brother was born 4 years later. My mother had a difficult labor at my birth, and I was not expected to live. My mother tells me that when she first saw me in my father's arms, she was shocked by my misshapen face, with red markings on my mouth and left ear, left from the forceps delivery. She was also concerned because she knew that my father had wanted a boy. My father, however, pronounced me "the prettiest baby" he'd ever seen, and I was always his favorite.

The Depression was difficult for my parents until my father found steady work on the railroad in Birmingham. His father and his oldest brother, John, both worked for L & N, and the family lived only a few blocks from the "yard." I was the first grandchild of the Strickland family and was born 2 months after the death of my grandmother, Ida Ruth Strickland. In her memory, I was given a good Southern double name, Bonnie Ruth. She had been ill for several years and may have also suffered from an affective or schizophrenic disorder, a condition that was to affect my beloved Uncle John after he joined World War II.

My mother taught me to read and to learn numbers at an early age. Uncle John also read to me and took me on trips through the city. My mother would return to northwest Florida regularly to visit her family, and I was one of innumerable cousins playing together near the river swamp or going to the beach. As I grew older, I learned to fish and to shoot, and I was never happier than when I was alone in a boat in the river swamp. My uncles and cousins took me fishing and frog gigging and pointed out the alligators sunning on the river bank. All the cousins were responsible for helping grub fish bait before dawn to deliver to various camps and stores. I learned to drive a pick-up truck when I was 12.

Growing up in Birmingham was very different from life in Florida. My mother and father divorced when I was 7, and my mother bought a house jointly with her sister. She took a job as a waitress, and my brother and I stayed with a series of live-in housekeepers until we were old enough to be on our own and handle the household chores. We continued to see our father regularly and spent holidays with his side of the family. My mother was also likely to have various cousins living with us, as well as Uncle John when he was not hospitalized.

Our new home was across the street from a public park and a library. I soon acquired a library card, and reading became a favorite pastime. I attended public elementary school, and as early as I can remember I wanted to be a schoolteacher when I grew up. Occasionally, especially as I played outdoors or in the park, I would fantasize about becoming a major sports figure, but there were few women in sports at that time. Although there was ample time to play outside, especially through the long Alabama summer evenings, I always knew that it would be necessary for me to go to work as soon as I could to help support the family. I did take an after-school and summer job in the library across the street when I was about 12. Because I was so completely enamored of books, work in the library was never tedious.

I had several other interests aside from reading. I was intrigued with radios and usually had a crystal set in some state of disrepair. I also had a chemistry set and built a laboratory under our back porch. This was not an altogether safe arrangement because my understanding of chemistry did not range further than developing crude magnesium bombs that I detonated in the backyard. Our backyard contained a basketball goal, and I spent uncounted hours shooting baskets or batting tennis balls against the wall of our house. I also played football and other team sports in the park and competed in various horseshoe tournaments. I was a tough kid, not afraid of much and willing to fight at any opportunity. My mother insisted that I take piano lessons, but she had little luck in turning me from my tomboy ways. I was active in Girl Scouts and Southern Baptist church groups, but my first love was sports.

A neighbor, Eunice Foster, taught me to play tennis, and by the time I started high school, I was good enough to make the boy's tennis team. I played in tournaments around the Southeast and won the Alabama State Girls' Doubles title when I was 16; I was nationally ranked for my age group. While I was playing tennis that summer, my brother pitched for the Little League team that won the national championship. He also became an outstanding tennis player and eventually completed Clemson University on a full tennis scholarship. He is a dentist now and lives with his wife and two daughters in Greenville, South Carolina. We fought as children, but we became quite close as adults and visit each other whenever we can.

In high school, I took college preparatory courses such as Latin and physics, but my interest kept returning to sports. I played softball in the summer, basketball in the winter, and tennis whenever I could. Although I was not a great swimmer, I completed enough Red Cross life-saving courses to become a Water Safety Instructor, and I was named the outstanding female athlete in my senior class. I was vaguely thinking about pursuing a professional tennis career, but my physical education teacher, Louise Pope, encouraged me to attend college. Most girls in my neighborhood married as soon as they finished high school; the boys either found jobs or joined the military. Mrs. Pope, however, sent me to her alma mater, Alabama College for Women, where I competed for and was awarded a physical education scholarship.

During high school, I had been eager to leave home and be on my own. The summer I graduated, I rented a room and found a job at a swimming pool in one of the public parks. I met a different crowd of friends, including several who were in trouble with the law. One young man whom I dated that summer was sent to the state prison the next fall for vehicular homicide. Others were involved in petty theft. We all corresponded for a while, and I visited the prison to see Pete on a couple occasions.

Few of my friends went to college, and my family was in no position to support me financially. Scholarships, waiting tables, lifeguarding, and delivering newspapers and movie theater programs all combined to provide my tuition, housing costs, and spending money. My Red Cross experience helped me land a summer job in Montevallo, Alabama, where the college was located. I taught swimming and lifeguarded at the local swimming area, a creek that wandered through the town. Low tuition and residence hall fees were also a great help. For about $750, I could attend college year-round, be housed and fed, and have my health care needs met and my clothes laundered.

I loved college. I found a faculty of predominantly female professors that seemed to take a special interest in me. Although I majored in physical education and took few of the substantive courses that would have helped me in graduate school, I still received an excellent education. Being in a women's college also allowed me to participate in extracurricular activities that might have ordinarily been closed to women. I became involved in theater lighting and was responsible for the lighting of several college productions. I also helped build sets, paint, and move scenery, as well as act in several plays (usually I was the male villian). I was often asked to be responsible for the lighting when various performers came to the campus, so I attended classical music performances and lectures that I might not have heard otherwise. During my junior year, the college became co-education. In many ways, I think that I had the best of all college worlds.

My college years, 1954 to 1958, also marked a period of considerable social change in the South. Black students began attending the major Southern universities for the first time. Eisenhower was president, and White Southerners were reacting to a perceived attack on their way of life. I don't recall feeling prejudiced toward Blacks and was particularly delighted when I learned that some of my faculty were supporting efforts at integration. But being raised as a Southerner, I felt a powerful sense of place and a strong sense of concern, especially when the Klan marched through our campus. My prejudices were against Yankees (anyone outside the few southeastern states) and those people, including the Klan, who seemed to have dogmatic ideas about how Southerners should behave. Although I had many Jewish friends, I never met a Catholic until I was a junior in high school. Also, as far as I knew, I never met a Republican.

Most of my college courses were in physical education. The school was rightly proud of a long history of training high school and occasionally college physical education teachers. Not only did we take the typical skill courses, such as basketball and golf, but we also had several basic biology courses. Even at this small women's college, I had the opportunity to work on a cadaver. I recall that the instructor, Dr. Gideon Nelson, scraped away a few cells on the arm of the body of an elderly Black man and said, "Look, the color is not even skin-deep."

In addition to electing to take physical education, I chose courses in English, philosophy, and psychology. Because I stayed at the college to work during the summer, I also had the opportunity to take additional classes. One summer I memorized parts of the Shakespeare plays and tried to teach them to the young swimmers. I was also proud that during the four summers I lifeguarded, I rescued 23 youngsters from the creek. Not all these were in great danger, but I occasionally pulled out unconscious and nearly drowned kids.

My last summer at the creek, a Boy Scout troop asked me to teach them to swim so that they might earn their merit badges. The boys were from a poor mining community in central Alabama, not far from the college, and most had never seen a body of water as large as the creek. At the end of the summer, I was invited to a picnic at their school grounds to award the badges. I umpired as the boys played baseball on a red clay field against a team from another, equally poor community. It was a hot August afternoon, and I stood in the Alabama sun and thought to myself that this would be my life—as a rural schoolteacher. I was attracted and disturbed at the same time.

In our small college, we had two psychology professors, Katherine Vickery and Herbert Eber, and about a half dozen psychology majors. One of my friends, Ginger Flowers, was taking a testing course with Herb Eber. She asked if I would be willing to take a Wechler Adult Intelligence Test so she could practice administering it. I suspect that she thought that it wouldn't take us long, and I agreed on the condition that she would tell me my score. I was trying so hard to make a good impression on this sophisticated psychology major that I can still recall some of my responses to the test she administered in a dormitory room. Ginger never told me my score, but Herb Eber called me in, and he invited me to take some more tests. He mentioned that he thought I might be interested in pursuing a career other than in physical education. I told him that I was interested in English or philosophy, and he asked "Why not psychology?" I had actually taken several courses in psychology, had been reading *The Return of Bridey Murphy* (a book about life before birth), and was practicing hypnosis in the dorm (I was altogether frightened when it seemed to work). I explained that I did not know many psychologists, none, in fact, but him and Dr. Vickery, and I thought psychologists as a group might be somewhat strange. Dr. Eber said I would fit right in.

Dr. Eber was the only clinical psychologist in that part of Alabama, and he was a consultant for numerous agencies, including the Alabama School for the Blind and the state mental hospital. He would often take students with him to help with testing. I recall that on one of our trips, I asked him what caused schizophrenia. No doubt I was thinking about my Uncle John, who remained hospitalized with a psychotic disorder. He was in a Veterans Administration hospital not far away, and I visited him regularly, always curious about his condition and wondering if mental disorders ran in the family.

Drs. Eber and Vickery were master teachers who insisted that I complete some independent research. I finished two projects before I was graduated—one concerning the relationship between strength and flexibility and the other concerning the effects of sleep deprivation on cognitive and motor responses. Dr. Eber suggested that I compute a factor analysis for one of the studies and sent me to a certain page in a statistics book. I eventually finished it (by hand in those days), and this was my complete exposure to math or statistics in college. I also had no foreign languages or physical sciences.

In the fall of my senior year, Dr. Eber asked what I would earn if I remained in Alabama teaching physical education. Starting salaries then were $2,700. Dr. Eber said that if I applied to graduate school in psychology, I might receive some financial assistance. By this time, I was taken with the notion of going to graduate school, and psychology had certainly captured my interest. Dr. Eber suggested that I apply to several programs and attend Ohio State University if I were accepted there. He also thought that I should specialize in clinical psychology, although I was not certain what that entailed. Dr. Vickery was convinced that I should go to Harvard and be an experimental psychologist. As it turned out, I was accepted into all the schools to which I applied, except Harvard. A letter came back to Dr. Vickery bemoaning my undergraduate major. All the programs to which I was accepted offered me some kind of an assistantship, except for Ohio State.

Dr. Eber and I then laboriously handwrote a letter to Julian Rotter saying that Ohio State was my first choice if I could receive any financial assistance. A letter came back from Dr. Rotter later that spring offering me a research assistantship of $2,400 on one of his projects. The letter arrived as I was on my way to play in a golf tournament. I still recall my uneasiness when I realized that my next school year would be spend in the North, among Yankees and possibly with snow. Dr. Eber comforted me by reminding me that the half-time research assistantship would pay almost as much as a full-time teaching job and that I could always come home if I wanted. My physical education faculty urged me to go on to Ohio State but to major in physical education.

From 1958 to 1962, when I was in graduate school there, Ohio State had a very exciting program with a strong emphasis on personality theory. Rotter had published *Social Learning and Clinical Psychology* (1954), and Kelly had published his two-volume *The Psychology of Personal Constructs* (1955). Other faculty members in the clinical psychology program were also quite productive, and each new student immediately joined a research team led by one of the faculty. The students in my class came from distinguished schools, including Harvard, and from some foreign countries. I recall that, in my first clinical psychology class, some students talked about their prior training with B. F. Skinner and Carl Rogers. These names were only vaguely familiar to me, and I knew that I would be hard-pressed to keep up with my classmates. The class included several women and some minority members. Even in the 1950s, Rotter was committed to a diversified student body. I now suspect that the faculty had admitted a kid from Alabama with a double Southern name, thinking that I was Black. I often asked Dr. Rotter how I happened to be accepted. He would smile and say I was part of his aid to the culturally deprived. He also told me later, not altogether in jest, that he had never thought that I would survive the program because I didn't speak the language. Actually, I talked little in class the first few years because I knew so little about what we were studying. And, I was terribly homesick. In Ohio, I met Republicans for the first time, and I was surrounded by Yankees. For a while, I roomed with one of the Black women in the program who was from the South. At least she and I ate the same food and talked the same way, and both of us had double names.

We were immediately involved in our course work, in our research, and in our clinical work. Most of us were on Veterans Administration (VA) summer clerkships that also included several days during the school year when we traveled to the VA hospital in Chillicothe, Ohio. On one of these trips, our VA supervisor, Robert Albrecht, took us to a ward filled with patients from World War I. This ward housed older men who were organically impaired from the ravages of syphilis. I recall that Albrecht told us that we would never see this again because syphilis could now be controlled. The advent of my graduate schooling also coincided with the beginning uses of psychotropic medication for the severely mentally ill. Nevertheless, I saw my share of straitjackets and bizarre behavior, always puzzled as to the causes of the severe mental disorders.

Some of my first research in graduate school was done with Douglas Crowne, who with David Marlowe was developing a measure of social desirability or need for approval. My master's thesis was in investigation of conformity as a function of high need for approval (Strickland & Crowne, 1962). Crowne and I also completed several other studies using need for approval to predict verbal conditioning (Crowne & Strickland, 1961) and premature termination of psychotherapy (Strickland & Crowne, 1963). All of us were also involved in the early development of Rotter's Internal–External Locus of Control Scale, which assesses the degree to which individuals can be considered "internal" (believing that the events that happen in their lives are contingent on their own behavior) or "external" (believing that events are caused by powerful others or are beyond one's personal control and understanding). My doctoral dissertation found that internal subjects were more likely than external subjects to be aware of reinforcement and extinction conditions in a "learning without awareness" paradigm. Subjects with high need for approval were more likely than subjects with low need for approval to verbally condition. Those subjects who showed learning without awareness extinguished more slowly than subjects who were aware of the contingencies (Strickland, 1970).

My internship experiences crossed several facilities. In the summer of 1960, I was at the Palo Alto VA, where some of the early pioneers of behavior theory, such as Leonard Ullman and Leonard Krasner, were on the staff. Albert Bandura and Gregory Bateson were consultants, and interns had a rich clinical experience across a number of theoretical approaches. Most of my time was spent on a ward for chronic schizophrenics, and I was part of a milieu therapy team that consisted of Ben Finney, a psychologist who was my immediate supervisor; the head nurse; and a psychiatrist, Richard Worthington. Little did we know that one of our very good aides, Ken Kesey, was then taking notes on the ward and was writing his book, *One Flew Over the Cuckoo's Nest* (1962). I could recognize some of our patients in his book, but I never thought he was fair to the head nurse.

My academic-year internship was spent in the out-patient service of the Ohio State Hospital in Columbus. This hospital had been the setting for *The Snake Pit* (Ward, 1946), a book written by a patient and made into a movie. The internship setting had several excellent supervisors, including Vincent O'Connell and Jane Gavin. We were also exposed to alternative therapies such as Gestalt and experiential theory.

The Ohio State program was at least as good as or better than Herb Eber had promised. Much of my work was completed with Jules Rotter, but I was also influenced by the other clinical faculty members—Shep Liverant, Doug Crowne, Ed Barker, Al Scodel, and

George Kelly. As best I could tell, women were treated equally with men, although some of the faculty had concerns that the female students would marry and leave psychology. My classmates all became close friends and later became productive and well-known psychologists. Ralph Cebulla, Herbert Getter, Zeinab El-Ghatit, Dick Lanese, Herbert Lefcourt, Conrad Schwartz, Jay Stack, and Norman Watt were all in my class. Barbara Henker and Pearl Gore Dansby both came with their master's degrees and graduated with our class.

When I finished Ohio State in 1962, all of us were looking for academic jobs. I interviewed for positions at several major universities and at a few colleges. A clinical director at a well-known Midwestern university wrote back to say that, although my record was very good, they had decided to hire a *man*. Dr. Rotter, my major adviser, was visiting Emory University in Atlanta when he learned that they had an opening; I was eager to return to the South and was pleased when I was offered the position at Emory.

The Emory Psychology Department was small when I joined it, and I served both on the faculty and in the Counseling Service. I was the only woman in the department and one of only a few in the university. In 1964, I was asked to become dean of women, and at age 27, I found myself in charge of housing and security for 1,800 women students. I enjoyed working with student leaders and, like Dr. Eber, sent several women students on to psychology graduate programs whether they had originally planned to go or not. After 3 years as the dean of women, I returned to the Psychology Department, which by then had attained American Psychological Association (APA) approval for its clinical psychology program. Jay Knopf, as chair, and Al Heilbrun, as clinical director, attracted outstanding faculty. I worked especially closely with Joe Thorpe, Marshall Duke, and Steven Nowicki on some shared research. Realizing that there was no generalized internal–external scale for children, Steve Nowicki and I developed the Nowicki–Strickland Children's Locus of Control Scale, which eventually became the instrument of choice for much of the internal–external research with children (Nowicki & Strickland, 1973). Marshall Duke helped develop additional versions of the scale to be used with different age groups, extending from preschool children to primary school children to the elderly. Much of our published research covered various predictions and descriptions as to how internal locus of control serves as an adaptive mediating variable for children's behavior (Strickland, 1972, 1973; Zytkoskee, Strickland, & Watson, 1971).

Graduate students, and some undergraduates, were always involved in my ongoing research, and we tackled several different problems. Joseph Doster, for example, predicted patterns of self-disclosure (Doster & Strickland, 1969, 1971), and we were all interested in prejudice and interpersonal interactions (Proenza & Strickland, 1965; Strickland, 1971; Strickland, Doster, & Thorpe, 1969; Strickland & Shaffer, 1971; Strickland & Weddel, 1972). A study of special interest that I helped supervise was a dissertation by Norman Thompson that was a consideration of the mental health status of gay men and lesbians in relation to heterosexual controls. This research was perhaps the first to show that homosexual men and women from a noninstitutionalized or nonclient population were similar in their reported mental health to that of heterosexuals. This was also the first study to include a large sample of lesbians—thus moving this literature toward a consideration of women as well as men (Thompson, McCandless, & Strickland, 1971).

Another study that I conducted with undergraduates was a first of sorts. Gore and Rotter (1963) showed by paper-and-pencil measures that internal Black students were significantly more likely than external Black students to report they would engage in civil rights activities. In the spring of 1963, the Southern Student Non-Violent Coordinating Committee (SNCC) held a meeting in Atlanta. Many Black SNCC participants, most of whom were living in situations of constant danger, agreed to complete Rotter's I–E scale. I found that Black SNCC activists were significantly more internal than a matched control group of college students (Strickland, 1965). This research was eventually named a Citation Classic and is one of the few studies that demonstrates a relationship between generalized expectancies and social activism. Zachery Sank and I (1973) repeated this study a decade later and found internals more moderate and externals more militant in regard to extreme social action.

The mid-1960s were a time of increasing interest in civil rights and social justice in the South. I served as an expert witness for some of the protestors in their legal battles, and I found myself joining many of those people of whom I had been suspicious while I was growing up. I began playing tennis with a real Yankee Quaker, June Youngblut. She introduced me to several Catholic nuns and priests, including Father Phillip Berrigan, who were in Atlanta for various demonstrations and protests to combat segregation. I found myself attending the marches, going to meetings at Dr. Martin Luther King, Sr.'s church, and generally becoming involved in the movement. I met Dr. King, Jr. at the first integrated dinner ever held in Atlanta on the occasion of his receiving the Nobel Prize. Our introduction was brief, but I still remember his warmth and charismatic manner. Indeed, he kept saying that he was glad to meet me. I was at the Southeastern Psychological Association meeting in Roanoke, Virginia, when I heard of his death. I immediately returned to Emory to see if we could be of help in the funeral arrangements. Emory students, who had never participated in civil rights activities, covered the switchboard for the Southern Christian Leadership Conference and met out-of-town visitors as they arrived in Atlanta. Some students sat with the King children at their home. Our friends in the Black community appreciated our help but eventually told us to leave the downtown area because "Atlanta was going to burn again," and they wanted us to be safe. As it turned out, there was no violence, and the city stayed quiet.

Promotion and salary advances were increasingly difficult to come by at Emory, especially, I think, for a woman. The first time I was recommended for promotion to associate professor by my department, the dean delayed the decision for a year. My tenure decision was also delayed. In 1972, I took my first sabbatical from Emory and spent 9 months at the University of Hawaii. Although I had enjoyed living in the South, the excitement and fun of Hawaii led me to think about looking for another position. I let old friends from graduate school know that I might be interested in a move. Norman Watt told me of an opening for a full professor of psychology at the University of Massachusetts at Amherst, and I interviewed for it. The department was very attractive and offered me a salary almost double what I was receiving at Emory. I took the position in September 1973, and, again, I was pleased to be a member of an excellent faculty. I also found myself one of some 15 women in our large department. I had previously been unaware of my need for and appreciation of other women faculty; in fact, there had been only about a half dozen at Emory College. I now found them a tremendous source of support. I also became active in the Faculty Senate Committee on the Status of Women and eventually chaired that group. Although I was happy as a professor, department members asked me to become the Director of Graduate Studies. And, when our department chair left in 1976, I agreed to serve as chair, a position I held for almost 5 years. In 1982, a new chancellor, Joseph Duffey, invited me to be his associate, and I worked with him for a year. Chancellor Duffey was well experienced in education and politics, and I learned a lot from him.

During my administrative stints, I still taught both graduates and undergraduates, supervised research and clinical activities, and saw a limited number of private clients. My research interests focused on the relation of generalized expectancies, such as internal locus of control beliefs, to health and adaptive behaviors (Strickland, 1977a; 1977b; 1978; 1979; Strickland & Janoff-Bulman, 1980), with a special concern for mood and depression. Daniel Hale, a graduate student, had moved with me from Emory to the University of Massachusetts and we continued our work on the manipulation of affect and subsequent cognitive and social behaviors (Hale & Strickland, 1976; Hale & Strickland, 1986; Strickland, 1976; Strickland, Hale, & Anderson, 1975). I was also particularly interested in the ways in which individual sensitivities to common foods and environmental pollutants could lead to depression (Strickland, 1981, 1982). A dissertation (King, 1981) that I supervised was the first study with carefully controlled double-blind conditions to demonstrate a relationship between food and chemical sensitivites and behavioral and emotional symptoms. I also supervised several theses and dissertations investigating sex differences in depression, and our research team, which was predominantly women, presented these findings at various professional meetings. My research in depression and in women's health was also no doubt influenced by my bout with uterine cancer in 1976. Fortunately, all the malignancy was removed, and there has been no reoccurrence. I do, however, find myself with special interests in mind–body interactions (Strickland, 1984, 1987; Strickland & Kendall, 1983).

In graduate school, we had all been encouraged to join the APA and to subscribe to the journals of interest to us. I became a member in 1963 but was not particularly active until Hans Strupp asked me to chair the first Equal Opportunity and Affirmative Action Committee of the Division of Clinical Psychology. With others, I helped establish the Section on the Clinical Psychology of Women, and in 1983 I became the second female president of the division. I served on the APA Council of Representatives for two terms, was on the editorial boards of five psychology journals, and was appointed to the Advisory Council for the National Institute of Mental Health. In all these responsibilities, I have tried to speak for women and others who have not had a strong voice in the past. I am also particularly proud of having been named alumna of the year at my undergraduate college, having received a distinguished teaching award, and having been named the chancellor's lecturer with a medal for distinguished service to the University of Massachussets at Amherst.

Having been trained as a scientist-practitioner and with a commitment to human welfare, I found that my interests crossed almost every aspect of organized psychology. I am a fellow in five divisions. I have been involved in teaching and research. I have completed insurance forms for my private clients as well as research grant applications. I was chair of the Council of Graduate Departments in Psychology at the same time that I chaired the Board of Professional Affairs. I have also been active in the Association of Women in Psychology and in the Feminist Therapy Institute. Many friends, especially women, encouraged me to run for president of APA, and I gained the support of a number of different groups. I was elected and began one of the most exciting periods of my life. In 1987, APA has 95,000 members and affiliates and is faced with a number of organizational demands that result from the extraordinary growth and success that we have achieved. I love being at the center of these activities and working closely with other psychologists to effect change. Traveling for APA also allows me to see old friends and students. Indeed, the students I have taught are a great source of pride for me. Another special satisfaction is being approached by women who say how much they appreciate my activities on their behalf.

When I look back on my life in psychology, I often wonder what forces moved me toward this exciting field. Perhaps it was the specter of mental illness in my father's family; perhaps it was the energy in my mother's. One of my mother's brothers was killed by a tax revenuer, probably because he was bringing illegal whiskey into the country. Some of my cousins became counterfeiters; some became counselors; a few stayed near the river to make Tupelo honey. But most of us tried to leave the river swamp in whatever way we could. One female second cousin received her doctorate in music; another became a high level computer consultant. Male cousins joined the military; female cousins married and moved away to raise families. Still, we all return whenever we can. I have a beach house close to Apalachicola and spend most of my free time there.

In Massachusetts, I helped design and build my present lakefront home. In the summer, I still play softball (in a feminist league), and I have learned to enjoy winter sports, like downhill skiing. New England is rather like the South in giving people a powerful sense of independence. I like it here. Close friends, faculty, and students have become my extended family, and my academic parents are those special mentors who have helped me pursue higher education.

In 1984, I spoke at the annual meeting of the Clinical Divison of the Georgia State Psychological Association. Herb Eber attended, and I beat him again in tennis after 26 years. Mostly though, I thanked him for sending me off to Ohio State. I also try to stay in touch with my other college teachers and with Jules Rotter, who changed my life when he offered me a research assistantship. And recently, I visited my high school teacher, Louise Pope, who helped me go to college so many years ago. She told me that I had been dependable and hardworking in high school, and she said that I would have been successful in whatever I undertook. I don't know. I do know that psychology opened doors for me and unlocked vistas of which I never dreamed. I still marvel that this kid from the south side of the steel mills in Birmingham and the river swamps of northwest Florida has been allowed a life of research, teaching, clinical practice, and professional service. I know of no higher calling.

REFERENCES

Crowne, D. P., & Strickland, B. R. (1961). The conditioning of verbal behavior as a function of the need for social approval. *Journal of Abnormal and Social Psychology, 63*, 395–401.

Doster, J. A., & Strickland, B. R. (1969). Perceived child rearing practices and self disclosing patterns. *Journal of Consulting and Clinical Psychology, 33*, 382.

Doster, J. A., & Strickland, B. R. (1971). The disclosing of verbal material as a function of information requested, information about the interviewer, and interviewee differences. *Journal of Consulting and Clinical Psychology, 37*, 187–194.

Gore, P. M., & Rotter, J. B. (1963). A personality correlate of social action. *Journal of Personality, 31*, 58–64.

Hale, W. D., & Strickalnd, B. R. (1976). Induction of mood states and their effect on cognitive and social behaviors. *Journal of Consulting and Clinical Psychology, 44*, 155.

Haley, W., & Strickland, B. R. (1986). Interpersonal betrayal and cooperation: Effects on self-evaluation in depression. *Journal of Personality and Social Psychology, 50*(2), 386–391.

Kelly, G. A. (1955). *The psychology of personal constructs* (Vols. 1 & 2). New York: Norton.

Kesey, K. (1962). *One flew over the cuckoo's nest*. New York: Viking.

King, D. S. (1981). Can allergic exposure provoke psychological symptoms? A double blind test. *Biological Psychiatry, 16*, 3–19.

Nowicki, S., & Strickland, B. R. (1973). A locus of control scale for children. *Journal of Consulting and Clinical Psychology, 40*, 148–154.

Proenza, L., & Strickand, B. R. (1965). A study of prejudice in Negro and White college students. *Journal of Social Psychology, 67*, 273–281.

Rotter, J. B. (1954). *Social learning and clinical psychology*. Englewood Cliffs, NJ: Prentice-Hall.

Sank, Z., & Strickland, B. R. (1973). Some attitudinal and behavioral correlates of a belief in militant or moderate social action. *Journal of Social Psychology, 523*.

Strickland, B. R. (1965). The prediction of social action from a dimension of internal–external control. *Journal of Social Psychogoy, 66*, 353–358.

Strickland, B. R. (1970). Individual differences in verbal conditioning, extinction, and awareness. *Journal of Personality, 38*, 364–378.

312   *Personal Perspectives*

Strickland, B. R. (1971). Aspiration responses among Negro and White adolescents. *Journal of Personality and Social Psychology, 19,* 315–320.

Strickland, B. R. (1972). Delay of gratification as a function of race of the experimenter. *Journal of Personality and Social Psychology, 22,* 108–112.

Strickland, B. R. (1973). Delay of gratification and a belief in internal locus of control among children. *Journal of Consulting and Clinical Psychology, 40,* 338.

Strickland, B. R. (1976). The affective disorders. In J. Calhourne (Ed.), *Abnormal psychology: Current perspectives* (2nd ed., pp. 159–184). New York: Random House.

Strickland, B. R. (1977a). Approval motivation. In T. Blass (Ed.), *Personality variables and social behavior* (pp. 341–356). Hillsdale, NJ: Lawrence Erlbaum Associates, Inc.

Strickland, B. R. (1977b). Internal–external control of reinforcement. In T. Blass (Ed.), *Personality variables and social behavior* (pp. 219–280). Hillsdale, NJ: Lawrence Erlbaum Associates, Inc.

Strickland, B. R. (1978). Internal–external expectancies and health-related behaviors. *Journal of Consulting and Clinical Psychology, 46,* 1192–1211.

Strickland, B. R. (1979). Internal–external expectancies and cardiovascular functioning. In L. C. Perlmuter & R. A. Monty (Eds.), *Choice and perceived control* (pp. 221–231). Hillsdale, NJ: Lawrence Erlbaum Associates, Inc.

Strickland, B. R. (1981). Psychological effects of food and chemical susceptibilities. *Voices: The Art and Science of Psychotherapy, 17,* 68–72.

Strickland, B. R. (1982). Implications of food and chemical susceptibilities for clinical psychology. *International Journal of Biosocial Research, 3,* 39–43.

Strickland, B. R. (1984). Levels of health enhancement: Individual attributes. In J. D. Matarazzo, N. E. Miller, S. M. Weiss, J. A. Herd, & S. M. Weiss (Eds.), *Behavioral health: A handbook of health enhancement and disease prevention* (pp. 101–113). New York: Wiley.

Strickland, B. R. (1987). Menopause. In A. Blechman & K. Brownell (Eds.), *Handbook of behavioral medicine for women* (pp. 41–47). New York: Pergamon.

Strickland, B. R., & Crowne, D. P. (1962). Conformity under conditions of simulated group pressure as a function of need for social approval. *Journal of Social Psychology, 58,* 171–181.

Strickland, B. R., & Crowne, D. P. (1963). Need for approval and the premature termination of psychotherapy. *Journal of Consulting and Clinical Psychology, 27,* 95–101.

Strickland, B. R., Doster, J., & Thorpe, J. (1969). Early impressions and later confirmation in interpersonal judgments. *Journal of Perceptual and Motor Skills, 28,* 1095–1096.

Strickland, B. R., Hale, W. D., & Anderson, L. K. (1975). Effect of induced mood states on activity and self-reported affect. *Journal of Consulting and Clinical Psychology, 43,* 587.

Strickland, B. R., & Janoff-Bulman, R. (1980). Expectancies and attributions: Applications for community mental health. In M. S. Gibbs, J. R. Lachenmeyer, & J. Sigal (Eds.), *Community psychology: Theoretical and empirical approaches,* (pp. 97–119). New York: Gardner.

Strickland, B. R., & Kendall, K. E. (1983). Psychological symptoms: The importance of assessing health status. *Clinical Psychology Review, 3,* 179–199.

Strickland, B. R., & Shaffer, S. (1971). IE, IE & F. *Journal for the Scientific Study of Religion, 10,* 366–369.

Strickland, B. R., & Weddel, S. C. (1972). Religious orientation, racial prejudice and dogmatism. *Journal of Scientific Study of Religion, 11,* 395–399.

Thompson, N. L., McCandless, B. R., & Strickland, B. R. (1971). Personal adjustment of male and female homosexuals and heterosexuals. *Journal of Abnormal Psychology, 78*, 237–240.

Ward, M. S. (1946). *The snake pit.* New York: Random House.

Zytkoskee, A., Strickland, B. R., & Watson, J. (1971). Delay of gratification and internal versus external control among adolescents of low socioeconomic status. *Developmental Psychology, 4*, 93–98.

REPRESENTATIVE PUBLICATIONS

Strickland, B. R. (1977). The approval motive. In B. B. Wolman & L. R. Pomer (Eds.), *International encyclopedia of neurology, psychoanalysis, and psychology* (Vol. 2, pp. 86–87). New York: Human Sciences Press Periodicals.

Strickland, B. R. (1984). Psychologist as department chair. *Professional Psychology, 5*, 730–740.

Strickland, B. R. (1984). This week's Citation Classic (Prediction of social action from a dimension of internal–external control). *Current Contents, Social and Behavioral Sciences, 16*(5), 20.

Strickland, B. R. (1985). Over the Boulder and through the Vail. *Clinical Psychologist, 38*, 52–56.

Strickland, B. R. (1987). Apprenticeships in health psychology. In G. Stone, S. A. Weiss, J. D. Matarazzo, N. Miller, J. Rodin, G. Schwartz, C. Belar, M. Follick, & J. Singer (Eds.), *Health psychology: A discipline and a profession* (pp. 351–360). Chicago: University of Chicago Press.

Strickland, B. R., & Calkins, B. S. (1987). Public policy and clinical training. *Clinical Psychologist, 40*(2), 31–34.

Strickland, B. R., & Halgin, R. (1987). Integration of clinical, counseling, and social psychology. *Journal of Social and Clinical Psychology.*

Strickland, B. R., & Haley, W. E. (1980). Sex differences on the rotter IE Scale. *Journal of Personality and Social Psychology, 39*, 930–939.

PART IV

PERSPECTIVES ON PATTERNS OF ACHIEVEMENT

CHAPTER 20

Synthesis and Resynthesis: Profiles and Patterns of Achievement 2

Agnes N. O'Connell

> *I have brought you here so you will know forever the silences in which are our beginnings, in which we have an origin like water.*
> —*"The Journey" (Eavan Boland, 1987)*

The structure of our knowledge about eminent women in psychology can be analyzed on three levels (O'Connell, 1983; Runyan, 1984): the universal level applying to all women; the group level applying to women in psychology; and the individual level applying to particular individuals. In essence, every woman is in certain respects like all other women, like some other women, and like no other woman (Kluckhohn & Murray, 1953, p. 53).

On the individual level, the autobiographies in this volume present the complex reality of the lives, experiences, and personalities of these distinguished women. On the universal level, Nancy Felipe Russo describes the social and historical context shared by women in psychology living during the same period of history. On the group level, this chapter provides an analysis and synthesis of the similarities and differences in the personal and professional lives of these women. In addition, by selectively integrating parts of the first volume of *Models of Achievement: Reflections of Eminent Women in Psychology* (O'Connell & Russo, 1983), this chapter examines transhistoric and time-specific trends and patterns.

The data for this analysis and synthesis are based on the autobiographies, on the biographical information forms completed by the authors, and on the authors' curriculum vitae. Through study of these sources, a range of variables and their relationships to one another have been identified. After several readings, categories were established, and content analysis was undertaken. The number of variables in this volume is greater than the number of variables in the first volume. Selective data in the first volume are used in conjunction with the data in this volume to gain insights into trends and patterns.

Although no claim is made that the women in this volume represent a scientific sample of outstanding women in psychology, the contents and analyses do illuminate their lives, experiences, and achievements from universal, group, and individual perspectives across time.

FROM THE BEGINNING: AFFILIATION, ACHIEVEMENT, AND FAMILIES OF ORIGIN

Sixteen of the 17 eminent women in this volume were born in a 30-year period beginning in 1906. Leona E. Tyler, Anne Anastasi, Marie Skodak Crissey, and Erika Fromm were born between 1906 and 1910; Lillian E. Troll, Olga E. deCillis Engelhardt, Patricia Cain Smith, Jane Loevinger, and Frances K. Graham were born between 1915 and 1918; Janet Taylor Spence, Dorothy Hansen Eichorn, Carolyn Robertson Payton, and Martha T. Mednick were born between 1923 and 1929; and Martha E. Bernal, Florence L. Denmark, and Bonnie R. Strickland were born between 1931 and 1936. Lois Hayden Meek Stolz was born in 1891. They were born in various regions of the United States: the East, Northeast, South, Southwest, and West. One was born in Frankfurt, Germany.

These women share some commonalities with the women in the first volume of *Models of Achievement*. Firstborns are overrepresented. Twelve (71%) of the 17 women in this volume are firstborns, including two only children. In addition, one woman (Olga deCillis Engelhardt) was born after a 5-year interval and therefore was likely to have benefited from the parenting and privileges generally reserved for firstborn children (Mellilo, 1983). Combining the women in both volumes, 22 (65%) of the 34 women are firstborn or only children. Another 4 (12%) were born after a 5-year interval. The data clearly define a significant relationship between achievement and birth order for high-achieving women.

The collective experience of these women, however, does not support a relationship between achievement and lack of a male sibling (Hennig & Jardim, 1977). Although 2 of these eminent women had no siblings, 15 did (Table 1, Column 4). Half of all siblings were male. Eight had one or more brothers; of these, 5 had no sisters. Ten had one or more sisters; of these, 7 had no brothers, and 3 had both brothers and sisters. For the total 34 models of achievement, 21 had one or more brothers, 19 had one or more sisters, 10 had both sisters and brothers, and 4 were only children.

If the seeds of achievement "are sown within families of orientation" (Featherman, 1978, pp. 2–3), then the occupational choices of the siblings of these eminent women are noteworthy. Many of the 28 living siblings are in occupations that require high levels of education. There are 7 teachers, 3 lawyers, 2 professors, 2 businessmen, 2 company presidents, 1 department chair, 1 physician, 1 physicist, 1 psychoanalyst, 1 dentist, 1 engineer, 1 social worker, 1 nurse, 1 accountant, 1 photographer, 1 translator, and 1 office manager. These occupational choices may reflect parental values, support, and encouragement toward academic and career achievement.

The women recall their parents as creating "an environment where intellectual pursuits were fostered" (Olga deCillis Engelhardt) and as "avid intellectuals" (Lillian Troll). "My family had an almost mystical belief in the power of education to change the condition of life" (Martha Mednick); "It was a given in my family that I would go to college" (Carolyn Robertson Payton). It is clear that the parents of these eminent women "placed a high value on education" (Frances Graham).

What contributes to parental emphasis on achievement? Is it related to parental education and occupational attainment?

Table 1 shows the occupations of the fathers and mothers of these eminent women. Six (35%) of the fathers and 9 (53%) of the mothers can be identified as professionals. An additional 5 (30%) of the fathers and 2 (12%) of the mothers are engaged in business or entrepreneurial endeavors. For this group of women, in contrast to those in the first volume, there is a decrease in percentage of fathers engaged in professional, business leadership, or entrepreneurial positions (65% vs. 88%) and an increase in the percentage of mothers so engaged (65% vs. 47%). Fathers were better educated than mothers, with 42% of the fathers and 24% of the mothers graduating from college or professional school. However, a substantial 29% of the women had at least one parent whose formal educa-

TABLE 1
Demographic Variable of Eminent Women in Psychology: Families of Origin

Eminent Woman and Date of Birth	Place of Birth	Birth Order	Siblings[a]	Father's Occupation	Mother's Occupation
L. H. J. Stolz October 19, 1891	Washington, DC	2	BW	Lawyer	Homemaker
L. E. Tyler May 10, 1906	Chetek, WY	1	WBBB	Painting contractor	Teacher/ homemaker
A. Anastasi December 19, 1908	New York City, NY	1	W	Attendance officer of board of education	President of piano factory
M. S. Crissey January 10, 1910	Lorrain, OH	1	WS	Realtor/ paralegal	Teacher/ homemaker/ realtor
E. Fromm December 25, 1910	Frankfurt, Germany	1	WBSBSSBB	Physician	Homemaker
L. E. Troll September 24, 1915	Chicago, IL	1	WS	Social worker	Social worker
O. E. D. Engelhardt August 26, 1917	New York City, NY	4	SSSWB	Tailor	Homemaker
P. C. Smith October 28, 1917	Minneapolis, MN	1	W	Banker	Social worker/ teacher

		BBWSB	Lawyer/justice	Teacher/musician/homemaker
J. Loevinger February 6, 1918	3		Lawyer/justice	Teacher/musician/homemaker
F. K. Graham August 1, 1918	1	WB	Engineer	Librarian
J. T. Spence August 29, 1923	1	WS	Business manager	Social worker
D. H. Eichorn November 18, 1924	1	WS	Accountant	Manager/administrator
C. R. Payton May 13, 1925	2	SW	Restaurant owner	Homemaker
M. T. Mednick March 31, 1929	1	WB	Dressmaker/tailor	Dressmaker
M. E. Bernal April 13, 1931	2	SWS	Automobile salesman	Bilingual teacher
F. L. Denmark January 28, 1932	1	WS	Lawyer	Musician/homemaker
B. R. Strickland November 24, 1936	1	WB	Railroad Worker	waitress

[a]W = eminent woman, B = brother, S = sister.

tion consisted of elementary school or elementary school and the beginning of high school.[1]

Approximately a third of the women in the present volume come from backgrounds that are difficult to identify in terms of parental occupation, education, or financial situation as especially nurturant of high achievement. In fact, several write of the considerable difficulties they encountered in this regard. Most notable are Martha Bernal, whose family valued education but believed that "education and careers were for men only;" Bonnie Strickland, who describes herself as a "kid from the south side of the steel mills in Birmingham and the river swamps of northwest Florida;" and Leona Tyler, who describes her family as "on the verge of poverty."

Regardless of occupational and educational attainments of parents, in all instances the eminent daughters surpassed their mothers' (and, with one exception, their fathers') educational attainments by earning a doctorate. The exception was Erika Fromm, whose father was a physician. This finding regarding occupational and educational attainments of the eminent women is largely similar for the women in the first volume, with four exceptions: the mother of Mary Henle and the fathers of Katharine Banham, Margaret Ives, and Mamie Phipps Clark were physicians.

The mothers of these eminent women had an average of 2.8 children, with a range from 1 to 8 children. Most (10) of the mothers had 2 children each; 2 had 1 child, and another 2 had 5 children each. Of their eminent daughters, 53% became mothers, including one (Marie Skodak Crissey) who did so as a stepmother. This percentage is a substantial increase over the 29% who became mothers in the first volume and may reflect a more accepting social context for the integration of motherhood and career achievement for these younger women.

CONTINUATION AND INTEGRATION: ACHIEVEMENT AND AFFILIATION

Marital Patterns

Eighty-eight percent of the 17 eminent women in this volume mar-

---

[1] High levels of formal education for a substantial percentage of the population are a relatively recent occurrence. In 1960, college was completed by 7.7% of the population; in 1970, by 10.7%; in 1980, by 16.2%; in 1984, by 19.6%. Of those completing college in 1984, 23.9% were White men, 16% were White women, 10.5% were Black men, 10.4% were Black women, 9.5% were Hispanic men, and 7.0% were Hispanic women. In 1984, median years of school completed for all races ranged from 11.0 years for Hispanic women to 12.6 years for White men (SAUS, 1986).

ried sometime during their lives (Table 2), in contrast to 76% of the 17 eminent women in the first volume and in contrast to only 42% of 22 "first generation American women psychologists" (born between 1847 and 1878). Furumoto and Scarborough (1986) listed and described this first generation in a format and style defined in the first volume of *Models of Achievement* (1983). The significant increase in occurrences of marriage among women in psychology over time seems to reflect the historical and social context. The greater acceptance of women as professionals is related to the increased occurrence of marriage for educated women. The married percentage (88%) found in this present group approaches the percentage (94%) for women in the general population (Glick, 1975; Rohrbaugh, 1979; SAUS, 1986).

For the present group, the age at first marriage averages 28.8 years and ranges from 21 years (Martha Mednick and Florence Denmark) to 56 years (Marie Skodak Crissey); median age is 25 years. In addition to an increase in the occurrence of marriage, there is a decrease in the median age at first marriage in contrast to the first volume. For the eminent women in the first volume, the median age at marriage is 27 years. For women in the general population, the median age at first marriage reached an all-time high of 23.3 years in 1985.[2] The postponement of first marriage seems to be related to educated, middle-class, career-minded life styles, but societal acceptance of women as professionals tempers the extent of the delay. The eminent women in these two volumes seem to have been pioneers for current trends in later marriages.

Although marriages were postponed, more eminent women—like others in the general population— married than remained single. Fifteen of the 17 women married. Eight who married are still married to their first husbands; 2 are widowed; 5 are divorced; and 1 is remarried. Of the 8 marriages before the doctorate, 5 ended in divorce; none of the 7 marriages after the doctorate ended in divorce. Yet, achieving the doctorate does not seem to be related to length of marriage nor to divorce per se. The doctorate was earned as much as 11 years *after* the divorce (Carolyn Robertson Payton) and 15 years *before* the divorce (Florence Denmark). The mean length of marriage is 15 years (the median is also 15 years), with a range from 2 years (Martha Bernal) to 36 years (Lillian Troll). The median duration of marriage for the general population since 1960

---

[2] For the general population, the median age at first marriage ranged from 20.5 to 21.2 years for the period 1920 through 1947; in 1956, it reached a low of 20.1 years; between 1960 and 1980, it ranged from 20.3 to 21.8 years; in 1985, it reached a high of 23.3 years (HSUS, 1975; SAUS, 1986).

TABLE 2

Demographic Variables of Eminent Women in Psychology: Marital Patterns

Eminent Woman	Age at First Marriage	Marital Status	Husband's Occupation	Age at First Child	Children
L. H. M. Stolz	46	Widowed	Physician		None
L. E. Tyler		Single			None
A. Anastasi	24	Married	Psychologist		3 stepchildren
M. S. Crissey	56	Married	Psychologist		1 daughter
E. Fromm	27	Married	Business executive	29	2 daughters
L. E. Troll	25	Divorced	Engineer	30	1 son
O. E. D. Engelhardt	33	Married	Professor of English and medievel literature	39	2 sons

Name	Age	Marital status	Occupation	Spouse's age	Children
P. C. Smith	24	Married	Psychologist		None
J. Loevinger	26	Married	Chemistry professor	27	1 daughter 1 son
F. K. Graham	22	Married	Physician	25	2 daughters 1 son
J. T. Spence	36	Widowed	Psychologist		None
D. H. Eichorn	22	Married	Minister/chaplain	30	1 son
C. R. Payton	22	Divorced	Police detective		None
M. T. Mednick	21	Divorced	Psychologist	28	2 daughters
M. E. Bernal	27	Divorced	Economist		None
F. L. Denmark	21	Divorced	Orthodontist	27	2 daughters 1 son
B. R. Strickland		Married Single	Publisher		3 stepchildren

Marital status as of 1987.

has not exceeded 7.2 years.[3] Although these women were about as likely to marry and to divorce as those in the general population, the duration of their marriages is approximately twice as long as the marriages of women in the general population. Both marriage and divorce can act as modifiers of career plans and goals, but there is little or no evidence that either was detrimental to long-range career achievement for these eminent women.

Marital Partners

The first husbands of these eminent women, like the husbands of the women in the first volume, are predominantly professionals. There are 7 psychologists and/or professors, 2 physicians, 1 orthodonist, 1 engineer, 1 economist, 1 minister, 1 business executive, and 1 police detective. These marriages to a large degree are marriages of professional couples who have combined the multiple roles of career, marriage, and child rearing. Some of the couples did not have children due to physical problems (Anne Anastasi), late marriages (Lois Meek Stolz and Janet Spence), or other reasons.

For the women who were married and childless or single (47%), there was greater flexibility in career choices and in choosing a continuous career pattern. Career patterns were affected by a great number of variables, including relocating with a spouse (Dorothy Hansen Eichorn, Olga deCillis Engelhardt, Frances Graham, Jane Loevinger, Martha Mednick, and Janet Taylor Spence) or changing educational plans to remain in the same location as a prospective spouse (Florence Denmark). In one instance, a husband relocated with his wife (Lillian Troll), but she relocated with him more often. Outcomes of relocating or not relocating varied, bringing both new opportunities and barriers to education and career advancement.

Husbands generally were very supportive, providing encouragement and new possibilities. Dorothy Hansen Eichorn accepted her husband's proposal of marriage only when he convinced her that it *was* possible to go to graduate school and be married at the same time. Frances Graham's husband introduced her to "electrophysiological recording" and helped her overcome her "resistance to learning about electronics."

---

[3] The median duration of marriage is approximately 7 years: It was 7.1 years in 1960, 7.2 years in 1965, 6.7 years in 1970, 6.5 years in 1975, 6.8 years in 1980, and 7.0 years in 1981 and 1982 (SAUS, 1986).

The person one marries has a great influence on personal and professional life style. Being married to another psychologist brings with it the camaraderie, shared understanding, and informal learning that make such partnerships stimulating and rewarding. In productivity (number of articles published, papers presented at conventions, books published, or grants received), husbands of psychologists are the most productive of any group, but wives of psychologists surpass other women psychologists (Bryson, Bryson, Licht, & Licht, 1976).

Being married to a psychologist brings entree into networks of psychologists, but being married to a professional in another or allied field can bring entree into networks that bring broader perspectives. Jane Loevinger described the benefits she gained from contacts with natural scientists—contacts made possible through her husband, a chemistry professor; among these benefits are insights that have served her as a psychologist.

Children and Parenthood

Of the 13 married women in the first volume 38% had children. Among, the 15 married women in this volume, 60%[4] had children, including stepchildren. Three had 2 children each—2 daughters, 2 sons, and a mixed pair; 2 had 1 child each—a son or a daughter; and 2 had 3 children each—2 daughters and 1 son. Average number of children born to these women is 2.1.[5] Average age at birth of first child is 29.4 years. The women who had 3 children each were 27 years and 30 years at the birth of the first child; the women who had 2 children each were 27 years, 28 years, and 39 years at the birth of the first child; and the women who had 1 child each were 29 years and 30 years at the birth of the first child. The children were born after 1 to 8 years of marriage, with an average of 4.75 years. These ages at birth of first child and years after marriage are considerably longer than the ages and years after marriage for birth of first children for the general female population.[6] However, the

---

[4] It is approximated that 83% of the women in the general population are mothers (Rohrbaugh, 1979, pp. 175, 194).

[5] The fertility rate during the Depression years was 2.3 children, the lowest level on record up to that time; the highest fertility rate was 3.8 children, recorded in 1957; in 1973, the fertility rate was 1.9 children; in 1984, it was 1.8 children. The birth rate remained around 15 per 1,000 population from 1973 through 1978; in 1979, the figure rose to 15.6; in 1980, it reached 15.9; in 1983, it dropped to 15.5 (Dolan & Stanley, 1982; Glick, 1975; SAUS, 1986; Trotter, 1987).

[6] The birth of the first child generally occurs within the first 24 months after marriage (Van Dusen & Sheldon, 1976).

age at birth of first child seems to be indicative of current trends among career women to delay birth of first child.

Parenting requires juggling of multiple roles. Child care was facilitated by spouses, hired help, and a shifting of emphasis from career to family on a temporary basis. In some instances, parenting was a shared endeavor between wife and husband (Dorothy Hansen Eichorn), but in many instances the parent with primary responsibility for child care was the mother (Olga deCillis Engelhardt, Erika Fromm, Lillian Troll, Jane Loevinger, Frances Graham, Martha Mednick, and Florence Denmark). Careers continued on a full-time or part-time basis or were interrupted for a period of child rearing. In some instances, the time-out provided new motivation and direction (Lillian Troll). Achievement and affiliation continued to be salient as child rearing was woven into the fabric of the women's lives: "High achievement motivated people remain high achievement motivated in everything they do" (Lillian Troll). Returning to a career after interruption temporarily required a steep climb—"You start out at a somewhat lower rung" (Olga deCillis Engelhardt)—but there was general consensus among the women that family was a first priority. Overall, marriage or children did not have a long-term effect on scientific production for these women or for the eminent women in science studied by Cole and Zuckerman (1987).

What about the children? What becomes of the children of psychologists? What becomes of the children of eminent "working mothers"? They become highly educated achievers. The 10 girls and 7 boys born to the 8 women in this volume are now: 4 college or graduate students, 3 college professors, 2 social workers, 1 physician, 1 chemist, 1 attorney, 1 engineer, 1 labor organizer, 1 executive manager, 1 actress, and 1 musician. It appears that these women were role models of achievement for their own children and that the ambience of dual professional parents encouraged and supported achievement in education and occupation.

ACHIEVEMENT: EDUCATIONAL AND PROFESSIONAL PATTERNS

Educational Patterns

To become eminent psychologists was not the childhood aspirations of these women. Many came to psychology through a circuitous route. In fact, considerable diversity in majors is apparent in their undergraduate lives. In addition to the 9 who chose psychology as a major or part of a double major, 8 chose other undergraduate majors: in education (Marie Skodak Crissey, Martha Mednick, and Lois Meek Stolz), in English (Leona Tyler), in health, physical education, and recreation (Bonnie Strickland), in home economics (Carolyn Robertson Payton), in history (Florence Denmark), in premedicine (Lillan Troll), and in sociology (Olga deCillis Engelhardt). Often, the women chose double majors (Denmark, Smith, and Troll). Of those who earned a masters degree, all but 1 (Martha Bernal) earned that degree in psychology. All earned a doctorate in psychology (Table 3).

Many women in the first volume also came to psychology through a circuitous route. In addition to psychology, eight different majors were represented in their undergraduate degrees. All but 1 woman earned her doctorate in psychology. There seems to be continuity in this pattern for the women in both volumes.

For the women in the present volume, the range in years from baccalaureate to completion of doctorate is 2 years (Anne Anastasi) to 30 years (Lillian Troll), with a mean of 7.9 years and a median of 5 years. The age at doctorate ranges from 21 to 52 years. The mean age at doctorate is 28.8 years, and the median is 26 years. The remarkable Anne Anastasi began Barnard College when she was 15 years old, was graduated at 19 years, and earned her doctorate at 21 years. Leona Tyler was graduated from college at 19 years; Frances Graham also was graduated from college at 19 years and earned her doctorate at 23 years. Patricia Smith earned her doctorate at 24 years. In comparison with the median age at doctorate in psychology and the social sciences and the median time lapse from bachelor's degree to doctorate, these women's median age at doctorate is lower, and their median time lapse from bachelor's degree to doctorate is shorter.[7]

Lillian Troll, an exemplar of achievement in a different way, illustrates the possiblities in career change. Troll was 52 years of age when she was awarded her doctorate. She is admirable not only for the adaptability, courge, and motivation that enabled her to earn a doctorate at middle age but also for her subsequent accomplish-

---

[7] The mean number of years from completion of baccalaureate to completion of doctorate in the field of psychology was 8.2 years for 1930–1939 and a high of 9.4 years for 1960–1961; in 1983, it was 8.9 years, and the median age at doctorate in psychology was 32.0 years. Median age at doctorate in the social sciences for 1983–1984 was 32.7 years, and the median time lapse from bachelor's degree to doctorate was 9.7 years (Harmon, 1963, 40; HEW, 1968, p. 64; HEW, 1985; SAUS, 1985).

TABLE 3
Education and Interests of Eminent Women in Psychology

Eminent Woman	BA/BS	MA/MS	Doctorate	Graduate Support	Interests
L. H. M. Stolz	1921 Education George Washington University	1922 Psychology Columbia University Teachers College	1925 Psychology Columbia University Teachers College	Scholarship, assistant, and fellowship, Columbia University Teachers College	Child development Developmental psychology
L. E. Tyler	1925 English University of Minnesota	1939 Psychology University of Minnesota	1941 Psychology University of Minnesota	Assistant, University of Minnesota	Counseling Individual differences
A. Anastasi	1928 Psychology Barnard College		1930 Psychology Columbia University	Assistant and lecturer, Columbia University	Testing Research and development

Name				Position	Research interests
M. S. Crissey	1931 Education Ohio State University	1931 Clinical Psychology Ohio State University	1938 Child Development Psychology State University of Iowa	Research assistant, State University of Iowa	Child development Mental retardation Intelligence testing Clinical psychology
E. Fromm			1933 Psychology Frankfurt, Germany		Psychoanalysis Hypnoanalysis Projective techniques Diagnostic testing
L. E. Troll	1937 Psychology/ Premed University of Chicago	1966 Human Development/ Psychology University of Chicago	1967 Human Development/ Psychology Chicago University of	Fellowship, University of Chicago	Clinical psychology Formation and dissolution of relationships Develpomental psychology
O. E. D. Engelhardt	1939 Sociology Hunter College	1940 Comparative Psychology Columbia University	1944 Experimental Psychology Columbia University	Instructor, University of Connecticut	Comparative psychology Experimental psychology Social psychology Tests and measurements Industrial/organizational

TABLE 3
(Continued)

Eminent Woman	BA/BS	MA/MS	Doctorate	Graduate Support	Interests
P. C. Smith	1939 Mathematics and Psychology University of Nebraska		1942 Industrial Psychology Cornell University	Assistant, Northwestern University and Bryn Mawr College Fellowship, Cornell University	Industrial/organizational psychology Scaling Research design Measurement Performance Perception
J. Loevinger	1938 Psychology University of Minnesota	1938 Psychometrics University of Minnesota	1944 Psychology University of California at Berkeley	Assistant, University of Minnesota Lecturer, University of California at Berkeley	Ego development Psychoanalysis Personality Construct validity Measurement
F. K. Graham	1938 Psychology Pennsylvania State University		1942 Psychology Yale University	Fellowship, Pennsylvania State University Fellowship, Yale University	Experimental psychology Neuropsychology Developmental psychology Psychophysiology

Name	Degree 1	Degree 2	Degree 3	Financial support	Areas of specialization
J. T. Spence	1945 Psychology Oberlin College	1949 Psychology University of Iowa	1949 Psychology University of Iowa		Clinical psychology Personality Social psychology Test construction
D. H. Eichorn	1947 Psychology University of Vermont	1949 Psychology Boston University	1951 Psychology Northwestern University	Teaching assistantship. Northwestern University	Physiological psychology Developmental psychology Experimental psychology Statistics
C. R. Payton	1945 Home Economics Bennett College	1948 Clinical Psychology University of Wisconsin at Madison	1962 Counseling/ Student Personnel Administration Columbia University Teachers College		Clinical psychology Industrial/organizational psychology Minority issues
M. T. Mednick	1950 Education City College of New York	1952 Psychology City College of New York	1955 Psychology Northwestern University	Scholarship, City College of New York Scholarship, Northwestern University	Psychological testing Psychology of women Women and achievement Clinical psychology Creativity

TABLE 3
(Continued)

Eminent Woman	BA/BS	MA/MS	Doctorate	Graduate Support	Interests
M. E. Bernal	1952 Psychology Texas Western College	1957 Special Education Syracuse University	1962 Clinical Psychology Indiana University	Scholarship, Indiana University Fellowship, Indiana University	Psychophysiology Behavior modification Parent training Minority mental health
F. L. Denmark	1952 History/ Psychology University of Pennsylvania	1954 Psychology University of Pennsylvania	1958 Social Psychology University of Pennsylvania	Teaching and research assistant, University of Pennsylvania	Psychology of women Gender roles Leadership and status Social psychology Minority group achievement
B. R. Strickland	1958 Health, Physical Education, and Recreation Alabama College for Women	1960 Psychology Ohio State University	1962 Clinical Psychology Ohio State University	Research Assistant Ohio State University	Clinical psychology Personality Social psychology Psychology of women

ments, perspectives, and insights. Her life and career illustrate that significant contributions to psychology are not the province of any particular age group. She, like the other eminent women in these volumes, turned the possiblity for lifelong growth and achievement into actuality.

Four of the doctorates were earned before 1940 (Lois Meek Stolz in 1925, Anne Anastasi in 1930, Erika Fromm in 1933, and Marie Skodak Crissey in 1938). The vast majority were earned between 1940 and 1967; 6 were earned in the 1940s; 3 were earned in the 1950s; and 4 were earned in the 1960s. In contrast, 12 of the 17 women in the first volume earned the doctorate in the 1920s and 1930s.[8,9]

Thirteen received graduate support. Five received fellowships; of these, 3 had assistantships or scholarships as well. Nine received teaching or research assistantships; 3 received scholarships. In addition, 1 (Olga deCillis Engelhardt) was an instructor at the University of Connecticut while earning her doctorate there.

Nine received a doctorate in psychology; 2 received a doctorate in clinical psychology; and 1 each received a doctorate in child development, counseling, human development, experimental psychology, industrial psychology, and social psychology. As shown in Table 3, graduate training does not necessarily predict interests. Interests varied widely and encompassed a broad range of subdisciplines in psychology. These interests changed as opportunities arose and curiosity and challenge motivated new directions and goals.

Although this group of eminent women is younger than the group previously studied, they, nonetheless, are pioneers, ground breakers, and innovators. They have made major breakthroughs in academe, industry, and government; in professional organizations, social action, and therapy; in research, training, and psychological testing.

These women are researchers, teachers, consultants, and leaders. In almost 100 years, the American Psychological Association (APA),

---

[8] The number of doctorates awarded to women in all fields increased substantially between 1920 and 1983–1984. Sample years and number of doctorates awarded to women are: 1920 (93), 1930 (353), 1940 (429), 1950 (643), 1960 (1,028), 1970 (4,000), 1978 (8,500), 1983 (10,657)—Hew, 1968, 1985; SAUS, 1981).

[9] In 1983, 47.5% of the doctorates awarded in psychology were awarded to women, compared to 33.6% of doctorates in all fields. In 1984, 50.1% of the doctorates awarded in psychology were awarded to women, compared to a projected 34.2% of doctorates in all fields (APA Committee on Women in Psychology, 1986; HEW, 1985; SAUS, 1985).

founded in 1892, has had 7 women as presidents. To be elected president, the highest office of the national organization, is to be recognized and endorsed by colleagues as a leader in psychology. Two of the 7, Mary Whiton Calkins (1905) and Margaret Washburn (1921), whose biographies were included in a special issue of the *Psychology of Women Quarterly* (O'Connell & Russo, 1980), are deceased. The other 5 have become presidents since 1972; Anne Anastasi (1972), Leona E. Tyler (1973), Florence L. Denmark (1980), Janet Taylor Spence (1984), and Bonnie R. Strickland (1987). The lives and accomplishments of these 5 are preserved in their own words in this book.

In addition to the very notable distinction of being members of an elite group, these women have made major theoretical contributions (Table 4) to the understanding of individual differences and creative thinking (Leona Tyler), test construction and interpretation (Anne Anastasi, Janet Taylor Spence, and Leona Tyler), environmental and experimental factors of psychological development (Anne Anastasi), achievement and achievement motivation (Janet Taylor Spence and Florence Denmark), gender identity (Spence and Denmark), locus of control (Bonnie Strickland), and counseling and psychotherapy (Tyler and Strickland).

Carolyn Robertson Payton, winner of the Distinguished Professional Contributions Award of APA, achieved national distinction and high office when she became the first woman director of the U.S. Peace Corps and a presidential appointee to the Board of Directors of the Inter-American Foundation. A commonality among these eminent women is that they were often first. Martha Bernal was the first Mexican-American woman to earn a doctorate in psychology, Erika Fromm developed the first psychological laboratory in a Dutch mental hospital, Olga de Cillis Engelhardt was the first woman industrial/organizational psychologist to head a division of business and management, and Lois Meek Stolz established the first Child Care Service Centers at Kaiser Shipyards during World War II. They were pioneers in landmark work on women and on gender issues (Florence Denmark, Janet Taylor Spence, Martha Mednick, and Lillian Troll), on minorities (Carolyn Robertson Payton, Martha Bernal, Martha Mednick, and Bonnie Strickland), on ego development and its measurement (Jane Loevinger), on biological determinants and correlates of behavior (Dorothy Hansen Eichorn), on perinatal anoxia (Frances Graham), on assessment of brain injury and mental retardation (Frances Graham and Marie Skodak Crissey), and on techniques for evaluation and training (Marie Skodak Crissey, Olga deCillis Engelhardt, and Patricia Cain Smith).

TABLE 4
Major Innovations of Eminent Women in Psychology

Eminent Woman	Innovations
L. H. M. Stolz	Examined the relationships of fathers to their children born while fathers were at war. Research on the effects of maternal employment and influences on parent behavior. Established Child care Service Centers at Kaiser Shipyards, serving nearly 3,800 children during World War II.
L. E. Tyler	Theory and practice of counseling psychology. Theoretical contributions to the understanding of individual differences and thinking creatively. Fourth woman to become president of APA.
A. Anastasi	Significant theoretical contributions to test construction and interpretation, environmental and experiential factors of psychological development, nature and identification of psychological traits. Differential psychology and psychological testing. Third woman to become president of APA.
M. S. Crissey	Developed special education programs, school psychologist, and school social work programs in public schools. Participant in Iowa studies examining mental development of adoptive and mentally retarded children. Research on mental development and environmental stimulation.
E. Fromm	Established first psychological laboratory in Dutch mental hospital. Theoretical and experimental research in the application of hypnosis and psychoanalysis. Interpretation and application of Rorschach and other projective tests.
L. E. Troll	Research on development throughout life span; family transmission of culture and values; family interrelations and intergenerational relations. Gender differences and discrimination in late adulthood.
O. E. D. Engelhardt	Consumer behavior and preference, techniques for executive/management training and evaluation. First woman industrial/organizational psychologist to head a division of business and management.

TABLE 4
(Continued)

Eminent Woman	Innovations
P. C. Smith	Identified situational and individual variables of industrial monotony. Developed Behaviorally Anchored Rating Scales (BARS), a behavioral guide for assessing employee performance as well as a means of assessing the initial interview. Improved criteria in job performance and satisfaction.
J. Loevinger	Developed theory of ego development and method of measurement. Work on test construction, construct validity, and reliability theory.
F. K. Graham	Developed Graham–Kendall Memory for Designs Test and similar tests to assess brain injury in children. Landmark research on perinatal anoxia. Introduced blink modulation paradigm and linked heart rate deceleration to Skolov's "orienting reflex" (cardiac-orienting hypothesis). First woman to receive the Distinguished Contributions Award of the Society for Psychophysiological Research.
J. T. Spence	Theoretical contributions to the understanding of achievement and achievement motivation and to the reconceptualization of masculinity, femininity, and gender roles. Constructed numerous assessment instruments, including scales for measuring anxiety, personality characteristics, and attitudes. Sixth woman to become president of APA.
D. H. Eichorn	Landmark longitudinal research in human development, including psychological determinants and correlates of behavior. Innovator in the Berkeley and Oakland studies.
C. R. Payton	First woman to become director of U.S. Peace Corps. Presidential appointee to the Board of Directors of the Inter-American Foundation. Research and emphasis on specific issues of minority women.
M. T. Mednick	Research on creativity. Significant contributions to the psychology of women and to women and achievement. Landmark research in the area of achievement in Black women, focusing on motivational and personality factors.

TABLE 4 *(Continued)*

Eminent Woman	Innovations
M. E. Bernal	Parent-training techniques for conduct-problem children. Psychophysiological responses in schizophrenic and autistic children. Developed extensive training materials for predoctoral and postdoctoral students to serve the mental health needs of minority groups. First Mexican-American woman to receive PhD in psychology. Served as President of the National Hispanic Psychological Association.
F. L. Denmark	Significant contributions to the understanding of leadership and status, gender roles, gender differences, and specific factors affecting achievement among minority groups. Fifth woman to become president of APA.
B. R. Strickland	Demonstrated that Black social activism could be predicted by generalized expectancies (i.e., belief in internal locus of control). Established reliability and construct validity for expectancy variables of locus of control and need for approval. Developed children's locus of control scale. Research in psychotherapy, depression, and women's health. Seventh woman to become president of APA.

They describe themselves as activists (Bernal, Crissey, Denmark, Mednick, Payton, and Strickland) as well as academicians, researchers, and consultants.

Despite their outstanding and varied accomplishments when asked to identify their most significant contributions to psychology, many refer to their roles as teachers and mentors. These distinguished women are extraordinary not only in their accomplishments but in their sense of generativity as they guide students' toward their own unique contributions. They truly are exemplars of high-level professionals who have integrated achievement and affiliation.

Professional Patterns

These distinguished women often held multiple positions simultaneously in various combinations of academe, industry, and government; as professors, deans, chairs, directors, supervisors, researchers, therapists, consultants, and entrepreneurs. The ivy league and seven sisters colleges and the public and private institutions that employed them are listed in Table 5 and include Harvard

University (Martha Mednick), Barnard College (Anne Anastasi and Frances Graham), Columbia University Teachers College (Lois Meek Stolz), Cornell University (Patricia Cain Smith), Stanford University (Lois Meek Stolz and Jane Loevinger), University of California at Berkeley (Dorothy Hansen Eichorn, Jane Loevinger, and Leona Tyler), University of Chicago (Erika Fromm and Lillian Troll), University of Michigan (Martha Mednick, Marie Skodak Crissey, and Lillian Troll), and University of Pennsylvania (Florence Denmark), among others. The women hold the highest ranks in academe: professor, professor emeritus, dean, dean emeritus, and director. A consistent finding is that neither marital status (single, married, or divorced) nor the presence or absence of children is predictive of attaining the highest ranks in academe for these women and the women in the first volume. The routes to the highest academic ranks include (a) a strong, almost continuous commitment to academe (Anne Anastasi, Florence Denmark, Frances Graham, Martha Mednick, Janet Taylor Spence, Bonnie Strickland, and Leona Tyler), (b) significant work primarily as a researcher (Jane Loevinger and Dorothy Hansen Eichorn), and (c) an established reputation as a psychologist in positions allied to academe (Martha Bernal, Erika Fromm, Lois Meek Stolz, and Lillian Troll) or in positions outside academe (Olga deCillis Engelhardt and Patricia Cain Smith). Marie Skodak Crissey, who remained in other settings, is renowned and has been honored by APA as a community psychologist for her work in applied settings. The movement between academe and other settings is overlapping, sequential, and in both directions.

Several of the women have become professor emeritus and have continued their lives of high achievement. Olga deCillis Engelhardt went on to become the first woman industrial/organizational psychologist to head a division of business and management; she later became dean of the College of Business and Management at Northeastern Illinois University. Patricia Cain Smith continues as executive director of her own firm, Cain-Smith Associates. Lillian E. Troll went from professor emeritus at Rutgers University to professorial rank at San Jose State University and the University of California at San Francisco. Others (Anne Anastasi[10] and Leona E. Tyler), like those mentioned, continue to write and publish professionally. Their lives illustrate lifelong achievement.

Recurrent threads through the employment histories of these women are the ability to integrate interests with opportunities and

---

[10] Dr. Anastasi was awarded the National Medal of Science by President Reagan in 1987.

TABLE 5
Major Professional Positions

Eminent Woman	Institutions	Title	Dates
L. H. M. Stolz	American Association of University Women Adult Education Program	Educational Secretary	1924–1929
	Columbia University Teachers College	Director, Child Development Institute; Professor of Education	1929–1939
	State of California	Lecturer	1938–1941
	Collaboration Center on Child Development, University of Chicago	Research Associate	1939–1940
	State of California, Coordinator for Care of Children in Wartime	Assistant to Governor	1942–1943
	Child Service Center, Kaiser Shipyards, OR	Director and Consultant	1943–1945
	Stanford University	Visiting Professor, Lecturer, and Professor	1945–1957
		Professor Emeritus	1957–1984

TABLE 5
(Continued)

Eminent Woman	Institutions	Title	Dates
L. E. Tyler	Junior High School, Mountain Iron, MN	Teacher	1925–1933
	Delzuan, MN	Teacher	1933–1934
	Muskesgon Heights, MI	Teacher	1934–1938
	University of Minnesota	Graduate Assistant	1938–1940
	University of Oregon	Instructor through Professor	1940–1965
	University of California at Berkeley	Visiting Professor	1957–1958
	University of Amsterdam, Holland	Visiting Professor	1962–1963
	University of Oregon	Dean, Graduate School	1965–1971
		Professor Emeritus	1971
		Dean Emeritus	1971
A. Anastasi	Barnard College	Instructor	1930–1939
	Queens College, City University of New Yrok	Assistant Professor and Department Chairperson	1939–1946
	Fordham University	Associate Professor	1947–1951
		Professor	1951–1979
		Professor Emeritus	1979

	Position	Institution	Dates
M. S. Crissey	Assistant State Psychologist	Board of Control of State Institutions, Des Moines, IA	1934–1936
	Assistant Director	Flint Guidance Center	1938–1942
	Director		1942–1946
	Lecturer	University of Michigan	1942–1957
		Private practice	1946–present
	Director, Psychological Services	Dearborn Public Schools, MI	1949–1969
E. Fromm	Research Associate	Department of Psychiatry, Wilhelmina Gasthuis, Amsterdam, Holland	1934–1935
	Director	Psychological Laboratory, Het Apeldoornsche Bosch, Apeldoorn, Holland	1935–1938
	Research Associate	Department of Psychiatry, University of Chicago	1939–1940
	Child Psychologist		1943
	Supervising Psychologist	Veterans Rehabilitation Center, Chicago	1943–1948
	Supervising Psychologist	Institute for Juvenile Research	1951–1953
	Assistant Professor	University of Illinois Medical School	1952–1953

TABLE 5
(Continued)

Eminent Woman	Institutions	Title	Dates
E. Fromm *(continued)*	Northwestern University	Assistant Professor to Associate Professor	1954–1961
		Director of Psychotherapy Training	1955–1961
	University of Chicago	Professor, Department of Psychology and Behavioral Sciences	1961–1976
	National Academy of Professional Psychologists	Teaching Faculty	1974–1977
	University of Chicago	Professor Emeritus	1976
		Professorial Lecturer, School of Social Service Administration	1976–present

L. E. Troll	Michael Reese Hospital, Chicago	Psychological Intern	1937–1938
	Child Study Department, Chicago Public Schools	School Psychologist	1938
	Lincoln State School and Colony, IL	Psychologist	1940
	University of Chicago	Research Fellow	1939–1940
	Pine Manor Junior College, Wellesley, MA	Instructor	1942–1943
	Personnel Research Section AGO, War Department, Washington, DC, New York	Personnel Technician	1941–1942 1943–1945
	Child rearing, then partial involvement with nursery school teaching, directing, and remedial reading.		1938–1958
	Newton Public School, MA	School Psychologist	1957–1963
	California State Department of Mental Hygiene	Research Analyst	1964
	California State Department of Education for Project Talent	Special Consultant	1964–1965
	Committee on Human Development, University of Chicago	Project Coordinator	1965–1967

TABLE 5
(Continued)

Eminent Woman	Institutions	Title	Dates
L. E. Troll *(continued)*	Merril–Palmer Institute, Teaching and Research	Senior Research Associate	1967–1970
	Department of Psychology Wayne State University	Associate Professor	1970–1975
	University of Southern California Ethel Percy Andrus Gerontology Institute	Visiting Professor	1973
	University of Michigan	Visiting Professor	1973–1974
	Rutgers University	Professor	1975–1986
		Department Chairperson, University College Psychology Department	1975–1982
	Gerontology Certificate Program Rutgers University	Chairperson	1976–1982
	University of British Columbia	Visiting Professor	1983–1986
	Rutgers University	Professor Emeritus	1983
			1986
	San Jose State University	Professor	1986–present
	University of California at San Francisco	Professor	1986–present

O. E. D. Engelhardt	Psychological Corporation	Assistant to Supervisor of Marketing Research	1942–1943
	University of Connecticut at Storrs	Instructor	1943–1951
		Assistant Professor	1946–1951
	Industrial Relations Center, University of Chicago	Research Associate	1950–1952
		Assistant Professor	1952–1955
	Campbell Soup Company	Psychological Consultant	1954–1956
	Child rearing		1957–1965
	Valparaiso University	Lecturer	1965–1966
	North Central College	Professor	1966–1981
		Chairperson, Department of Psychology	1974–1981
		Chairperson, Department of Social and Behavioral Sciences	1980–1981
		Professor Emeritus	1981

TABLE 5
(Continued)

Eminent Woman	Institutions	Title	Dates
O. E. D. Englehardt *(continued)*	Northeastern Illinois University	Professor; Director, Division of Business Management	1981–1983
		Professor; Dean, College of Business and Management	1983–present
P. C. Smith	Aetna Life and Affiliated Companies, Hartford, CT	Personnel Intern; Consultant to Hartford Hospital	1942–1944
	Salmon Association, Washington, DC	Director of Personnel Division	1944–1949
		Director of Research	1949–1963
	Wells College, Aurora, NY	Lecturer	1948–1949
	Ithaca College, Ithaca, NY	Lecturer	1948–1949
	Cornell University, Ithaca, NY	Assistant through Full Professor	1949–1966
	Cain–Smith Associates, Ithaca, NY, and Bowling Green, OH	Executive Director	1951–present
	Bowling Green State University	Professor	1966–1980
		Professor Emeritus	1980

J. Loevinger	Stanford University	Acting Instructor	1941–1942
	University of California at Berkeley	Lecturer	1942–1943
	Washington University	Instructor	1946–1947
		Research Psychologist	1950–1953
	Jewish Hospital, St. Louis	Research Associate	1954–1960
	Washington University	Research Associate Professor	1960–1971
		Research Professor	1971–1974
		Professor	1974–present
F. K. Graham	St. Louis Psychiatric Clinic	Psychologist; Acting Director	1942–1944
	Department of Psychiatry, Washington University	Instructor	1942–1948
	Barnard College	Instructor	1948–1951
	Department of Psychiatry and Department of Pediatrics, Washington University	Research Associate	1952–1957
	Department of Pediatrics, University of Wisconsin	Research Associate; Professor	1957–1986
	University of Wisconsin	Lecturer through Professor	1962–1986
	University of Delaware	Professor	1986–present

TABLE 5
(Continued)

Eminent Woman	Institutions	Title	Dates
J. T. Spence	Northwestern University	Assistant to Associate Professor	1949–1960
	Veterans Administration Hospital, Iowa City	Research Psychologist	1960–1964
	University of Texas at Austin	Professor	1964–1979
		Asbel Smith Professor	1979–present
D. H. Eichorn	Institute of Human Development, University of California at Berkeley	Junior Research Psychologist to Research Psychologist	1951–present
	Child Study Center, University of California	Administrator	1960–present
	Society for Research in Child Development	Executive Officer	1971–present
	Institute of Human Development, University of California at Berkeley	Associate Director	1975–present

C. R. Payton

Livingstone College	Instructor	1948–1953
Elizabeth City State Teachers College	Dean of Women	1953–1956
Virginia State College	Associate Professor	1956–1959
Howard University	Assistant Professor	1959–1964
U.S. Peace Corps	Eastern Caribbean Country Director	1964–1970
Howard University	Director, Counseling Sevices	1970–1977
U.S. Peace Corps	Director	1977–1978
Center for Multicultural Awareness	Director	1979–1980
Howard University	Dean, Counseling and Career Development	1980–present

TABLE 5
(Continued)

Eminent Woman	Institutions	Title	Dates
M. T. Mednick	Chicago, IL	Teacher	1951–1952
	Hospital, Hines, IL; Veterans Administration Mental Hygiene Clinic, Chicago, IL	Clinical Intern	1952–1955
	Harvard University	Fellow	1956–1957
		Research Associate	1957–1958
	University of Michigan	Research Associate	1959–1960
	Institute for Social Research, University of Michigan	Research Associate	1960–1964
	University of Michigan	Associate Professor of Psychology in Nursing	1964–1967
	University of Michigan	Extention Service Teaching	1967
		Lecturer, Department of Psychology	1965–1967
	Institute for Social Research, University of Michigan	Research Associate	1965–1967
	Howard University	Associate Professor	1968–1971

M. T. Mednick (*continued*)	National Academy of Public Administration, Washington, DC	Consultant	1969–1970
	Geomet, Incorporated, Rockville, MD	Consultant	1971–1972
	Center for Social Research on the Kibbutz at Givat Haviva, Israel	Visiting Research Associate	1972
	Laboratory of Psychology National Institute of Mental Health, MD	Visiting Fellow	1974–1975
	University of Connecticut at Storrs	Professor	1976–1978
	Howard University	Professor	1971–present
	University of Hawaii at Manoa Honolulu	Visiting Professor	1984
	Kibbutz Research Institute and Women's Center, University of Haifa, Israel	Visiting Researcher	1985
	Harvard University	Visiting Scholar	1984–1985
M. E. Bernal	University of Arizona	Assistant Professor	1963–1964
	Neuropsychiatric Institute, University of California at Los Angeles	Senior Psychologist and Assistant Professor in Residence	1964–1971
	University of Denver	Professor	1971–1986
	State University of Arizona	Professor	1986–present
	Hispanic Research Center	Associate	1986–present

TABLE 5
(Continued)

Eminent Woman	Institutions	Title	Dates
F. L. Denmark	University of Pennsylvania	Teaching assistant to Instructor	1952–1958
		Research Assistant	1952–1955
		Clinical Supervisor	1955–1958
	University of Pennsylvania Hospital Survey Research, Inc.	Psychologist Research	1955–1956
		Interviewer	1957
	Queens College	Lecturer	1959–1966
	Daniel Starch and Staff, Mamaroneck, NY	Research Analyst	1960
	Testing and Counseling Center, Queens College	Counselor	1961–1964
	Hunter College and Graduate Center, City University of New York	Instructor through Professor	1964–present
		Thomas Hunter Professor	1984–present

B. R. Strickland	Emory University	Assistant to Associate Professor	1962–1973
	University of Massachusetts at Amherst	Dean of Women	1964–1969
		Professor	1973–present
		Chairperson, Department of Psychology	1976–1977
			1978–1983
		Associate to Chancellor	1983–1984

the flexibility to shift employment settings and direction. There are many valuable lessons to be learned and an instructive model for current and future generations in the variety of employment patterns of these women and in the earlier group of 17 eminent women.

BARRIERS, COPING STRATEGIES, AND INFLUENTIAL HISTORICAL EVENTS

Barriers

Because the women in this volume are younger as a group than the women in the first volume, and the historical and social context of their lives is more contemporary, it might be expected that they would experience less overt discrimination and fewer restrictions on educational and professional opportunities. To a limited extent, this is true. But, the overt discrimination and restrictions they experienced are significant (Table 6). Their contributions, seminal and definitive, were made in environments that ranged from benign to hostile, from accepting to rejecting. At times they were neither accepted nor rejected as professionals; they were tolerated (Lois Meek Stolz and Leona Tyler). They faced barriers of sexism, racism, anti-Semitism, ageism. They were denied admission to medical schools (Erika Fromm and Lillian Troll), to honor societies (Patricia Cain Smith), and to educational seminars (Frances Graham) because they are women. Some mention restricted job opportunities and denial of positions due to their sex (Marie Skodak Crissey, Jane Loevinger, and Patricia Cain Smith); others mention delayed advancement and inequitable salaries (Leona Tyler, Erika Fromm, Janet Taylor Spence, Florence Denmark, and Bonnie Strickland). Some mention discrimination because they are Black, (Carolyn Robertson Payton) or Hispanic (Martha Bernal) or Jewish (Jane Loevinger) or too old (Lillian Troll).

Several mention discrimination in education and employment settings based on their marital status. Being married restricted educational opportunities. Dorothy Hansen Eichorn was denied entry into a psychology graduate program at Harvard because she was not viewed seriously. "The faculty could not waste their time" on married women. With a male wage earner/spouse women's employment and salary were viewed as superfluous. During the Depression, women were resented for taking a job; jobs were to be reserved for men (Frances Graham). Later, women were offered inequitable salaries (Florence Denmark) or were denied financial aid (Patricia

TABLE 6
Barriers and Coping Strategies of Eminent Women in Psychology

Eminent Woman	Barriers	Coping Strategies
L. H. M. Stolz	Administrative demands interfered with time for research.	Flexibility, assertiveness; set limits and conditions.
L. E. Tyler	Family believed "psychology'" compromised Christian beliefs. Advancement delayed because a woman.	Persistence, adaptability, flexibility, determination. Defined priorities.
A. Anastasi	None mentioned.	Task oriented.
M. S. Crissey	Denied positions on three occasions because a woman.	Flexibility, developed alternative professional possibilities, excellence.
E. Fromm	Denied admission to medical school, status, and equitable salary because a woman.	Strong determination, perseverence, flexibility, adaptability.
L. E. Troll	Denied admission to medical school due to quota for women. Role conflict hindered career development. Ageism, denied admission to doctoral program due to age.	Flexibility, adaptability, determination, strength, perseverance. Relocated.
O. E. D. Engelhardt	Lack of women role models in academe. Role conflict interrupted career development. Disruptions and relocations.	Found role model in professional organization. Strong determination, flexibility, adaptability. Kept current on developments in psychology while child rearing.
P. C. Smith	Refused admission to honor society because a woman. Denied financial aid because a married woman. Limited job alternatives and expanded work load.	Perseverance, resourcefulness, determination, excellence. Kept marriage a secret until graduation. Hard work. Set priorities and goals.

357

TABLE 6

(Continued)

Eminent Woman	Barriers	Coping Strategies
J. Loevinger	Denied assistantship because Jewish. Denied faculty positions because a woman.	Determination, assertiveness, perseverance, flexibility.
F. K. Graham	Denied access to educational seminars because a woman. Dual-career family job conflict.	Persistence, flexibility. Negotiated for own and husband's positions before relocating. Considered her own and husband's careers when relocating.
J. T. Spence	Antinepotism. Advancement delayed because a woman.	Flexibility, adaptability, determined to grow professionally with each opportunity.
D. H. Eichorn	Financial. Denied access to graduate program because a married woman. Issues of dual-career family.	Hard work. Flexibility, adaptability, resourcefulness.
C. R. Payton	Limited educational and academic opportunities because Black. Believed corporate position not feasible because Black.	Set priorities. Strong determination, integrity, strong self-esteem, persistence, flexibility.
M. T. Mednick	Issues of dual-career family. Relocating with husband limited opportunities. Antinepotism.	Resourcefulness, persistence, adaptability, flexibility. Relocated for own career.
M. E. Bernal	Conflict between career goals and cultural expectations for women. Lack of Mexican-American colleagues.	Strong determination, perseverance, endurance, integrity, resourcefulness.
F. L. Denmark	Denied equitable salary because a married woman. Advanced more slowly because a woman. Role conflict.	Persistence, assertiveness, flexibility, determination. Set priorities. Resourcefulness.
B. R. Strickland	Financial. Denied academic position because a woman. Advancement delayed because a woman.	Hard work. Perseverance, determination, resourcefulness, flexibility. Relocated.

Cain Smith) because their husbands could support them. Martha Mednick and Janet Taylor Spence were denied positions due to anti-nepotism policies.

In addition to these barriers in the societal context, there was also the barrier of role conflict experienced by several of the married women. Career advancement often was in direct conflict with being a wife and mother according to both external and internalized societal prescriptions. The solutions to this conflict varied, but many chose part-time work and/or an interruption of career for a period of child rearing. Yet, despite institutional barriers and the challenge of role conflict, these women did make astoundingly productive contributions to psychology.

Coping Strategies

Personality, intelligence, motivation. Recurring themes in these autobiographies are the persistence, resourcefulness, and flexibility of these women in the face of obstacles. They showed strength, determination, and dedication. When one pathway was blocked, they chose another (Dorothy Hansen Eichorn, Lillian Troll, Jane Loevinger, Carolyn Robertson Payton, and Janet Taylor Spence). They took risks, changed direction, and relocated. When advancement was delayed at one institution, they moved to a more receptive institution (Bonnie Strickland and Martha Mednick) or persisted until advancement came (Florence Denmark). They were multitalented and used these talents well in a variety of settings and in a variety of capacities. They relocated with spouses and, despite limited opportunities, worked at the most interesting positions they could obtain (Janet Taylor Spence and Martha Mednick). They faced isolation and exclusion with determination and dedication (Martha Bernal, Frances Graham, and Olga de Cillis Engelhardt). They were open to change and to new experiences; learning was an integral part of their lives. They strongly valued achievement in education and occupation; they were very highly motivated to be productive. Lois Meek Stolz (1891–1984) had a professional life that spanned over 70 years; she continued to be professionally productive into her 90s.

Mentors and professional and social networks. These remarkable women were aided by both male and female mentors. The ratio of identified mentors is three men to two women. In Volume 1, men also outnumbered women as mentors due to their larger numbers in the field. With the increasing percentage of women earning their doctorates in psychology, it is likely that in future decades this trend will tend to diminish as more women become mentors. Some of the male mentors mentioned are Robert Hollingsworth, Otto Klineberg, Clark Hull, Max Wertheimer, Robert Woodworth, J. P. Guilford, T. A. Ryan, Robert Underwood, Albert Pepitone, Julian Rotter, and George Kelly; the female mentors include Helen Thompson Wooley, Helen Koch, Bernice Neugarten, Pauline Sears, Nancy Bayley, and Mary Reuder. Martha Mednick identifies Janet Taylor Spence and Leona Tyler as mentors; all three have autobiographies in this volume. Florence Denmark identified Virginia Staudt Sexton, who wrote the Foreword. Janet Taylor Spence identified her husband, Kenneth Spence, as a mentor.

Professional socialization and the formation of critical links in professional and social networks so necessary to reaching eminence in psychology or in other fields were facilitated by the mentors (Clawson, 1980; Levinson, 1978). The mentor relationship provides credibility and shortens the time needed to prove oneself. The mentors provided access, information, advice, support, knowledge, challenge, guidance, and visibility for the aspiring professionals. Recommendations for educational programs, assistantships, and positions often came from mentors, professors, or members of a woman's professional network (Anne Anastasi, Bonnie Strickland, Lois Meek Stolz, Martha Mednick, and Janet Taylor Spence, among others). Social networks were also a means of entree.

Influential Historical Events

All the women experienced World War II; some also witnessed the Great Depression, and a few lived during World War I as well. These major historical events had less effect on the lives and careers of these women in comparison with the women in the earlier volume because many were not born or were children when one or more of these events occurred. Leona Tyler, Marie Skodak Crissey, Erika Fromm, and Lillian Troll were born or were children during World War I. Carolyn Robertson Payton, Dorothy Hansen Eichorn, Janet Taylor Spence, Frances Graham, Jane Loevinger. Patricia Cain Smith, and Olga de Cillis Engelhardt were children during the Great Depression. Bonnie Strickland, Florence Denmark, Martha Bernal, and Martha Mednick were children during World War II.

Lois Meek Stolz, the oldest woman in both volumes, pioneered in providing child-care facilities for working mothers at the Kaiser plants during World War II. She also served as assistant to the governor of California, coordinating the care of children during wartime. More than a half century later, as we approach the 21st century, the concept of child care in conjunction with place of employment is still considered avant garde by some sectors of the work world, but not by all. Some corporations and academic institutions do provide day care for the children of their employees. The time lag in integrating pioneering work into the fabric of mainstream society can be excruciatingly slow, and it often seems that the wheel of social change must be invented and reinvented again and again before it is accepted as worthy.

In general, there was some increase in job opportunities for women during World War II because positions had been vacated by men. But, for this group of women, another significant impact of World War II on career and family life came as an aftermath of the war. The aftermath of World War II, and the decade of the 1950s, brought the empasis on the family—fostered by a "togetherness" zeitgeist—to a new realization. The influence of this new realization is evident in the career paths of several of the women (Lillian Troll, Martha Mednick, Jane Loevinger, Frances Graham, Olga deCillis Engelhardt, Florence Denmark, and Erika Fromm). Martha Mednick writes, "My college classmates retired to have children and my male peers had wives who were all PHTs (putting hubby through)." Lillian Troll and Jane Loevinger write of the impact that Betty Friedan's work (1963) had on them. Friedan wrote of the "crisis in women's identity" and the "forfeited self." Her work called attention to the hidden conflict in choices based on societal prescriptions of the feminine role. For some women in this volume, role conflict was a challenge to achievement, a challenge met and resolved.

The social activism of the 1960s and 1970s brought major philosophical changes that had a lasting impact on the lives and careers of these women. Women's liberation, civil rights, racial integration, peace through negotiation, and college student unrest fueled the demonstrations of this period. Carolyn Robertson Payton became regional director of the "Eastern Caribbean Country" of the U.S. Peace Corps and later the first woman to become director of the U.S. Peace Corps. Bonnie Strickland, Martha Mednick, Martha Bernal, Marie Skodak Crissey, and Florence Denmark made social activism a part of their professional lives and research. Historical and social influences played a significant role in shaping the lives of these women.

TRENDS AND PATTERNS: PROFILES ACROSS TIME

Are there variables that are related to eminence across time? Are there variables that are influenced by historical or social context?

Is there a single profile for eminent women in psychology? Is it transhistoric or time-specific?

The variables that are related to eminence—regardless of historical or social context for the 34 woman in these two volumes—are birth order and demographics on a family of origin; educational institutions, graduate support, and years from baccalaureate to doctorate; marital status and marriage partners; coping strategies toward barriers; and mentors and colleagues. A clear profile emerges, a profile that is transhistorical. The eminent women who fit this profile come from privileged, well-educated, middle-class families that valued high levels of achievement in education and occupation. They were firstborns in families that were professional or entrepreneurial. The women attended prestigious colleges (Ivy League or Seven Sisters institutions), remained single or married professional men, and remained childless. They went from baccalaureate to doctorate in less time than others in the doctorate population, received graduate support, and had an impressive list of mentors and colleagues and good professional and social networks. They persisted in the face of discrimination and other barriers to contribute ideas, approaches, and definitive work to psychology. In one way or another, parts of this profile fit all the women in these volumes. But, there are substantial deviations and other variables to consider.

Time-specific historical and social forces contributed to the change in profile for education. For women born between 1891 and 1914, choices for graduate training were limited. Few institutions offered degrees in the new science of psychology, and the institutions that did tended to be ivy league or seven sisters institutions. For women born between 1915 and 1936, the sites of formal education included a range of colleges and universities, including state institutions. Although ivy league and seven sisters institutions continued to be good choices, other choices became available. For the younger women, a wider distribution of degree-awarding institutions are represented. This is an important variation in the transhistorical profile.

Another variation was facilitated by the greater access to professional training. For women whose families of origin were not privileged, professional training came into reach. Although being born into an educated, professional, and/or wealthy family continued to be advantageous in achieving eminence, achievement now became accessible to women who were not from a family privileged in at least one of these ways. It also became possible to achieve eminence when educational and occupational achievement for women was not a family value due to cultural, religious, or other beliefs or circumstances. With the doors of opportunity cracked open, love of learning led these women to high achievement.

At the same time, the profile for marital status began to reflect the changing social context. Marriage and parenthood were more likely to become part of the texture of life for eminent women born later rather than earlier. For the 18 women born between 1891 and 1914, 14 married. Of these, 21.4% had children. For the 16 women born between 1915 and 1936, 14 married. Of these, 71.4% had children. This dramatic increase in parenting seems to reflect the demise of the perception that women must choose career *or* marriage and parenthood. These women were pioneers in "having it all." It seems appropriate to conclude that historical and societal influences contributed to this change and to the expansion of profiles. These profiles now include single, married-without-children, married-with-children, and single-parent variations. All these profiles are represented among these women. Marital choice did not exclude achieving the highest academic ranks or the mantle of eminence.

With all these changes and variations, is the tranhistorical profile still valid? Yes. The profile continues to represent several eminent women, and parts of the profile continue to fit even larger numbers. As a group, the 34 predominantly firstborn women went from baccalaureate to doctorate in less time than others; received graduate support; had an impressive list of mentors and colleagues and good professional and social networks; married professional men; and persisted in the face of discrimination and other barriers to contribute ideas, approaches, and definitive work to psychology.

Are there exceptions even to these parts of the profile? Yes. For example, 21% of the women took more than a decade to go from baccalaureate to doctorate (Thelma G. Alper, Katherine M. Banham, Ruth Howard, Carolyn Robertson Payton, Carolyn Wood Sherif, Leona E. Tyler, and Lillian E. Troll). These women represent the four marital categories. The reasons for the extended period of time vary but include financial circumstances, family considerations, and lack of opportunity. Other women suffered from a paucity of mentors and colleagues. Although earning the doctorate in a brief period of time is a predictor of later achievement and the presence of mentors, colleagues, and social and professional networks important to achievement, there does not seem to be any one insurmountable variable in the face of talent, ability, determination, and strong motivation. Several of the eminent women write of their struggles but also of their belief that the *chance* to succeed exists alongside the challenge to overcome obstacles: "Few of my friends went to college, and my family was in no position to support me financially. Scholarships, waiting tables, lifeguarding, and delivering newspapers and movie theater programs all combined to provide my tuition, housing costs, and spending money" (Bonnie Strickland). "Throughout my life, however critical I might be of this country, I have felt grateful for the opportunities of which I availed myself. They would most likely not have existed had I lived in Mexico" (Martha Bernal). "I learned, as all children in public school, that I was an American and as such was guaranteed the pursuit of happiness, equality, and justice. I learned that lesson well and have continuously struggled to achieve these rights as a minority and as a woman" (Carolyn Robertson Payton).

As a group, the women persisted despite professional and personal obstacles, focused on the task at hand, and brought their considerable talents to bear. It is no less true of the later 17 than it is of the earlier 17:

> They were risk-takers, self-reliant, energetic, and flexible. They had great curiosity following their interests and inclinations into new subdisciplines and new opportunities. They found that solving one problem uncovered others. They saw the world as it was and as it might be. Their lives were marked by complexity of purpose, by weaving and reweaving of endeavor, by the forward movement of progress. They made wide use of support systems, professional and social, but were not afraid to be pioneers and go it alone. Their lives resound with integration and complexity. (O'Connell, 1983)

The 17 women in this volume are innovators continuing in the pioneering spirit established from the very beginning of psychology. These women are younger, more contemporary, but pioneers nonetheless. Pioneers continue to be needed to show us the way. The trail is not sufficiently well blazed so that pioneers are no longer necessary (Gruber & Wallace, 1981). A new vision of women as exemplars and achievers has yet to emerge. The world has undergone major transformations, but as we approach the 21st century, equal access to education, employment, and advancement remains a too rarely realized ideal. Women continue to confront a glass ceiling that prevents equitable representation, tenure, advancement, and recognition at the most prestigious universities and elsewhere.

The history of psychology needs to integrate the formidable contributions made by women—contributions made from the very beginning of psychology as a science—if it is to be an accurate history and if a new vision of women is to be realized. The women in this volume, like their predecessors, have brought us to the forefront of knowledge with the streams of their professional work. They have helped shape the profession of psychology, the history of the 20th century, and the quality of our lives. They are insipirational role models of achievement for now and for the future.

ACKNOWLEDGMENTS

Thanks to Mary Anne Hone, Frank Hone, Thomas D. O'Connell, Nancy Felipe Russo, and Ira Sugarman for their comments. Thanks also to Barbara Priestner-Werte for her assistance in the content analyses of the autobiographies. This work was made possible by a separately budgeted research grant from Montclair State College.

REFERENCES

APA Committee on Women in Psychology. (1986). [*Report on women in psychology.*] Washington, DC: APA.

Boland, E. (1987). The journey, In E. Boland, *The journey and other poems*, (pp. 39–42). New York: Carcanet.

Bryson, R. B., Bryson, J. B., Licht, M. H. & Licht, B. G. (1976). The professional pair: Husband and wife psychologists. *American Psychologist, 31*, 10–16.

Clawson, J. G. (1980). Mentoring in managerial careers. In C. B. Dear (Ed.), *Work, family and the career: New frontiers in theory and research* (pp. 144–165). New York: Praeger.

Cole, J. R., & Zuckerman, H. (1987, February). Marriage, motherhood and research performance in science. *Scientific American*, pp. 119–125.

Dolan, B., & Stanley, A. (1982, February 22). The new baby bloom. *Time*, pp. 52–58.

Featherman, D. (1978). *Schooling and occupational careers: Constancy and change in worldly success*. Madison: University of Wisconsin, Center for Demography and Ecology.

Friedan, B. (1963). *The feminine mystique*. New York: Norton.

Furumoto, L., & Scarborough, E. (1986). Placing women in the history of psychology: The first American women psychologists. *American Psychologist, 41*, 35–42.

Glick, P. C. (1975, February). A demographer looks at American families. *Journal of Marriage and the Family*, pp. 15–26.

Gruber, H. E., & Wallace, D. B. (1981, August). *Integrative strategies in creative lives*. Paper presented at the annual meeting of the American Psychological Association, Los Angeles.

Harmon, L. R., et al. (1963). *Doctorate production in the United States, 1920–1962*. Washington, DC: National Academy of Sciences.

Hennig, M., & Jardim, A. (1977). *The managerial woman*. New York: Anchor-Doubleday.

HEW. (1985). *Digest of educational statistics, 1985*. Washington, DC: National Center for Educational Statistics.

HEW. (1985). *The condition of education, 1985*. Washington, DC: National Center for Educational Statistics.

HSUS. (1975). *Historical statistics of the United States: Colonial times to 1970* (Pt. 1). Washington, DC: Bureau of the Census.

Kluckhohn, C., & Murray, H. A. (1953). Personality formation: The determinants. In C. Kluckhohn, H. A. Murray, & D. Schneider (Eds.), *Personality in nature, society and culture* (p. 53). New York: Knopf.

Levinson, D. J. (1978). *The seasons of a man's life.* New York: Knopf.

Mellilo, D. (1983). Birth order, perceived birth order, and family position of academic women. *Individual Psychology: Journal of Adlerian Theory, Research, and Practice, 39,* 57–62.

O'Connell, A. N. (1983). Synthesis: Profiles and patterns of achievement. In A. N. O'Connell & N. F. Russo, (Eds.), *Models of achievement: Reflections of eminent women in psychology* (pp. 297–326). New York: Columbia University Press.

O'Connell, A. N., & Russo, N. F. (Eds.). (1980). *Eminent women in psychology: Models of achievement* [Special issue]. *Psychology of Women Quarterly, 5*(1).

O'Connell, A. N., & Russo, N. F. (1983). *Models of achievement: Reflections of eminent women in psychology.* New York: Columbia University Press.

Rohrbaugh, J. B. (1979). *Women: Psychology's puzzle.* New York: Basic.

Runyan, W. M. (1984). *Life histories and psychobiography: Explorations in theory and method.* New York: Oxford University Press.

SAUS. (1981). *Statistical abstracts of the United States* (101st ed.). Washington, DC: Bureau of the Census.

SAUS. (1985). *Statistical abstracts of the United States* (105th ed.). Washington, DC: Bureau of the Census.

SAUS. (1986). *Statistical abstracts of the United States* (106th ed.). Washington, DC: Bureau of the Census.

Trotter, R. J. (1987, May). You've come a long way, baby. *Psychology Today,* p. 38.

Van Dusen, R. A., & Sheldon, E. B. (1976). The changing status of American women: A life cycle perspective. *American Psychologist, 31,* 106–115.

Index